BUSINESS DATA PROCESSING SYSTEMS

SECOND EDITION

LAWRENCE S. ORILIA   NANCY B. STERN   ROBERT A. STERN

JOHN WILEY & SONS
SANTA BARBARA   NEW YORK   LONDON   SYDNEY   TORONTO
A WILEY/HAMILTON PUBLICATION

This book was set in 10 point Melior by Graphic Typesetting Service. The text and cover were designed by Janet Bollow, copyediting was done by Judyl Mudfoot. Chuck Pendergast and Jean Varven supervised production. Printing and binding was done by Kingsport Press.

Library of Congress Cataloging in Publication Data:

Orilia, Lawrence.
Business data processing systems.

"A Wiley/Hamilton publication."
Includes index.
1. Business—Data processing. I. Stern, Nancy B., joint author. II. Stern, Robert A., joint author. III. Title.
HF5548.2.0687 1977 658'.05 77-2660

ISBN 0-471-65700-X

Printed in the United States of America.

10 9 8 7 6 5 4 3 2 1

PREFACE TO THE SECOND EDITION

By its very nature, a book on systems analysis and design becomes obsolete very quickly, far more quickly than most other types of books. The major purpose of this new edition is to update the material, paying particular attention to new developments in data processing. A second purpose, of equal importance in the eyes of the authors, is the pedagogic revision of the material, a revision designed to provide the student with the best possible understanding of the material. It is generally recognized in the computer field that systems analysis and design is a uniquely difficult subject to incorporate in a text because it is on a higher level than most other data processing subjects and because it, of necessity, reflects the orientation of the instructor. As teachers of systems analysis and design for many years, we have incorporated in this new edition material that has been discussed with many different instructors, reflecting many different perspectives toward the subject. We have also incorporated many changes based on our understanding of student needs and problem areas. Our testing of the text has resulted in a revision that we feel will effectively satisfy student and instructor needs. While an effort to be "all things to all people" generally results in a weakened approach, in this case such an effort provides the best possible perspective on the subject.

The book has been extensively revised in both organization and subject matter. A unit approach is used, consisting of five major areas:

I. Introduction to Systems Concepts
II. Basic Design Considerations
III. Information Processing
IV. Project Controls and Management
V. The Systems Package

The major additions to subject matter are in the chapters on file design, hardware, data communications, and MIS. New topics discussed include minicomputers, HIPO/IPO, CICS, and editing of data. These additions are designed to provide the student who has had some basic introduction to data processing with a far greater depth of understanding and with a heightened perspective, one which will enhance his[1] ability to analyze and design systems.

A separate chapter has been included on controls and feedback to emphasize these important elements of a system. In addition, a separate chapter is devoted to planning tools, including such topics as CPM, PERT, Gantt charts, HIPO/IPO, and simulation. An appendix on computer characteristics has been added to provide the student with an appreciation of hardware costs, speed, and specifications.

The text includes general questions at the end of each chapter, to facilitate and enhance the level of classroom discussion. The workbook that is to be used with the text has been extensively revised as well. The simulated company used in the first edition has been revised and simplified. This new approach will better enable the student to develop a systems package systematically, chapter by chapter.

The authors wish to thank the following reviewers for their helpful comments while the manuscript was being prepared: Professor Bobby McDowell, Joliet Junior College; Professor Ida Mason, Lehigh Community College; Professor Richard Manthei, Joliet Junior College; Professor Howard Granger, City College of San Francisco; Professor Carl A. Friedman, Federal City College; Professor Mike Marlow, Parkland College; Professor Vernon Hoffner, Eastern Michigan University.

[1]We use the masculine pronoun only because no viable alternative as yet exists. Educational and job opportunities in data processing and systems analysis are available both to women and to men. We do not assume that a systems analyst will be male—nor that a keypunch operator will be female.

ABOUT THE AUTHORS

Lawrence S. Orilia is currently Associate Professor of Computer Science at Nassau Community College in Garden City, New York. He has held that position since 1969. Prior to that Professor Orilia worked in industry as an industrial engineer and a systems analyst. He received his Ph.D. from the University of Sarasota.

Nancy Stern did her undergraduate work at Barnard College, and graduate work at New York University and the State University of New York at Stony Brook. Ms. Stern has held several teaching positions in the area of data processing and mathematics in various New York area schools. In addition to her teaching experience, Ms. Stern has worked as a technical writer, an educational consultant and a programmer analyst. She has written several data processing textbooks.

Robert A. Stern has graduate degrees from New York University and St. Johns University School of Law. He has worked in industry as a systems analyst and as an industrial engineer and has taught data processing at Nassau Community College in Garden City, New York. In addition, he is the co-author of several textbooks in various areas of data processing.

CONTENTS

UNIT I

INTRODUCTION TO SYSTEMS CONCEPTS

CHAPTER **1**

SYSTEMS STUDIES—AN OVERVIEW

As we look about us, we often observe operations and procedures that could be performed in a better way. As a student, for example, you may have encountered a cumbersome registration procedure that caused you to question the efficiency of the system. As systems analysts, we are concerned with devising the most efficient and economical systems or procedures to accomplish given tasks within a company.

This textbook discusses the study of business systems. A **business system** is defined as an organized method for accomplishing a business function. There are two types of systems studies:

1. Where a system currently exists, but a new or revised one is considered desirable
2. Where a present system does not exist, but a new set of procedures is nonetheless considered desirable

In the first case, we must perform *analysis* on the current system and then *design* a new one. In the second case, only the design phase is necessary. We shall generally consider systems that require analysis and then redesign, since this case encompasses all aspects of the other.

Analysis of a system is the procedural study of its operations with an attempt to discover its basic problem areas. Determining why a system is not operating properly decreases the likelihood that the new design will produce the same problems.

The systems analyst should recognize that it is not necessarily true that everything currently being performed in a system needs revision. Three major items must be determined when performing a systems study:

1. *What* should be improved or revised
2. *How* it should be improved or revised
3. *How much* it will cost compared to current operations

Sometimes the study of a system involves the analysis of whether the company should acquire data processing equipment to better serve its needs. When the acquisition of computer equipment becomes an element in the analysis, we call this a feasibility study. That is, a **feasibility study** is an independent analysis to determine whether a company should acquire data processing equipment.

The systems study we are considering focuses on an existing set of operations that needs improvement. The analyst must be aware of all existing or proposed constraints or limitations while he or she is performing the study to improve this system. For example, the company may already have a computer with two disk drives and four tape drives. If the analyst thinks an optical scanner would improve the system, he must be prepared to justify its cost in a feasibility study.

This chapter is designed to acquaint the student with the basic approach necessary in a systems study. Each topic outlined here will be discussed in depth in the next few chapters. The purpose of this chapter is to present the entire picture of a system before evaluating each of its elements.

A **systems study** is a descriptive and analytical report to the management of a company. It includes at least the following:

1. An analysis of the present system, with evaluations of its efficiency and cost
2. The design of the proposed system, with an evaluation of its cost
3. A plan to test and then implement the new system

ANALYSIS OF THE PRESENT SYSTEM

The analysis of the present system will uncover major problem areas that must be eliminated. Suppose that as a systems analyst you have been asked to investigate a company's present payroll system for employees paid on an hourly basis. The first step of analysis is the collection of data by analyzing procedures and forms, and by interviewing people who work with the system. As a systems analyst, you observe, for example, that a weekly payroll listing (Figure 1.1) is produced by the computer each week when payroll checks are prepared.

The payroll listing lists *every* employee for whom the computer has produced a payroll check, and shows for each employee what deductions were subtracted from gross earnings to arrive at net pay. This report is reviewed by the manager of the payroll department before the checks are released for dis-

PAYROLL LISTING — DATE XX / XX / XX

PAGE XX

EMPLOYEE NUMBER	NAME	GROSS EARNINGS	FICA	FED. W/H	STATE W/H	HOSP.	UNION DUES	BOND	MISC.	NET
1034	JANET AKINS	160.00	9.36	25.60	8.00	4.80	1.55	0.00	0.00	110.69
1027	MARTIN BROWN	800.00	46.80	128.00	40.00	5.20	1.55	0.00	0.00	578.45
2076	JOAN BYMES	180.00	10.53	28.80	9.00	0.00	0.00	2.50	0.00	129.17

Figure 1.1 Weekly payroll listing.

tribution. If any check seems unreasonably high, the week's timecard for the employee involved is pulled out, along with the payroll records that indicate the employee's hourly rate of pay. The calculations are then performed manually, and if there is a discrepancy between the figures on the payroll listing and those calculated manually, the check produced by the computer is destroyed and a new one is issued manually.

It is very time-consuming for the payroll manager to review each week a payroll report that lists *all* the hourly employees working for the company. An interview with the payroll manager revealed that only a few checks require investigation each week.

After the data on the system have been amassed, the second step in analysis begins: integrating all the elements within the system so that the entire system is seen and its basic problems placed in perspective. The basic tool for representing the system as a whole is the systems flowchart. A **systems flowchart** is a diagram that shows how the system operates. The flowchart in Figure 1.2 gives an overview of the entire system being analyzed.

A determination of cost factors is the third step in analysis. It is necessary to compile cost figures on every phase of a system so that it becomes obvious which operations and procedures cost too much relative to their output.

If the production of the weekly payroll listing by the computer and the time expended in reviewing the entire listing cost several hundred dollars each month, then this cost may be disproportionately high relative to the usefulness of the listing.

Once all aspects of a system have been thoroughly studied, the analyst must prepare a problem definition. This is the fourth and final step in analysis. In the **problem definition**, the analyst specifies the major problem areas within the current system and outlines how a new system will eliminate them.

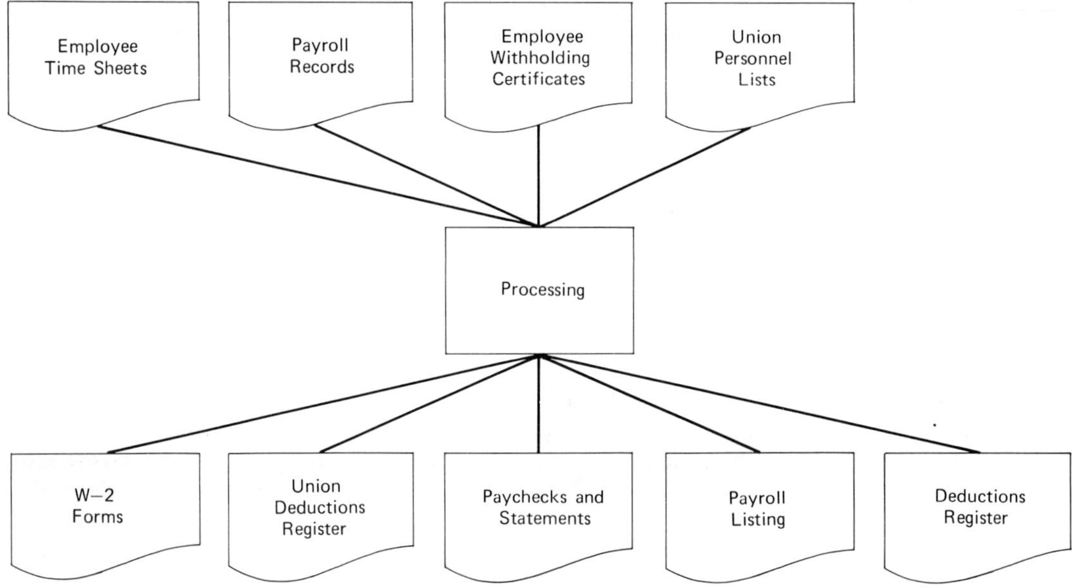

Figure 1.2 Overview of payroll system.

This is the formal document on the analysis of the system. It is generally submitted to the management of the company for review. If management is satisfied that a new system will alleviate the current system's problems, then the analyst is instructed to begin the design phase. If not, the study is abandoned. Most often, management gives its consent to continue, unless changes within the company necessitate policy changes.

DESIGN OF THE PROPOSED SYSTEM

The analyst begins the design phase by devising more significant output. The output in our example needs revision, since it costs too much to prepare and utilize, and since it is not providing information as effectively as possible.

One way to cut down the cost and time of preparing reports is to devise what is commonly called an **exception report.** This type of report highlights the critical problems—the "exceptions" to smooth operations. An exception payroll listing is shown in Figure 1.3.

This report lists only paychecks that are unreasonable. That is, only the "exceptions" to a reasonable payroll are listed. The criteria for determining what is an unreasonable paycheck must be reviewed by the analyst with the businessperson for whom the new system is being designed. A primary benefit of

EXCEPTION PAYROLL LISTING — DATE XX / XX/ XX

PAGE XX

EMPLOYEE NUMBER	NAME	HOURS WORKED	HOURLY RATE	GROSS EARNINGS	FICA	FED. W/H	STATE W/H	HOSP.	UNION DUES	BOND	MISC.	NET
1027	MARTIN BROWN	200	4.00	800.00	46.80	128.00	40.00	5.20	1.55	0.00	0.00	578.45

Figure 1.3 Exception payroll listing.

this type of report is that it is easier for someone to note problems without wading through lines and lines of information that require no attention.

The second step in the design phase is the redesign of other files, as required. Changes in output may necessitate revisions of input.

Once input and output files have been revised, the new processing steps must be outlined. This is most often done in a systems flowchart. Consider the flowchart in Figure 1.4, which shows how timecards are processed.

When the design effort has been completed, the analyst must prepare **documentation,** which describes the detailed design and provides an economic justification for it. The

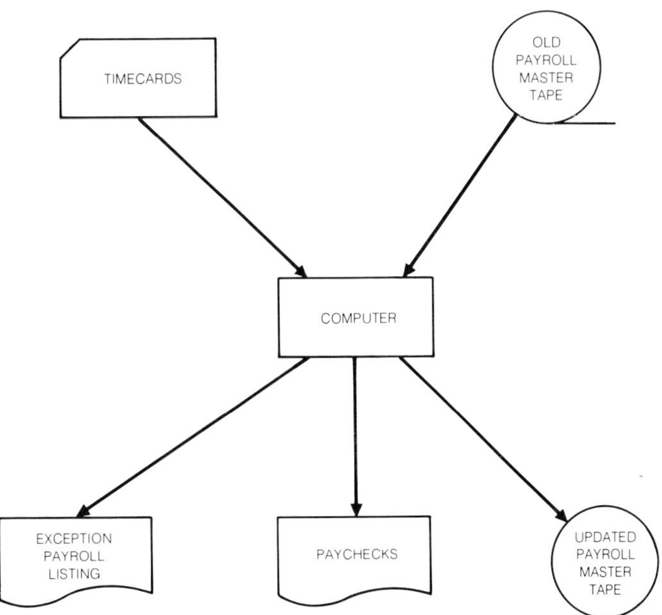

Figure 1.4 Processing of timecards.

documentation must be submitted to management, which determines whether implementation should begin. In addition to the formal design, the analyst should include alternative system designs from which management can make a realistic choice.

Since there are often several good alternatives for improving a system, an interesting question arises. Which alternative should we choose to implement? If all the alternatives yield the same benefits, such as supplying the necessary reports on a timely basis, then the solution is rather easy. The cost of designing and implementing each alternative must be evaluated to select the alternative that best satisfies management's goals or objectives.

TESTING AND IMPLEMENTING THE SYSTEM

Thus far, we have illustrated how analysis of the present system and design of the proposed system might be handled in a systems study. Now let us look at the other items in the study. We must plan to test the proposed system, and then to implement it. First, we will discuss the testing of the system.

In the above system, we have decided that an exception payroll listing instead of a full payroll listing should be produced. A programmer will thus have to modify a program that is already in existence. It is advisable to create some fictitious "test" timecards. In addition, a test payroll file should be created. To test out the effectiveness of the program, deliberate errors should be incorporated in these timecards and in the payroll file. Then the timecards and the tape should be given to the programmer to run with the revised program as an experiment or test. If the computer prints out an exception payroll listing *identical* to the one the analyst obtained by using pencil and paper, then the test has been performed successfully. However, suppose the result is a computer report that is incorrect. At this point, the analyst determines why the test has failed and then takes corrective action. The error could result from the analyst's misunderstanding of the system, from an error in the programmer's logic, or from an employee's misunderstanding.

The purpose of the systems test is to reveal inherent weaknesses in the proposed system before it is put into full operation. Once we are satisfied that the proposed system has been tested satisfactorily, we are ready to implement the system. Since implementation may involve training people to follow new procedures, a careful plan must be set up to ensure that the new system will operate smoothly. For example, it may take clerks some time to accustom themselves to filling out new forms or to using computer reports. In addition, new forms, in the beginning, may be improperly filled out or incorrectly distributed throughout the company.

A common practice in implementing a new system after it has been tested is to perform a **parallel run.** While the old system continues to operate, the new system will be run at the same time, in parallel. This has several benefits. First, if the results from the new system are not identical to those of the old system, something is wrong, and the analyst must correct the weaknesses that were not discovered in a test run. Another benefit from a parallel run is that no information is lost while people are getting accustomed to the new system and how it operates. The old system will continue to generate the needed information. Once the parallel run has proved that the new system works, the old system can be completely eliminated.

The parallel run is expensive, since it usually requires the use of additional people, temporarily, to permit a given system to operate in two different ways at the same time. It should be pointed out that every new system does not need to be implemented by a parallel run. For example, we may decide to implement a system with minor changes completely as of a given time on a given date, without a parallel run. This type of implementation is good if:

1. The procedures to be followed are simple.
2. No great loss of information or damage is expected to occur if something should go wrong on implementation. In other words, if something that was not anticipated occurred, any lost information could easily be obtained by returning to the old system.

The systems analyst should include the following in the implementation plan:

1. The type of implementation (parallel run or immediate implementation, for example).
2. The time schedule for the implementation—when it will start and how long it will continue until the new system is fully operational.
3. The schedule for ordering any new forms and/or hardware needed to implement the new system.
4. The schedule for determining when training of people in-

volved in the new system will be conducted. In addition, how the training will be performed should be mentioned. Will employees be trained by individual instruction, by group discussion, by written instructions, or by some combination of these techniques?

SUMMARY

A systems study is a report to management. It points out where improvements can be made in an existing system. It then shows the costs of the existing system and of the proposed system. A plan to test the proposed system and then to implement it is included so that management can see what would happen if they accepted the proposal.

In preparing the systems study, the analyst must draw on experience in the following areas:

1. Methods of collecting data, such as interviews, the review of procedures, and a study of documents used
2. Systems flowcharting
3. Forms and file design
4. Cost analysis
5. Capabilities of computer hardware and software

QUESTIONS

1. What fields appear on the exception payroll listing (Figure 1.3) that are not on the full payroll listing (Figure 1.1)? Why have these fields been added?
2. What criteria might be used to determine whether the details for a particular paycheck should be listed on the exception payroll listing because that paycheck is for an unreasonable amount?
3. What are the major inputs and outputs for this payroll system?

CHAPTER **2**

THE SYSTEMS ANALYST

Though the primary purpose of this text is to introduce the concepts of analysis and design, we must not overlook the individual primarily responsible for system changes—the analyst. The analyst's role, purpose, and scope of activities are too often misunderstood. This chapter will discuss these topics, as well as describe the various methods employed by the analyst for the collection of data.

THE ANALYST

A **systems analyst** is the staff employee responsible for analyzing existing systems and for designing new, more efficient ones. He or she must scrutinize each system, determine its weaknesses, and, based on the problem areas discovered, make recommendations for revised systems.

The analyst must maintain an expertise that transcends individual departments. He will be called on to investigate many systems in different areas. The analyst must be capable of making professional evaluations of all of them. While the analyst should have a basic understanding of the workings of each department within the company, he need not be an expert on each to make valid recommendations.

The chief asset the analyst must possess is a logical and systematic method of thinking. The analyst must be trained to think logically, analytically, and thoroughly. He must be capable of determining the cause of a problem quickly and precisely. It is hoped that this text will help train a potential analyst to think systematically.

Obviously, the characteristics of a good analyst are not developed overnight. These qualities are developed through a combination of hard work, self-evaluation, and practical experience. Before we review some of these qualities, let us discuss the typical background of the analyst.

In the majority of cases, systems analysts have been in the data processing field for many years. A conservative estimate, for the average analyst, is between eight and ten years. During these years, the analyst gains experience that gives him a sense of what has or has not worked in other companies or data processing installations. This experience provides an invaluable education, one that unfortunately cannot be completely provided by a textbook. Experience often provides the analyst with initial, potential solutions. Repeatedly in a systems effort, an initial solution becomes a point of departure toward a more comprehensive design.

Many analysts develop their experience as they "come up through the ranks." That is, analysts start as data clerks or operators and work their way to the position of programmer. From that point, depending upon opportunities within a company and the attributes of the individual, a programmer may enter a supervisory position (e.g., programming manager) or become an analyst. All prior experience will prove a valuable asset, regardless of the individual's future direction. Should the position of analyst be selected, entry into management is still eventually possible. In fact, it is becoming more common for higher management to select systems analysts to fill executive positions precisely because of their qualifications and experience.

The reader should be cautioned against concluding that systems analysts must have an electronic data processing (EDP) background. Many analysts originally began their careers in other fields, for example, as efficiency experts or industrial engineers. It is this type of individual that brings cross-specialization into the data processing field and helps round out the systems staff in a company. Potential analysts may be employed in a computer-aligned field, such as accounting, mathematics, marketing, transportation, or sales.

Industrial engineers (IEs) are frequently attracted to the position of systems analyst. The background of the IE—a broad spectrum of engineering/manufacturing courses, experience requiring cost analysis and economic justification with a practical emphasis on cost-saving measures—lends itself to the field of systems analysis.

Formal education for an analyst can be valuable both professionally and practically. In a typical data processing or business program, the analyst will be instructed in concepts and techniques applicable in business. A formal education will also help develop the logical thought patterns required of the analyst, and refine the badly needed skills of verbal and written communication. Do not underestimate the importance of carefully developing both forms of communication. It is imperative that the analyst be capable of communicating with all company personnel.

A major difficulty in data processing is the inability of staff employees to communicate properly with department personnel. An analyst must understand an existing system in its entirety before he can begin to study it. The chief method for learning about a system is communicating with those who operate within it. The problems that arise in attempting to extract information about a system from one who understands it are great. The analyst must (1) be able to establish confidence so that department employees can speak freely without fear of reprisal or loss of job and (2) be able to direct an interview so that he extracts all the necessary information in as little time as possible.

In addition to developing verbal skills, the analyst must learn to clearly document data and to write proposals. We must remember that, at the conclusion of any investigation or project, a report must be written to document the work completed. Quality work will be enhanced when properly presented in a well-written report. Likewise, a poorly written and presented report can negate the finest efforts of an analyst. Analysts must continually work at maintaining their written skills. These skills can be mastered with continuous work and experience.

The analyst, unlike many company employees, must possess the maturity and integrity to operate independently. Because of the nature of his job, he is permitted to proceed at his own pace, a pace generally established by the environment within which he operates. The analyst proceeds from analysis to design when he thinks the time is right. The analyst prepares guidelines for management indicating his evaluation of the time each task will take. The real test of the analyst's ability does not come until the system design is implemented. Supervision throughout the assignment, then, becomes difficult, and personal motivation must provide the necessary impetus for timely completion.

One should never consider the work of an analyst a one-shot assignment. The analyst's work is not solely within the confines of the current project, nor does the analyst's involvement cease at the completion of the project. Overall, the analyst's chief responsibilities are the following:

1. To analyze existing systems and design alternate systems for selection by management
2. To investigate and develop system recommendations that are consistent with management objectives
3. To supervise the implementation of any system and ensure that all system constraints are explicitly satisfied

In conclusion, the analyst must possess practical experience, good communication skills, exposure to business organizations, some formal training, and a logical methodological approach to problem solving. Employing all of these qualities, the analyst will be capable of making critical judgments and developing sound recommendations on systems. An individual possessing the proper balance of business experience and a logical mind has the right combination for effective analysis and good design work.

Having discussed the characteristics of an analyst, let us now turn our attention to the environment within which the analyst works.

THE SYSTEMS GROUP

As we initially noted, the systems analyst works within the data processing department strictly in a staff capacity. That is, the analyst operates as a consultant, an advisor to management. As a staff member, the analyst can never directly initiate any activity. The analyst prepares recommendations for presentation to management. High-level executives will accept or reject these recommendations. No action on any project can be instituted without management's approval and direction. Once a project is undertaken, the analyst will ensure that the system is properly implemented.

The analyst is a functional and vital part of the systems group. However, the systems staff is not solely responsible for the development of solutions to data processing problems. The systems group is merely one of the components of a data processing unit or department. Normally the data processing unit is composed of the following groups: the systems group, the programming group, and the operations group (see Figure 2.1). The data processing department is under the direction of a director of data processing, with each of the groups supervised by a manager (programming manager, operations manager, and systems manager).

The entire data processing department has a staff responsibility. In many organizational structures, the data processing

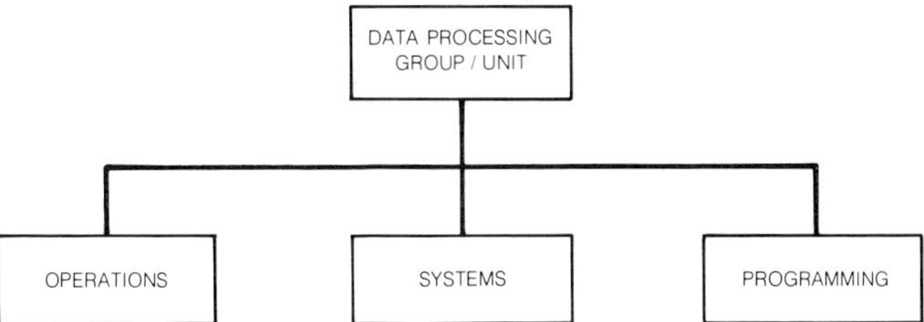

Figure 2.1 Data processing unit.

(DP) department reports directly to the comptroller or vice-president of a company. This organizational arrangement permits the direct flow of sensitive material with a minimum of interference and distortion. Any project undertaken by the DP department is always instituted with the direct approval and responsibility of the comptroller or vice-president. The DP department has no power to direct the implementation or initiation of any activity within a company.

Systems analysts work within the **systems group.** This group has the responsibility for the analysis of existing conditions and the creation of new, more effective systems. With the approval of management, the systems group will implement newly designed systems.

The **programming group** is responsible for the technical programming of the system and the maintenance of all data files within the computer.

The **operations group** has the responsibility for the physical operation of the computer.

The relationships among the three groups composing the DP department are totally dependent on the company in question. There is a good deal of variation from one company to the next. Once the system is designed, the analyst must work with the programmer to ensure that they obtain the proper perspective on each task. In some organizations, the programmers work for analysts and are directly responsible to them. Other companies, in an effort to develop competent systems personnel, utilize programmer/analysts who design the new systems and then program the new segments themselves. However, once the programs within the system have been written, tested, and debugged, the system can be implemented. That is, the new system can begin to function on a regular basis. At this point, computer operators within the data processing unit must be familiarized with the workings of the system. They must be given both the schedule for performing specific tasks and the requirements of each task. Thus each group of analysts, programmers, and computer operators within the data processing unit must work closely with the others to ensure proper implementation of each system.

COLLECTION OF DATA

As we have stated, the analyst must proceed logically through all phases of analysis and design to effectively evaluate and implement a system. Obviously, in order to study and evaluate the elements of a system, the analyst must amass all of the available data pertaining to the system under study. This phase of the analyst's work is referred to as the **collection of data** and will be discussed in this section.

Need for Accurate Collection of Data

The accurate collection of data is essential for a thorough analysis. *All* aspects of the system must be evaluated in depth. The careless omission of a single factor could drastically alter the analyst's interpretation of the system. Similarly, the smallest fact, misunderstood, could cause the analyst to make unnecessary and illogical revisions in the system. The analyst must strive to collect data that are all-inclusive and in proper perspective.

There are four primary goals that must be considered when collecting data:

1. Understanding the objectives of the system; that is, broadly, what management expects the system to accomplish
2. Understanding the requirements of the system; that is, specifically, what processing and output must be obtained from the system
3. Understanding how the objectives and requirements are met, through the careful analysis of operations and procedures
4. Understanding the problem areas of the system: deficiencies, malfunctions, extremely expensive processing, ineffective operations, unprotected or uncontrolled operations, flaws, and defects

In short, analysis must uncover any areas that could be more suitably performed in another manner. Note that, in a broad sense, all the elements of a system must be studied when collecting data—objectives, constraints, inputs, outputs, processing, controls, and feedback.

These goals are the basic objectives of collecting data. While the analyst is amassing data, he or she should center efforts on *investigation* rather than analysis. An experienced systems analyst will make judgments on certain aspects of the system as it is studied but will remain flexible and open to suggestion until *all* the data have been collected. While data are being collected, basic problem areas will become evident. The analyst must, however, maintain his objectivity until all data have been evaluated, since some justification for apparent problems might then become evident.

How Data Are Collected

The three basic means for collecting data are:

1. Studying procedures manuals
2. Evaluating forms
3. Interviewing department representatives

Data are first collected by reviewing written documents on the system. The analyst can often obtain an objective idea of how the system functions by examining the procedures manuals and the forms utilized within the system. Interviews with department representatives, however, are the most informative and accurate method for obtaining data on the system. The interview technique has the advantage of reviewing actual operations firsthand with the people who perform them. These employees can shed light on the system and its basic flaws far better than any written document.

The interview method of collecting data is generally the last one. The analyst first learns about the system from procedures manuals and written reports so that he does not take up valuable time of the interviewees. With a general idea of the system from what he has read, the analyst interviews department representatives, asking them pertinent questions that came up as he reviewed the written documents.

Procedures manuals. Most companies or organizations have formal written manuals containing the procedures and operations to be followed for each system. These **procedures manuals** are the first items to be studied when collecting data, since they are useful in describing the basic workings of the system.

The objectives and requirements of each system are clearly and concisely stated in the procedures manual. Thus, from these documents, we obtain a general idea of how a system *should* function.

Consider the following statement of objectives of a personnel system as noted in a procedures manual:

PROCEDURES MANUAL
I. Introduction

A. Purpose of the management personnel system. Management employees in this company have many capabilities, a wide variety of training and experience, and numerous interests. The management personnel system is designed to record, for full-time management employees below officer level, certain of the more important items of information on these matters, as well as job and salary histories, and to provide a means of ready access and summarization of the data thus recorded. It is the basis for studies that may be used in reaching important company decisions.

From the above entry, the analyst obtains a general idea of the objectives of the system. Once these objectives are clearly understood, the analyst must learn how effectively they are met by the actual operations within the system. This personnel system has, as its ultimate aim, the creation of accurate reports to management on the status of the employees so that major company decisions can be more easily reached. Any inefficiency or flaw in the system that thwarts this objective must be corrected.

Although objectives and requirements of the system to be studied are contained in a procedures manual, this document is not a reliable method of obtaining data on the *actual* operations of the system. The manuals are often out of date, and the procedures indicated are sometimes not followed. It is almost inevitable that a written description of operations and procedures will contain some broad generalizations that become obsolete almost as soon as they are written.

EXAMPLE 1. A systems analyst is studying an accounting system. In collecting data, he observes the following in the procedures manual:

PROCEDURES MANUAL
II. Accounting

A. Ordering of material. All parts and material must be ordered through the project administration department two weeks prior to desired delivery date.

The analyst, as an integral part of his company, is aware that an organization change two years ago has made the sentence above obsolete. The project administration department was eliminated, and its functions were reassigned to several other departments.

This excerpt from a procedures manual, while presenting data on the system, contains a fundamental error. The analyst should always read such documents, recognizing that some entries may be incorrect. The analyst may recognize errors immediately if he is familiar with current company policy. If not, he can recognize them later when he talks with department employees. The analyst should note any obvious errors, like the above, so that corrections to the manual can be made. A new employee who checks the procedures manual for rules on ordering material may not be aware of its obsolescence. It is an added responsibility of the analyst, while revising the existing system, to see that the manual is updated.

Basic problem areas in the system itself may also become evident while studying these manuals. Consider the following example:

EXAMPLE 2. A systems analyst is studying a personnel system. In collecting data, he observes the following in the procedures manual:

PROCEDURES MANUAL
III. Personnel

A. Notification of change in salary or status. A supervisor will notify the payroll department of a change in an employee's status. This notification will contain: name, social security number, new salary, new level, new department.

The supervisor will also notify the personnel department of a change in the employee's status. This notification will contain all of the above in addition to supervisor's name, last promotion date, and previous salary.

The experienced systems analyst might well question why there is not a *single* form for a change in salary or status, containing *all* data required by both the payroll and personnel departments. In this way, one form can be sent to the payroll department; when the data have been recorded, the form can then be transmitted to the personnel department. A single form avoids: (1) the duplication of effort required for filling out two forms, and (2) the increased potential for error when two forms are used.

Before finalizing his analysis of the manual, the analyst should question department representatives in an interview, because there may be a reason why obvious inefficiencies cannot be corrected.

In short, then, procedures manuals remain a useful method for collecting data. As well as listing objectives and requirements of the system, these documents will always give a general idea of how the system, as originally instituted, should function.

For systems without procedures manuals, the task of amassing data is more difficult. The analyst must obtain *any* written document that has been on file since the system was established. These include letters from management, or the original analyst, or perhaps the department manager. Letters often indicate the intent or purpose for implementing the system. Other documents that may prove helpful include the original analyst's notes on the system and legal contracts. Labor agreements indicating a company's contractual obligations are important to the analyst. Though the analyst might wish to recommend changes in how a task is performed or in data distribution, the company could be prohibited from making such changes because of a labor contract. Examination of all sources of information, then, is essential.

Evaluation of forms. The printed form is the most widely used single medium for transmitting information. It is generally the most important tool used by management in decision making.

When collecting data, the analyst must become familiar with *all* forms utilized within the system. He must know the exact nature of the data presented on the forms, as well as the distribution of forms. It is important to notice which department representative receives each document and where it is sent after it is used.

An illustration or chart is often a useful method of representing forms distribution. The experienced analyst develops his own illustrations, but Figure 2.2 will serve as an example.

There is an analytic method for studying forms in order to design better, more efficient ones. This method will be discussed in Chapter 4, since the design of new forms cannot begin until after all data have been collected and evaluated. In our present discussion, the analyst evaluates forms for the primary purpose of understanding the system. Later, the analyst will analyze forms for the primary purpose of designing more efficient ones.

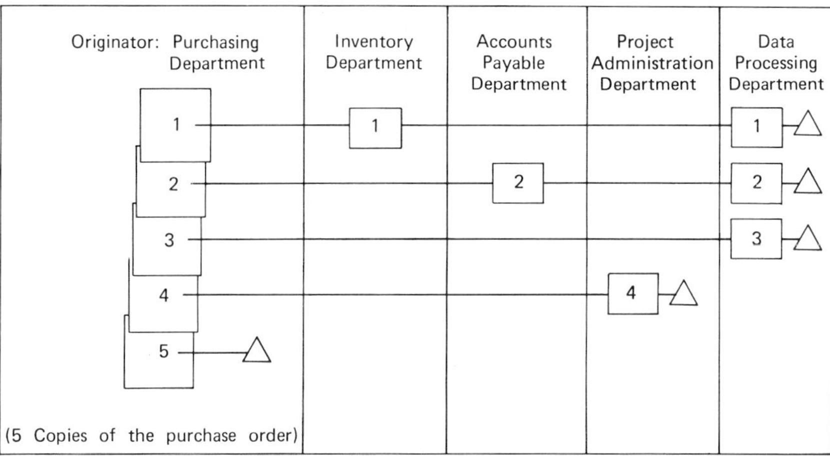

Figure 2.2 Forms distribution chart for purchase order. (△ denotes report filed.) It is an easy task to follow the distribution of forms from an illustration.

We evaluate forms so that we can better understand the system. Forms illustrate what information is required within the system and how it is used. In evaluating forms, inefficiencies within the system often become evident. Each printed document should be analyzed with the following questions in mind:

1. Are there any unnecessary items of information on the form? If employee name and social security number appear on a personnel report, for example, is employee number really required?
2. Is there any unnecessary or inefficient distribution of forms? Let us take as an example the manager who requires all forms used by his department to pass through his office before they are distributed. The analyst must determine if (a) there is no justifiable reason for this except the lack of trust that the manager exhibits toward his subordinates, or if (b) he is merely ensuring that distribution has, in fact, been made, in case some intended recipients are not receiving copies.
3. Are there manually prepared forms that would be more efficiently prepared by a computer?

If a clerk spends one week of every month preparing a report that could be created in five minutes on a computer, the analyst must consider this an inefficiency requiring correction in a new design.

4. Are there some forms that could be combined into a single, comprehensive report?

These questions, which are raised by the analyst while studying forms, must be followed up during the interview. The department representative may know a reason why some forms cannot be combined into a single document or why an inefficient distribution of forms cannot be altered. The interview, then, is the next step in the collection of data. The following checklist, illustrating the types of questions that are apt to be asked during an interview, will assist the analyst in evaluating forms and their distribution.

1. Who uses the report or form? A list should be prepared of people currently receiving or using a form, indicating who receives which copy (copy 1, copy 2, etc.). The informal distribution of reports is also a source of information. Imagine the embarrassment of corporate officials if a profit and loss statement revealing a substantial loss became public. If a competitor had knowledge of your inventory levels on critical parts, your company could be forced into paying exorbitant prices on these parts.
2. How often is a form used? After compiling a list of the personnel using a form, the analyst must ascertain how frequently each person uses the form. For example, a list of suspended credit card accounts would probably be employed by a sales clerk repeatedly in the course of a day, and an automobile reservations clerk would refer to a report indicating the day's rentals throughout the day. Compare the usage of these two reports to the potential use of monthly personnel action change reports that list changes of address and marital status.
3. How much of the information on the form is used? Here, the analyst is attempting to determine who uses what information. Checking the efficiency of the form is a necessary function. Is the report still of value, or have conditions changed so markedly that a revision of the form is in order? The analyst should determine whether a user's informational requirements have diminished so that the data required by the user can be found on another report. Possibly a current report, prepared exclusively for the analyst, can be eliminated.
4. Is the data on this report necessary for:
a. making decisions on some form of action?
b. keeping you informed on current conditions?

c. checking the accuracy of other matters?
d. establishing control of other matters?

Questions 4a through d examine the purpose of the form and the timeliness of the information presented. Will the data on the form be employed by management to control some aspect of business? If so, are the data provided the most current and up-to-date data available? The answers to questions 4a through d will help the analyst determine how vital the particular form is to management, how important the data on the report are, and how the data are used.

5. What would be the effect on your work if you:
a. did not receive the report at all?
b. received it less frequently?
c. received less information than at present?
d. received more information than at present?

These questions are patterned after those in question 4. They are designed to elicit the same type of responses from the user. The analyst is attempting to determine how essential a form is to the user and what data are required and used.

6. What other reports or data are prepared from this report? Often data contained in a report as the output of one operation become the input to another processing activity. Here, the analyst is ascertaining what data are used as input to develop new data. Clearly, if a report is altered, the operations dependent upon that report as input will be affected.

7. Can the data on a report be obtained from any other source? If a report is redesigned, there is a possibility that some of the data available on the old report will not be provided in the new report's format. If and when this type of situation occurs, the analyst must determine if the eliminated data items can be derived from another source or form. It is possible that another existing output can provide the same data and satisfy the user's need.

8. Is the report easy to read and use? The answer to this question will be rather subjective and dependent upon the views of the user. The analyst will develop a sense for the evaluation of user responses. All user replies must be weighed and evaluated with regard to the user's attitude. Often, workers displaced from jobs they thought were solely theirs by the reorganization of a company that results from the installation of a computer system will deliberately taint their responses to put any computer-prepared reports in a questionable light.

9. How long do you keep your copy? What is the retention period for copies of the report received? Must the user retain

previous copies of a report to compile yet another report? The analyst may observe that the user retains copies of everything when they are not needed. The storage costs as well as the personnel costs involved could be staggering.

10. How and where do you file it? The analyst is trying to determine storage requirements for the form. Are all special cabinets and holders needed and justifiable? When stored, is the form easily accessible? How quickly can data be found and used?

11. How often do you refer to it after its original use? This question ties together almost all of the prior questions. The point here is reuse of a form for the compilation of data (e.g., a history of monthly sales) or for informational purposes (e.g., looking up previously completed sales data to find a particular piece of information).

The analyst will use this checklist of questions when interviewing a user of a form. The answers obtained, coupled with the analyst's own evaluations, will assist in the analysis of a form. Though we have not spoken specifically about outputs from a terminal device using a visual display, the checklist can be effective in the evaluation of this type of output as well. A more thorough discussion of outputs, both visual and printed, is provided in Chapter 4.

Interviewing department representatives. The most important source for the collection of data is the interview. Once the analyst has a fundamental understanding of the system through the evaluation of manuals and forms, he can learn details from interviews.

Before talking with department representatives, the analyst must take time to prepare for the interview. The analyst must learn the role and function of each employee to be interviewed. An **organization chart** (as illustrated in Figure 2.3) is a representation of where each employee fits into the organization. A chart of this kind is available in most companies and is helpful in determining the specific role of each department representative. It is important, in each interview, for the analyst to know the organizational level of the employees with whom he is speaking.

The analyst must also obtain approval from supervisors to interview any clerks or other nonmanagement employees. Then a meeting schedule must be established with all interviewees.

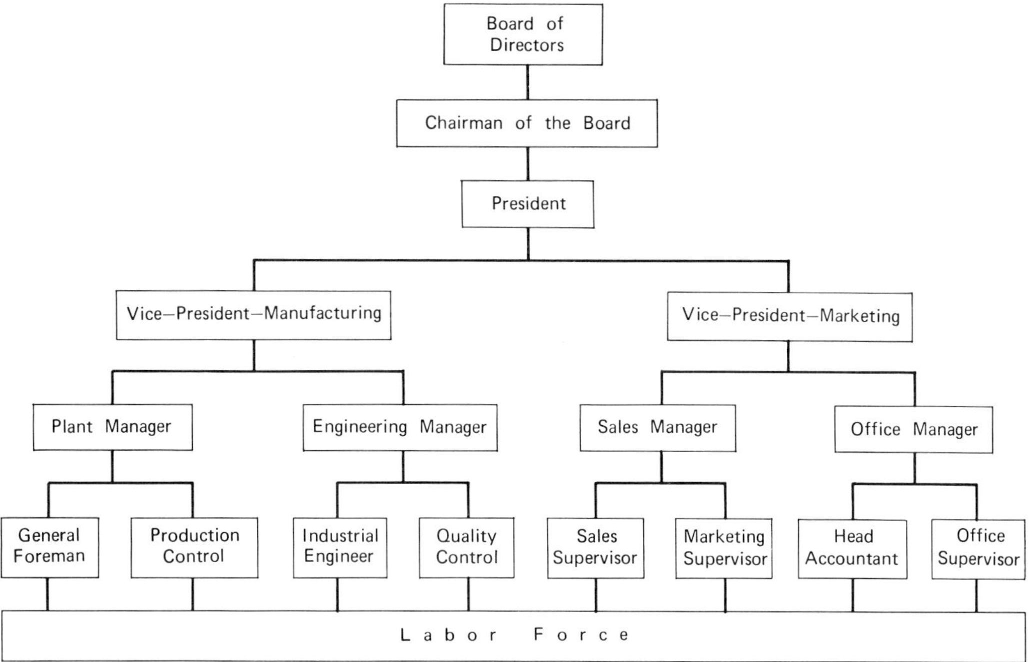

Figure 2.3 Organization chart.

By thorough preparation for the interviews, the analyst can present himself as an organized and reliable professional. The analyst should always arrange an interview, indicating why he wants to meet with the specific employee and how much time he expects the interview to take.

Once the preparation has been completed, the analyst will attempt to learn all the fine points of the system from the interview. What was learned from the manuals is how the system, if it were operating properly or ideally, would function. What the analyst hopes to learn by an interview is how the system actually functions.

One must keep in mind that the most difficult problem the analyst will face is communication with department representatives. Analysts must train themselves to ask pertinent questions and to make certain that they fully understand all of the answers. Too often, difficulties in communication make for an unsuccessful interview. If the analyst gives an inaccurate impression of his purpose, the interviewee will often become unresponsive.

Above all, the analyst must be tactful. Many people are initially uncooperative in an interview; they think that it is a waste of valuable time. Similarly, many are fearful of data processing personnel. Employees often feel that systems analysts will attempt to "replace" them with computers. Still others have difficulties handling their own jobs, which makes them antagonistic when specific questions are raised about their system. When dealing with department employees, then, a tactful approach is a fundamental necessity.

The analyst, therefore, must learn how to establish an effective rapport with people. If this is not done, the analyst will undoubtedly learn little from the interview.

It is important for the analyst to take notes at the interview. These notes summarize major points, which might otherwise be forgotten, for future evaluation.

Several points must be learned or clarified in an interview:

1. *Objectives and requirements of the system.* You will recall that procedures manuals list the objectives and requirements of the system. They must, however, be reaffirmed and clarified in the interview. Sometimes the objectives and requirements of the system, as noted in the manual, are not the same as those a department representative sees. When a discrepancy exists, it is possible that the goals represented in the documents may be unrealistic with present manpower, or that time and growth have altered the stated goals, or that the department does not fully understand the stated aims. In any case, a precise understanding of the objectives and requirements of the system is essential before any analysis can be undertaken.
2. *Functions of the interviewees.* Each department representative should state his tasks clearly and explicitly. He must also state his functions in relation to other employees in the department. The analyst will often note that the way in which an employee views his responsibilities is not the same as the way others view them. Perhaps he is too engrossed with his job to understand its relation to others. Or perhaps an employee's hostile attitude makes for a strained relation with others that affects the efficiency of the system. In any case, all points of view provide a better understanding of the tasks involved.
3. *Cost of each operation.* The analyst must determine the cost of each operation. Since the ultimate aim of a systems analysis is a more efficient system, the analyst must be totally familiar with all cost factors. The department representative must indicate the time he spends on each job. These data should be substantiated, if possible. The analyst must also ob-

tain salary figures on all interviewees. These data are used for a cost analysis, which is discussed in detail in Chapter 12.

4. *Overall impressions of the system.* It is generally a good idea to ask employees about their impressions of the system. First, it enables them to express an opinion on matters in which they are involved. It also enables them to contribute to the analysis and subsequent design of the system.

Often their impressions and attitudes shed light on fundamental problem areas within the system. Some employees have valid suggestions that could be incorporated in a new design.

Sometimes, however, these impressions tend to be too subjective to be meaningful. The experienced analyst must learn to judge the feedback and place it in its proper perspective.

The following is a checklist of general items that represent the type of information the analyst must learn to extract from interviews:

a. Timing of each task. Do the present procedures and operations utilize too much time and effort of the employees? Can monetary savings be realized with new or revised operations?

b. Accuracy of output data. Does inaccurate reporting result in duplication of effort? Similarly, are the output data reliable enough for the department to have faith in them?

c. Flexibility of procedures. Is the present system so rigid and inflexible that minor changes require major revamping?

d. Capacity. Can the present system handle larger volumes that would result from normal growth?

e. Acceptance. Does the present system meet with any major resistance?

Let us consider the following illustration of how an interview can further the analyst's understanding of a system.

EXAMPLE. A systems analyst is studying a payroll system. According to the procedures manual, a rigorous schedule for the maintenance of payroll data must be followed:

Monday (each week). All new employees begin work on a Monday. On the Monday that they begin work, new employees must fill out questionnaires that are to be delivered to the payroll department by 5 P.M.

Tuesday (each week). Questionnaires on all new employees are delivered to Mrs. Jones, a keypunch operator. Each questionnaire must be keypunched into 10 employee record cards. The keypunching task must be completed by 5 P.M. and delivered to the control unit.

Wednesday (each week). The employee record cards on all employees (including the new hires) are used for the preparation of paychecks, which must be delivered to all employees by 3 P.M. on Friday.

On interviewing the clerks in the payroll department, the analyst learns that approximately 100 new employees begin work each Monday. Since each new hire requires 10 employee cards, approximately 1,000 cards must be keypunched on Tuesday by Mrs. Jones, who also has additional responsibilities on that day.

The analyst determines that this schedule is probably difficult, if not impossible, to maintain. All interviewees, however, indicated that no difficulties in the schedule were encountered.

Through the careful prodding of one clerk, the analyst finally learns that, in fact, the schedule was seldom met and many new employees did not receive their first paychecks until their second week of employment.

It is important to observe that, except for a single clerk, no payroll representative wanted to "indict" any member of his department by revealing a deficiency in the system. Each asserted that the schedule was maintained.

These difficulties with the department representatives resulted from the fact that the interviewees misunderstood the role of the analyst. They did not trust him. They did not realize that the analyst's prime function is to increase the efficiency of the system and not to find fault with individuals.

Once the deficiency in the schedule was noted, the analyst could recommend either (1) additional keypunch assistance for Mrs. Jones, or (2) that the new employees fill out their questionnaires when they are hired, prior to their actual starting date.

The point of this illustration is that the proper rapport between the analyst and the department representative will lead to an effective interview, which will ultimately result in a more efficient system.

After the interview, all data must be verified. The subjectivity of each individual must be placed in its proper perspective. Questionnaires distributed to a sample group of employees are often a good method for verifying data learned in an interview. The questionnaire enables an analyst to extract key information in a relatively short time.

When all data have been collected by the analyst, it is imperative that he write an interpretation of each job within the system.

It is during and after the interview that basic flaws in the system will become evident to the analyst. The analyst should verify that these flaws do, in fact, exist by again questioning department representatives to make certain he understands all facets of the system.

In summary, data are collected in three basic ways: the study of procedures manuals, the evaluation of forms, and the interviewing of department representatives. The first two methods give the analyst a fundamental understanding of the system. The last method provides all the detailed data that make his understanding thorough and complete. The interview technique, then, is the most important method for collecting data. The analyst must prepare for the interview, understand each representative's role, and schedule each interview. The analyst must maintain a tactful approach during each interview and follow up the interview with verification of the data. Once all the data have been collected, they must be evaluated and analyzed so that basic flaws within the system become evident. It is the analyst's basic responsibility to find these flaws and then to correct them.

GLOSSARY

Forms distribution chart. A graphical analysis of the distribution of the copies of a form within a company.

Management personnel system. A system designed to maintain a complete status on company personnel and the significant trends within the personnel area.

Organization chart. A representation of where each individual fits into the organization.

Payroll system. A system that maintains company payroll records, prepares and distributes payments to company employees, and satisfies all legal requirements.

Procedures manuals. Printed documents in which all procedures utilized within a company are explained in detail.

QUESTIONS

1. Examine the job opportunities section of your local newspaper and compile a list of requirements for systems analysts. Include data on the following particular items:
   a. Salary range offered/sought

   b. Years of experience desired
   c. Type of past experience:
   programming
   analysis
   type of equipment worked with
   d. Educational background (minimum degree requirements)
   e. Type of industrial experience (e.g., federal, military, marketing, reservations)
2. Think about the last interview in which you were involved, and answer the following:
   a. Were you at ease? Did the interviewer try to put you at ease?
   b. Do you think your appearance was OK, or were you improperly attired?
   c. Did you prepare yourself for the interview and review potential responses to questions you considered appropriate? Did it show?
   d. Were you intimidated? Was it evident? Why?
   e. Did you project a feeling of confidence?
3. Prepare a list of similarities between an interview and a first dating experience.
4. Find a newspaper or magazine article that includes an interview. Evaluate both the questions and the answers. Construct a fictitious interview that you think would have elicited more newsworthy information.
5. Indicate what you consider the most important characteristics an analyst should possess.
6. It has sometimes been stated that a systems analyst's job requires a large amount of public relations expertise. Do you agree or disagree and why?

CHAPTER **3**

FUNDAMENTAL CONCEPTS OF ANALYSIS AND DESIGN

We have defined a **system** as an organized method for accomplishing a business function. It is important, at this point, to have a clear perspective on the elements that constitute a system.

A system is built of individual elements, or building blocks, each contributing to form an organized, integrated entity. The analyst must understand each of these elements and also the relationships among them. Design of new or revised systems cannot begin until the analyst fully understands the existing system.

Analysis is the separation of a system into its basic elements so that each can be studied individually and in relation to the others. The objective of analysis is a realistic and keen insight into a system and its problem areas, so that an improved system can be designed. Thus design work cannot commence until analysis is completed. The analyst conceptualizes ideas for a new system while analyzing but does not formalize them until analysis is complete.

The typical system to be analyzed would be a manual business system, where the goal is conversion to data processing equipment, or a small computer system, where the goal is conversion to a larger, more encompassing computer system. We shall consider both types of systems.

To facilitate the understanding of a system, we represent it as having seven basic elements. These elements are shown in Figure 3.1.

The analyst must amass data on a system from all available sources. He will then have a *general* concept of the system in its entirety. Analysis begins with a thorough and detailed study of the elements in Figure 3.1. Once the current system and its weaknesses are fully understood, the analyst is in a position to propose one or more alternatives to management.

The elements of **control** and **feedback** are concerned with the minimizing of errors and the procedures necessary to

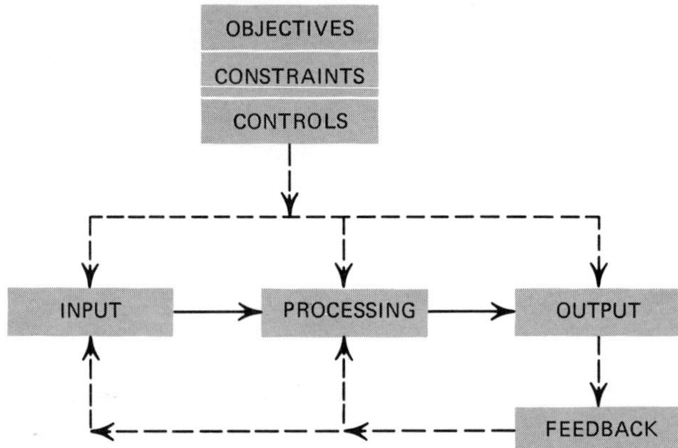

Figure 3.1 Overview of systems elements.

make adjustments when errors occur. Since these elements are important to every system, they will be considered separately in Chapter 11.

We will now discuss each of the other basic elements in a system so that you will know what to consider when analyzing a system and designing a revised one.

OBJECTIVES

The systems analyst must be aware of management's requirements from the system, in a broad sense. That is, management's goals and **objectives** must be understood. For example, one of a company's objectives might be to establish a computerized accounts receivable system so that a customer can walk into any branch store and have a clerk tell him his balance due immediately.

A determination of the objectives must come *first*. The analysis of a system must determine how well it meets the stated objectives. Thus, before an evaluation of a system's problem areas can begin, an understanding of the objectives is essential.

Another reason for determining objectives prior to formal analysis is to provide the analyst with an appreciation of the type of know-how he will need for the particular system. For example, an analyst, while studying the objectives of an accounts payable system, learns that all accounts must be paid within ten days of the billing date in order to receive a discount. If the analyst is not familiar with the method generally used for establishing discounts, he should learn it before attempting to analyze the present system.

In short, the analyst must be fully aware of *how* business functions are used to meet the stated objectives. Sometimes this requires formal training in specific business areas. Experienced analysts can often rely on previous business exposure, while neophytes must learn about these business functions as they are called on to study them.

Note that there is nothing sacred about stated objectives. It is possible that after analysis is completed, the analyst will recommend to management a modification of the objectives, based on his previous experience. Management might concur with the idea of having a real-time system that can provide them with immediate information concerning any aspect of the operation of the system, for example.

Typical objectives that an analyst may encounter when designing systems are the following:

1. Management in a department store would like to know the distribution of sales by product line each day.
2. Management in a bank would like terminals in each branch office to facilitate personal check cashing. The teller will dial the computer via touchtone telephone, enter the account number and the amount of the check, and receive an audio response to indicate if the check can be cashed.
3. Management in a department store would like to have a computer generate purchase orders whenever the stock level for an item reaches its predetermined reorder point.
4. Management in a public utility company desires a monthly computer-generated sales forecast in order to plan equipment needs.
5. Management in a retail store would like to have machine-readable charge slips to facilitate updating of accounts receivable records.
6. Management would like the ability to receive the company's financial statement immediately on request.

CONSTRAINTS

After the analyst determines the objectives of the present system, he must study its **constraints.** Now that he understands what the company specifically wants, he must learn what limitations have been applied. These constraints will sometimes indicate areas that must be maintained in the subsequent design even though they appear inefficient.

Typical constraints are as follows:

1. **Legal.** Certain information must be saved and specified reports prepared in a particular format for tax purposes. The analyst might be capable of designing these reports to be more meaningful, but he will not be able to do so because of the tax constraint. Similarly, the analyst may feel that the design of certain outputs, such as the W-2 withholding form in a payroll system, is inefficient. He may, in fact, have a better design. However, there is little the analyst can do when legal constraints have been imposed. In the case of the W-2 form, the federal and local governments dictate what the form should look like, how many copies there should be, and when it must be sent to employees.
2. **Cost.** Frequently management may be willing to settle for a system that just satisfies its needs instead of an optimum one that operates in the best possible manner, but whose cost to design is considered excessive. This is a realistic consideration, since it takes time and manpower and, therefore, money to analyze and design systems. Some business systems require one or more man-years to analyze, design, and implement. Cost factors are generally considered the most limiting constraint. Management sometimes establishes monetary limits that the analyst considers too binding, but within which he must nevertheless function. Thus an existing system may prove to be inefficient or cumbersome because it was bound by severely limiting cost factors.
3. **Hardware.** Often an analyst must analyze and design with the management directive that all systems must be adapted to the computer **hardware** or equipment currently available in the company's computer installation. This can certainly constrain an analyst, since he must work with the equipment on hand unless he can justify major changes.

Additional equipment not presently installed in the company that the analyst considers an asset to his system, such as an optical scanner, must be justified from a cost standpoint. For any additional hardware requirements, the analyst must perform a **feasibility study** to determine the feasibility of acquiring such devices. For companies with no existing computer facilities, the analyst must perform a feasibility study prior to any design work. The computer system that is deemed feasible becomes the equipment constraint for the new design. Studying the constraints of a given system will provide the analyst with some insight into *why* the system operates as it does. Some of the system's problem areas will, no doubt, be due to the existing constraints. When this is the case, the analyst will attempt to convince management in his formal analysis that the current constraints are too limiting. Sometimes this can result in more suitable limitations for a new or revised system. Keep in mind, however, that management does not issue constraints merely to thwart the analyst. Such directives are deemed necessary by management, which has keener insight into the best policies for the company as a whole. An element that would improve a particular system may not be wise for the company's total structure.

OUTPUT

After objectives and constraints are fully understood, the analyst must determine what is *broadly* required as **output.** He must also observe what is *specifically* provided. Sometimes the differences between desired output and what is provided are indeed striking!

While an analyst is studying existing output, he must keep in mind relevant ideas for revised output in future design work. Based on experience and on a complete comprehension of how a particular system functions, the analyst will need to recommend to management new or revised reports that can readily be obtained from a computerized system.

The analyst must consider more than just existing reports when he considers output. Current systems usually have "saved" information in the form of updated files that can be used for producing reports in the future. In addition, the information that is saved might be useful in providing answers to the specific inquiries of management regarding a particular system. Sometimes an entire report is not necessary, and a specific item of data would be sufficient.

Thus an understanding of existing output can make for a more effective utilization of available data in a revised system.

When a system is operated manually, the most common form of output is the printed form. For systems that currently utilize computers, printed forms as well as magnetic tape files, magnetic disk files, and punched cards are common output forms.

In designing outputs for the new system, the analyst must basically consider several points.

1. He must be certain that management will receive all necessary reports in the new system.
2. He must be innovative enough to recommend to management new reports that can yield important information. Man-

agement may be accustomed to having certain reports prepared manually. Executives may not realize the capability, flexibility, accuracy, and speed of a computerized system. It is the analyst's task to explore these facets and to familiarize management with the computer's ability.

3. He must be attuned to the needs of the company so that he can perhaps suggest outputs other than printed reports, such as cathode ray tubes and audio response units.

The analyst must remember one critical point: He can only make recommendations; he cannot dictate. If management chooses to continue to use some reports the analyst considers inefficient, that is its prerogative. Perhaps some reports might easily be combined in a computerized system. However, management may be accustomed to doing things in a particular way and may be reluctant to change at this time. Keep in mind, also, that management personnel possess critical data on the company as a whole that may not be available to the analyst. These data may necessitate a rejection of some of the analyst's proposals.

In designing new reports to recommend to management, it is a good practice to design a sample form that has representative data on it. The form should be an exact replica of what management can expect to see if the new design is put into operation. If a multiple-copy form is being suggested, all copies should be included in the sample, with different color schemes and notations for each copy as deemed necessary or desirable by the analyst. In this manner, management can readily see some of the benefits of the analyst's design work. They are particularly concerned with the output of the system, since this is something with which they are familiar and which they depend on for decision making.

PROCESSING

When analyzing a system, the analyst must recognize what processing operations are performed to achieve the desired results. The logic must be completely evaluated so that the goal of each operation is understood in proper perspective. The analyst will ultimately be required to evaluate the processing performed to determine if output data are efficiently produced, or if some better method might be suggested.

Keep in mind that the analyst must be innovative in his approach toward computer processing. Because a group of tasks or operations is performed a certain way in the present system does not necessitate a similar approach in the proposed one. The use of a computer allows the analyst a greater degree of flexibility than was feasible in a manual system or a unit-record one. Perhaps several independent operations can be combined into a single computer program, thereby reducing errors.

It is also possible that the analyst may recommend on-line processing to replace batch processing in a particular system. In **batch processing** a group or batch of inputs is processed at one time. For example, at the end of each day all charge slips in a department store are keypunched, and the punched cards used to update an accounts receivable master file. **On-line processing,** on the other hand, enables immediate updating of data on a master file via terminal devices. Thus, when a customer purchases something on a charge account, it is possible to enter this information into the computer at the time of the sale.

It is essential, while designing the processing steps, for the analyst to remove himself from the intricacies of the present system. He must design a total system, utilizing computer equipment, without limiting himself to the present approach.

A common tool used for organizing ideas during the design of processing steps is the systems flowchart. These flowcharts depict the relationships among inputs, processing, and outputs. They make it easier to review the proposed system with management, instead of requiring them to wade through numerous pages of narrative. In addition, flowcharts give the programming staff clear insight into the workings of the system.

The design of processing steps involves more than just determining relationships of inputs, processing, and outputs. It includes the establishment of schedules for producing the various outputs. The analyst must designate which outputs will be produced daily, weekly, monthly, etc. This schedule is useful for management when they are reviewing the proposed system. In addition, it is also valuable for the operations section of the data processing unit, since they will eventually have the responsibility for turning out the desired reports.

The analyst must also clearly define all calculations and procedures to be performed when computer files are to be updated or when specific reports are generated. Again, this will be of interest to management as well as to the programmer.

INPUT

Now that the analyst appreciates the processing necessary to produce the outputs under the present system, he must look at the inputs that are used. **Input** is the data that will be fed into the system to serve as the basis for desired outputs. This input may typically be on media such as paper, punched cards, magnetic tape, and magnetic disk, when computers are utilized in the present system, or on ticket stubs, time sheets, and bills in manual systems.

The analyst must know the properties of each major type of input so that he can incorporate the appropriate ones in the new system when design work begins. The advantages and disadvantages of each type must be clearly understood. Factors such as relative cost, processing speed, storage capability, and handling characteristics must be considered.

The answers to the following questions will provide a clear insight into the nature of the input for the system that the analyst is studying:

1. Can the analyst trace back where all information used for processing is derived?
2. How often is each type of input generated?
3. If there are codes or abbreviations used for input, does the analyst have complete lists of them?
4. What happens to input information in order to make it machine-readable, if this is required? For example, is input on certain documents keypunched? If so, what happens to the documents after keypunching of information from them is performed?

When designing the new system, the analyst must consider two basic types of inputs:

1. **Source documents** must be designed so that all information necessary for processing will be supplied. These documents should be designed in a manner analogous to the design of outputs mentioned above. That is, sample forms with typical entries should be provided.
2. The analyst must decide what **files** will be needed to retain data for producing desired reports when they are required. A decision must be made as to whether card files, tape files, disk files, etc., will best suit the system being designed. As an example, an analyst designing a real-time system will probably consider incorporating disk files in his design because of the random-access feature.

In designing files to be used in processing, the analyst will find file layouts very useful. A **file layout**[1] shows, for each different type of record in each file, the name of each field, its length, and its location within the record. With this type of drawing, management can easily see the type of information that will be stored. They may suggest additional fields that may prove valuable in the future. Management may, for example, envision a need in the future to perform certain statistical studies. The programmer will obviously need file layouts in order to be able to write the necessary programs.

If a file, such as a card file, is to serve as an intermediary file between source documents and the files that are to be updated, then layouts and specific instructions are required here also. If information is to be keypunched from certain documents, for example, then card layouts that show the fields on each card, and keypunch instructions should be included in the design of the inputs. If there will be codes used on various inputs, then the analyst must either establish complete lists of codes or else take existing lists, if they are adequate, and include them in his design. Where possible, lists of codes should conform to existing ones to avoid confusion when the new system becomes operational.

TESTING AND IMPLEMENTATION

It is important to realize that the design of a new system involves more than just the design of various elements discussed above. The analyst must prepare a plan to install the new system if management approves the design. This plan must include the following items:

1. The system must undergo a *systems test* once all programs have been written and the training of departmental personnel is completed. The analyst prepares sample data that will encompass all possible cases. The data are stepped through the system in much the same way as a normal run. The major difference is that the analyst remains in control of the data throughout all processing. If the computer produces reports that differ from what the analyst calculated with pencil and paper using the same data, then there is a problem. Either the programmer has made errors in logic, or the analyst may have misunderstood certain calculations, or departmental employees have erred. The purpose of a systems test is to make sure

[1]File layouts will be discussed in detail in Chapters 5 and 6.

that the system functions as intended. If the test is successful, management can determine exactly how the system will operate when it is completely implemented.

2. The analyst must allow time to *train* the personnel who will be involved in the new system. All procedures must be explained to the people who will be using them. It will also make the system function more effectively if each individual sees exactly where he stands in the operation of the entire system.

3. The *type of implementation* must be made clear to management. A common plan of implementation is known as a **parallel run.** Essentially, this means that the new system will be run initially at the same time that the current system is working. In other words, the new system will parallel the current one. In this way, people can become familiar with the new system while all reports are generated under the current one. One of the advantages of a parallel run is that it gets the momentum going under the new way of doing things without jeopardizing any system's continuity. The obvious disadvantage is that it involves additional expense for two groups of people to be working on the same system at the same time—one group doing it the old way, and the other doing it the new way.

The analyst must include in his plan the time period for which a parallel run will continue before the old system is completely dropped and the new one is permanently established.

A parallel run is especially useful if the analyst is implementing a complicated procedure. However, on occasion, certain systems can be implemented immediately. This is the case when the new system is relatively simple and, if anything should go wrong at the outset, it is easy enough to revert immediately to the original way of doing things.

4. The analyst must consider the need to *follow up* on the new system after it has been operational for some time. Approximately three months after the new system is working, the analyst should check back to determine if the system is operating in the way that he intended. He may find that some people are no longer following the procedures exactly. There may be several reasons for this. Perhaps the people on the job have found a better way of performing some particular aspect of the system. It is also possible that new personnel have not received the proper training. In any event, the analyst may find it desirable to modify the system at this point or to update the documentation.

The following checklist is provided as a guide to ensure that all aspects of design have been adequately considered by the analyst.

1. Are management's objectives for the new system thoroughly understood?
2. Can any recommendations be made to management to expand or to modify these objectives?
3. Are all legal constraints known concerning the new system?
4. What is the deadline for having the design work completed?
5. When does management want the new system fully implemented?
6. What is the computer configuration the company has now?
7. Is any additional hardware and/or software already on order?
8. Are all reports that management wants from the new system fully understood?
9. Can any additional reports be suggested to management?
10. Are all calculations understood for the required processing?
11. Can other forms of output be recommended?
12. What controls can be built into the system that would facilitate processing?
13. What changes to input can be made to enhance the quality of output?
14. Can a plan for installation be easily implemented?
15. Have feedback procedures been adequately prepared?

GLOSSARY

Analysis. The separation of a system into its basic elements so that each can be studied individually and in relation to the others.

Batch processing. The processing of data in groups or batches rather than individually. This sort of processing is more efficient but cannot be used in systems where immediate access to information is necessary.

Constraints. Limitations placed on the analyst by specific legal, cost, and/or hardware restrictions.

Control. The process of minimizing data processing errors.

Feasibility study. The determination of a business or a system's computer requirements.

Feedback. The procedures necessary to make adjustments when errors occur.

Hardware. Computer equipment.

Input. Data that enter a system.

Objectives. Management's requirements from the system.

On-line processing. The processing of data immediately, as they enter the system. This type of processing is utilized when immediate access is a necessary requisite.

Output. Information produced by a system.

Parallel run. The simultaneous operation of the newly designed system with the existing one.

System. An organized method for accomplishing a business function. A system consists of individual elements that need to be studied both independently and interactively.

QUESTIONS

1. Define the term "system."
2. Distinguish between the terms "systems analysis" and "systems design."
3. Suppose you are asked to design a new system for which the analysis has already been completed. That is, the present analyst is to be reassigned, and you are to take over his assignment. Prepare a list of general questions you will need to ask the analyst.
4. Do you think that management's relationships with its employees are important variables in analyzing a system? Defend your position.
5. Suppose you have completed your analysis of an existing system and have determined that a new design is simply not cost-justifiable at this time. You know, however, that the vice-president is very eager for a new design. What would you do and why?
6. List and explain the systems elements, paying particular attention to the interactions among these elements.
7. Do you think it is useful or necessary for a systems analyst to have programming experience? Explain your answer.
8. Suppose the analysis and design of a very large system necessitates the use of several analysts. Would it be best to segment their tasks so that one is responsible for inputs, another for feedback, etc.? Or would this sort of segmentation lead to problems? Explain your answer.

UNIT 

BASIC DESIGN CONSIDERATIONS

CHAPTER **4**

FORMS DESIGN

The output of printed data for use is generally the most important product of a computerized system. The outputs produced by the computer, whether they be printed on paper or displayed on some sort of terminal device, provide a summation of activities within the system and data critical to management for decision-making purposes. Needless to say, with the high volume of activity normally occurring within business today, the output provided by a computerized data processing system is vital to the management of a company.

In the vast majority of cases, the primary output of a computer is in the form of a printed report. Thus the design of printed documents falls within the realm of the data processing area and becomes a prime responsibility of the analyst. But let us not deceive ourselves. Though a prime consideration of the analyst is the printed form, the analyst must be equally concerned with every document employed within a computer system. In order to optimize computer productivity and to facilitate the creation of effective reports, the analyst must be concerned with source documents and input forms that are used within a system. Specifically, the analyst must:

1. Analyze documents/outputs used within the system and determine those that require revision
2. Design new or revised document/outputs (based upon the prior analysis) that will more promptly reflect the informational needs of the system

First, let us consider the analysis of existing forms or outputs.

ANALYSIS OF EXISTING FORMS AND OUTPUTS

The impetus to analyze a particular document or output may emanate from the following sources:

1. A current or projected user, department head, or manager may ask the analyst to examine an existing document or output for completeness, accuracy, or future use.

2. The analyst may discover weaknesses or shortcomings of an output of the system while examining other aspects of the system.
3. Within a more formal or major systems study, in which the entire systems staff may be involved, the detailed analysis of any forms or outputs would not occur until after a clear definition of the problems encountered within the system is written. (The concept of a formal problem definition is discussed in Chapter 15.)

To ascertain whether a form or output is adequately fulfilling present or projected needs, we must initially examine its existing format, in its entirety, and consider the following questions. The answers to these questions will be of considerable value in the analysis of documents or outputs.

1. *Is the purpose of the form or output clearly indicated by its title?* How many times have you or your family received a letter from a company or store and been unable to determine its significance? How many times has an advertisement from an insurance company been mistaken for a bill, or worse yet, a bill mistaken for an advertisement? Both of the above illustrate forms that were not properly and clearly identified.
2. *Is the source of the document (i.e., department, section, company, person) easily identified?* Have you ever received a bill and not known where to send the payment? How about a memo from someone whose name was illegibly scribbled, in which no other identifying data were provided?
3. *Is the entire form or output legible and intelligible? Are all the characters or letters easy to read and to understand?* Some motor vehicle departments provide examples of the manner in which numbers should appear on license forms to assist in the processing of data. In some states, consumer protection laws require that the lettering on a contract be of a certain size so that it is easy to read. On many cathode ray tubes (CRTs), the characters S and 5, 3, and 8, or 2 and Z are so similar that frequent operator errors occur.
4. *Is the space provided for the insertion of data or for answers to questions adequate?* If the response you seek is more than a yes or a no answer, or quite long, then sufficient space for an answer must be provided. If you are seeking data in the form of written responses, then it is pointless to give almost no space for the respondent to write. Hopefully, if sufficient space is provided, the response will be more lucid and more meaningful to you.

5. *Are critical data placed prominently?* Items that are important to the receiver of a form should be highlighted in some way to catch the eye. Examples of data items that should be accentuated are: the last date of payment of a bill, finance or special payment charges, the date to appear in court, the minimum payment required. Often these items are blocked, placed within borders, or have large arrows pointing to them.

6. *Is the form easily filed or stored?* For the most part, forms or punched cards should be compatible with the filing system employed within the firm. Legal papers (8½ × 14 in.) may not be suitable or economically justifiable for a company whose filing system employs an 8½ × 11 in. storage file.

Many companies and agencies employ punched cards for invoices, bills, or checks (e.g., telephone company, utility companies). Using a punched card facilitates the distribution of bills and checks (only one document must be prepared), the processing of payments or reconciliation of accounts (the cards can be directly input to the computer), and the eventual storage of the cards (these documents can be neatly stored in card files).

7. *Does the composition and/or color of an output form lend itself to easy reading or use?* Multicolor forms are more easily handled and distributed by both company personnel and the consumer (e.g., the client receives the yellow copy and the company retains the blue).

Many forms employ perforations to facilitate the tearing of the form in half, so that the consumer retains half as a record of the bill and encloses the other half with the payment. When an analyst designs a form that uses the idea of perforations, he must ensure that it is operationally sound. How many times have you attempted to "tear along the dotted line" and wound up with a jagged piece of paper in one hand and the remnant of the bill in the other hand? Perforations, when used, must permit the form to be easily separated.

If a number of lines of data must be referenced by a clerk to handle a transaction, then the use of a visual display terminal is not possible, since after the screen is completely filled with data, each new line of data that is added would destroy a previous entry. Thus the output of the transaction must be handled in segments or via terminal devices that permit the printing of all data required.

8. *For a paper document, does the number of multiple carbon copies result in illegible and unusable copies?* Though we would like to type, at one time, ten copies of a form (using

carbon), it is highly improbable that the last few copies would be readable and usable.

9. *Is the cost related to a form or output commensurate with its use?* The cost of any form or output must be economically justifiable. A form used solely by three internal company personnel would not generally warrant a cost of $10 per form.

However, if the form would serve the work of six people, this cost might be justifiable. It is the analyst's responsibility to perform cost analysis as part of the design effort. For example, though a company might desire to have its clerks enter data to the computer via terminals, the entire cost of such a project might be prohibitive. A cost analysis would provide some rationale for deciding whether to undertake such a vast project.

All of the prior questions are designed to permit a thorough examination of any form or output. Each analyst, drawing on his or her experience, will employ each of these questions differently, depending on the type of application being investigated. These questions should be revised to suit the particular application under investigation.

During the analysis phase, the analyst should draw on any resource available to supplement the information obtained by answering the questions above. A resource that could prove invaluable to any analyst is the representative or sales person of a company that specializes in paper products used in DP installations. These sales representatives are abreast of the latest developments in their field. They can demonstrate a wide range of standard forms, carbon-backed paper, carbonless forms, and computer-oriented paper products. There may exist a type of form that can be readily adapted or modified for your purposes. If nothing else is learned, the analyst will gain an insight into the current state of the paper products/forms market. This information will be of value in future analysis and design projects.

As stated, the variety and scope of answers obtained by the analyst will assist in the evaluation of any form or output. Though the previous questions will provide the analyst with data about the existing use of a form or output, one factor not yet considered is possible future use. The future use of a printed form or output is of considerable importance in the decision to redesign and weighs heavily against factors relating to current usage. The analyst must develop a "feel" for how the form or output is to be used in order to effect a successful and usable design. Let us, therefore, discuss some factors that relate to the future use of a form or output that an analyst must review at the time design work begins.

1. *Will the form or output service the same group of people and number of departments?* The analyst must compare the people currently using the form or output against the people who are scheduled to use it. In doing this, the analyst will determine whether:

a. The same number of copies of a printed report is required or the quantity must be increased or decreased. It may be necessary to order a new multicarbon form, to alter the manner in which the form is produced, or to change distribution of the form so that not everyone currently receiving the report will continue to receive it. In the case of outputs (printed or visual) prepared by some form of terminal device, can an existing format satisfy a new user? If it can, this will save an additional systems and programming effort and, thereby, company dollars and resources. Here, it is important to determine who really needs a report. This sounds much easier than it actually is. Most people are reluctant to admit that they do not use an output, for a variety of reasons (e.g., people will think they are not working, they might miss something, insecurity about their job status). Often, the answer to the question, "Do you now use this report or plan to use this report?" is a stock "Yes!" The analyst must specifically determine who uses what data, when, and how. Only then will the analyst's recommendations on the distribution of an output be of value.

b. Items of data must be added to, or deleted from, the existing format to strengthen the usefulness of the form or output. Here, a change in user requirements could cause specific data items within the report to become obsolete or extremely vital. Thus, within the overall format, some data items could be deleted while others are added, or existing data items could be shifted to highlight their importance.

2. *Will the output be prepared solely with the use of existing media?* This factor requires an analysis of the means of preparing a report and its availability to users. Many considerations must be reviewed by the analyst. For example, will a report be prepared manually or by machine? When a company converts to a computer-oriented system from a manual one, the composition and appearance of forms used within the sys-

tem change radically. Just as informational needs change within a company, so, too, the priority of reports or outputs will vary. As a result, a printed report once prepared partially by hand may be prepared entirely by computer (e.g., in a data collection system that feeds directly to a distant computer for on-line processing, as with an automated manufacturing system). A report originally prepared by a printer on a daily basis carries urgently needed information that could be made immediately available to users via a visual display terminal (e.g., a CRT tied directly into the stock exchange maintaining a status on the volume of business a Wall Street firm is transacting).

3. *Will the physical appearance of a printed form or visual output be altered?* Many companies regularly change their advertising symbols or names, or redesign the stationery used for all correspondence. Any of these conditions could result in a revision of a company's printed forms. Consider the alteration of a company's monthly customer charge statement (e.g., that of a retail store). A change in where or how the customer's name and address are to be printed will necessitate the redesign of the form and involve the analyst. The analyst must determine the nature of the change and translate this change into terms or specifications acceptable to the programming staff. In addition, he must determine the length of time this revision will last.

Likewise, to facilitate the entering of data on a visual display terminal (CRT), the physical appearance of information on the screen of the terminal must conform to a predetermined format. In addition to changes necessitated by equipment requirements, a newly implemented operational procedure might require alterations in existing forms or outputs. For example, in an effort to control the improper or illegal use of credit cards, businesses have instituted somewhat elaborate checking procedures. These controls have necessitated changes in both printed forms and output because space must be provided for credit control entries (i.e., the entry of approval codes on the charge slip prior to the completion of the transaction and the display, on a terminal, of the customer's current credit balance as the credit check is performed).

4. *Will new data be made available to management?* Data prepared by computer, either provided on a printed report or displayed via terminals, can supply new information to management heretofore too difficult or too costly to provide.

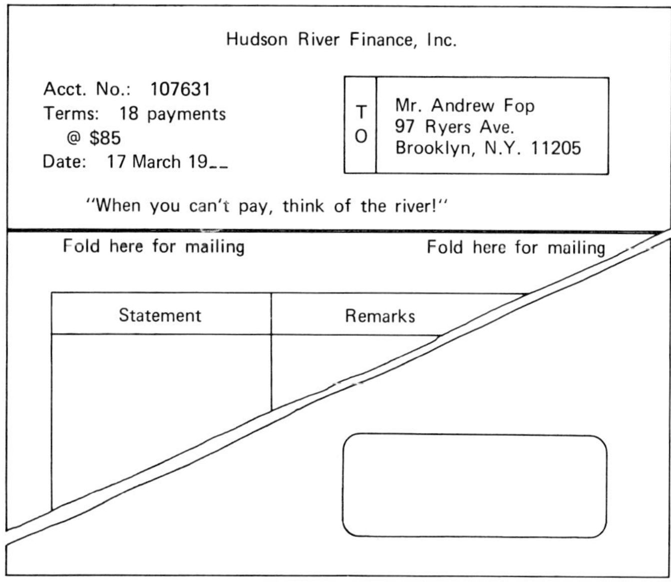

Hudson River Finance, Inc.
Acct. No.: 107631
Terms: 18 payments
@ $85
Date: 17 March 19__
TO
Mr. Andrew Fop
97 Ryers Ave.
Brooklyn, N.Y. 11205
"When you can't pay, think of the river!"
Fold here for mailing
Fold here for mailing
Statement
Remarks

Figure 4.1 New invoice and envelope.

Let us consider an example involving the redesign of a company's printed invoice. Previously manually prepared, the invoice will be prepared automatically by computer. To permit computer preparation and the usage of window (see-through) envelopes, redesign is necessary. Here, savings accrue by eliminating the manual preparation of invoices and the addressing of envelopes. Figure 4.1 illustrates the new form and envelope.

Each change or redesign is dependent on the requirements or purposes imposed on the form. There is no standardized set of rules that indicates when a change will be required. In general, when the benefits that will accrue from changing the form outweigh the expense (wasted stock on hand, set-up charges for printing plates, different binders, etc.) and inconvenience (retraining company personnel to use the new form), a change is justified.

After analysis, the analyst will decide whether to redesign the given form. Before a new form can be considered, all other company documents must be examined to determine whether any existing form, with minor changes, could satisfy the new requirements.

The analyst may find it advantageous to design a computer-generated output. Prior to this, he must familiarize himself with the printer device of the computer. Careful study of the equipment manual is mandatory. This manual describes the operating controls, specifications, and limitations of the specific machine. Data such as carriage controls, printing speeds, form specifications, printer characteristics, and machine operations are invaluable when the analyst is designing printed outputs.

The analyst should list all the types of data with their proposed positions on the document under design. Each entry should be evaluated to ensure that it is essential to the form.

A **printer spacing chart,** illustrated in Figure 4.2, is extremely useful to the analyst. By actually laying out the data fields, the analyst can visualize the form's eventual format. Computer-printed documents require the use of this chart, so that programmers know the requirements for a program.

Don't become confused. The printer spacing chart is not restricted to the design of printed documents. The printer spacing chart can be used when designing any type of document (input, source, or summary) or an output to be employed with any type of terminal device. Basically, where the spacing of data is essential, the printer spacing chart should be used. Similarly, to ensure the proper spacing of data across the page, the printer spacing chart is useful.

Let us note some of the physical characteristics on the printer spacing chart. The chart provides for 150 printing positions—15 columns composed of 10 printing positions each. The number of characters composing the print line varies from 80 to 144 print positions depending upon the manufacturer of the printer. Similarly, visual display, teletypewriter, or CRT terminals can have output areas ranging from 60 to 120 characters. It is the responsibility of the analyst to determine the characteristics of the equipment employed within the system prior to any design effort.

The use of the printer spacing chart permits the analyst to experiment with different techniques while designing any form or output. The most effective design may be selected without any extensive delay after considering many and varied types of formats. The following recommendations will be helpful when using a spacing chart in designing:

1. Boldface type can be used to highlight headings, special notes, or dates.
2. Numeric fields should accommodate the largest possible entry.

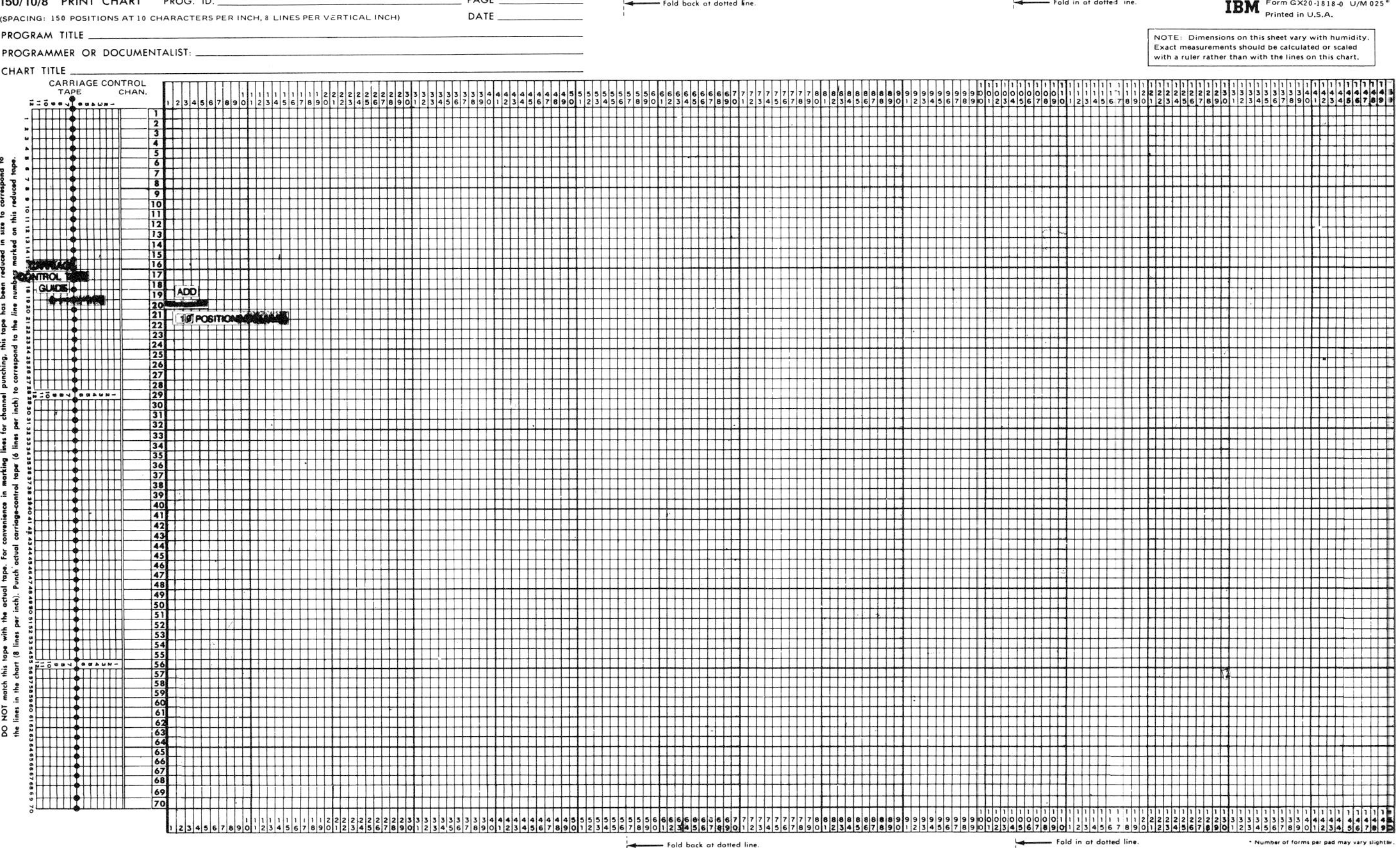

Figure 4.2 Printer spacing chart (courtesy IBM).

3. Filing codes, dates, or identification numbers should be placed near the top of the form or output on the terminal.
4. Specifically for printed documents, when multiple copies are required, color codes can assist in routing copies. Clerks remember that the pink copy is sent to the supply department, the green copy to the accounting department, etc.
5. Use a heavy or double-ruled line to segregate sections of the data. This technique is frequently used with preprinted forms. The double or heavy lines can be created on a report by a programmer; however, the programming effort can be prohibitive. Double lines are particularly effective to highlight data that are output via a terminal.
6. Incorporate controls or checks for the protection of payrolls, accounts payable, special checking accounts, or cash disbursements. This will ensure that checks are prepared properly.
7. The inclusion of a form number is necessary for most preprinted forms.

Figure 4.2 illustrates a completed printer spacing chart for a proposed computer printout.

A great deal of an analyst's work is related to the preparation of printed forms of some type. As a result, the analyst must be aware of considerations particularly relevant to printed documents. The next section deals specifically with the printed media.

PRINTED MEDIA

The selection of the appropriate type of paper on which to print a report is a design consideration of the analyst. The following terms describe paper types generally available.

1. Standard (stock) paper
2. Preprinted forms

Standard or stock paper is the most widely used paper size. Its uniform width, ready off-the-shelf availability, and adaptability to any type of printer permit general usage within any company. By using stock paper sizes, system costs can be reduced and controlled.

Whereas stock paper can be purchased without special effort and without additional cost, preprinted forms are somewhat different. Custom-tailored to satisfy a particular company need, preprinted forms are costlier, limited in use, and may require special handling. These forms, used primarily for outgoing company correspondence, represent a form of advertising. Common examples of preprinted or **customized forms** are customer invoices with special letterheads and payroll or special checks issued by a company. Figure 4.3 illustrates customized card formats.

The new applicant card has a single-purpose usage within the registration procedure of a college. The other card represents a form of advertising, while serving the functional purpose of recording data. Each card was designed for a specific purpose, and its usage is limited to that purpose.

It should be noted that with stock paper, the page and column headings, identifications, page numbers, and the like can be computer-generated to make the data more intelligible.

Figure 4.3 Preprinted card formats.

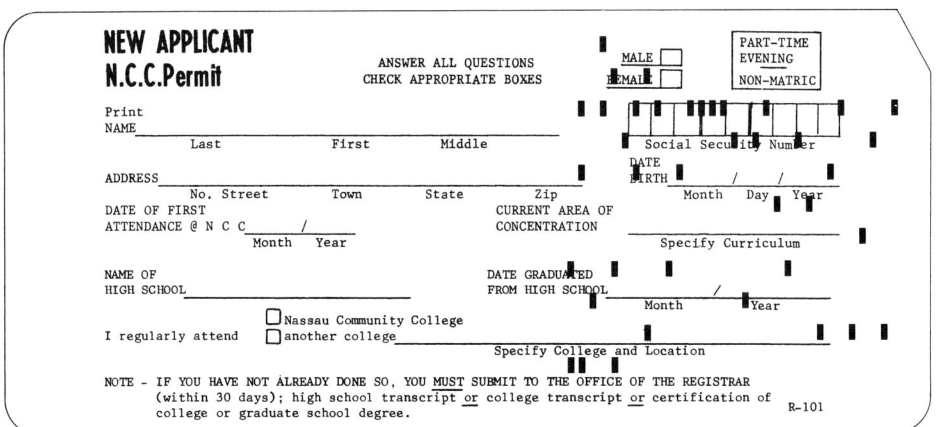

NEW APPLICANT
N.C.C.Permit

ANSWER ALL QUESTIONS
CHECK APPROPRIATE BOXES

MALE ☐
FEMALE ☐

PART-TIME
EVENING
NON-MATRIC

Print NAME ____ Last First Middle

Social Security Number

ADDRESS ____ No. Street Town State Zip

DATE OF BIRTH __/__/__ Month Day Year

DATE OF FIRST ATTENDANCE @ N C C __/__ Month Year

CURRENT AREA OF CONCENTRATION ____ Specify Curriculum

NAME OF HIGH SCHOOL ____

DATE GRADUATED FROM HIGH SCHOOL __/__ Month Year

I regularly attend ☐ Nassau Community College ☐ another college ____ Specify College and Location

NOTE - IF YOU HAVE NOT ALREADY DONE SO, YOU MUST SUBMIT TO THE OFFICE OF THE REGISTRAR (within 30 days); high school transcript or college transcript or certification of college or graduate school degree.

R-101

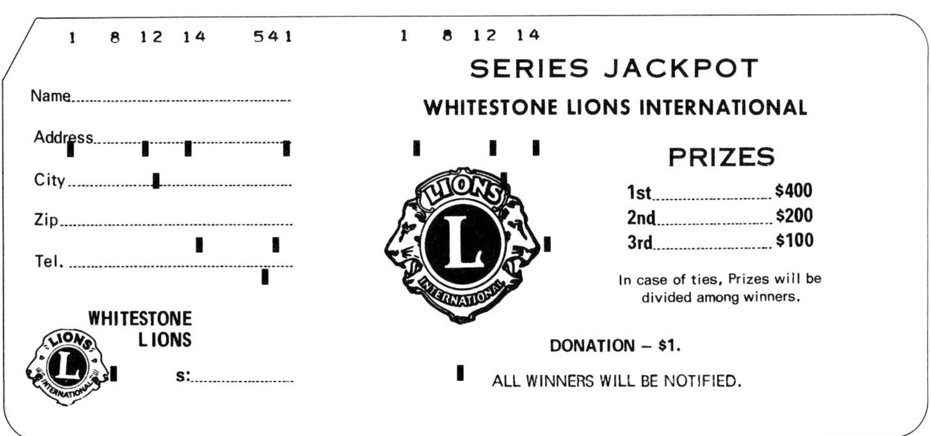

1 8 12 14 541

Name

Address

City

Zip

Tel.

WHITESTONE LIONS

S:

1 8 12 14

SERIES JACKPOT

WHITESTONE LIONS INTERNATIONAL

PRIZES

1st $400
2nd $200
3rd $100

In case of ties, Prizes will be divided among winners.

DONATION – $1.

ALL WINNERS WILL BE NOTIFIED.

Also, precise alignment is not required. Another advantage of stock paper is that slight changes in the format of reports do not make existing inventories of paper stock obsolete, as they might with preprinted forms.

A general rule of thumb is: If the report remains within the company, it may be prepared on standard paper with computer-generated headings. The analyst should attempt to standardize all reports and their formats. This will result in:

1. Purchase of fewer special paper sizes, thus reducing paper supply inventories
2. Standardization of the type and size of binders and filing supplies
3. Quicker processing and handling of forms
4. Reduction in the set-up time of form-feeding devices, since the operator will not be required to unload the printer and replace standard paper with a special-sized form

The analyst must also consider a form's eventual storage and handling. Both standard paper and preprinted paper forms can have one or both of the following characteristics:

1. They appear on continuous forms
2. They can be marginally punched

Let us consider each of the above.

A **continuous form** is a series of connected sheets, each form being individually prepared. After printing has been completed, the individual sheets are easily separated by the perforations between forms.

A **marginally punched form** presents a different format and problem. The term "marginally punched" refers to the uniformly spaced holes placed in the margin on each side of the form. These holes are required to accurately feed paper through the printing device. **Pin-fed** is another term used to designate forms utilizing this principle. If no control were used in feeding paper to the printer, slippage would occur with today's high-speed machines.

Figure 4.4 pictures the federal W-2 form. This is a continuous, marginally punched, pin-fed, side-by-side, customized form. Notice that all forms are connected and would subsequently be separated along the perforations.

Margins

When designing a form, space should be allotted for the marginal perforations required on pin-fed forms or for possible binding. Most forms have a perforation of ½ in. on either side. A minimum of one print position should be left between the first machine-printed character planned and the perforation.

If binding is a consideration, space may be allotted at either the top or the side of the form. Some reports are bound using the marginally punched perforations. This eliminates the necessity of providing additional space for binding. It is an accepted practice to let the form-feeding holes remain on internally used reports. When binding is necessary, data should not be printed too near the margin provided, since, after binding, reading that data may become difficult. Binding a report at the top can be accomplished without sacrificing the form's readability. Binders are available that use binder holes or pressure-held fasteners.

Carbons

The proper use of carbon copies can effect substantial savings, when they are incorporated in a design. When large numbers of copies of a form are required, however, increasing the number of carbons used is not always a satisfactory solution. When many copies are used, the legibility of the last copies is very poor. The use of split carbons, special carbons, or a limit to the maximum number of carbons are ways of effectively controlling the quality of copies. Split carbons are used when some, but not all, data must be specifically placed on respective copies of a form. Instead of a full carbon between copies, split carbons are placed over the fields requiring duplication.

When a reduction in the number of copies is desired, the designer may use the following techniques:

1. Side-by-side printed reports (Figure 4.4) duplicating the data on each. This technique is sometimes called "two-up."
2. Consolidated reports that can be used by many departments.
3. Sequence routing of reports between departmental personnel, in lieu of simultaneous distribution, where time permits.
4. Mechanical or photographic reproductions. A rule of thumb states: With forms of eight parts or less, carbons can effectively be used without smudging to render legible copies.

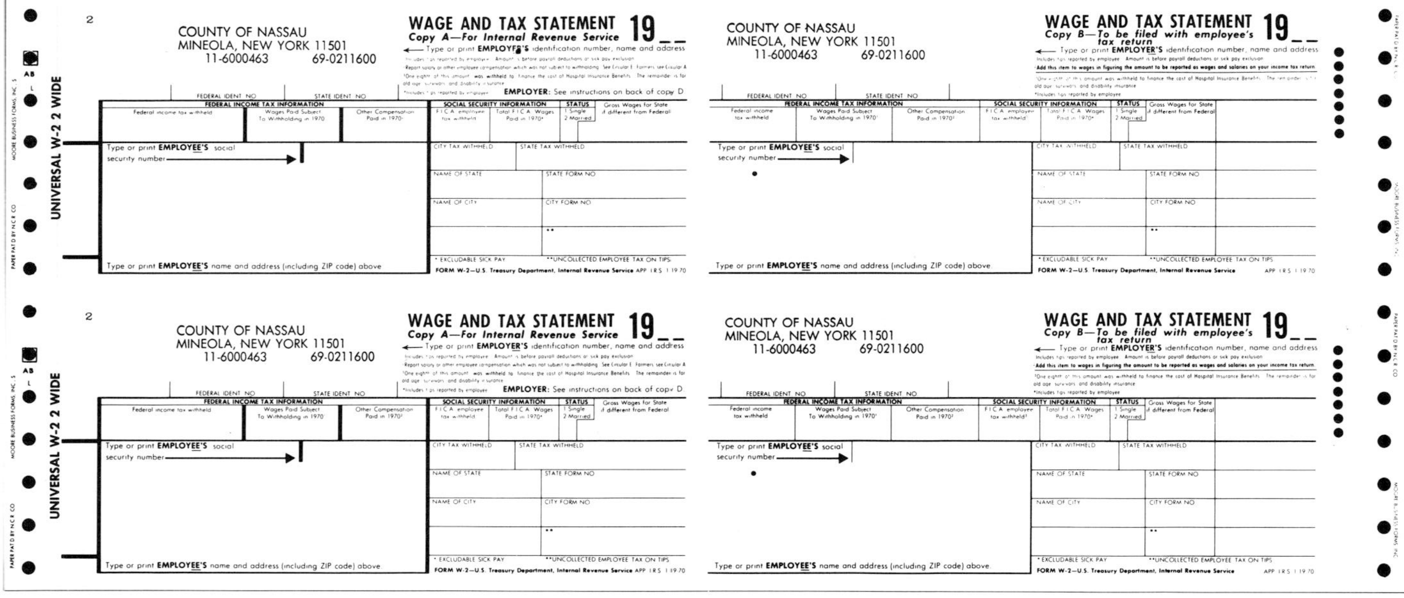

UNIVERSAL W-2 2 WIDE

2

COUNTY OF NASSAU
MINEOLA, NEW YORK 11501
11-6000463 69-0211600

WAGE AND TAX STATEMENT 19__
Copy A—For Internal Revenue Service

← Type or print **EMPLOYER'S** identification number, name and address

EMPLOYER: See instructions on back of copy D

FEDERAL IDENT NO | STATE IDENT NO

FEDERAL INCOME TAX INFORMATION			SOCIAL SECURITY INFORMATION		STATUS	
Federal income tax withheld	Wages Paid Subject To Withholding in 1970	Other Compensation Paid in 1970	F.I.C.A. employee tax withheld	Total F.I.C.A. Wages Paid in 1970*	1 Single 2 Married	Gross Wages for State if different from Federal

Type or print **EMPLOYEE'S** social security number →

CITY TAX WITHHELD	STATE TAX WITHHELD
NAME OF STATE	STATE FORM NO
NAME OF CITY	CITY FORM NO
	**

Type or print **EMPLOYEE'S** name and address (including ZIP code) above

* EXCLUDABLE SICK PAY **UNCOLLECTED EMPLOYEE TAX ON TIPS

FORM W-2—U.S. Treasury Department, Internal Revenue Service APP I.R.S. 1-19-70

COUNTY OF NASSAU
MINEOLA, NEW YORK 11501
11-6000463 69-0211600

WAGE AND TAX STATEMENT 19__
Copy B—To be filed with employee's tax return

← Type or print **EMPLOYER'S** identification number, name and address

Includes tips reported by employee. Amount is before payroll deductions or sick pay exclusion

Add this item to wages in figuring the amount to be reported as wages and salaries on your income tax return

One eighth of this amount was withheld to finance the cost of Hospital Insurance Benefits. The remainder is for old age, survivors and disability insurance

*Includes tips reported by employee

FEDERAL IDENT NO | STATE IDENT NO

FEDERAL INCOME TAX INFORMATION			SOCIAL SECURITY INFORMATION		STATUS	
Federal income tax withheld	Wages Paid Subject To Withholding in 1970	Other Compensation Paid in 1970	F.I.C.A. employee tax withheld	Total F.I.C.A. Wages Paid in 1970*	1 Single 2 Married	Gross Wages for State if different from Federal

Type or print **EMPLOYEE'S** social security number →

CITY TAX WITHHELD	STATE TAX WITHHELD
NAME OF STATE	STATE FORM NO
NAME OF CITY	CITY FORM NO
	**

Type or print **EMPLOYEE'S** name and address (including ZIP code) above

* EXCLUDABLE SICK PAY **UNCOLLECTED EMPLOYEE TAX ON TIPS

FORM W-2—U.S. Treasury Department, Internal Revenue Service APP I.R.S. 1-19-70

UNIVERSAL W-2 2 WIDE

2

COUNTY OF NASSAU
MINEOLA, NEW YORK 11501
11-6000463 69-0211600

WAGE AND TAX STATEMENT 19__
Copy A—For Internal Revenue Service

COUNTY OF NASSAU
MINEOLA, NEW YORK 11501
11-6000463 69-0211600

WAGE AND TAX STATEMENT 19__
Copy B—To be filed with employee's tax return

Figure 4.4 Wage and tax statement printed using a side-by-side format.

The types of carbons available to the analyst are:

1. *One-time carbons.* These are used once and then thrown away.
2. *Carbon-backed paper.* A carbon surface is placed on part or all of the reverse side of the original copy.
3. *Chemically-coated paper.* Chemicals on interfacing sheets react when pressed together by a type bar or stylus (e.g., bank deposit slips, laundry tickets).

The general guide to usage is:

1. When a small number of copies is required or carbons are available and easily used, a one-time carbon is preferred.
2. If carbons are unusable or undesirable, a chemically-coated copy may service that need properly.
3. When additional writing on a form is required and slippage of carbons is a problem, carbon-backed paper can be effectively used.
4. If specific data must be limited to particular copies, to avoid the placement of too much data, split carbons may be employed.

In general, the analyst should consider all of the possibilities discussed in completing his design. A checklist of some kind should be used by the analyst to ensure the completeness of his effort. The following checklist is offered to the reader as a sample.

CHECKLIST OF CONSIDERATIONS

1. Equipment

What equipment is available within the computer system in general, and exactly what equipment is being made available for the specific user? Often the devices available at an installation cannot be used for any number of reasons.

Of the equipment that is available for use, what are the physical characteristics of each device, and which specific features does each have? Frequently, a device can possess a special feature whose use might enhance the output of data or ease the entry of data into the system. Likewise, a special feature might not be supportable by the system and is, therefore, useless. It is the responsibility of the analyst always to check the capabilities of the computer system and determine what the equipment can or cannot support. Imagine the embarrassment of the analyst who orders equipment and upon installation discovers that it is not compatible with the main computer. This problem is encountered frequently when an attempt is made to add a device (especially a terminal) to an existing computer system produced by a different manufacturer.

2. Improved Distribution of Copies

Is the number of copies of a report justifiable, and are the proper people receiving the report?

3. Volume and Frequency of the Report

Is a report needed weekly or daily, and can its preparation and frequency be justified? Many times, the data drawn from a weekly report, which stands alone, might be of greater value than if grouped together with similar data prepared on a monthly basis. The compilation of a document comparing when reports are prepared to when they are actually needed, or used, might be of value to the analyst.

4. Storage and Filing Considerations

How long should a report or form or check be kept, and when should it be filed? For example, what legal restraints are placed on IRS employee records, customer charge accounts? These considerations would affect how essential data must be stored and who is permitted to have access to them. Should IRS data be kept in a fireproof vault? Should bank payroll checks be stored in a safe and accounted for by number?

Very often, storage considerations are glossed over and disregarded. This is not one of the analyst's most creative jobs, but one that requires the utmost attention and precision. Here again, the manufacturers of various forms and storage devices can provide invaluable assistance.

5. Special Requirements

What special factors are required for the preparation of each form? What special forms are to be used, and how should they be handled? Will special distribution of a report be required, or will special time constraints be applied to specific reports such that the computer operators need special instructions? Answers to these questions are often neglected, but unless accounted for early in the design phase, they can create serious implementation problems.

6. Cost

The cost associated with the preparation of any printed form is always a prime consideration of the analyst. Once again, the cost of preparing a form must be justifiable. A customized form might cost too much to prepare and distribute. Thus the analyst would need to redesign the form or modify the form's preparation in order to work within economic constraints.

Up to this point, our discussions have generally focused on printed documents, with particular emphasis on their preparation by computer. However, there is another means available for the preparation of data within report form. Today, in ever increasing instances, more data are being made available via terminal devices. The device most commonly used is the visual display terminal, referred to as the **CRT** (cathode ray tube, a television picture tube used to display data on a screen similar to that of a television set). Let us turn our discussion toward this topic and review considerations peculiar to terminal outputs.

TERMINAL OUTPUTS

Because of technological developments within the computer field, the terminal has gained undisputed acceptance and is an integral part of many computer installations. Visual display terminals are being used in motor vehicle bureaus, supermarkets, school systems, air traffic control, and a host of other installations. There is a strong possibility that the analyst will encounter applications involving terminals, and he should be familiar with them.

Many of the considerations, in both analysis and design, that were applied to printed documents can be successfully applied to terminals. The initial problem faced by the analyst is determining which type of terminal would be best suited for the application. This is vital because each type of terminal has its own advantages and limitations.

For example, a **teletypewriter terminal,** also known as a **self-documenting terminal,** prints its output on paper. This continuous printed record provides the user with a permanent record of output. The clerk employing the terminal device merely has to examine this **hard-copy output** to observe any of the previously completed transactions.

The only serious limitation to the teletypewriter terminal is the length of the carriage—the number of characters it can print on one line. As a result, the report's output, on this kind of terminal, is normally concise, with very specific uses for specific data. Generally, this is also true when the terminal is employed as an input device.

The CRT or visual display terminal presents a somewhat different problem. Here, no permanent records are kept. The data appear in the form of characters on a television-like screen. This type of output is commonly referred to as **soft copy.** In many instances, a complete record must be capable of appearing on the screen at one time. The problem encountered by the operator at the CRT is that after the screen is completely filled with data, every new line of data added to the display destroys an existing line of data on the screen. There is no standard answer to this type of problem; the solution is normally determined by trial and error.

A partial solution to the above problem has recently evolved and is often referred to as **page formatting.** It consists of carefully identifying and limiting the number of data items that appears on the screen at any one time. Therefore, the user of the terminal will always know how much data will appear on the screen and exactly in what order. The complete contents of the screen is referred to as a "page," and the contents of that page are fixed. The user accesses the page of his choice and performs whatever operations are required with the line desired. As with the teletypewriter terminal, carriage length is a consideration. The paging technique can be applied to both input and output applications.

Today, in the majority of cases, terminals are employed primarily as inquiry stations, and the vast majority are of the visual-display type. Accordingly, the number of printed forms employed with the majority of terminal applications would be extremely limited and, for the most part, designed for typewriter-like devices. A continuous form, of stock size, would be used in this case. When designing outputs for any type of terminal, it is helpful to use a printer spacing chart for formatting.

Regardless of the specific device, terminals lend themselves to use as inquiry stations capable of inputting and outputting data. Problems particular to source documents are discussed in the next section.

SOURCE DOCUMENTS

Source documents require a different perspective. Whereas printouts are the final results of processing, **source documents** provide the data for input. Design of a source document is equally as important as design of a printout, but different requirements must be considered.

Initially, the steps in a source document design are similar to the steps used for printed outputs. Data must be gathered, in correct format, to complete the proposed source document.

The proposed form is outlined on a spacing chart. The considerations are:

1. The data on the source document should, where possible, be positioned to facilitate simplified manual coding or simplified operator reading.
2. The sequence of data should assist the keypunch operator, coder, or typist in extracting data from the form. The operator should read data fields off the form in a logical sequence. Thus hesitations because of misinterpretations or visually jumping across the form are eliminated.
3. Key figures should be blocked out if they require special usage. Highlighting these figures will reduce the operator's search time.
4. To distinguish between input areas used by two different users, shade or darken the area set aside for one user and have the instructions specify who completes what input area.
5. A trial period must test the source document. If a change is needed, actual usage will indicate the form's inefficiencies. People using a form are often the best critics of its design.

Keep in mind that source documents need not always be typewritten copies. A mark-sensed card, for example, can serve as a source document.

The examples that follow will reinforce many of the principles we have just discussed.

EXAMPLE 1. The document shown in Figure 4.5 was used by a department store's accounts receivable section to indicate the receipt of payment or a credit given to a customer. The form

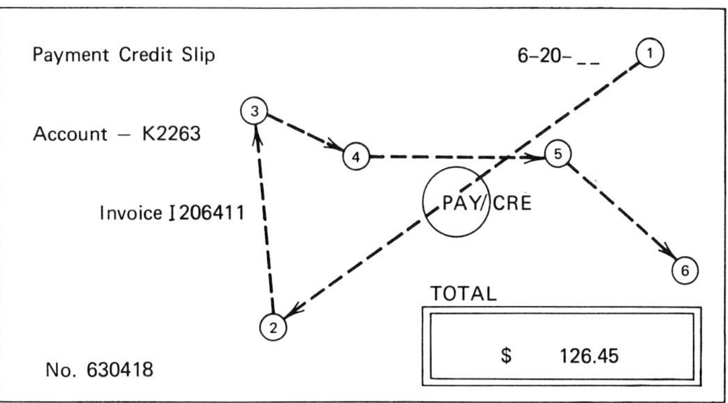
Payment Credit Slip

6–20–__

Account – K2263

Invoice I206411

PAY/CRE

TOTAL

$ 126.45

No. 630418

Figure 4.5 Payment/credit slip (noting the visual pattern required of a keypunch operator).

was manually completed and sent to be keypunched. It was batched into the accounts receivable system daily. In Figure 4.5, the dotted line and circled numbers indicate the visual pattern required of the keypunch operator. The symbol ① denotes the first item to be keypunched, ② the second item, and so on.

After analysis and discussion, the form was redesigned in the format shown in Figure 4.6. The itemized form number has been eliminated because analysis showed that the figure was never utilized. The operator's visual pattern and sequence is easier. This will avoid eye strain and will assist in reducing fatigue. Indentation will assist the operator in distinguishing the invoice number from the account number.

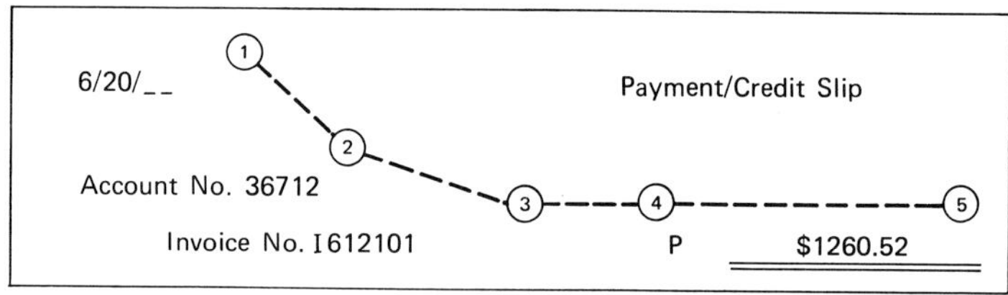

Figure 4.6
Redesign of payment/credit slip.

EXAMPLE 2. Air Chance Airways is converting its manual reservations system to a computer-generated one. The system will use terminals, at its airport counters, that are tied into the airline's main computer. A design for the terminal reservation code is required. After analysis of the data required to correctly make a reservation, the following facts are known:

1. The carriage-type positions available are numbered 1 to 80, complementing the existing computer system.
2. Name, date of departure, flight number, departing airport, size of party, their names, type of payment, and any special conditions relating to these reservations are the fields to be keyed.
3. Some type of confirmation must be given to the reservations clerk after the reservation has been made. Also, an error or deletion code must be available.

The following formats were laid out for the respective inquiries and responses. The initial inquiry asks for the status of the flight desired:

INQ 210 6/20 1245 JFK.

INQ equals entry code to the computer; 210 is the flight number desired; 6/20 is the day; 1245 is the time of departure; JFK is the departing airport; and the period denotes the end of a transmission.

The response to this inquiry is:

210 6/20 1245 JFK 90/12 120/26.

The response falls into the pattern of the inquiry. This permits a comparison that is a form of a checking for errors. Here, 90/12 is the number of existing reservations made in economy/first class; and 120/26 represents the configuration of the plane—the number of seats available in economy/first class.

To initiate a reservation, the agent types in:

RES 210 6/20 1245 JFK 3E SMITH,JOHN SP

The 3E reserves three economy fares for John Smith. The comma is used within the name field to separate last and first names. SP is the prefix to any special instructions that might be associated with this passenger. It begins after the name field. First-class fares would be noted by an F.

Any special comment would be completed at the end of the line. If additional space should be necessary, an asterisk, anywhere along the line, would continue the message to the next line. The computer's response to confirm this reservation is:

CON 210 6/20 1245 JFK 3E SMITH,JOHN.

EXAMPLE 3. The HO-HO Cupcake Company has instituted a computer-controlled inventory system. A feature of the system is the automatic completion of a purchase order when an inventory level falls below its prescribed limit. The purchase order must be printed on a customized, continuous, multicopy, split-carbon form. The design of the new form is the analyst's responsibility. The designed format is shown in Figure 4.7. The following points should be noted from this illustration.

1. The date is in the upper lefthand corner, for ease of filing. Purchase orders are filed by date of issue.
2. The purchase order number, machine printed, is next. The heavy line enclosing this figure highlights the entry for easy reference.

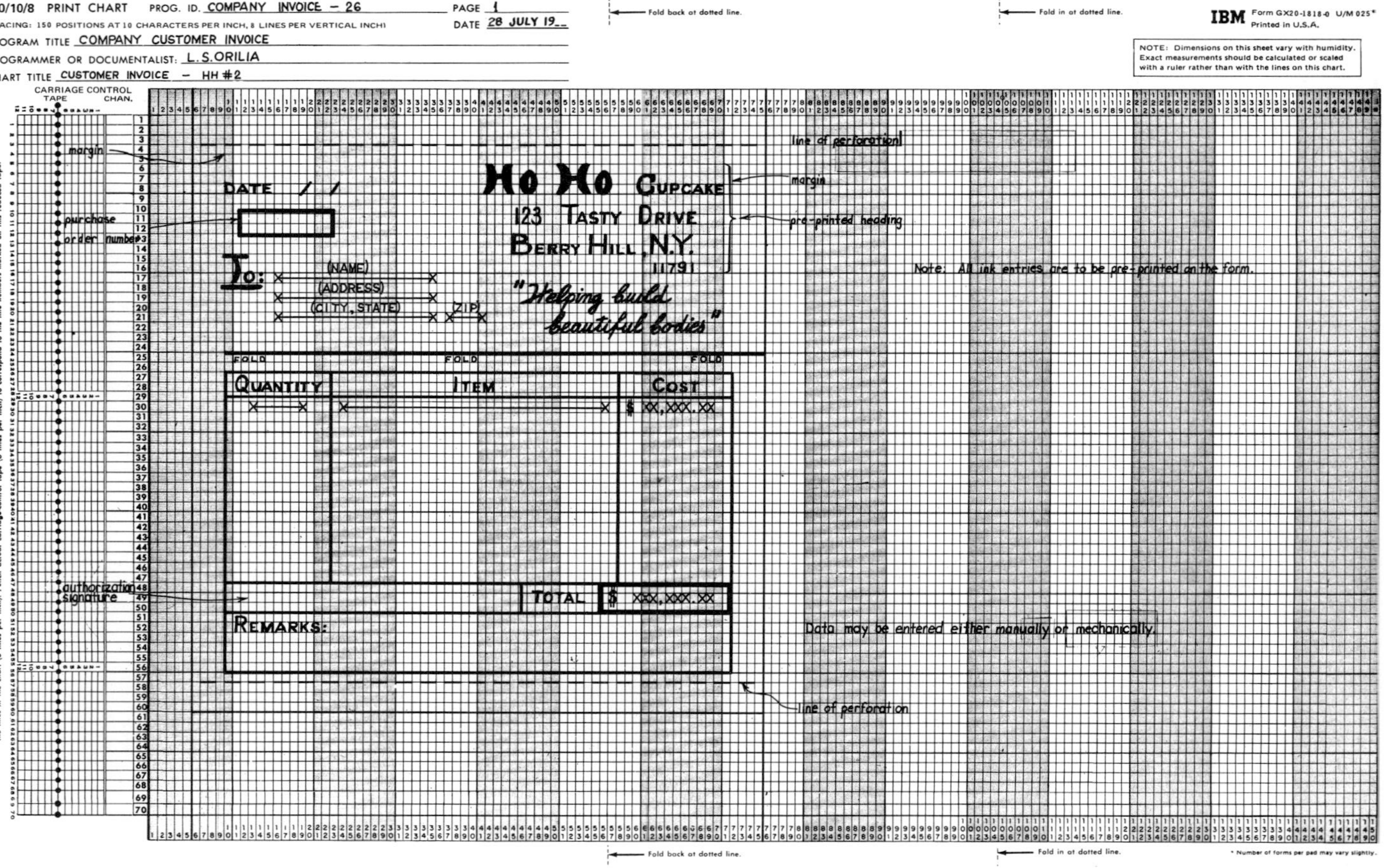

Figure 4.7 New design of purchase order.

3. The line for folding is used to facilitate correct folding. These forms are to be used within envelopes having transparent windows.
4. The authorization signature may be entered manually, if checking is desired, or mechanically for ease of completion.
5. Again, the heavy line is used to highlight the Total figure.
6. Adequate space has been provided for special instructions or entries that may be either manually or mechanically prepared.
7. Space for margins and perforations has been allotted.
8. Copies of the form will be sent to:
a. Accounting department, copy 2 (pink)
b. Inventory section, copy 3 (green)
c. Purchase department, copy 4 (blue)
d. Receiving department, copy 5 (yellow)
e. Supplier, shipping copy, copy 6 (white).

EXAMPLE 4. The following problem was brought to your attention by the use of a CRT—a terminal device with an attached television tube display for data and a keyboard with which to enter data similar to that of a typewriter. The problem was basically that the clerk operating the CRT terminal was having difficulty distinguishing between the requests for data made by the system and the respective responses, when both appeared simultaneously on the screen.

After interviewing the supervisor for the above clerk, and also some of the clerks, the problem was more clearly defined. The analyst, however, was no closer to the solution. One of the possible solutions was to reconstruct the physical display of data by having the request for data appear on one line and the clerks' response on the next line. This solution was logical, since from the interviews the analyst was able to conclude that the clerks found it difficult when both inquiry and response were on the same line. The solution, though, would involve rather extensive reprogramming, a delay of approximately six months, and an additional expense of several thousand dollars.

In addition to observing the clerks at their terminals, which permitted the analyst to observe their actual working conditions, the analyst also examined the CRT device and obtained a copy of the manufacturer's equipment manual (for the CRT in use). In reading the manual, the analyst noted that the CRT has a switch labelled "Half-Tone." The analyst was able to determine that this switch enabled entries made via the keyboard to appear at full (brightest) intensity on the viewing screen, while the computer's response to that data appeared at half of the full intensity. The switch was easily accessible by the clerks and could easily be activated or deactivated.

The split-tone (half-tone) feature of the terminal was readily available for use, since it already was standard equipment on the terminal device. Thus the display of characters in two different intensities, at the same time, could easily be incorporated into the operating procedures.

The use of the split- or half-tone feature was tested by the clerks, who found this solution satisfying.

The point here is that solutions to a problem do not always necessitate redesign, great expense, or lengthy projects. A solution to a problem may be sought from various sources, and the analyst must always remain alert to all of the available information and keep his options open.

EXAMPLE 5. In this example, we will describe the steps employed by the analyst from the inception of the analysis to the final and acceptable solution for one problem. This narrative will provide the student analyst with insight into the sequence of events and procedures followed by an analyst.

The request to analyze the form illustrated in Figure 4.8 originated from the registrar's office, through the data processing (DP) manager. An analyst was assigned to the project, and he immediately prepared a tentative or initial course of action:

1. Interview the registrar (the requestor of analysis).
2. Interview users of the form.
3. After analysis, prepare and write some type of problem definition.
4. Design and draft a series of alternate solutions.
5. Obtain approval for one solution and have it implemented.
6. Ensure that the form is tested using real data, incorporating the necessary modifications.
7. After a suitable testing period (6 months), reexamine the form and its use. Determine whether or not additional analysis and design are warranted.

The analyst made an appointment with the registrar, requesting that the registrar block out a two-hour period of time. This would ensure that sufficient time would be allotted for the interview and would also minimize interruption. From the interview, the analyst learned the following:

CYCLE MODULE SCHEDULE FORM

YEAR ________ CYCLE ________ DEPARTMENT ________ CHAIRMAN ________
Signature

MODULE				INSTRUCTOR	MODULE	Max. No.		1		2		Total Hrs.	DEPT.	Room Cap.
Name	No.	Sect.	Credit	Last name, & First Initial	Catalogue Title	Stud.	Cyc.	Days of Week Time	Room	Days . . . Time	Room			

Figure 4.8 Form that requires redesign. The form appears to be serviceable, with appropriate space provided for entries. However, the entry of data will reveal some of the shortcomings of the form.

1. The form was an input document that the registrar's office employed for scheduling of courses each semester.
2. The form was manually completed by the department chairperson, then transmitted to the registrar's office for additional information, which was put onto the form. Then it was sent to the DP department, where data on the form were keypunched on two course cards (referred to as 58 and 59 cards).
3. The registrar estimated that 60 percent of the course data received was incorrect and 33 percent of the data relating to courses had to be changed after the course cards were processed by the computer. The registrar felt that the majority of errors was attributable to poor completion of the form by the department chairperson and to bad keypunching.
4. A list of the institutional personnel who were involved with the form was obtained.

The analyst returned to the DP department offices and discussed his initial findings with the operations manager who supervised the keypunch activities and was involved with processing data related to the form. From this discussion, the analyst discovered the following:

1. The majority of errors resulted from incorrect completion of the form.
2. One out of every two cards keyed from the form required rekeypunching after verification.
3. One-third of the data entered by the registrar's office was incorrect.

The operations manager substantiated his comments by showing a log in which problems relating to the form were recorded. He also showed the analyst old completed forms that contained sample errors. Prior to the completion of the interview, the analyst asked permission to examine files containing old copies of the form, with related data, and permission to interview and work with the keypunch operators—this was a must. In addition, the analyst obtained examples of the 58 and 59 cards that are keypunched and the card format used for both cards (shown in Tables 4.1 and 4.2). On the 59 card, the * indicates that the class meets in more than one classroom and/or at a different time during the week, otherwise the fields are left blank.

After the conference with the operations manager, the analyst remained in the DP area and reviewed old copies of the forms. In this way, the analyst was able to familiarize himself with the forms, the types of errors made, and the types of information being keyed into the cards. This investigation also prepared the analyst for his interview with the keypunch operators. From the examination of previously used forms, the analyst concluded the following:

TABLE 4.1 FORMAT OF 58 CARD

Card Column	Field
1–4	module number
5–7	section number
8	cycle
9–11	module name
12–27	course title
28–29	credits/course
30–31	max. no. of students per class
32–44	prof. last name assig. to course
45	prof. first initial
46	hours code for class
47–49	actual hours for course (xx.x)
50–78	blank
79	digit 5
80	digit 8

TABLE 4.2 FORMAT OF 59 CARD

Card Column	Field
1–4	module number
5–7	section number
8	cycle
9–13	days of week class meets
14–24	time of day (xx*xx*-xx*xx)
25–27	room number
28–30	capacity of room/persons
*31–35	days of week class meets
*36–46	time of day (xx*xx-xx*xx)
*47–49	room number
50	department code (0 or 1)
51–53	hrs/week for course (xx.x)
54–57	hrs/term for course (xxx.x)
58	remedial code (0 or 1)
59	grade code (0 or 1)
60–78	blank
79	digit 5
80	digit 9

*These fields are used when a second classroom is necessary or when the class meets at different times.

1. That the estimate of rekeying one of two cards was correct (observed from the verification punches made by the IBM 129 keypunch).
2. That errors on the source document were extensive, indicating that the people initially completing the form were very careless and sloppy.
3. That 20 percent of the data added by the registrar was incorrect. (It was observed on the old form that some of the registrar's data were crossed out and replaced.)
4. By correlating the errors on forms with rekeyed cards, the analyst concluded that keypunch errors were at a minimum. Most errors were made when the keypunch operator could not read the form.

A sample composite form noting many of the commonly made errors in shown in Figure 4.9. During the examination of the forms, the analyst also compiled a list of errors made by people who filled out the form. This list would be compared to the list of errors he would compile while interviewing the keypunch operators, which was his next task.

The interview with the keypunch operators went slowly at

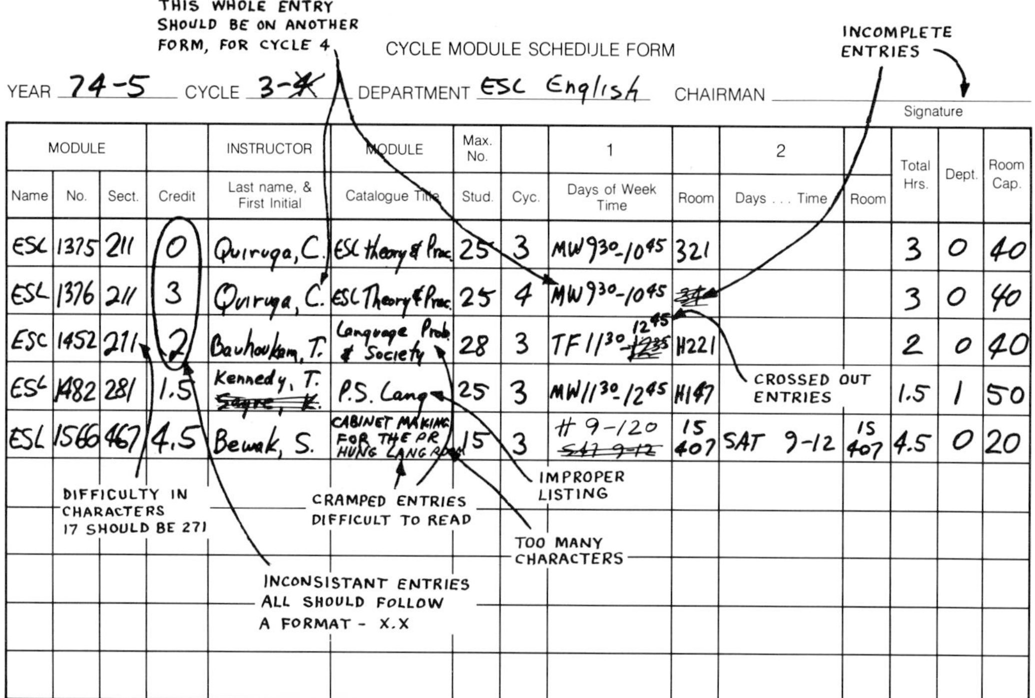

CYCLE MODULE SCHEDULE FORM

YEAR 74-5 CYCLE 3-~~4~~ DEPARTMENT ESC English CHAIRMAN ______ Signature

MODULE				INSTRUCTOR	MODULE	Max. No.		1		2				
Name	No.	Sect.	Credit	Last name, & First Initial	Catalogue Title	Stud.	Cyc.	Days of Week Time	Room	Days . . . Time	Room	Total Hrs.	Dept.	Room Cap.
ESC	1375	211	0	Quiruga, C.	ESC Theory & Prac.	25	3	MW 9^{30}-10^{45}	321			3	0	40
ESL	1376	211	3	Quiruga, C.	ESC Theory & Prac.	25	4	MW 9^{30}-10^{45}	~~321~~			3	0	40
ESC	1452	211	2	Bauhoukam, T.	Language Prob. & Society	28	3	TF 11^{30}-12^{45} (~~1235~~)	H221			2	0	40
ESL	1482	281	1.5	Kennedy, T. ~~Sayre, K.~~	P.S. Lang	25	3	MW 11^{30}-12^{45}	H147			1.5	1	50
ESL	1566	467	4.5	Bewak, S.	CABINET MAKING FOR THE PR HUNG LANG	15	3	# 9-120 ~~SAT 9-12~~	15 407	SAT 9-12	15 407	4.5	0	20

Figure 4.9 Completed form with errors made by users pointed out.

first, as they were suspicious of the analyst's motives. After reassurance about his objective, the operators were increasingly cooperative. The keypunchers agreed that their main problem was: difficulty in reading the form due to sloppy handwriting, incomplete entries, and an overall difficulty in reading the entire form. The analyst reviewed the list of errors that he had compiled to confirm some of the sources of error as described by keypunch operators when the form was used in keypunching.

After completing the interview of keypunch operators, the analyst felt that some interviews with the people who had completed the form would be enlightening. Accordingly, he arranged to have conferences with selected department chairpersons and registrar personnel. A profile of these responses follows:

1. The form was easy to fill out, but they didn't have the time to fill it out and recheck their work.
2. Errors were supposed to be caught by the DP department; it was not considered their responsibility.
3. Errors could be corrected on subsequent runs, when

courses were deleted or added and when students that registered for improperly offered courses would be forced to come back and reregister.

The analyst *objectively* recorded and compiled these responses as he completed this last group of interviews.

As the analyst progressed through the series of interviews, he began to formulate ideas and some solutions. However, he could not firm up any of the ideas until meeting the programmer manager. A determination of the formats necessary for the programs using the 58 and 59 cards as inputs was needed, and also a determination of what effect, if any, changes in the card formats would have on these programs. Two critical factors in this project were a severe shortage of programming personnel and the need to implement and complete any changes in seven weeks. Thus any reprogramming effort must be, by necessity, kept to an absolute minimum. The programming manager indicated that changes in the using programs would be required if any changes in the existing card formats were made and that he could allot, at a maximum, five man-days to the reprogramming effort.

With this last bit of information acquired, the analyst began the analysis and drew up the following major guidelines for his design.

1. The same card format would be adhered to, thereby minimizing the reprogramming effort and retraining of keypunch operators.
2. The people filling out the form must be, without their knowledge, restricted and forced into completing the form legibly and completely.
3. The new form must distinguish between data entered by the department chairpersons and data entered by the registrar.
4. The number of lines of data on one form would be reduced to three or four, since the space allotted for entries would be expanded, therefore permitting enlarged penmanship and, hopefully, clearer entries.

With these considerations in mind the analyst proceeded to the design of a new form.

In an effort to elicit clearer written responses, the analyst chose a boxed-character format. That is, the person completing the form would be able to write only one character inside a box. The analyst experimented with box widths of 1/8 in.,

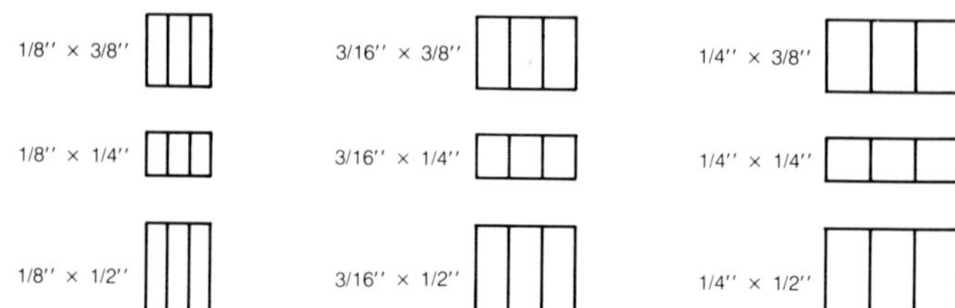

Figure 4.10 Sample of boxes tested by the analyst.

3/16 in., and 1/4 in., and heights of 1/4 in., 3/8 in., and 1/2 in. (see Figure 4.10). Sample forms employing combinations of each height and width were constructed and distributed to some users of the form and to the keypunch operators. This was accomplished to observe what configuration was easiest to read after data were entered.

The sample forms also provide each person who uses the existing form, and would use the new form, an opportunity for input. Thus the samples would assist in gaining acceptance of the form eventually chosen. The results of this experiment revealed an almost unanimous acceptance of the 3/16 in. wide and 3/8 in. high box. (See Figure 4.11.)

Employing this size box, the analyst designed a group of formats of varying lengths, as shown in Figure 4.12. Upon checking the available paper sizes, the analyst was informed that only 8½ × 11 in. and 8½ × 14 in. paper sizes were kept in stock and that no future expenditure for paper was antici-

Figure 4.11 Analyst's worksheet employed when experimenting with varied entry formats.

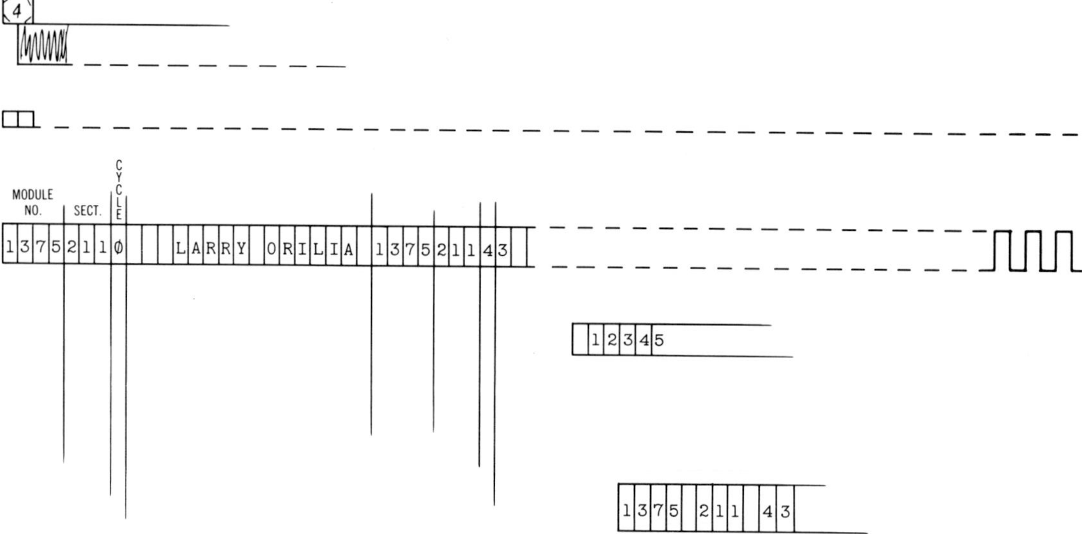

Format 1

79 80: 5 8

Field	Columns	Entry
MODULE NO.	1–4	ØØØØ
SECT. NO.	5–7	ØØØ
CYCLE	8	1
MOD. NAME	9–11	ADM
MODULE COURSE DESCRIPTION	12–27	FUND OF PUB ADM
CRED.	28–29	ØØ
MAX. STUD.	30–31	25
PROFESSOR'S NAME — LAST NAME	32–44	WESTEROFF
PROFESSOR'S NAME — F.	45	C
PROF. HRS. — COMP.	46–48	ØØØ
PROF. HRS. — DEV.	49–51	ØØ2
PROF. HRS. — REM.	52–54	ØØ2

79 80: 5 9

Field	Columns	Entry
CLASSROOM #1 — DAYS (M T W H F)	9–13	M
CLASSROOM #1 — TIME OF DAY (BEGIN TO END)	14–24	Ø2*ØØ-Ø3*15
CLASSROOM #1 — ROOM NO.	25–27	4Ø7
ROOM CAP.	28–30	Ø3Ø
CLASSROOM #2 — DAYS (M T W H F)	31–35	W
CLASSROOM #2 — TIME OF DAY (BEGIN TO END)	36–46	Ø2*ØØ-Ø3*15
CLASSROOM #2 — ROOM NO.	47–49	337
DESC	50	0
COURSE HRS. — PER WEEK	51–53	Ø25
COURSE HRS. — PER TERM	54–57	2ØØØ
P/R	58	Ø
P/S	59	Ø

Format 2

79 80: 5 8

Field	Columns	Entry
MODULE NO.	1–4	ØØØØ
SECT. NO.	5–7	ØØØ
CYCLE	8	2
MOD. NAME	9–11	ADM
MODULE COURSE TITLE	12–27	FUND OF PUB ADM
CRED.	28–29	ØØ
MAX. STUD.	30–31	25
PROFESSOR'S NAME — LAST NAME	32–44	WESTEROFF
PROFESSOR'S NAME — F.	45	C
PROF. HRS. — COMP.	46–48	ØØØ
PROF. HRS. — DEV.	49–51	1ØØ
PROF. HRS. — REM.	52–54	ØØØ

79 80: 5 9

Field	Columns	Entry
CLASS #1 (☐ CHECK FOR 2 RM) — DAYS (M T W H F)	9–13	M
CLASS #1 — TIME OF DAY (START TO END)	14–24	Ø2*ØØ-Ø3*15
CLASS #1 — ROOM NO.	25–27	407
ROOM CAP.	28–30	Ø3Ø
DESC	50	0
COURSE HRS. — PER WEEK	51–53	Ø25
COURSE HRS. — PER TERM	54–57	24ØØ
P/R	58	Ø
P/S	59	Ø
ROOM #2 — DAYS (M T W H F)	31–35	W
ROOM #2 — TIME OF DAY (START TO END)	36–46	Ø2*ØØ-Ø3*15
ROOM #2 — ROOM NO.	47–49	337

Figure 4.12 Samples of forms considered.

CYCLE MODULE SCHEDULE FORM
DEPARTMENT

MODULE NAME [1 2 3]

MODULE NO.	SECTION NO.	CYCLE	MODULE COURSE TITLE	CRED	MAX. STUD.	PROFESSOR'S NAME LAST NAME
4–7	8–10	11	12–27	28 29	30 31	32–39

79 80 [5 8] *

CHAIRPERSON / /7

	F.	PROF. HRS. DEV.	PROF. HRS. COMP.	PROF. HRS. REM.	ROOM #1 DAYS	ROOM #1 TIME START TO END	ROOM #1 ROOM NO.	ROOM CAP.
40–44	45	46–48	49–51	52–54	12–16	17–27 (* - *)	28–30	31–33

☐ CHECK FOR TWO RMS.

ROOM #2 DAYS	ROOM #2 TIME START TO END	ROOM #2 ROOM NO.
34–38	39–49 (* - *)	50–52

Format 3

Figure 4.12 Continued.

pated. As a result, the 8½ × 14 in. format was selected. The remaining consideration was the number of entries to be placed on one form. After discussion with the registrar, it was decided that two entries per form would permit greatest legibility.

Subsequently, the form was drawn up and 50 test copies were produced. Tests with the new form were instituted, and small adjustments were made to the form. Figure 4.13 depicts the final format selected and the one currently in use.

GLOSSARY

Continuous forms. A series of connected sheets, each form individually prepared. After printing has been completed, the individual sheets are easily separated by the perforations between forms.

MODULE NO. (4)	SECTION NO. (3)	CYCLE	MODULE COURSE TITLE (16)	CRED (2)	MAX. STUD. (2)	PROFESSOR'S NAME LAST NAME (13)
4 7	8 10	11	12 27	28 29	30 31	32 40

	PROF. HRS.				ROOM #1			☐ CHECK FOR RM #2	ROOM CAP.
	F.	DEV. (3)	COMP. (3)	REM. (3)	DAYS (5)	TIME (11) START TO END		ROOM NO. (3)	
41 44	45	46 48	49 51	52 54	12 16	17 27		28 30	31 33
						* - *			

ROOM #2		
DAYS (5)	TIME (11) START TO END	ROOM NO. (3)
34 38	39 49	50 52
	* - *	

Format 4

Figure 4.12 Continued.

CRT. A type of terminal that displays data on a screen (cathode ray tube) similar to that of a television set.

Customized forms. Forms specially designed to satisfy a particular company's need or purpose.

Hard copy. A term used to denote computer outputs that are in a readable format and that can be stored or filed.

Marginally punched form. A form with uniformly spaced holes placed in the margin on each side of the form. These holes are required to accurately feed paper through the printing device.

Pin-fed. The term used to designate forms with marginally punched holes.

Soft copy. A term used to denote those outputs, usually visual, that are not retained after usage.

CYCLE MODULE SCHEDULE FORM

DEPARTMENT

MODULE NAME [1 2 3]

79 80: 5 8

MODULE NO.	SECTION NO.	CYCLE	MODULE COURSE TITLE	CREDIT	MAX. STUD.	PROFESSOR'S NAME		PROF. HRS.		
						LAST NAME	F.	DEV.	COMP.	REM.
4–7	8–10	11	12–27	28–29	30–31	32–44	45	46–48	49–51	52–54
						* - *				

CHAIRPERSON / /7

79 80: 5 9

ROOM #1			ROOM CAP.	ROOM #2			DESC.	COURSE HOURS		R OR R	P/S CRE
DAYS	TIME	RM. NO.		DAYS	TIME	ROOM		PER WK.	PER TERM		
12–16	17–27	28–30	31–33	34–38	39–49	50–52	53	54–56	57–60	61	62
	* - *				* - *				•		

Figure 4.12 Continued.

Format 5

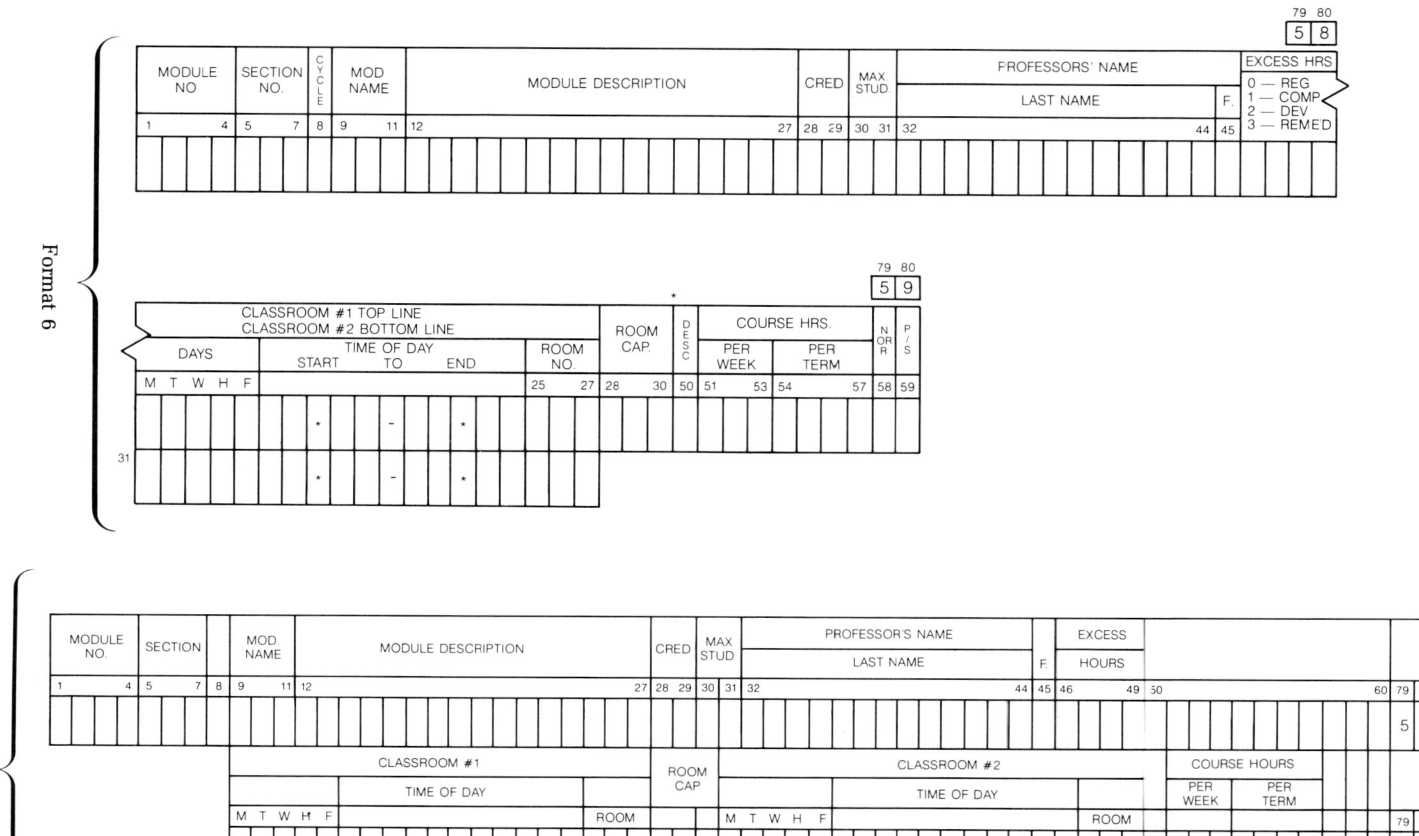

Figure 4.12 Continued.

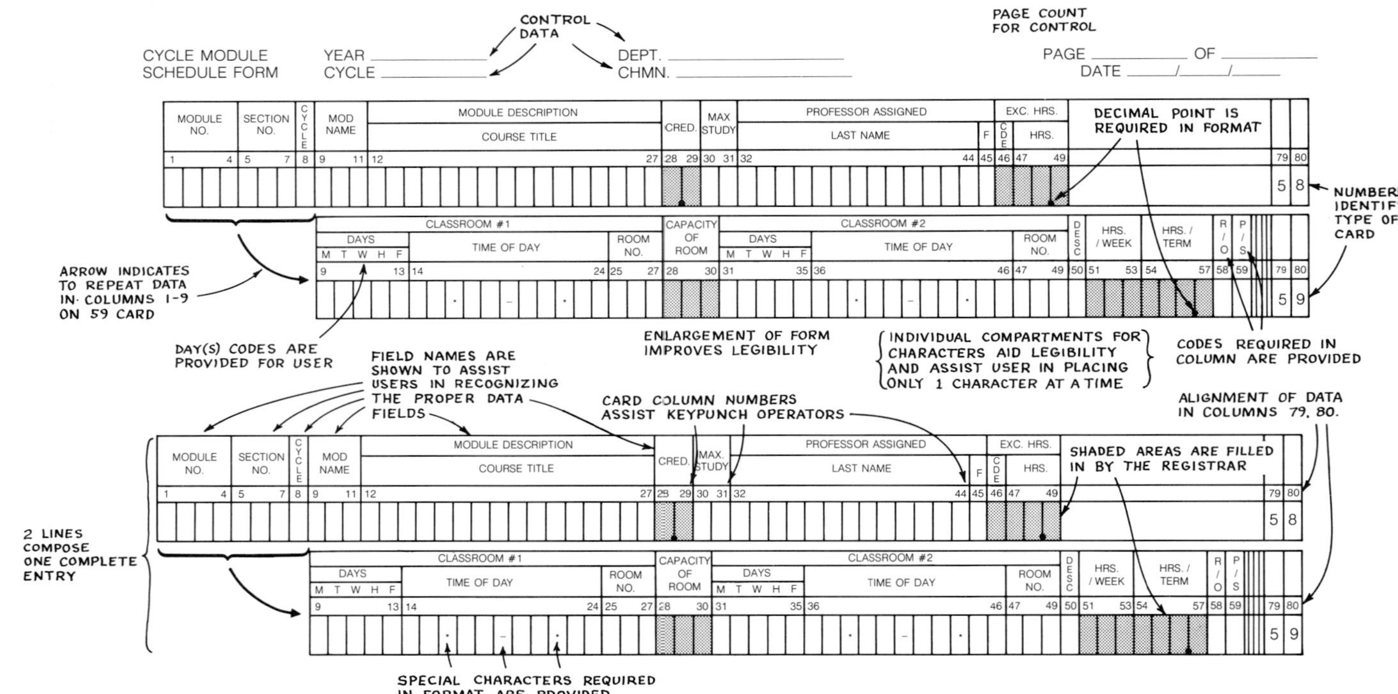

Figure 4.13 Final format selected by the registrar. Comments note special features incorporated by the analyst.

Source documents. Documents that provide the data for input to a system.

Teletypewriter terminal. A self-documenting terminal that prints its output on paper.

QUESTIONS

1. Take the nine questions concerning a form and apply them to a credit card bill, personal check, and company check. Note whether the documents satisfy each question, if applicable to the form.
2. Examine the forms you receive at work, school, or your home and prepare a list of them. Classify the forms on your list as to whether they are preprinted, standard, continuous, marginally punched (separated along their perforations after processing), chemically treated, etc.
3. *Sales Application.* Consider the sales performance report in Figure 4.14, which is produced by a computer.
   a. Was this prepared on a blank continuous form or a preprinted form? Explain your answer.
   b. Indicate the meaning of each field heading. Why do all the amount fields contain dashed lines?
   c. Describe the report.
   d. What is the significance of the two total fields at the bottom of this report?
4. *Accounts Receivable Application.* A major problem with many business organizations is the increasing number of customers who do not pay their bills or who pay them after lengthy delays. Both result in the loss of much money for the company. Late payments result in the loss of interest on money not received until bills are finally paid after 30, 60, 90, or more days. Most companies produce a report as part of the accounts receivable processing that indicates customers who have an unpaid balance for 30 days, 60 days, 90 days, or more than 90 days. This report is then transmitted to a specific employee for follow-up or to a collection or insurance agency that is contracted to collect from delinquent accounts. Assume that Figure 4.15 represents a computer-produced form used by a collection agency to assess these accounts.
   a. Describe the form and explain the purpose of each field. Place sample "computer-produced" output in the fields to ensure your understanding of the report.

SALES PERFORMANCE REPORT

DATE: 3/ 31 /

DIST. NO.	OFF NO.	SLSMN. NO.	DISTRICT, OFFICE OR SALESMAN	PRODUCT "A"	PRODUCT "B"	PRODUCT "C"	PRODUCT "D"	TOTAL BY SALESMAN	TOTAL BY OFFICE	TOTAL BY DISTRICT
1			NORTHEAST DIST							
	1		BOSTON OFFICE							
		5	J G CARGILL	2316 85	4819 37	3098 17	972 55	11206 94		
		43	A E JOHNSON	4018 61	3627 18	1085 36	2589 02	11320 17		
		77	G I ROSS	4001 35	3869 92	4781 03	1968 45	14620 75		
									37147 86	
	2		NEW YORK OFFICE							
		2	P E AKERS	3213 98	4890 97	1344 45	1861 03	11310 43		
		17	A K DEERING	3544 40	2315 86	3987 03	2932 23	12779 52		
		36	R T INGEBRETSEN	2843 16	3720 10	2815 77	1504 32	10883 35		
		79	F H RUSH	1444 83	2315 16	1591 47	1416 37	6767 83		
		89	T L WESTMORE	2429 76	3402 10	3295 14	2678 01	11805 01		
									53546 14	
										90694 00 *
2			MID COAST DIST							
	1		BALTIMORE OFFICE							
		3	B L BARNEY	5584 36	4715 96	3620 93	1926 18	15847 43		
		27	P W GOODE	3231 64	1780 41	4099 82	2078 68	11190 55		
8			SOUTHWEST DIST							
	1		DALLAS OFFICE							
		51	R X MILLER	5028 00	1858 95	2468 31	3769 70	13124 96		
		58	R M NORTH	2338 71	3066 30	3517 89	3010 53	11933 43		
									25058 39	
	2		EL PASO OFFICE							
		56	A R NELSON	5419 02	4380 65	3729 77	4380 91	17910 35		
									17910 35	
										42968 74 *
										872106 87 * *

Figure 4.14 Sales performance report.

CLASSIFICATION OF UNPAID
ACCOUNTS RECEIVABLE

LAWTON - BYRNE - BRUNER
INSURANCE
AGENCY COMPANY
401 PINE STREET • SAINT LOUIS, MISSOURI 63102
PHONE 621-5540

PRODUCER

MONTH

CUSTOMER CODE	NAME OF ASSURED	UNPAID BALANCE	30 DAYS	60 DAYS	90 DAYS	OVER 90 DAYS	BROKERS NOTES
	TOTALS ⟶						

Figure 4.15 Classification of unpaid accounts receivable.

b. Do you think that a standard continuous form could serve as well as this preprinted form?
c. Explain the shading used in the fields called 30 DAYS, 60 DAYS, 90 DAYS, and OVER 90 DAYS.
d. Can you tell from a first glance at the form that it is prepared by a machine?
e. Do you think that a form that listed every customer, his unpaid balance, if any, and the number of days that this balance was outstanding would serve the same purpose?

CHAPTER 5

CARD DESIGN

INTRODUCTION TO FILES

Before a systems analyst can create an integrated data processing system, he or she must design and structure each element within the system. First, the output required from the system must be created. When the output specifications have been completed, the analyst must design and structure all files so that they produce the desired output as efficiently and effectively as possible. This chapter will discuss the elements necessary to design those files.

A **file** is a group of records pertaining to a specific item. A payroll file, for example, contains all the payroll records within the company. A discussion of file design, then, will incorporate record format.

More than one file is often needed to produce the required output. Figure 5.1 illustrates a flowchart of an accounts receivable system. Notice that three files are necessary to produce the updated master file and output reports: new accounts file, daily transaction file, and accounts receivable master disk file.

Prior to designing files, the analyst must carefully consider three elements:

1. Required Output. As we have indicated, the analyst must examine all forms of output required from the system before he can determine what should go into the system.

2. Projected Output. The analyst must consider the possibility of future special requests or inquiries from management when designing files. That is, he must build into files enough data to satisfy possible requests on any pertinent item within the system.

Thus some data items that pertain to the system but are not *currently* required as output may be deemed important and relevant enough to be placed on a file. If management makes inquiries on these items at some later date, it is a simple task to retrieve them.

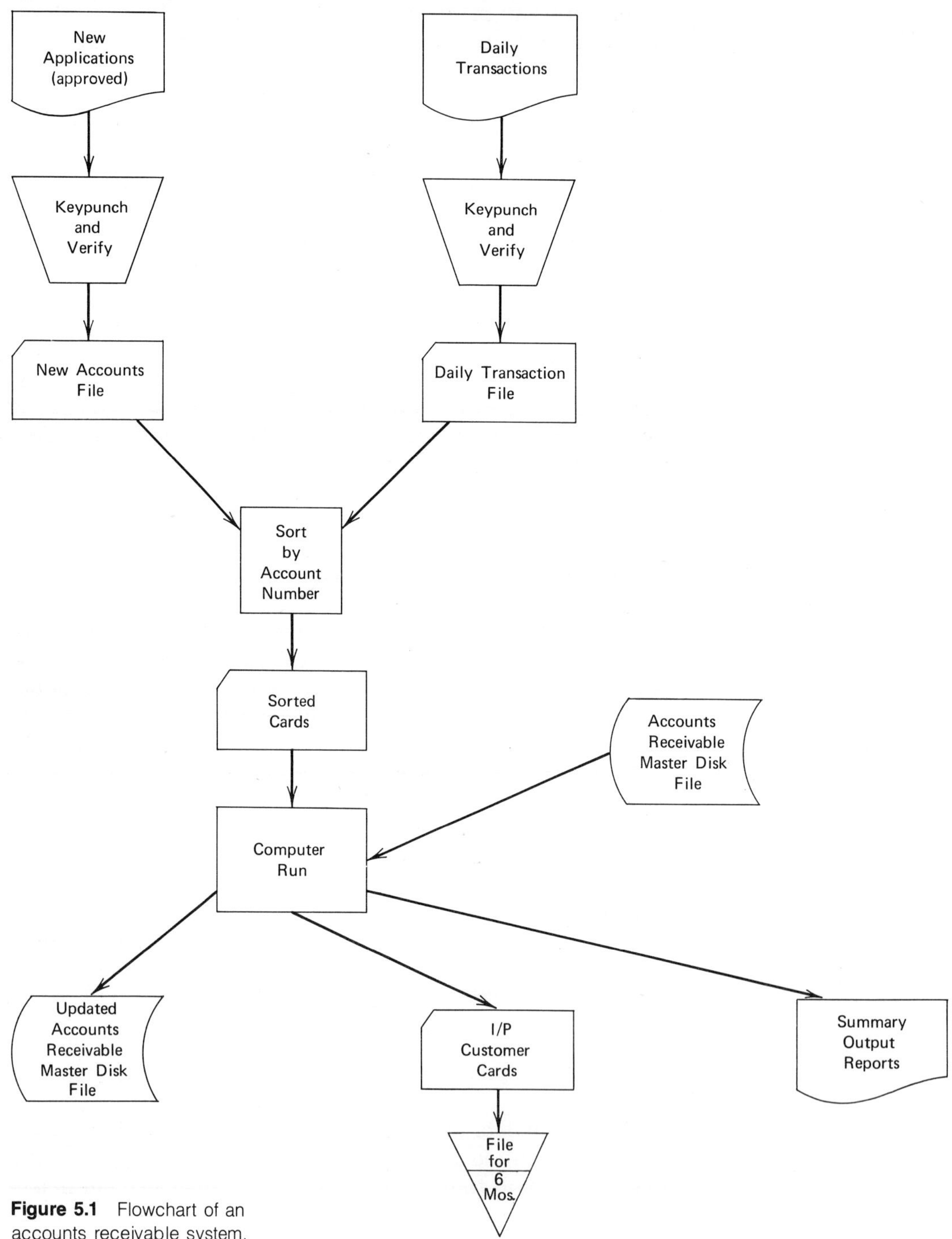

Figure 5.1 Flowchart of an accounts receivable system.

To determine which items might be requested in the future, the analyst can investigate previous inquiries made by management.

Projected output also includes output that may be required at some later date if normal growth trends continue. The analyst must attempt to design files so that normal growth trends will not result in major revisions. For this reason, it is often necessary to provide the file with additional data items that are not currently required for processing. The analyst may think that credit rating, for example, will be an important item in the future for an accounts receivable system, even though this item is not presently used.

Projected output cannot be determined as precisely and systematically as required output. Instead, the analyst must rely heavily on his understanding of the goals and objectives of the system and on experience. That is, it is not a simple task to build into a system provisions for future requirements. It is, however, important for the analyst to attempt to structure the files so that major revisions will not be required.

3. Interrelation of Files. The analyst cannot consider files within a system as independent entities. He must keep in mind the relationships between files. Sometimes a single file may be used to satisfy more than one system, or more than one requirement within an individual system. Many businesses utilize, for example, a payroll file as input to a personnel system.

Thus the analyst must be familiar with the file organization within the entire company. The utilization, where possible, of a file from another system will undoubtedly save the company both time and money.

After studying the above items, the analyst must determine what storage medium will best suit his file design. Should cards be used for a file? Would a tape file be more beneficial? Should a direct-access file be utilized?

This chapter is devoted exclusively to punched cards since the principles involved in designing card records and files are easily understood and are also applicable to other types of input/output media. In addition, while the use of punched cards has decreased in many computer installations due to the introduction of other keyboard entry systems, many small computer centers still use punched cards as a primary form of input. Other keyboard entry systems will be discussed in Chapters 6 and 9.

THE PUNCHED CARD—AN INTRODUCTION

Data are recorded on **punched cards** in the form of punched holes used to represent a code. Vast amounts of records are converted to these cards. Historically, machines were constructed to mechanically sense the holes, and then sort, merge, or otherwise compile the data.

The punched card usually contains 80 columns. Thus record size is restricted to 80 characters, or multiples of 80, when more than one card is used to represent a record.

Consider the timecard illustrated in Figure 5.2. Note that consecutive card columns that represent a unit of data are called a **field**. In other words, a field is a set of adjacent positions reserved for a specific purpose. The consecutive card columns 1 to 25 in the figure represent the NAME field. Card columns 26 to 50 represent the POSITION field, and so on.

Each field consists of characters. The NAME field has the character C in its first column (12-zone and 3-digit punches), an H in column 2 (12-8 punches). Note that if a person's name does not fill the whole field, the remainder of the field is left blank.

Figure 5.3 reviews the specific features of the 80-column punched card, including the Hollerith code.

Figure 5.4 illustrates the features of the 96-column card and

Figure 5.2 Timecard.

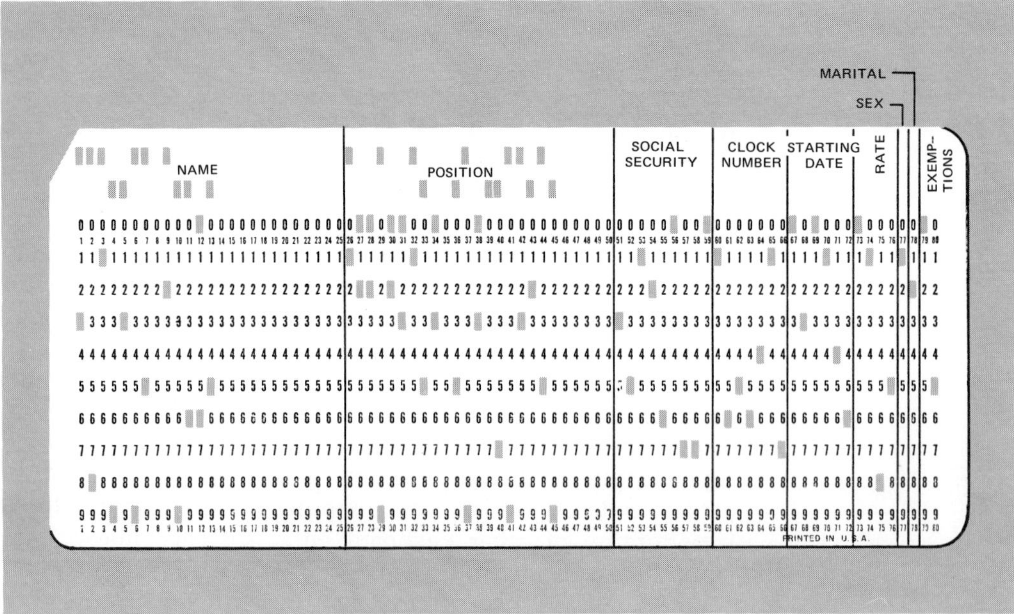

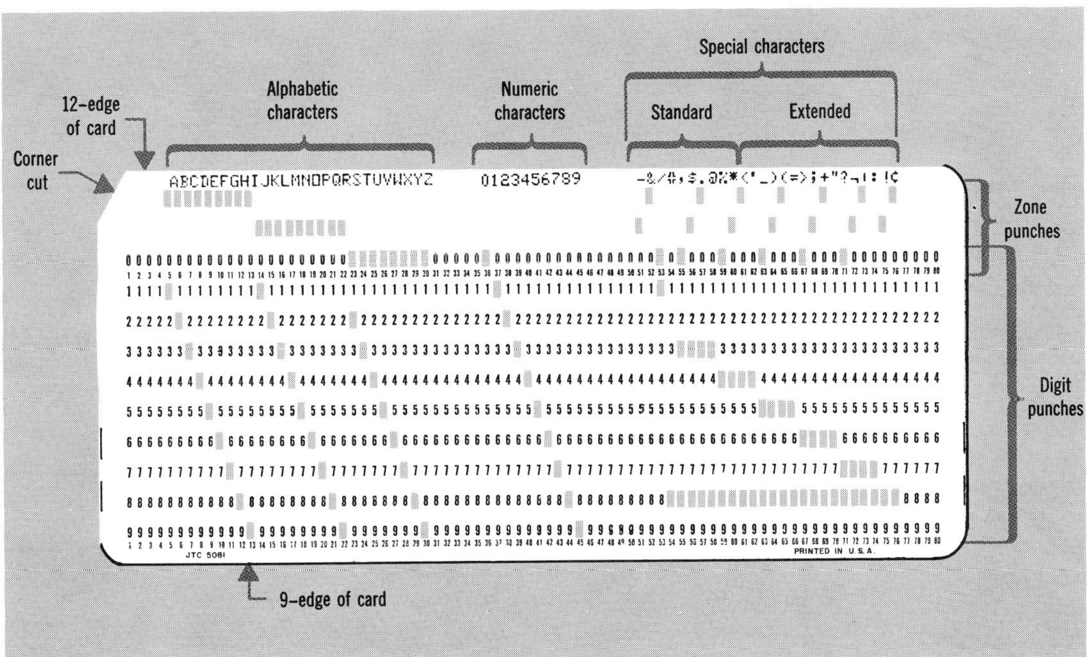

Figure 5.3 Review of Hollerith card.

the BCD (Binary Coded Decimal) code. Comparing the BCD code to the Hollerith code, notice that in BCD the letter A is represented by three punches: a B, an A, and a 1. The B and A punches together are equivalent to the 12-zone in Hollerith.

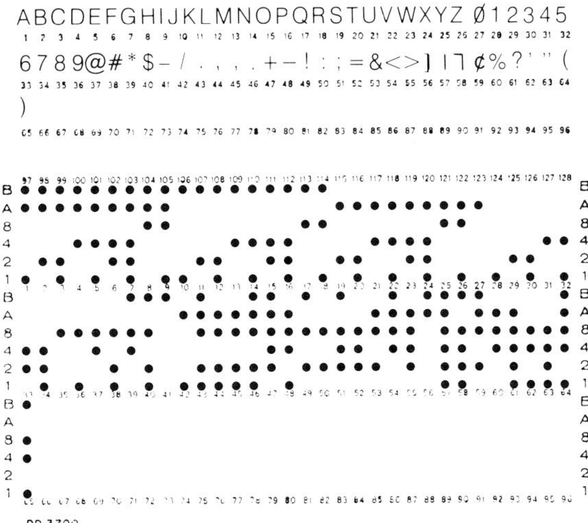

Figure 5.4 Illustration of a 96-column card.

Similarly, the B punch is the same as the 11-zone, and the A punch is the equivalent of the 0-zone. Notice also that instead of putting only one punch in a digit row for a number, the BCD code uses some combination of the 8, 4, 2, and 1 punches to add up to the particular number. Thus the letter I in Hollerith is a 12-zone and a 9 punch, whereas in BCD it is represented by B, A, 8, and 1.

RECORDING DATA ON PUNCHED CARDS

Punched card data can be input to a computer or to an electronic accounting machine (EAM), such as a sorter, collator, or accounting machine. A punched card is sometimes referred to as a **unit record** because a card typically represents a unit of information.

Use of Keypunch Machines

Generally, data are initially recorded on punched cards from information supplied in a printed report, called a **source document**. A device called a **keypunch machine** is used to convert written documents to punched cards. This device, not unlike a typewriter, needs an operator to press the appropriate keys representing characters so that the machine can punch corresponding holes in the card. (See Figure 5.5.) Using a keypunch machine, data are punched in the card according to

Figure 5.5 Keypunching of data.

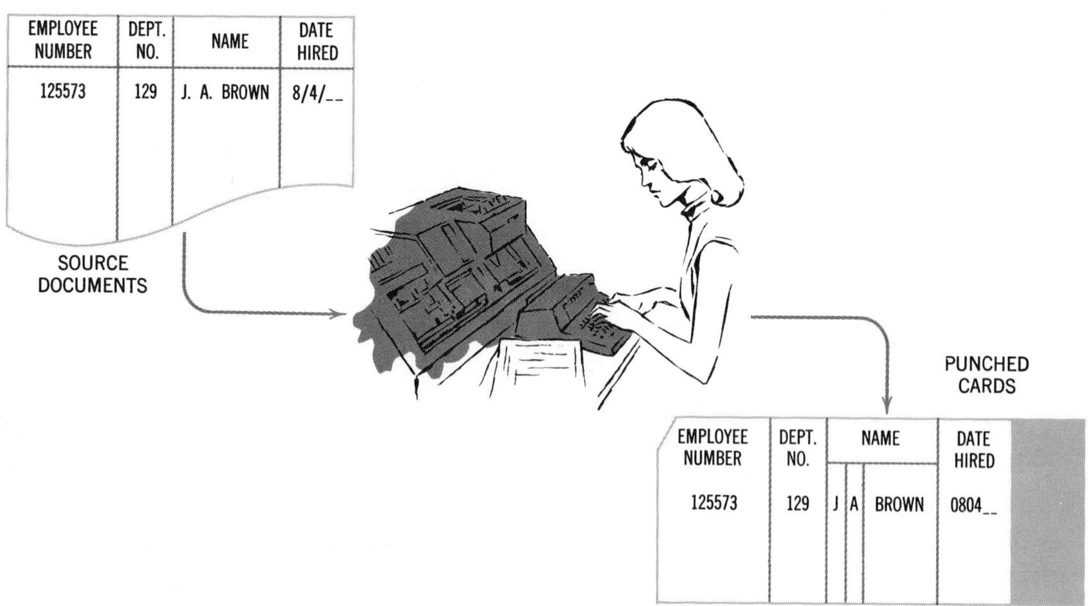

the Hollerith code and, if desired, the corresponding characters are printed on the top edge.

To ensure that data are correctly transcribed by the keypunch operator into a punched card, a card verifier device is used. This device resembles the keypunch machine. The operator uses the keypunched cards instead of blank cards. He then depresses the verifier's keys, as in normal keypunching. If he depresses a key that has not, in fact, been punched in the card, an error light goes on.

Correctly keypunched cards are typically notched on the right side, while incorrectly keypunched ones are notched *above* the column in error. Therefore all cards with right-side notches have been verified, and ones with notches on top are in error. (See Figure 5.6.)

Some keypunch machines are equipped with verifying ability so that a single machine can be used first to keypunch data and then to verify the keypunching.

Characteristics of Fields

Data fields can be classified in three ways:

Numeric—digits only
Alphabetic—letters and blanks only
Alphanumeric or alphameric—combination of letters, digits, and special characters, such as an ADDRESS field

Figure 5.7 is another sample data card. Columns 1 to 5 represent an AMOUNT, which is a *numeric* field. Columns 6 to 25 are used for an *alphabetic* NAME field. Data are represented differently in numeric and alphabetic (or alphanumeric) fields when fill characters are required.

Field sizes are generally established to accommodate the longest number of characters. That is, a LAST NAME field may be 25 characters in length because the longest name is that size. Since most names are shorter than this, part of the field will remain blank. Similarly, numeric fields, consisting of only numbers, are *right-justified* with leftmost positions generally *zero-filled*. That is, to represent 383 in an AMOUNT field in positions 1 to 5, 383 is put in the rightmost position (columns 3, 4, 5) with leftmost positions (columns 1 and 2) filled with zeros. (See Figure 5.7.) Thus 00383 has been placed in the field. The rightmost positions are sometimes referred to as *low-order* or units positions, and leftmost as *high-order* positions.

Alphabetic or alphanumeric data are placed in the *leftmost* or *high-order* positions with low-order positions filled with

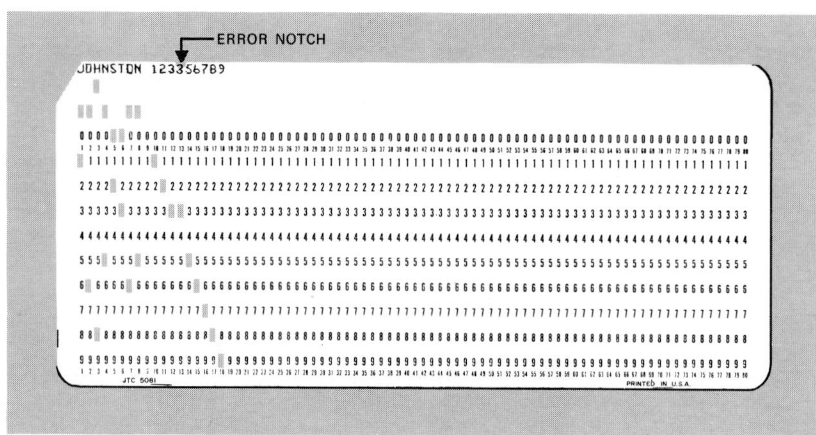

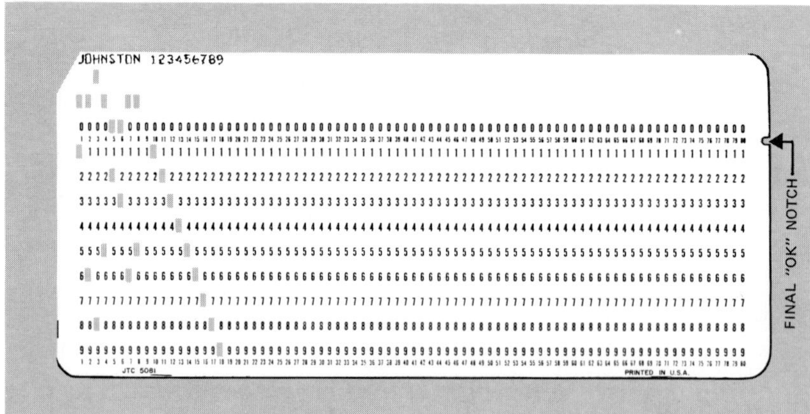

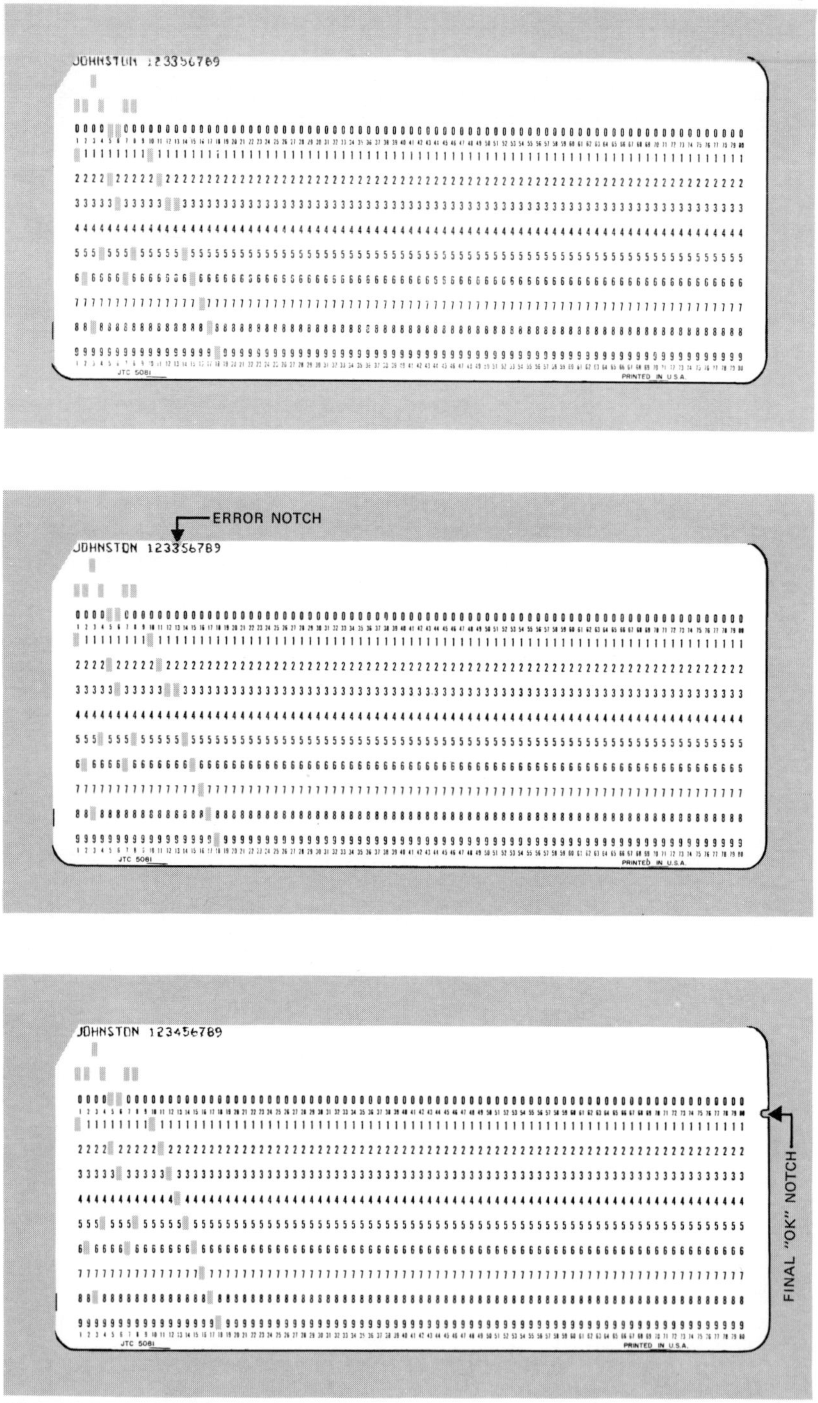

Figure 5.6 Verification of punched cards: *(a)* card is keypunched; *(b)* card is verified, and an error is detected in column 13, causing an error notch; *(c)* card is rekeypunched and successfully verified, resulting in a final OK notch on right side.

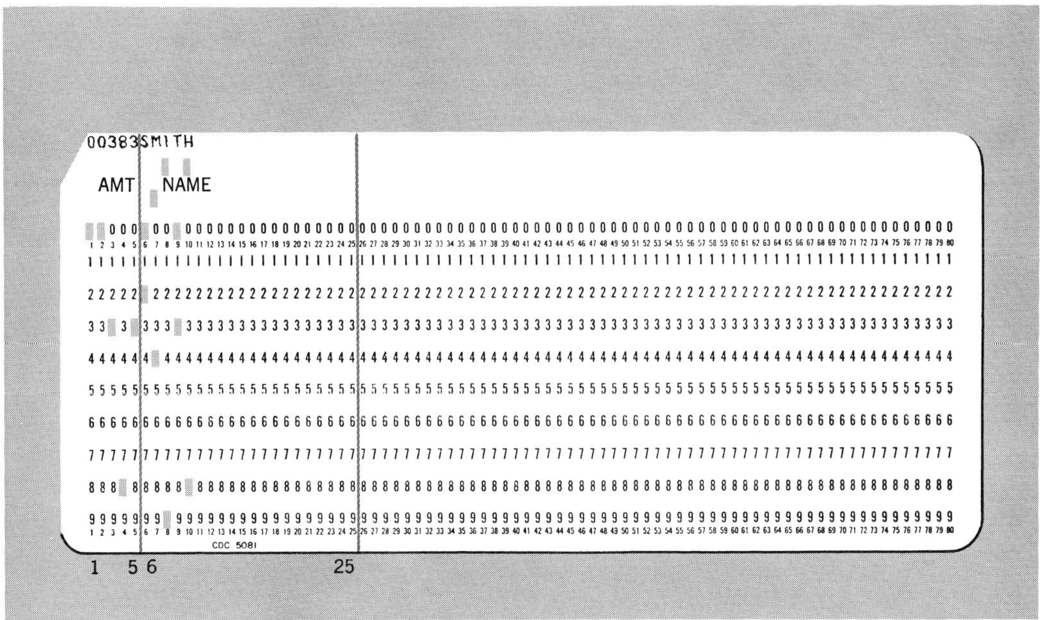

Figure 5.7 Sample data card 1.

blanks or spaces. Consider the LAST NAME field in columns 6 to 25 in Figure 5.7. The field size is 20 characters. The data, SMITH, consist only of five characters. The data are placed in the high-order positions with low-order positions left blank.

Elements of Card Design

As we have seen, the punched card is generally coded from information supplied on a source document. This source document is usually an established report that has been used successfully in a business area. When a procedure is automated, the source document is usually converted to a machine-readable form, such as a punched card. Time sheets, purchase orders, sales slips, credit return slips, applications for credit cards, and stock transfer sheets are examples of source documents that are generally converted to a punched card or to some other form of input for computer processing.

We have thus far seen that there are typically 80 positions on a card. This limits the size of most card records to 80 characters.

When designing card records, every effort must be made by the systems analyst, who is normally responsible for card design, to limit record size to 80 positions. If more characters per record are required, then two or more cards per record will be necessary. This, in essence, defeats the purpose of the unit-record concept and, where possible, should be avoided.

Since 80 characters per record is often a limiting factor, several design plans, discussed below, are generally implemented to ensure a concise card record. The businessperson must work closely with the systems analyst to determine that these design plans are appropriate for the specific system.

Where source document fields are not really useful or required, they are eliminated from the card format. The systems analyst must determine which fields are really unnecessary. By eliminating these fields from the card, a monetary savings may be realized. Concise card records that do not include unnecessary source document fields reduce the time required to keypunch cards and the time it takes the computer to process them.

Edit symbols such as a dollar sign, decimal point, or comma, and superfluous blanks are not entered on input cards. Consider the NAME field on the card illustrated in Figure 5.8.

The LAST NAME field appears *first* in many data cards, since it is better form to have major fields before minor ones, for identification and sorting purposes.

Figure 5.8 Sample data card 2.

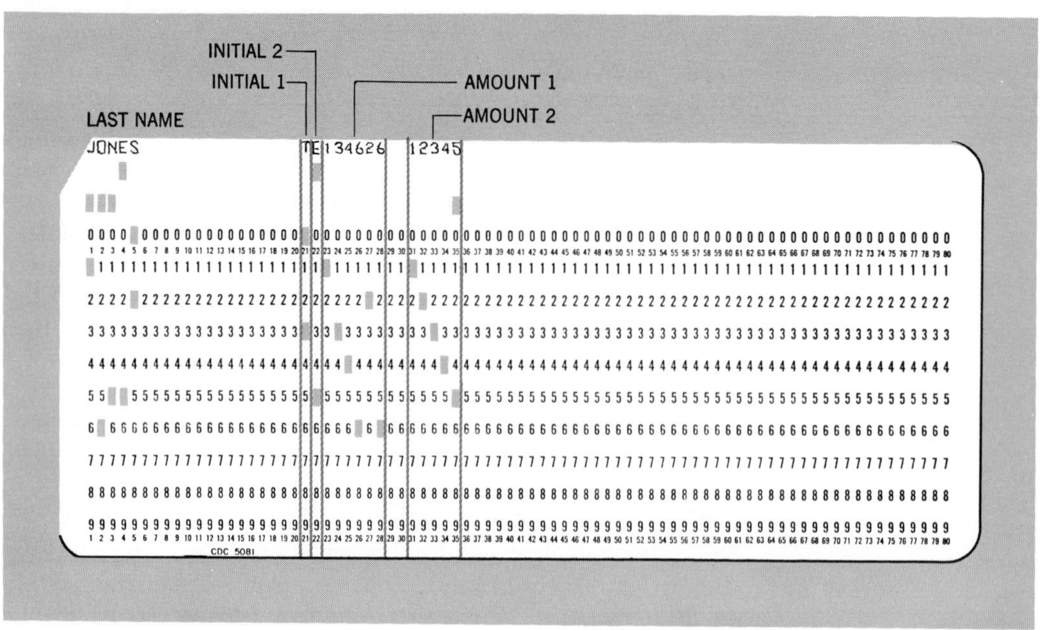

You will note that the initials are adjacent to the LAST NAME field, *with no spaces or periods in between.*

No blanks appear between initials on a card document, since such superfluous *blank columns* would utilize extra positions on the card. These additional positions are often not available if card records have many fields of data. Although printed output will incorporate these blanks or periods between initials for ease of reading, card input need only be read by unit-record devices, or computers, which readily accept concise data.

Thus the elimination of blanks, as superfluous characters, helps to ensure that most card records will fit the 80-character limit, making additional cards per record unnecessary.

The elimination of edit symbols, such as a dollar sign, comma, or decimal point, will result in a similar savings. The programmer need only indicate to the computer that the amount represents four integers and two decimal positions. The above AMOUNT 1 field results in a savings of three positions, since the dollar sign, comma, and decimal point are eliminated.

Thus an amount of $1,346.26 would be represented on a card as shown above. In addition, the computer cannot usually perform arithmetic operations if fields have special characters such as a dollar sign or comma included in the field.

Consider the DATE field (columns 52 to 57) on the card in Figure 5.9.

This represents a date of 01/20/77, with the slashes omitted to save space. This is another conventional method for eliminating edit symbols.

Operational signs are often noted in the units or low-order position of a field. That is, they do not occupy a separate position. If a negative numeric field is to be printed it would generally print as −12345 or 12345−, for example. To indicate negative amounts on a card, however, such representation of five positions for the amount and one for the operational sign would be wasteful.

The convention for input cards is usually to place an operational sign, if needed, in the low-order position of the field, *along with* the units digit.

That is, an AMOUNT field would be indicated as $1234\bar{5}$. A minus sign is a special character, coded as an 11-zone. Thus the field would appear as indicated in columns 31 to 35 of Figure 5.8.

In this way, a position would be saved for each signed numeric field. An 11-5 punch in a single column can also be considered as the letter N. Thus 1234N in a *numeric* data field means −12345 to the computer and to unit-record devices. That is, all arithmetic operations on this amount field will result in proper calculations. The computer is designed to treat 1234N in a numeric field as a negative 12345.

Similarly, 12J would be considered as −121 when coded in a numeric field. To program the computer to add 100 to this number would result in a sum of −21 or 2J.

Sometimes an operational plus sign, represented by an ampersand (12-punch) is placed over the units position of a field to represent a positive quantity. Note that the *absence* of a sign also implies a positive quantity.

The use of a plus sign, however, ensures that a sign was not inadvertently or incorrectly omitted. That is, in fields where many items have negative quantities, plus signs are used to denote positive amounts. In this way, all items are signed; thus negative quantities are less likely to be incorrectly coded as positive or unsigned amounts.

Plus signs are represented, in their low-order position, as a 12-punch in conjunction with the units digit. Thus 423 might

Figure 5.9 Sample data card 3.

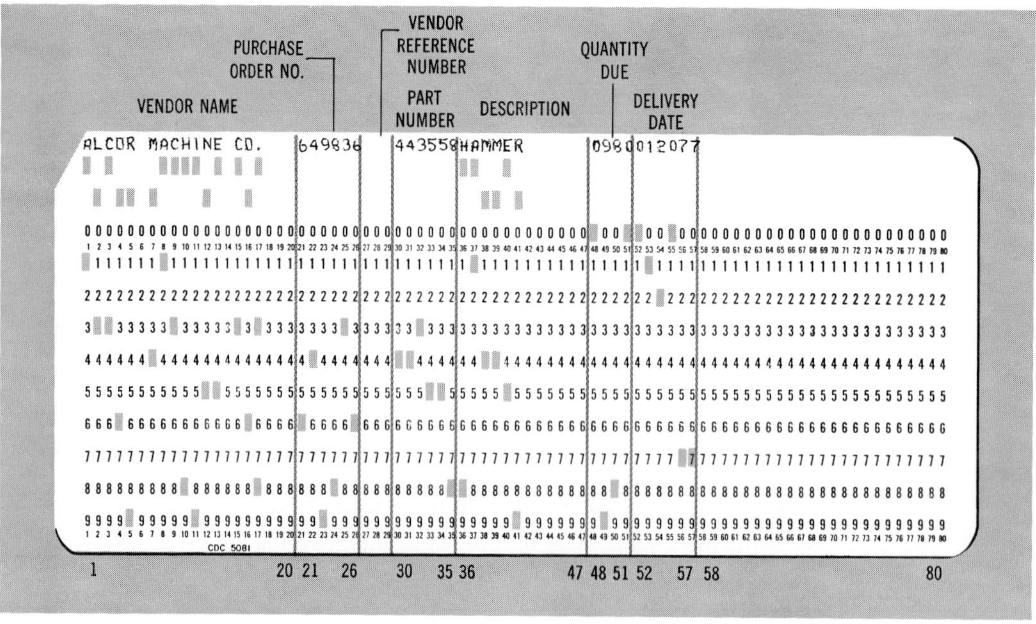

be a positive quantity in an AMOUNT field. This can also be coded as 42C (12-3 punches in units position).

Coded fields are often used to make data more concise. The use of codes on a card is an effective method of saving positions. Suppose, for example, that a retail establishment has 5,000 customer accounts. The card could be designed with a 20-position field for customer name. Each customer could, however, be given a coded ACCOUNT NUMBER, by which he will be known within the data processing department. Thus a 4-position coded ACCOUNT NUMBER representing accounts from 1 to 5000 would save 16 card columns. Similarly, certain payroll procedures often utilize an assigned EMPLOYEE NUMBER or a SOCIAL SECURITY NUMBER instead of NAME. This saves many storage positions and also is a more reliable identification field. Although two employees may have the same name, all employee numbers and social security numbers are unique.

Control punches or fields are often used to save space. Sometimes it is possible to conserve space on a card by utilizing the same positions for two mutually exclusive fields. Suppose, for example, that a transaction card can have *either* a 5-position AMOUNT OF CREDIT field or a 5-position AMOUNT OF DEBIT field. By using *six positions* on the card, we can provide for both these fields. That is, we can include a 5-position AMOUNT field with a sixth position as a CONTROL field. If the sixth position is a 1, for example, then AMOUNT is really equal to AMOUNT OF CREDIT. If it is a 0, then AMOUNT = AMOUNT OF DEBIT. In this way, we need only provide a *single* 5-position field.

To eliminate the need for a sixth position, we can incorporate that control punch into the AMOUNT field itself. An 11-punch, sometimes called an *X*-punch, over the units position can be used for control purposes and *not* to denote a sign. Thus $1387\overline{2}$ would be AMOUNT OF CREDIT equal to 13872, while 13872 in the same positions would indicate an AMOUNT OF DEBIT equal to 13872.

In short, the systems analyst must make every effort to limit a card record to 80 positions so that multiple cards per record are not required. The above five methods of (1) eliminating unnecessary fields (2) eliminating edit and superfluous symbols, (3) placing operational signs in the low-order position of a numeric field, (4) using coded fields, and (5) using control punches are the most frequently used methods for conserving space on a card and thereby ensuring a concise record.

Data are also represented on a card in a logical sequence. That is, fields are *not* haphazardly arranged. The beginning fields on the card are usually those that identify card data or that serve as sort fields. We are not likely to find the date or an amount as the first field of a card, for example. NAME, ACCOUNT NUMBER, TRANSACTION NUMBER, SOCIAL SECURITY NUMBER are more likely fields used to identify the card or for sorting purposes.

After major fields are indicated on a card, the remaining fields are generally arranged as they appear on the original source document so that keypunch operators are not required to visually skip over fields. Figure 5.10 illustrates a conversion from a source document to a punched card. The included card punching or verifying instructions sheet is the document sent to the keypunch supervisor to ensure that the keypunching staff is provided with the information necessary to punch cards with data in the correct format and sequence.

At this point, we will indicate the hierarchy in which data are represented. We have thus far seen that records are composed of related fields. For example, an employee time card is a **record** of data containing a NAME field, HOURS WORKED field, and so on. A collection of related records is called a **file**. Thus a collection of *all* employee time cards would constitute a file. (See Figure 5.11.) These definitions of fields, records, and files apply to any type of input/output medium.

A card layout form is used to assist the analyst in positioning data within several card files. Consider the multiple-card layout form illustrated in Figure 5.12. This form is used to block out key fields within a card that are the same for each of several files.

Illustrative Card Designs

Let us consider some cards designed for specific systems, as shown in Figures 5.13, 5.14, and 5.15.

Types of Cards

The major use of the input punched card is for computer or EAM processing. That is, these cards are meant to be machine-read and interpreted, and thus are designed for ease of processing. They are also machine-prepared, usually with the use of a keypunch machine. Often they are not very "readable," since the coded fields and elimination of edit symbols reduce their readability. They do, however, usually contain the printed equivalent of the punched holes.

Some cards serve as *output* as well as machine-readable input. That is, a card can also be created as *output* from a com-

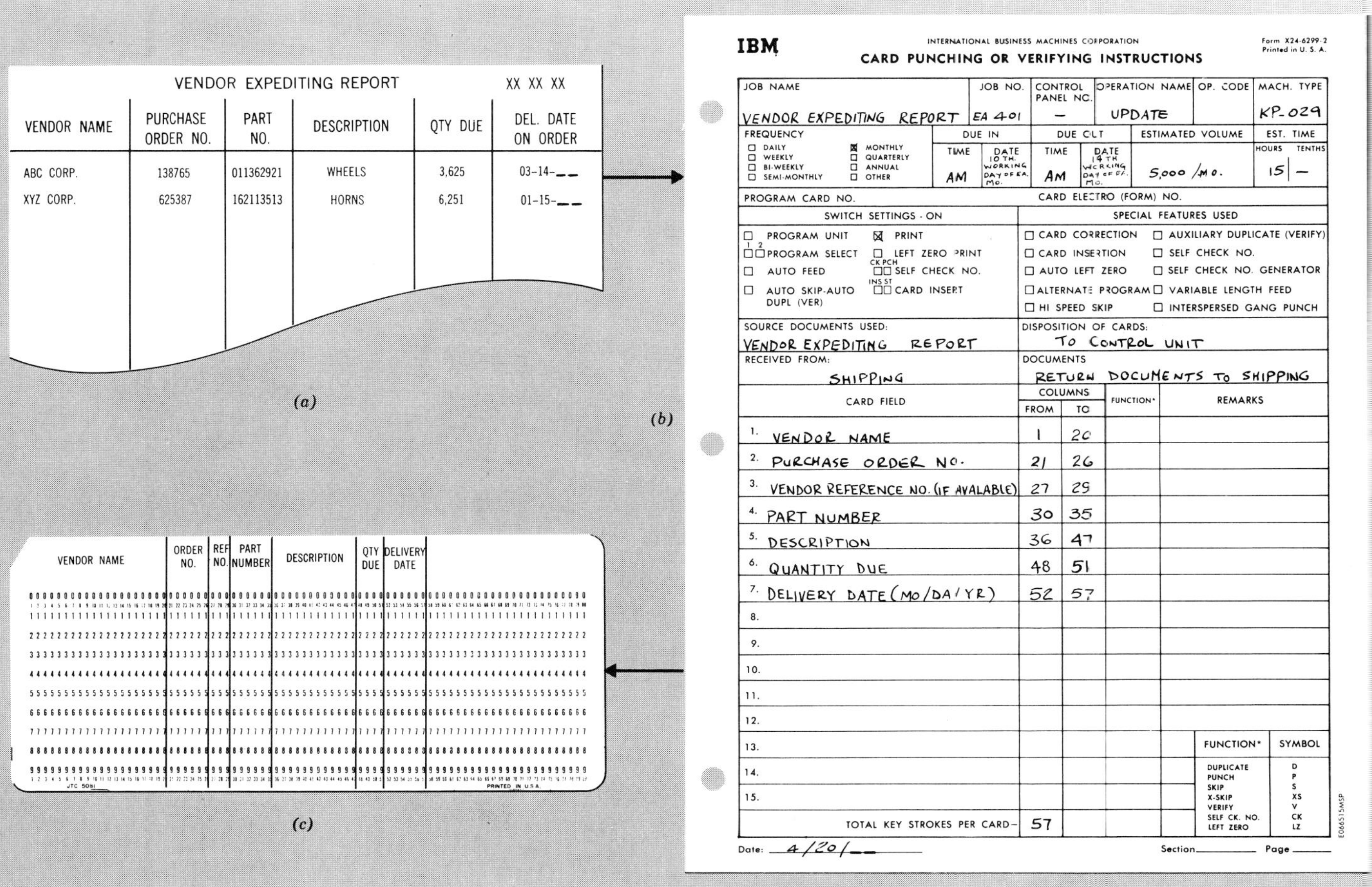

VENDOR EXPEDITING REPORT XX XX XX

VENDOR NAME	PURCHASE ORDER NO.	PART NO.	DESCRIPTION	QTY DUE	DEL. DATE ON ORDER
ABC CORP.	138765	011362921	WHEELS	3,625	03-14-__
XYZ CORP.	625387	162113513	HORNS	6,251	01-15-__

(a)

IBM

INTERNATIONAL BUSINESS MACHINES CORPORATION

CARD PUNCHING OR VERIFYING INSTRUCTIONS

Form X24-6299-2 Printed in U. S. A.

JOB NAME	JOB NO.	CONTROL PANEL NO.	OPERATION NAME	OP. CODE	MACH. TYPE
VENDOR EXPEDITING REPORT	EA 401	—	UPDATE		KP-029

FREQUENCY: ☐ DAILY ☐ WEEKLY ☐ BI-WEEKLY ☐ SEMI-MONTHLY ☒ MONTHLY ☐ QUARTERLY ☐ ANNUAL ☐ OTHER

DUE IN: TIME AM; DATE 10TH WORKING DAY OF EA. MO.

DUE OUT: TIME AM; DATE 14TH WORKING DAY OF EA. MO.

ESTIMATED VOLUME: 5,000 /MO.

EST. TIME: HOURS 15 TENTHS —

PROGRAM CARD NO.

CARD ELECTRO (FORM) NO.

SWITCH SETTINGS - ON

☐ PROGRAM UNIT ☒ PRINT
☐☐ PROGRAM SELECT ☐ LEFT ZERO PRINT
☐ AUTO FEED ☐☐ SELF CHECK NO.
☐ AUTO SKIP-AUTO DUPL (VER) ☐☐ CARD INSERT

SPECIAL FEATURES USED

☐ CARD CORRECTION ☐ AUXILIARY DUPLICATE (VERIFY)
☐ CARD INSERTION ☐ SELF CHECK NO.
☐ AUTO LEFT ZERO ☐ SELF CHECK NO. GENERATOR
☐ ALTERNATE PROGRAM ☐ VARIABLE LENGTH FEED
☐ HI SPEED SKIP ☐ INTERSPERSED GANG PUNCH

SOURCE DOCUMENTS USED: VENDOR EXPEDITING REPORT

RECEIVED FROM: SHIPPING

DISPOSITION OF CARDS: TO CONTROL UNIT

DOCUMENTS: RETURN DOCUMENTS TO SHIPPING

	CARD FIELD	COLUMNS FROM	COLUMNS TO	FUNCTION*	REMARKS
1.	VENDOR NAME	1	20		
2.	PURCHASE ORDER NO.	21	26		
3.	VENDOR REFERENCE NO. (IF AVALABLE)	27	29		
4.	PART NUMBER	30	35		
5.	DESCRIPTION	36	47		
6.	QUANTITY DUE	48	51		
7.	DELIVERY DATE (MO/DA/YR)	52	57		
8.					
9.					
10.					
11.					
12.					
13.					
14.					
15.					
	TOTAL KEY STROKES PER CARD—	57			

FUNCTION*	SYMBOL
DUPLICATE	D
PUNCH	P
SKIP	S
X-SKIP	XS
VERIFY	V
SELF CK. NO.	CK
LEFT ZERO	LZ

Date: 4/20/__ Section______ Page______

E06651SMSP

(b)

(c)

Figure 5.10 Conversion of source document to punched card.

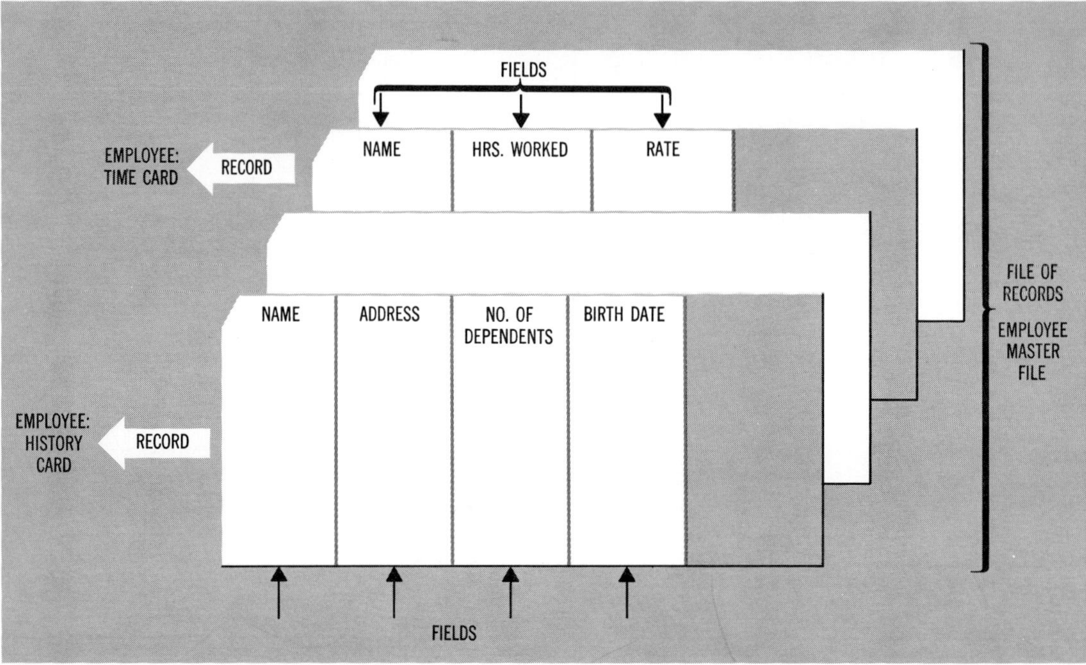

Figure 5.11 Related fields in records within a file.

puter or from specific EAM devices such as a **reproducer.** A typical example is a utility bill created on a punched card by a computer, which serves as output to be read and interpreted by a customer, as in Figure 5.16. The customer is instructed to return this card, or bill, with the payment. He is also urged not to "bend, fold, staple, or mutilate" the card, since it will later serve as input to the computer to update the customer's account.

Timecards are also often created by a computer with just EMPLOYEE NAME and NUMBER. These cards are then additionally punched by special machines to denote the hours worked for each employee.

In short, a punched card can be created or keypunched from a source document to serve as *input* to a computer or EAM device. In addition, a punched card can serve as *output* from a computer or EAM device. When a card is created as output, it will usually be reentered into the data processing flow at some later date as input. Thus the utility bill or the timecard is only an intermediate form of output, since it will eventually serve as input again.

Some cards are punched *manually* by a hand device, and

IBM

INTERNATIONAL BUSINESS MACHINES CORPORATION

MULTIPLE-CARD LAYOUT FORM

GX24-6599-0
Printed in U.S.A.

Company ABC CO.

Application INVENTORY CONTROL SYSTEM by N. STEARN Date 1/1/ Job No. 3A Sheet No. 1

PART NO.	DESCRIPTION	QTY. INTO STOCK	QTY. ISSUED STOCK	QTY. BACK ORDER	UNIT OF MEAS.	UNIT PRICE $	¢		LOT CONTRACT NO.	
1–7	8–27	28–32	33–37	38–42	43–46	47–50	51–52	53–69	70–74	75–80

PART NO.	DESCRIPTION	QTY RECEIV-ED	QTY REC'VD MO.	YR.		LOT CONTRACT NO.	
1–7	8–27	28–32	33–34	35–36	37–69	70–74	75–80

1–80

1–80

1–80

1–80

Figure 5.12 Multiple-card layout form for inventory control system.

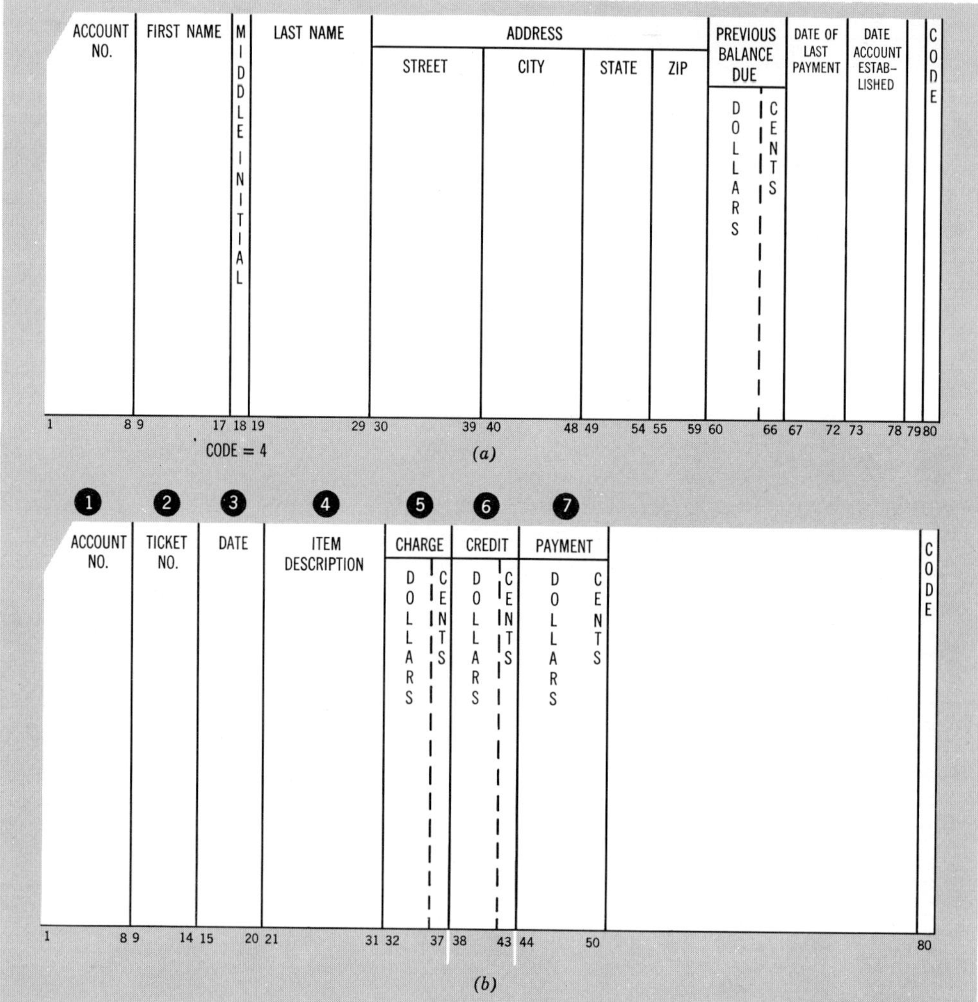

Figure 5.13 Accounts receivable card records: (*a*) name-and-address card; (*b*) transaction card for sales slips, credit slips, payment notices, memos. The following fields are keypunched, depending on the source document:
Sales slip: fields 1, 2, 3, 4, 5, 8 are filled; code = 1
Credit slip: fields 1, 2, 3, 4, 6 are filled; code = 2
Payment memo: fields 1, 3, 7, 8 are filled; code = 3

are called **Port-A-Punch cards** (Figure 5.17). Other cards are manually marked by a special electrographic pencil. These marks on the card can then be interpreted by a special machine and converted to conventional punched cards. These cards are called **mark-sensed cards** (Figure 5.18). Many students have used these for taking multiple-choice tests. The answers are mark-sensed by the student with the special pencil.

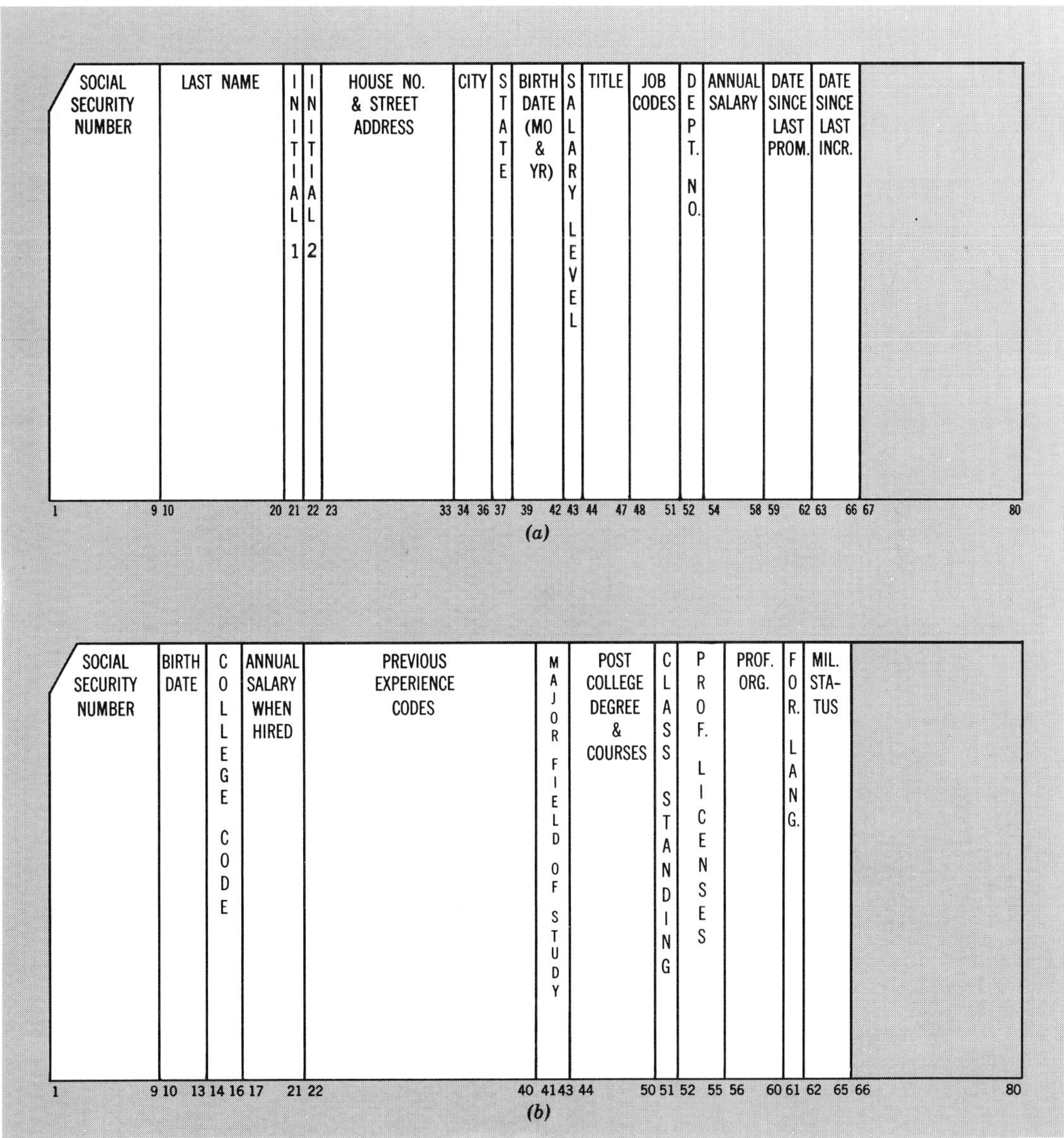

Figure 5.14 Personnel card records for salaried employees: (*a*) change-in-status personnel card; (*b*) new employee personnel card.

They are then converted into the appropriate Hollerith configuration on the same card, by a special machine. Both Port-A-Punch and mark-sensed cards eliminate the need for a conversion from a source document to a machine-readable form, thereby saving a data processing cost. That is, the card itself serves as a source document. An employee from a water com-

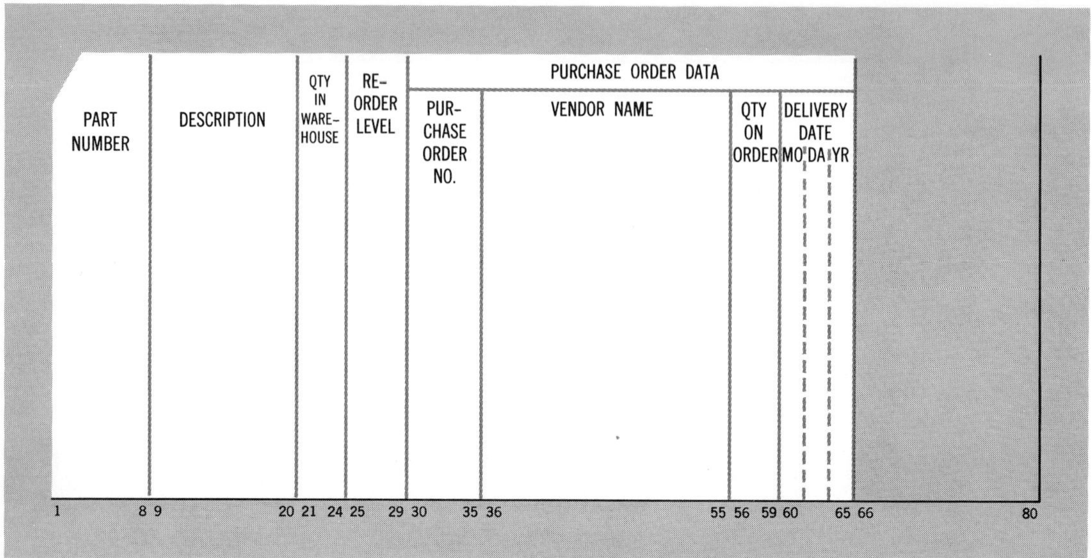

Figure 5.15 Inventory card record.

pany, for example, can use either Port-A-Punch or mark-sensed cards to punch or mark water meter figures that he obtains from each home meter. In this way the cards can serve as input to a data processing machine.

In short, cards can serve multiple purposes in data processing systems. The card in Figure 5.19 was produced by a computer. Then a special electronic accounting machine called an **interpreter** printed the information in the boxes so that it could be read by customers. While card punch devices of

Figure 5.16 Utility bill on a punched card (courtesy IBM).

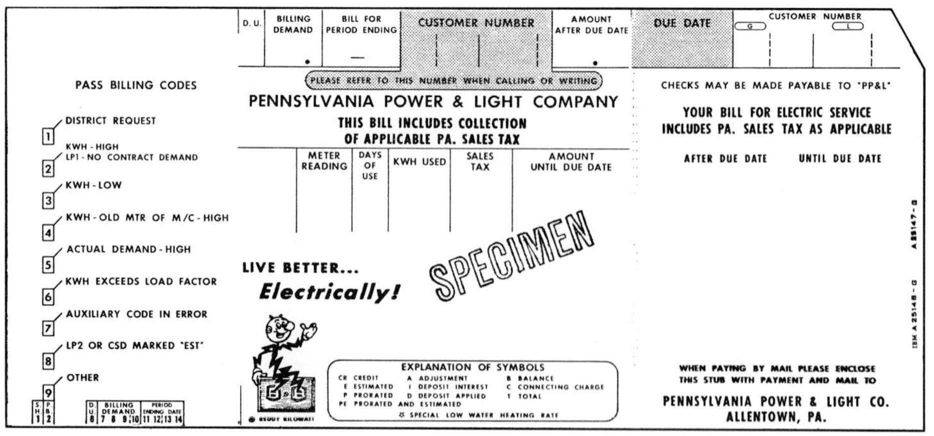

computer systems can be equipped with the ability to print the information while they are punching, such equipment is too expensive for many applications. In general, then, peripheral EAM devices, such as the interpreter, are still in use for operations that are feasible for computers to perform but that can be performed at lower cost on these devices.

Similarly, cards such as the one in Figure 5.19 are sometimes reentered into a computer system. In such cases, information is added to these cards with the special mark-sense pencils or even by keypunch machines. Note in Figure 5.19 the numbers at the right of the illustration. These numbers are filled in with special mark-sense pencils by an operator to record payments. The mark-sensed information is then either converted to punched holes or entered into the computer directly. Note, then, that mark-sensing need not be the only op-

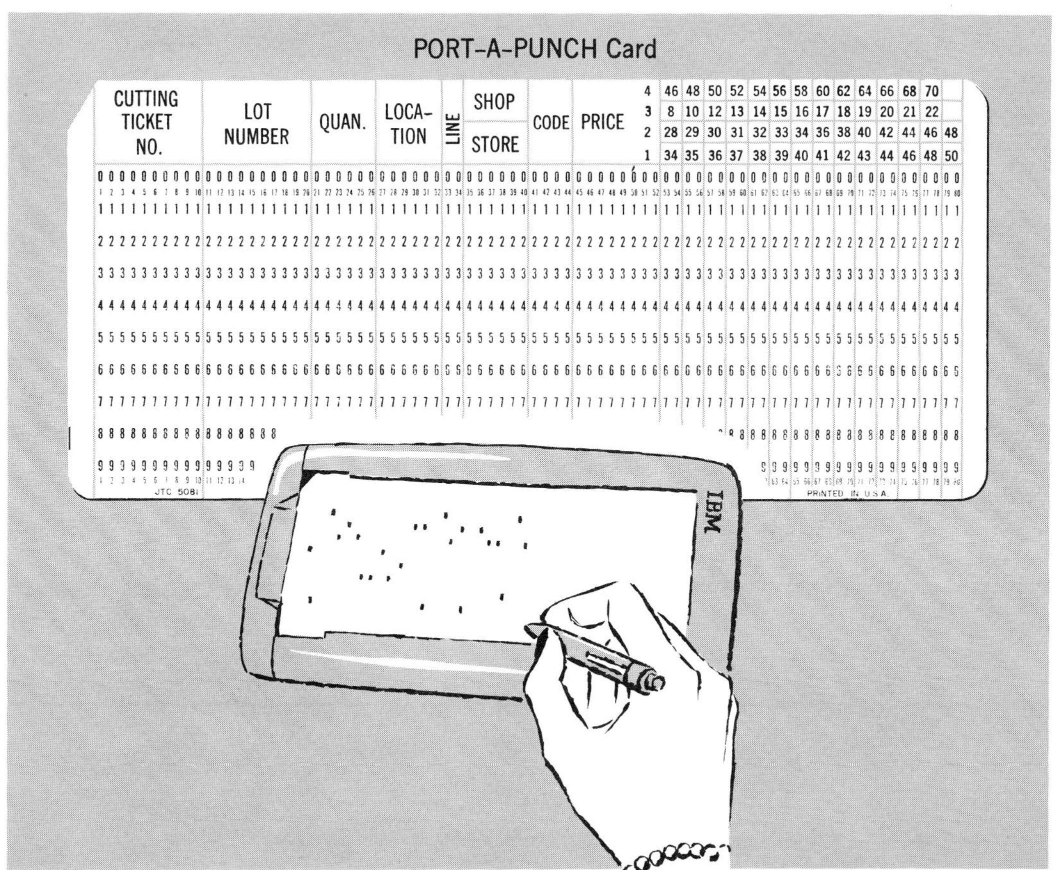

Figure 5.17 Punching a Port-A-Punch card.

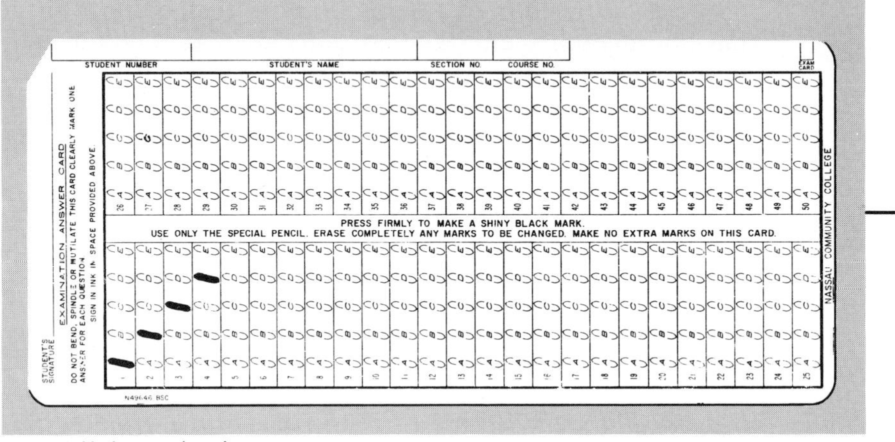

***(a)* Mark-sensed card**

***(b)* Reproducer (Courtesy IBM)**

Figure 5.18 Mark-sensing and the reproducing punch: (*a*) mark-sensed card; (*b*) reproducer (courtesy IBM); (*c*) mark-sensed card with punches.

***(c)* Same mark-sensed card with punches**

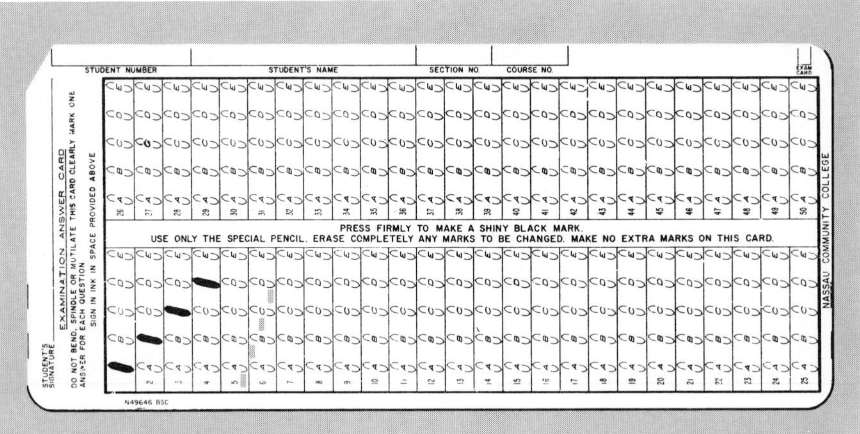

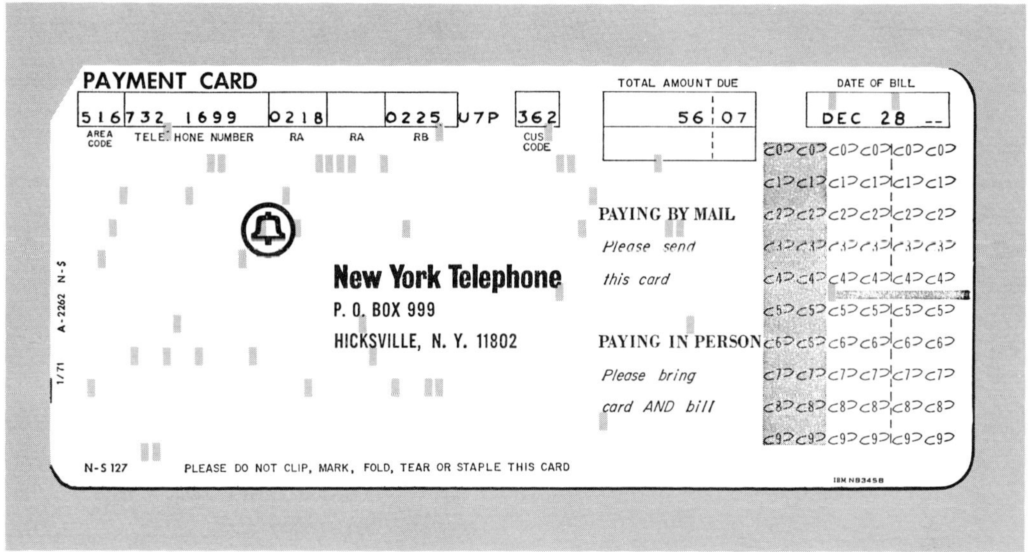

Figure 5.19 Sample utility punched card.

eration performed on the card. Cards such as the one in Figure 5.19 can serve several different purposes and can be used by several different machines, thus eliminating multiple record keeping.

Advantages and Disadvantages of Punched Card Processing

We can see that the punched card has numerous uses in industry. As indicated, it is the most widely used storage medium in small-scale computer installations.

Its basic advantages include the fact that data recorded on cards are machine-accessible *and* manually accessible as well. That is, computers and EAM devices can utilize card data, while manual methods can still be utilized to extract specific records since the data punched on the card may also be printed on the face of the card. (Most keypunch machines have printing facility, but most card punch devices do not.)

Another important consideration is the relatively economical method by which cards can be processed.

There are, however, several inherent disadvantages to card processing that must be realized by all business and data processing students. The relative convenience of card processing decreases with increased numbers of cards. That is, large numbers of cards are cumbersome to process. Cards within a file can often be lost, misplaced, dropped, or missorted. Operator time is greatly increased with large numbers of cards. Operators must constantly feed these records into the appropriate machines. Magnetic tapes and disks, discussed in Chapter 6, do not have these disadvantages.

The card reader of a computer and the EAM devices utilize essentially mechanical methods of sensing holes in a card. Mechanical devices often jam, causing the loss of many hours of machine time. These devices, then, are not as efficient as others that rely solely on electronic equipment. Similarly, mechanical devices are notoriously slow. Some card readers, for example, can read *an average* of 1,000 cards per minute. This speed, although seemingly fast for a layman, is very slow compared to the *billionths* of seconds in which the computer can process the data, once they are read. We shall see that other computer forms are much faster.

Thus, while cost is minimal, efficiency is limited with punched cards. Similarly, physical limitations often adversely affect card processing. The previously mentioned factor of 80 positions per record is a distinct disadvantage. Some records do not lend themselves to 80-character formats. Also, humid weather conditions result in warped cards, which cause mechanical devices to jam.

In short, the punched card is the basic form of input. Most computer centers utilize the card as input, often to be converted to a more efficient medium at some later date. Only small computer centers, however, utilize the punched card as a *primary* form of input. Such small companies usually have limited amounts of data, and for these the card remains the most economical and efficient medium. In larger companies, the disadvantages and inefficiencies of the punched card make other storage media more desirable.

GLOSSARY

Field. Consecutive positions that represent a unit of data.

File. A collection of related records.

EAM devices. Electronic accounting machines such as collators, reproducers, accounting machines, and interpreters.

Keypunch machine. Device used to convert source documents to punched cards.

Mark-sensed card. Card that is manually marked by a special electrographic pencil. These marks on the card can be interpreted by a special machine and converted to punched cards.

Port-A-Punch card. Punched card whose punches are manually produced by a hand device.

Punched card. Card on which data are recorded in the form of punched holes.

Record. A collection of related fields.

QUESTIONS

1. What are the basic advantages of card processing?
2. What are the basic disadvantages of card processing?
3. How should fields of data be arranged on a card?
4. Suppose information relating to a specific record is 90 characters long. Suppose, in addition, that the record must be transcribed onto cards. What are the various options open to you to minimize problems with the system?
5. What are the various ways in which errors in card processing can be minimized?
6. Indicate the various types of cards with which an analyst should be familiar, and specify the characteristics of each.
7. Provide at least two examples of the ways in which people come into contact with punched cards in their everyday lives.
8. What are the various machines that could be used in conjunction with card processing in a data processing environment?
9. What are the differences between representation of numeric data on a card and the representation of nonnumeric data?
10. What is the purpose of a card punching or verifying instructions sheet?

CHAPTER 6

DESIGN OF HIGH-LEVEL FILES

MAGNETIC TAPE PROCESSING—AN INTRODUCTION

A magnetic tape is a *high-speed* medium that can serve as input to, or output from, a computer. It is a common file type for medium- or large-scale processing.

A magnetic tape drive is the device that can either read a tape or write onto a tape. It has a **read/write head** that is accessed by the computer for either reading or writing. (See Figure 6.1).

Magnetic tape drives function like home tape recorders. Data can be recorded, or written, onto a tape and "played back," or read, from the same tape at a later date. If data are written on a tape, previous data in that area are written over or destroyed. For this reason, computer centers must take precautions to protect important tapes that should not inadvertently be written over.

A typical magnetic tape is 2,400 to 3,600 feet long and ½ inch wide. The tape is made of plastic with an iron-oxide coating that can be magnetized to represent data. Since the magnetized spots or **bits** are extremely small and not visible to the human eye, large volumes of data can be condensed into a relatively small area of tape. Information from an entire 80-column card, for example, can typically be stored on one tenth of an inch of magnetic tape, or less. The average tape, which costs approximately $25, can store approximately 20 million characters. After a tape file has been processed and is no longer needed, the same tape can be reused repeatedly to store other information.

Because tape drives read data *electronically* by sensing magnetized areas, and write data electronically by magnetizing areas, tapes can be processed at very high speeds. Data can be read or written at speeds of from 100,000 to 300,000 characters *per second*.

Thus tape files are frequently used for large volumes of data. One tape can store hundreds of thousands of records, transmit and receive data at very high speeds, and store the data in a compact form. In many medium- or large-scale companies, **master files** for payroll, accounts receivable, accounts payable,

(a)

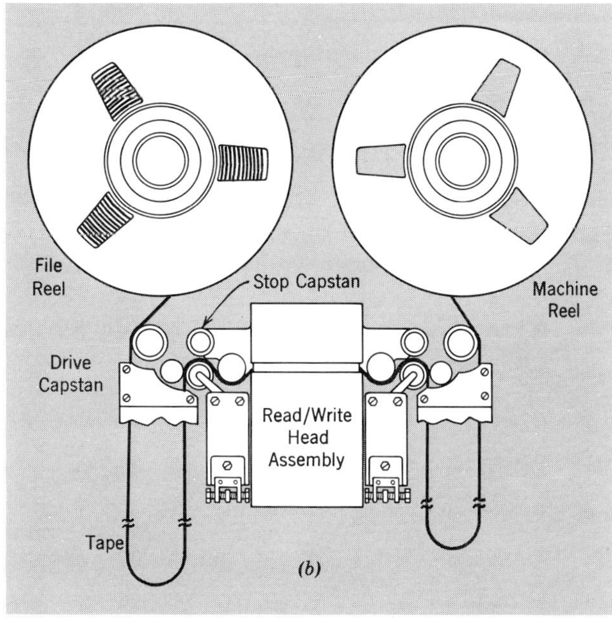

(b)

Figure 6.1 *(a)* Magnetic tape drive (courtesy Burroughs Corp.); *(b)* read/write head for tape (courtesy IBM).

inventory, and so on, are stored on tape. A master file is the main data file that holds all current information for a specific department or system.

A record on a tape may be any size, as long as it is physically consistent with the size of core storage. That is, it is not feasible to create 5,000-position records using a 4,000-position computer, since the output area (5,000 positions) must be located in storage. Aside from this limitation, tape records may usually be any size. Keep in mind, however, that extremely large records sizes are more difficult to process.

Because of a tape's capacity to handle large volumes of data in a relatively short time, it is ideally suited for **batch processing,** or processing in cumulative groups.

The tape files may be created by:

1. A tape drive of a computer system. The tape serves as output when it is the product of a computer run. The data are initially entered from some other device, such as a card reader, and then converted, by the computer, to magnetic tape.

2. A **key-to-tape encoder** or converter (Figure 6.2). This device is similar to a keypunch machine. It requires an operator to code data from a source document to a magnetic tape via a typewriter-like keyboard. The operator depresses a specific character key, and the device converts it to the appropriate magnetized coding. Tapes encoded in this manner can be verified by the same device to ensure their accuracy.

The key-to-tape equipment in use today can be divided into two basic categories:

1. Stand-alone encoders, which, as indicated above, are used to convert source documents to a magnetic tape.
2. Key-to-tape preparation systems, which include a small computer with a core capacity of 8K (8,000) to 16K, a tape drive, and from 6 to 64 key-entry stations. With the use of this processor, data keyed in by an operator can be formatted, verified, edited, and then placed on a tape for use by the standard computer at the installation.

In short, tape is a very common file medium for high-speed, voluminous processing. It does, however, have several inherent disadvantages, discussed below.

Data recorded on a tape can only be processed **sequentially.** That is, to access a record with transaction number 254 from a tape file that is maintained in transaction number sequence, we must read past the first 253 records. We instruct the computer to read a record; test if it contains transaction number 254; and, if it does not, to read the next record. Thus 254 records are read. There is no convenient method to instruct the tape drive to skip the first few inches of tape or to go directly to the middle of the tape.

Thus, unless all or most records from a tape file are required for processing *most of the time,* this method could become inefficient and costly.

If an inventory file is created on tape with 100,000 records and only a handful of these are required to print a report, then tapes may not be the best file type to use. Processing time and thus cost would be excessive, since most of the file must be read even to process only a small number of records. Sequential processing is beneficial only when *most* records on the file are required for normal processing in sequence. Again, master payroll, accounts receivable, and accounts payable files are ideally suited to magnetic tape, since most records are required for processing during normal runs. We must read an

Figure 6.2 Keytape encoder (courtesy Honeywell). Simple keyboard — operating ease is one of the many advantages of Honeywell's Keytape devices. The units bypass conventional punched card preparation by transcribing information directly onto magnetic tape from the keyboard. Typing and control functions are similar to those on a keypunch machine, easing the task of keypunch operators in learning to use the devices.

entire payroll file, for example, to print checks; thus a tape file is suitable.

Another disadvantage of tape processing is that a given tape can usually be used *either* as input or output during a single run, but cannot serve as both an input/output medium. That is, an **updating** application, or the process of making a master file of data current, generally requires the master file as input and the creation of a *new* physical tape. Consider the update illustration in Figure 6.3.

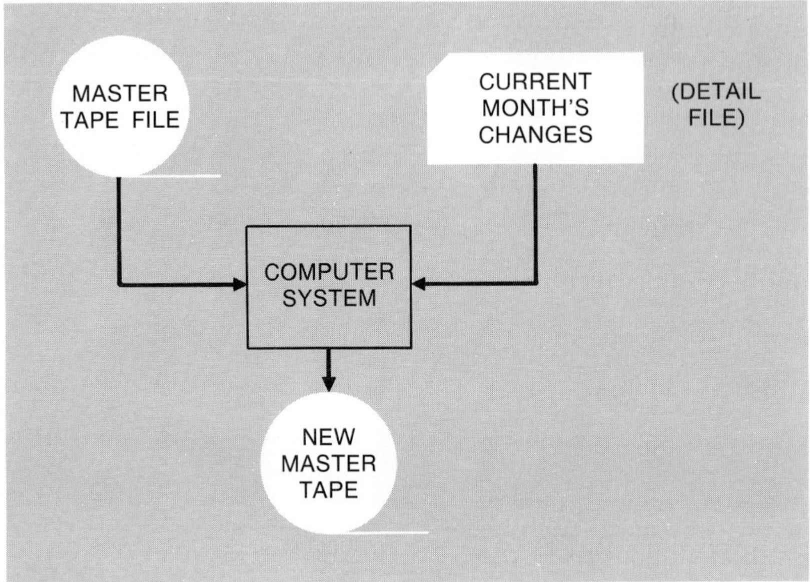

Figure 6.3 Update procedure using magnetic tape.

A new tape must be created that, in effect, rewrites the information from the previous master tape and adds the current month's changes. The input master tape cannot be conveniently processed to add new records, delete some records, and make changes in existing records. A *new tape* must be created that incorporates master information along with the current changes.

This inability of the tape to be conveniently processed as *both* input and output during a single computer run results in several limitations. Since two tapes are required for such runs, *two* tape drives are necessary to process them. The necessity of reading many master records that have *not* changed during the present month, and recreating them without alteration on an output tape drive, results in increased processing time. That is, if only 30 payroll changes, for example, are needed to amend a 1,000-record master tape, then 970 master records that do not require revision must be read and rewritten onto the new tape. Keep in mind that although this inability results in increased processing time, the increased time is not usually excessive, since tape records are written very quickly. We would require tapes with hundreds of thousands of inactive records in order to substantially affect the processing time.

A third disadvantage of tape processing is the identification problem. Most medium- and large-scale computer installations have hundreds or even thousands of magnetic tapes, each utilized for a specific application. Because data recorded on these tapes are not "readable" or visible to the naked eye, it is often difficult to maintain identification of them. If a master accounts receivable tape is inadvertently written over, or used as *output* for some other job, for example, the result could be an expensive recreation process, since the writing of output would destroy the existing information. Several steps have been implemented at most installations to prevent such occurrences, or to reduce the extent of damage, should they occur:

1. Tape Labels. External gummed labels are placed on the face of each tape (see Figure 6.4), identifying it and indicating its **retention cycle,** or how long it should be maintained. These labels are clearly visible to anyone, so that chances for inadvertent misuse of a valuable tape are reduced. The problem with gummed labels, however, is that they sometimes become unglued. Their effectiveness is also directly related to the effort and training of the computer staff. If operators are negligent, then labels will not be used properly.

To make the identification of tapes more reliable, most programs include a built-in routine that, for output tapes, creates a tape label record that is produced as any other tape record, with magnetized bits. The label is the first record on the tape. When the tape is used as input, at some later date, then this first label record, called a **header label,** is checked as part of the program, to ascertain that the correct tape is being used.

Thus header labels are created on output tapes and checked on input tapes. This label creation for output and label checking for input is a standard procedure in most programs. Since it uses the computer to verify that the correct tapes are being used, there is less danger of manual inefficiency.

2. Tape Librarian. Most medium- and large-scale companies have numerous tapes that must be filed or stored, handled properly, and released for reuse when no longer required. Such companies employ a tape librarian to maintain the proper usage of tape files. If he or she performs the job properly, there will be less misuse or misplacing of tapes.

3. File Protection Ring (Figure 6.5). Available tapes that may be written on, or used as output, have a **file protection ring** inserted in the back. The tape drive is electronically sensitized

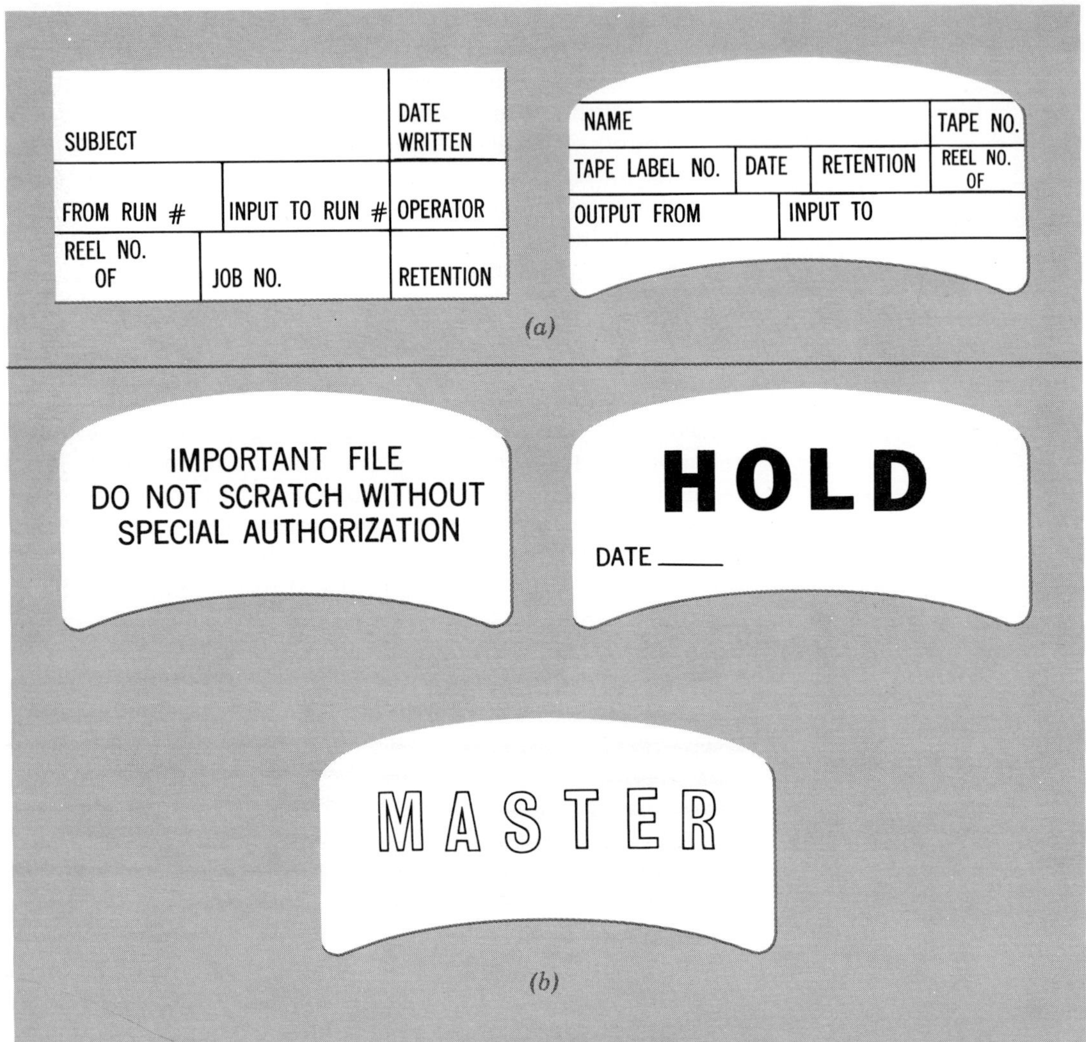

Figure 6.4 External tape labels: *(a)* two commonly used external labels; *(b)* three commonly used special-purpose labels.

so that it will *not* create an output record unless this ring is in its proper place. For tapes that are to be maintained and not written over, the ring has been removed. Thus, if an operator inadvertently uses such a tape for an output operation, the computer prints a message that tells him, in effect "NO RING—NO WRITE." If the operator is cautious, he will examine the external label, and hopefully, he will realize that he is using the wrong tape. If he is persistent, he will merely place a ring on the tape (any file protection ring fits all tapes)

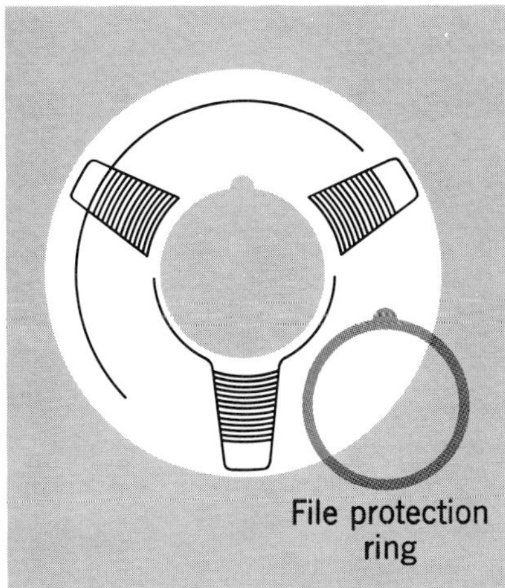

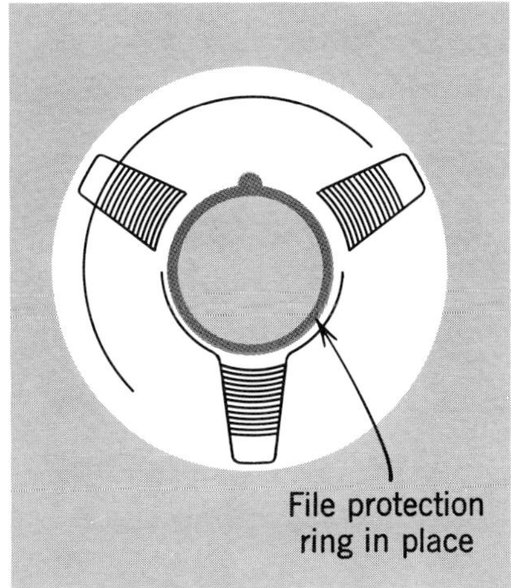

Figure 6.5 File protection ring, a plastic ring that fits into the groove in the tape reel. When the ring is in place, both writing and reading of tape records can occur. When the ring is removed, only reading can occur. In this way, the file is protected from accidental erasure.

and restart the job. Thus this method, alone, deters the misuse of tapes but does not totally solve the problem.

4. **Backup Tapes.** Since tapes can sometimes be written over or even become physically damaged, it is necessary to maintain backup tapes so that the recreation process, should it become necessary, does not become enormously costly and cumbersome.

Suppose the update procedure shown in Figure 6.3 is performed each month. After processing, it is best to store the old master tape and the detail records *along with* the new master tape. In this way, if some mishap should befall the new master tape, it is a simple task to recreate it from the two forms of input. Normally, we maintain *two* previous tapes as backup, in addition to the present one, in order to prevent any serious problem. Hence, the three **generations** of tapes maintained for important files are called the **grandfather-father-son** tapes. (See Figure 6.6.)

REPRESENTING DATA ON MAGNETIC TAPE

You will recall that data are recorded on magnetic tape on a thin film of iron-oxide coating. Many third-generation tapes have nine tracks on which to record data (see Figure 6.7), although seven-track tapes designed for second-generation computers are still widely used. We shall discuss nine-track tapes in detail.

Each of these tracks can be magnetized or demagnetized de-

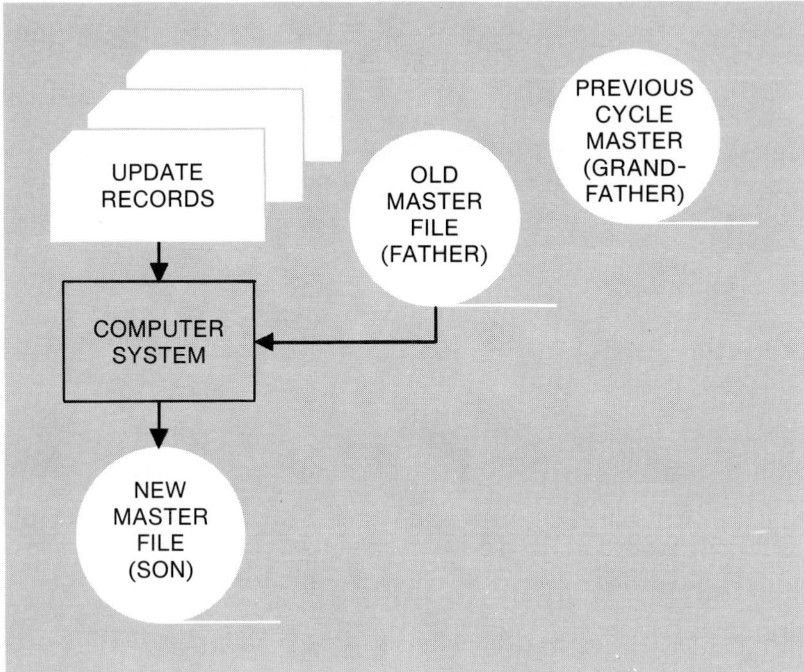

Figure 6.6 Grandfather-father-son method of file backup.

pending on the data represented. The coded representation of data on these nine tracks, labeled P and 0 to 7, is the *same* code used by the computer for the internal representation known as EBCDIC, or Extended Binary Coded Decimal Interchange Code. The Hollerith code, on a punched card which uses a combination of a single zone and a single digit, can be converted to this *9-bit* (**b**inary dig**it**) machine code. (See Figure 6.8.)

Figure 6.7 Nine-track tape.

ZONE PORTION

ZONE \ BITS	0	1	2	3
12 (for letters A–I)	1	1	0	0
11 (for letters J–R)	1	1	0	1
0 (for letters S–Z)	1	1	1	0
DIGITS	1	1	1	1

DIGIT PORTION

DIGIT \ BITS	4	5	6	7
0	0	0	0	0
1	0	0	0	1
2	0	0	1	0
3	0	0	1	1
4	0	1	0	0
5	0	1	0	1
6	0	1	1	0
7	0	1	1	1
8	1	0	0	0
9	1	0	0	1

Figure 6.8 Typical representation of data on a nine-track tape. Digit bits 4 5 6 7 correspond to binary values 8 4 2 1.

Disregarding the P-bit momentarily, we may represent any character using this combination of four zone and four digit bits.

The letter A, a combination of a 12-zone and a 1-digit in Hollerith, would be represented as indicated on tape in Figure 6.9.

A typical way to represent any *integer* on magnetic tape would be to use 1111, in the zone positions, in addition to the corresponding digit representation. Thus the number 172 in a numeric field will be represented as indicated also in Figure 6.9.

Note that the illustrated code is the same one the computer uses for internal representation of data. In essence, the 1s denote magnetized positions or current "on." The 0s denote demagnetized positions or current "off." Magnetic tape can be processed quickly by computer because no code conversion is required. Data are represented on tape in nine-track form, with each track having current "on" or "off," in the same way data are represented internally in the computer by nine core positions for each character, using current "on" or "off." Thus for the computer to read from or write onto magnetic tape is a high-speed process.

The P-bit corresponds to a **parity** or **check bit** and is used to check the coded representation of data.

When data are coded, both internally in the computer and on magnetic tape, there is a remote possibility that a single bit position can sometimes become demagnetized, or an "off" position can become magnetized. The parity or P-bit is used to determine if this error has occurred.

Figure 6.9 Representation of sample characters on a nine-track tape.

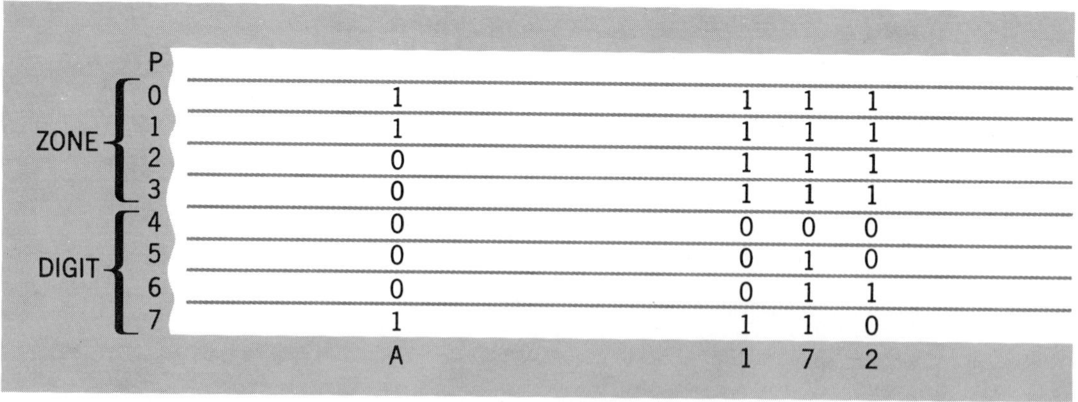

A: 12 Zone: 1100 Zone Bits
1 Digit : 0001 Digit Bits

8	4	2	1
0	0	0	1

172:Zone Bits: 1111
Digit Bits :

8	4	2	1	8	4	2	1	8	4	2	1
0	0	0	1	0	1	1	1	0	0	1	0

Odd parity is the utilization of an odd number of on-bits to represent *any* character. Figure 6.10 illustrates how the digit 5 is represented on tape.

Note that there are *six* bits on, not counting the P-bit. Using the concept of odd parity, the machine would automatically magnetize or "turn on" the P-bit.

Thus the complete codes for the number 7 and the letter A are denoted also in Figure 6.10.

The P-bit is used to ensure that an odd number of bits is always on for the computer that uses odd-parity checking.

For **even**-parity computers, the P-bit is used to ensure that an *even* number of bits is always on.

In short, the number of bits on must always be *odd* for odd-parity computers. Thus magnetic tapes typically utilize an odd number of bits for each character. During the reading of a magnetic tape, the number of bits on is checked to determine if, in fact, an odd number exists. If a single bit were inadvertently demagnetized or the current turned "off," or similarly an extra bit were magnetized, this would result in a parity error. The computer would not continue processing this tape until the problem was located.

Notice that this technique of parity checking only works when a *single* bit for a specific character is inadvertently misrepresented. If two bits are demagnetized, an odd number would still exist and no parity error would occur. Keep in mind, however, that the loss or gain of a single bit during processing is a remote possibility, but one that must nonetheless be properly handled; the loss of two bits, however, has almost no probability of occurring during processing and thus is simply not handled by most computers.

Figure 6.10 Representation of characters: 5, 7, A, B on a nine-track tape.

	Track	5	7	A	B
	P	1	0	0	0
ZONE	0	1	1	1	1
ZONE	1	1	1	1	1
ZONE	2	1	1	0	0
ZONE	3	1	1	0	0
DIGIT	4	0	0	0	0
DIGIT	5	1	1	0	0
DIGIT	6	0	1	0	1
DIGIT	7	1	1	1	0

Density

Millions of characters can be recorded on a single magnetic tape. Different tapes, however, have different storage capabilities. The **density** of a tape denotes the number of characters that can be represented in a given area of tape. Usually we indicate tape density as the *number of characters per inch*. The most frequently used densities are:

556 bpi
800 bpi
1,600 bpi

Bpi is an abbreviation for bits per inch. In effect, this indicates the number of characters per inch. Thus the most frequently used tape densities are 556 to 1,600 characters per inch.

Obviously, the larger tape densities enable the tape to store more characters. Some magnetic tapes have densities of up to 3,000 or more characters per inch.

Blocking

We have seen that tapes, unlike cards, can utilize any record size. The size of tape records is only restricted by the physical limitations of the computer.

Thus we may have 100-position tape records or 500-position tape records. When all records on a single tape file are the same size, we say that the file employs **fixed-length records.** When records on a single tape file have different sizes depending on the format of each record, we say that the file employs **variable-length records.**

Programming effort is simplified by using fixed-length records on a tape. Variable-length tape records require far more sophisticated programming and thus are not usually employed unless processing is optimized by utilizing records of different sizes.

We will, therefore, restrict our discussion to fixed-length tape records, where each record is the same size. The specific size of each record, however, is determined for each application by the systems and programming staff.

Many applications use, for example, 100 characters per record. We shall now see, however, that small records such as these can, if not handled properly, lead to inefficient processing.

Between tape records the computer automatically reserves a fraction of an inch of blank tape called an **interblock gap (IBG)**. Thus when a tape is created as computer output, it is created as shown in Figure 6.11.

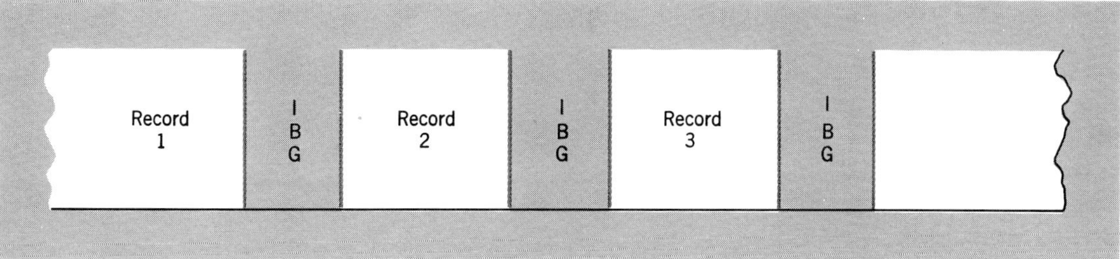

Figure 6.11 Physical records separated by interblock gaps on a tape.

For some tape drives, this interblock gap between records is ¾ inch; for others it is 3/5 inch. The smaller the IBG, the less wasted tape there is.

This blank area of tape called an IBG is a necessary part of tape processing. When a computer reads from a tape, it reads an entire record at the average rate of more than 100 inches per second. This is an extremely fast rate. Once a record has been read, and the computer senses its end, it requires a fraction of a second for the equipment to physically stop and cease reading because of the speed with which it functions. This concept is called **inertia.** It is similar to the automobile traveling 60 miles per hour that, after the brake has been applied, requires numerous feet before it actually comes to a full stop.

Thus a magnetic tape that is read or written at tremendous speeds needs a fraction of a second to physically stop after the end of a record has been reached. In this fraction of a second, a fraction of an inch of tape has been bypassed. That is, in the time it takes the read/write head of a tape drive to stop, an extra fraction of an inch of tape has been passed.

To accommodate for this inertia, each record, upon creation, is automatically written with a blank area of tape next to it. This blank area called an IBG is the exact size necessary to accommodate for inertia, so that when the fraction of an inch of tape has been bypassed, no significant data will be lost.

Thus each record has a blank area of tape called an IBG adjacent to it. Let us consider the size of the IBG to be 0.6 inches, which it is for some tape drives. If each tape record were 100 characters long, and the tape has a density of 800 bpi, we would have data represented on tape as indicated in Figure 6.12.

You will note that while each record occupies ⅛ (0.125) of an inch, each IBG adjacent to it uses 3/5 (0.6) inch. In effect, we would have more blank tape than recorded areas.

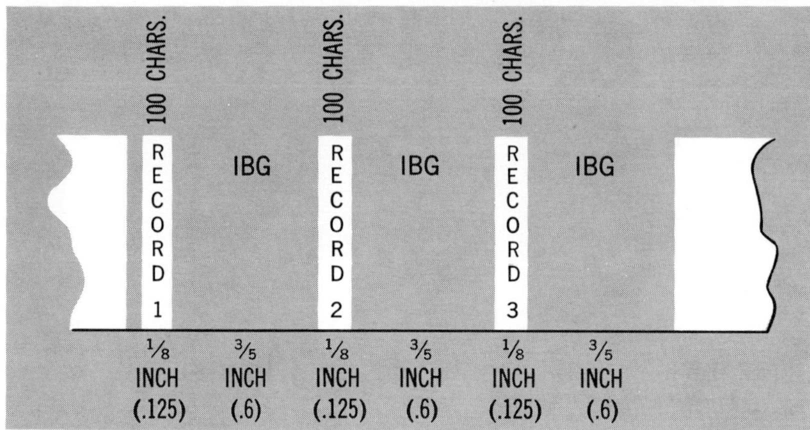

Figure 6.12 Physical representation of data on a tape — without blocking.

To alleviate this problem, the computer systems allow us to **block** or group tape records to make maximum use of the tape area. The systems and programming staff determines the size of the block, or the **blocking factor**, as indicated in Figure 6.13.

In this way, the computer processes eight records (as an example) as a group. If each record contained 100 characters, the physical record or block would contain 800 characters. At 800 bpi that would be 1 inch of tape. Thus we would have our 0.6 inch IBG between each inch of data. This is a distinct improvement over our previous example, where we had substantially more blank area than recorded data.

The blocking of data on tape does *not* represent very much increase of programming effort. Most modern computers have advanced input and output control systems that facilitate programming effort using magnetic tape or disk processing. The programmer is merely required to supply the blocking factor and the record size, and the computer itself will per-

Figure 6.13 Blocking of tape records. Blocking factor is 8; 8 records = 1 block.

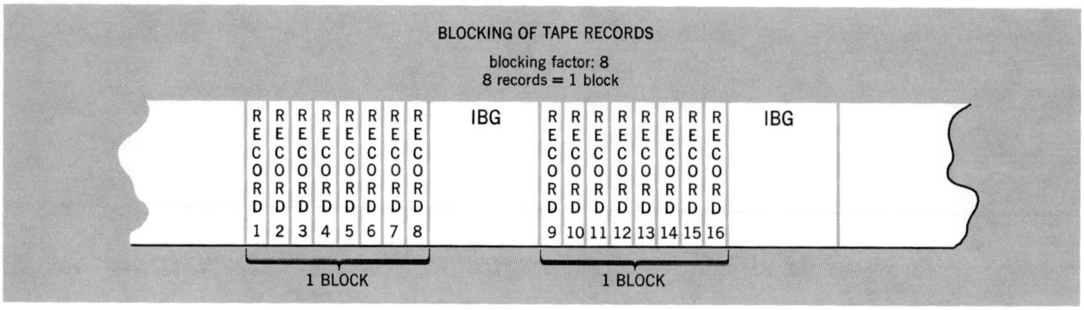

BLOCKING OF TAPE RECORDS

blocking factor: 8
8 records = 1 block

RECORD 1 | RECORD 2 | RECORD 3 | RECORD 4 | RECORD 5 | RECORD 6 | RECORD 7 | RECORD 8 | IBG | RECORD 9 | RECORD 10 | RECORD 11 | RECORD 12 | RECORD 13 | RECORD 14 | RECORD 15 | RECORD 16 | IBG

1 BLOCK
1 BLOCK

form the specific input/output functions. When a computer is instructed to read from a tape, for example, it reads a **physical record** or **block** into storage. (See Figure 6.14.)

It then makes the first **logical record**, record 1, available for processing. When it is instructed to read a second record, it does *not* go to the tape again, but makes record 2 *from storage* available for processing. Thus for the first eight READ TAPE commands, the computer accesses the tape only *once*. It then makes each of the logical records available *from storage* as they are called on by a READ TAPE command. On the ninth READ TAPE command, the computer must physically access the next block of eight records and place it in storage overlaying the previous eight records.

The creation of output tape records operates similarly. If the blocking factor is again 8, the computer will accumulate eight logical records in storage before it physically writes a block. Thus the first eight WRITE TAPE commands merely result in the accumulation of eight logical records *in storage*. The ninth

Figure 6.14 How blocked records are processed by a program. The first READ TAPE command causes a physical block of records to be read in by the control system, with record 1, from storage, then available for processing. Each succeeding READ command makes a record from storage available for processing, until the first block has been processed, at which point the next block is read from tape.

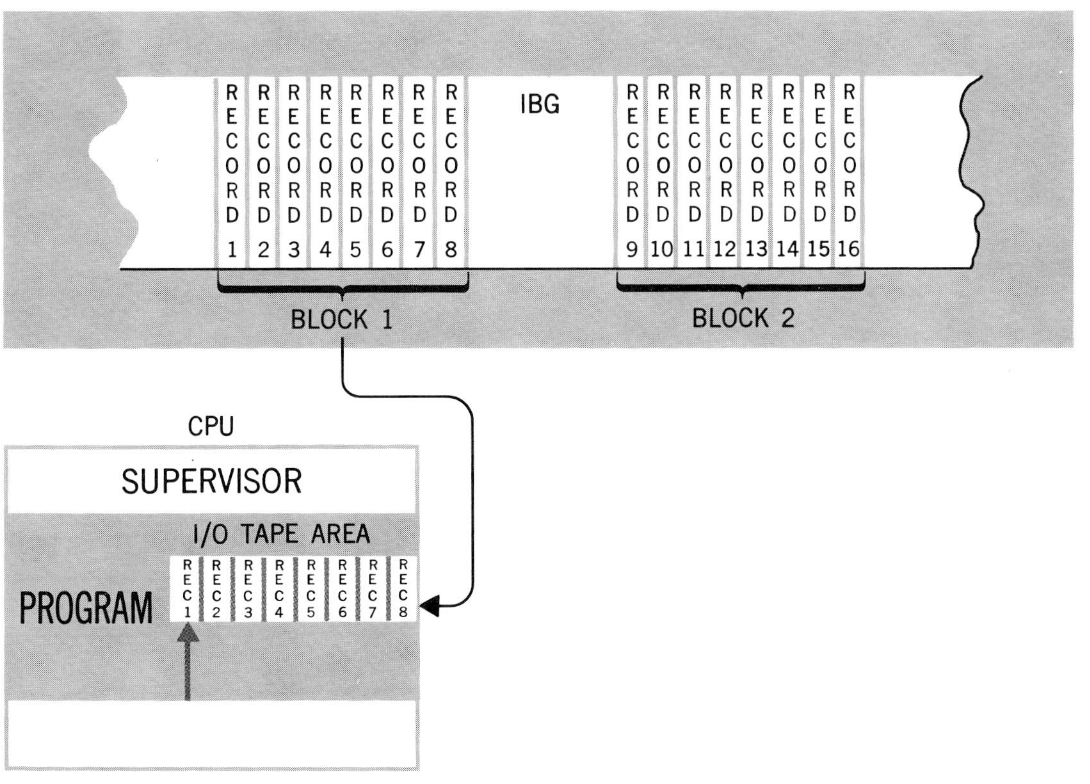

WRITE TAPE command causes the previous block of eight records to be created on tape and the ninth logical record placed in storage. Here, again, the computer accesses the tape only after every *eight records* have been processed.

In summary, tape records are blocked in an effort to make maximum use of the tape area. The blocking factor is determined by the systems and programming staff and is subject to the physical limitations of the computer. A record size of 1,000 and a blocking factor of 50, for example, would simply be too cumbersome or too large to be effectively handled by most computers. In addition, the larger the physical block, the more chance there is for transmission errors.

The programming effort required for blocking records is not very great, since the computer's input/output control system is capable of handling many of the details. The programmer is required to supply the record size and the blocking factor, and the computer can perform much of the internal processing. The programmer need only supply READ and WRITE commands and the blocking and deblocking is automatically handled.

The complex coding of the following can usually be eliminated by utilizing the computer's control system:

1. Tape labels (header labels for identification, trailer labels for summary or total information)
2. Creation of IBGs
3. Blocking of records
4. End-of-file conditions
5. End-of-reel conditions (where a specific file requires more than one physical tape reel)
6. Wrong-length-record errors (where programming or transmission errors result in a record that is not of the specified length)

The programmer need only specify the length of a logical record, and the control system will incorporate in the program a wrong-length-record check. Similarly, the programmer need only specify blocking factor, and blocking techniques will also be included.

Utility Programs for Tape Processing

The computer manufacturers have available for the user **utility** or packaged **programs** to handle many types of tape processing. For example, the coding of a program to sort a magnetic tape into a specified sequence is a cumbersome and intricate task. Such sorts are often a necessity, since a tape may be initially created in one sequence, but another sequence is required for specified output reports. For example, a payroll tape may be created in social security number sequence, but for purposes of preparing payroll checks for distribution, it must be sorted into department number sequence.

Most computer manufacturers supply utility sort programs for tapes where the programmer need only supply specification cards denoting:

1. Sort field or fields
2. Ascending or descending sequence
3. Alphabetic or numeric sequence

Similarly, a utility program to merge tapes, called a **merge utility**, creates one tape from several individual tapes. To create a tape from card records a **card-to-tape utility** can be utilized. A printed report can be written from a tape using a **tape-to-print utility**. In all these utility or prewritten, manufacturer-supplied programs, the programmer need only supply specification cards.

Note that these utility programs are of great value at many installations. Consider the case of a payroll department that has 50,000 cards, one for each employee in the company. To sort these cards would require much EAM machine and operator time. A card-to-tape utility program can be used to create a tape *duplicating* the card records, and a tape-sort utility can be used to sort it, in far less time than if the original deck of cards were processed manually.

We have seen the intricacies of tape processing. This should give the analyst a perspective on the specific ways in which tapes might be incorporated in a systems design.

MAGNETIC DISK—AN INTRODUCTION

The magnetic disk is another high-speed medium that can serve as either input to or output from a computer system. Like tape, it has an iron-oxide coating that is used to store millions of characters of data, typically 6 to 10 million, and over 60 million on some units. The magnetic disk drive is used to record information onto the disk and to read information from it.

Figure 6.15*b* illustrates a typical disk pack. The pack resembles a series of concentric disks similar to phonograph records that rotate on a vertical shaft.

(a) (b)

Figure 6.15 (*a*) Disk drive; (*b*) disk pack (courtesy Burroughs).

Each surface of the disk consists of numbered concentric tracks. Each track is used to store information. A read/write head is used to read information from, and record information onto, any of the tracks.

Disk processing has many of the same advantages as tape processing. It can store large numbers of records in a condensed area. The disk drive, like the tape drive, reads and records information electronically and thus is a high-speed device. Records on a disk can essentially be any length. They are not fixed, as is the case with 80-column cards, for example.

Disk processing, however, has some additional features that are not available with tape processing. A disk may be used for *either random or sequential* processing.

In addition to handling records in sequence, a disk has the facility to access records in some order other than the one in which they were originally recorded. The processing of records on disk is similar to the accessing of phonograph records from a juke box. By indicating that record 106 is required, for example, the mechanism is capable of accessing 106 *directly* without first reading records 1 to 105, as is required with tape processing.

The most common method for accessing magnetic disk records randomly is with the use of an **index.** During the creation of records, the computer establishes an index on the disk itself. The index indicates where each record is located. This is similar in concept to the index found at the end of a textbook, which indicates the page where each item of information can be located.

The disk index indicates the **address** or location of records that are stored on the disk. The address, in basic terms, refers to the surface number and track where a particular record can be found. A **key data field** in each record, as indicated by the programmer, is used by the computer as the basis for establishing address information in the index. As an example, if a payroll file is stored on disk, a key field would probably be SOCIAL SECURITY NUMBER or EMPLOYEE NUMBER, if this is to be used as a means of identification.

To access any disk record, then, the user need only supply a particular key data field, such as EMPLOYEE NUMBER 17537. The computer then "looks up" the corresponding disk address for this record from the index and seeks that record directly.

In addition, disks have the added advantage of permitting updates or changes in existing records *on the same disk.* In this way, a new disk need not be created to incorporate the current changes, as is required with tape processing. That is, the same disk can be used for *both* input and output. We can read a record from a disk and make changes in that record on the same disk; we can add records to the disk; we can delete records from the disk.

This type of processing is extremely advantageous for specific applications. Suppose, for example, a police department wishes to obtain information on three known criminals, immediately. Suppose, too, that the department maintains a 100,000-record criminal file. If the criminal file were on tape (a sequential medium), each tape record would be read, in sequence, until the appropriate ones were found.

To read 100,000 data records would require some time. If, however, the file were on a disk pack, then each of the three records could be accessed directly, in a much shorter time period. We merely supply the key data field, which may be ID NUMBER or PRISON RECORD NUMBER. Where time is critical and random processing is frequently required, disks are far more suitable than tapes. For **on-line processing**, or immediate processing of data, a disk file is usually used, since individual detail records can be used to update the disk file quickly and easily.

Businesses find innumerable uses for random processing. Large accounts receivable systems that may have master files with 50,000 customers may utilize a disk so that daily changes in a small number of these customer records can be performed quickly in an on-line environment (or even in a batch processing environment). The detail records, with the changes, need not be sorted. They can be used to look up the disk record, by providing the key field such as CUSTOMER NUMBER. Changes can then be made in existing accounts; new accounts can be added; and accounts with no balance or no activity in recent months can be deleted. All this can be performed on a single master disk; no recreation is necessary.

Notice that this type of random processing is time-saving only if a relatively small number of records need be altered on a relatively large file. If most of the records have some activity, then it is just as efficient to sort the detail cards and use a magnetic tape for the master file in a batch processing environment. In this way, the reading of the tape file will result in most of the records being processed. Thus excessive READ commands for bypassing records would not be a factor. Note, however, that tape processing would require a *new* output tape for each run.

It should be noted that a sequential file can also be established on disk, *without* the index, similar to a tape file. In such a case, the disk is essentially being used as a high-speed tape. In addition, there are other methods of file organization besides the one described above, which utilizes an index.

In short, a disk is extremely advantageous for processing records randomly (or directly), as well as sequentially. Disks do, however, possess some inherent limitations: (1) The disk drives are relatively expensive devices compared to others, such as tape drives. (2) Because of the sophisticated procedures required to process disks, a relatively small number of disk drives can be used at a given installation. Although eight or ten tape drives may be available with medium-sized computers, only two or four disk drives are usually permitted. (3) The identification of disk files, just as with tapes, often results in some problems. Since disk files, like tape files, cannot be visibly read, labels, both external (physically glued to the pack) and internal (programmed data labels) are required. (4) Tape update procedures usually result in a new master file that is created from the previous master file and a series of change records; the previous master can always be used as backup, should the new master be defective and a recreation process deemed necessary. Since update procedures on a master disk file add to or delete from the one master, recreation, if it becomes necessary, is very difficult.

Most disk files are created by computer output, although key-to-disk recorders are available. Like key-to-tape encoders, there are two types of key-to-disk encoders: stand-alone and key-to-disk preparation systems. The latter type, with the use of a small processor, formats, edits, and verifies disk data in addition to recording. The key-to-disk preparation system is far more prevalent in business today.

Because of the cost of these devices, most businesses still utilize other input media and then rerecord data onto a disk with a normal updating procedure. Master disk files, then, are usually converted from another input medium; they are still not generally created from a source document directly.

REPRESENTING DATA ON MAGNETIC DISK

We have already discussed the primary feature of magnetic disk—the *random-access* capability. We will now discuss, in greater depth, the distinguishing facets of a disk storage unit in order to present a comprehensive understanding of this important storage medium.

A typical disk storage unit consists of six platters, or **disks**, arranged in a vertical stack, called a **disk pack**, as shown in Figure 6.16.

Data can be recorded on both sides of the disk. There are, however, only *ten* recording surfaces, since the upper surface of the top disk and the under surface of the bottom disk cannot be utilized. Each of the ten recording surfaces is accessed by its own individual read/write head, which is capable of both retrieving and storing information.

Technically, the ten recording surfaces are numbered from 0

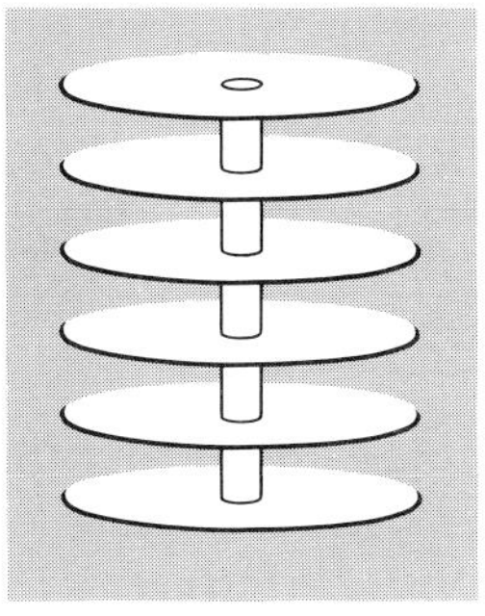

Figure 6.16 Typical disk pack.

to 9. The corresponding read/write heads, which access each of these surfaces, are similarly numbered. Figure 6.17 illustrates the relationship of the read/write heads to the disk pack.

Now that we have a general perspective on the composition of a disk unit, let us consider a typical recording surface. Each surface is composed of 203 concentric tracks numbered 000 to 202, as shown in Figure 6.18. Each track can store information in the form of magnetized spots. It may appear as if track 202 will contain far less data than track 000, but because of varying recording densities all 203 tracks store *exactly* the same amount of information. Typically, each track can hold a maximum of 3,625 characters or bytes.

It should be noted that ordinarily only 200 of the 203 tracks are used for storing data, since the remaining three are held in reserve in case any other track becomes defective.

The disk pack can therefore store approximately 7.25 million characters of information (10 surfaces × 200 tracks × 3,625 characters per track).

An important feature of the disk pack is the **cylinder concept**. One way of understanding this concept is to visualize, for example, all of the tracks numbered 050 *on the entire pack*, as shown in Figure 6.19.

The stack of vertical tracks can then be thought of as forming a hypothetical cylinder. There are, therefore, 203 cylinders on the pack, numbered 000 to 202.

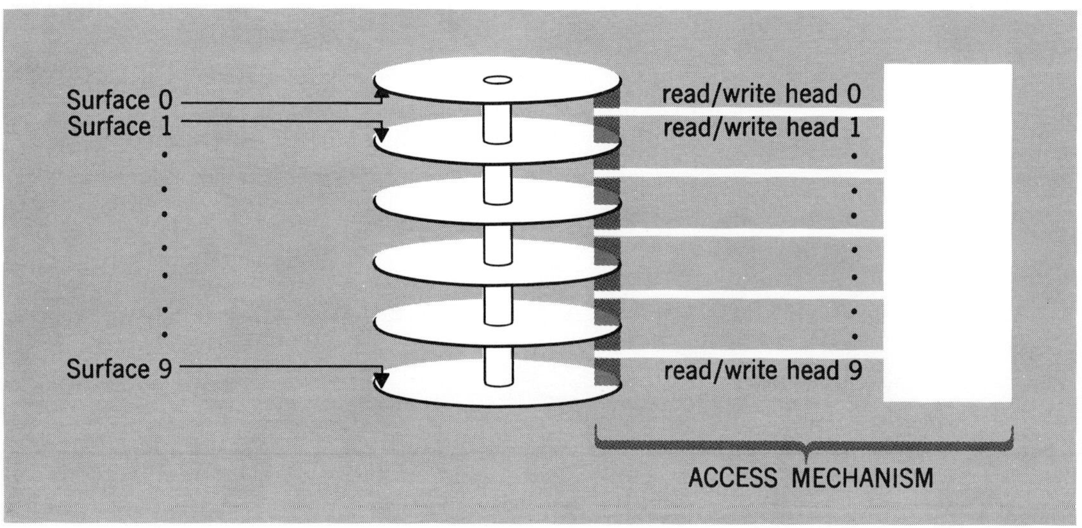

Figure 6.17 How data are accessed from a disk pack. Each read/write head accesses a specific surface. The read/write heads move in and out together as a function of the access mechanism.

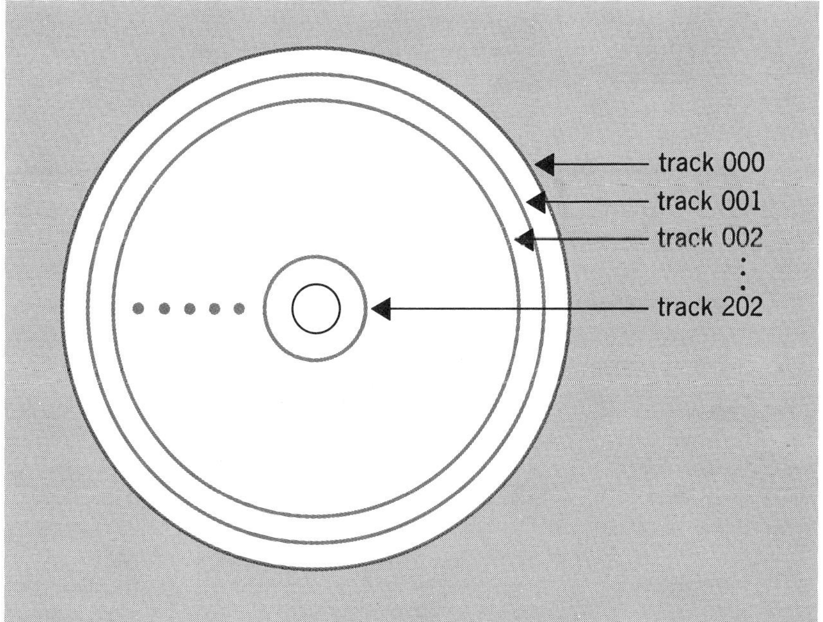

Figure 6.18 Tracks on a disk surface.

It is important to understand the cylinder concept, since data are stored by cylinder in order to reduce access arm movement. That is, once a track on a particular surface has been filled, information will subsequently be stored on the same track number within the cylinder, but on the next surface. As an example, suppose track 001 has just been filled on surface 7. The next data element will be stored on track 001 but on surface 8, within the same cylinder. The advantage of storing data in this manner as opposed to other means (such as storing information on an adjacent track on the same surface) is that time is saved in both storing and retrieving data. Since all read/write heads on the access mechanism move in and out *together* rather than independently, after writing data on a particular track it would be easy to access the same track on the next surface. If a particular track has just been filled with data, there is no need to reposition the access mechanism in order to proceed with the recording of additional information within the same cylinder. All that is required is that a different read/write head, *which is already in position,* be activated to continue the processing on the next surface. No movement of the access arm is required, as would be the case if the adjacent track were used instead.

Organization of Files on Disk

As was indicated previously, the term "file" refers to a collection of related records. We speak of an accounts receivable file, for example, as being the collection of all records of customers who owe money to the company. We will now discuss the various ways in which files can be stored on a disk storage unit. With an understanding of how disk files can be organized, business and data processing students will be able to see the advantages of utilizing disk storage for meeting the requirements of information processing today.

There are generally three different ways in which information can be organized on a magnetic disk: standard sequential, indexed sequential, and direct. We will now discuss each of these types of file organization in greater depth.

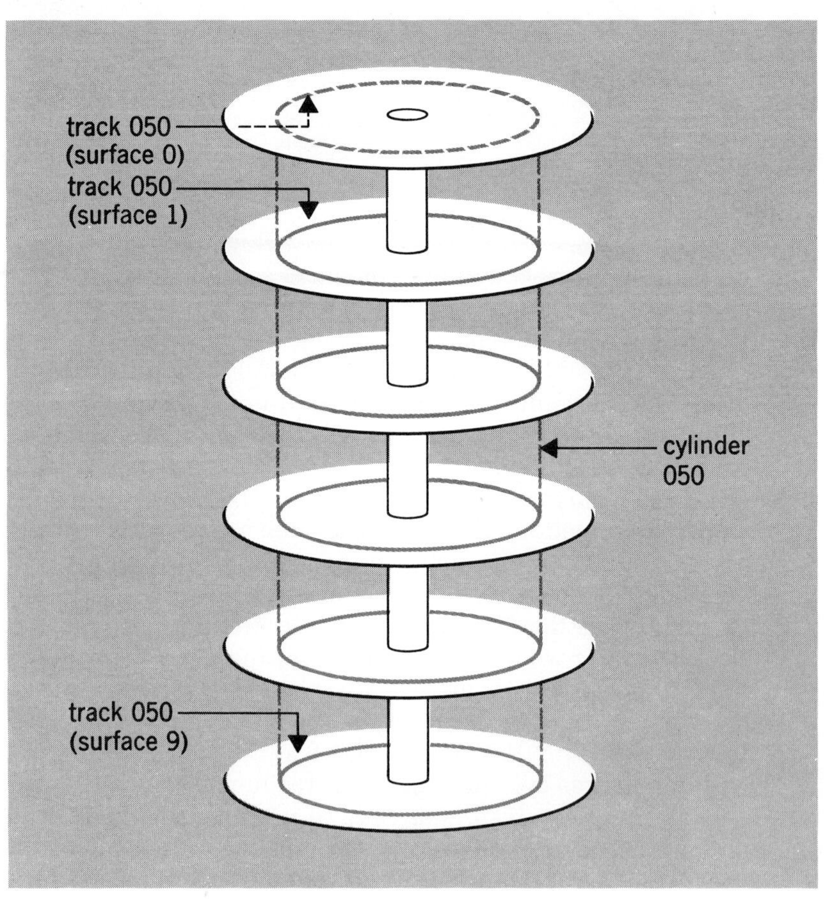

Figure 6.19 Cylinder concept on magnetic disk.

Standard Sequential File Organization. The simplest type of disk file organization is **standard sequential**. This type of file is identical in concept to the way in which information is stored on magnetic tape. Typically, the records to be stored on a standard sequential file are first sorted into some sequence such as customer number, part number, or employee number. When this sorted file is stored on disk, it is then relatively easy to locate a given record. The record with employee number 00986, for example, would be physically located between records with employee numbers 00985 and 00987.

The main disadvantage with this type of processing, however, is that if we want to access *only* the 986th record in a standard sequential disk file, the read/write heads must first read past 985 records in order to be in the proper position. This process of reading past records can consume valuable time. Thus this type of file is identical to a sequential tape file, as shown in Figure 6.20. Note that the part of the disk file illustrated appears in cylinder 000, the outermost cylinder.

In effect, then, a standard sequential disk file utilizes the disk as if it were a high-speed tape, with the added benefit that disk processing is many times faster than tape processing, since disk drives can access records more efficiently than tape drives.

Figure 6.20 Comparison of sequential disk and tape files.

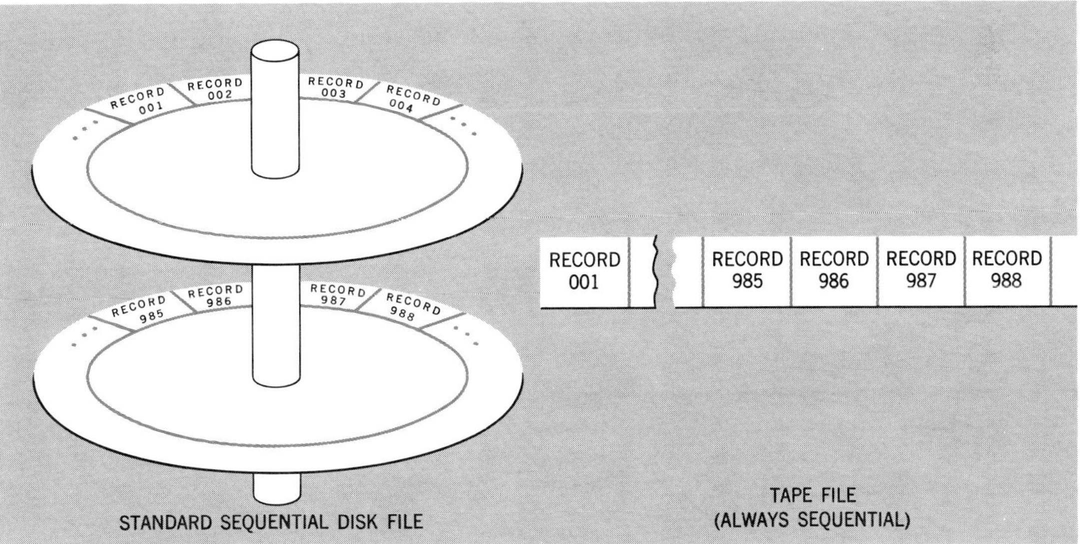

This type of file organization on disk is efficient only when there is a large number of records, such as in a major company's payroll file, and when most or all of these would be required for processing. In that case, little time would be wasted in locating a particular record, since the read/write heads would be passing over the previous records anyway in order to process them. However, if all or most of the records in a file are *not* ordinarily required during processing for a given run, then the access time of sequential processing can sometimes be too long to make this method efficient. For example, suppose a company has an inventory file with 10,000 records stored on a disk, with each record pertaining to a different part that is required by the sales department of the company. Suppose that most of the time the file is used to process only a small number of records. As an example, each day only those records pertaining to merchandise sold are updated to reflect the new stock status. If, on the average, only 1,200 different items are sold daily, of the total 10,000 items, then much processing time would be wasted if a standard sequential file were used.

Standard sequential file organization, therefore, is not an efficient method when only small numbers of records are required for processing from a relatively large file. Standard sequential file organization is also not an efficient method when records required for processing must be accessed in some sequence other than the one in which the file is organized. That is, when input is entered randomly to update or make inquiries about a sequential disk file, then this access method is extremely inefficient. Suppose, for example, that inquiries about an accounts receivable disk file are made periodically throughout the day. If such inquiries represent a significant volume and if they are entered randomly, then access time could be excessive unless another method of file organization were selected.

The two other commonly used methods of file organization for disk, indexed sequential and direct, offer alternatives to this processing problem. These methods of organization can utilize the disk pack's ability to access records in a random manner.

Indexed Sequential File Organization. An **indexed sequential** file is a method of organization that facilitates random processing of disk files. An index, or reference table, is maintained as information is recorded on the disk. This index essentially references a **key field** within each record of the file and indicates the corresponding address of that record. The key field, such as employee number or part number, within the disk record must be designated by the programmer as a unique field within the record. Thereafter, when a specific record is required for processing, the computer can check the reference table or index to determine the address or location of that record once the key field is supplied. The address for a disk record consists of the cylinder and track numbers. It should be noted that the index is stored on the same disk pack as the file that it references.

Once the address has been obtained from the index, the access mechanism can move directly to the appropriate cylinder without requiring the read/write heads to read past all the previous records in the file until the desired one is found. This concept is analogous to the index in the back of a book that has unique subjects (keys) and their corresponding page numbers (addresses). Thus a specific topic can be accessed from the index without having to read the book from the beginning until that topic is found.

The programmer states, for example, that the social security number of each record within the employee file is to serve as a key field. This is appropriate, since all social security numbers are unique. The computer then establishes the index on the disk with references to the addresses of employee records, based on their social security numbers. To access a specific record, the social security number of the desired record is supplied, and the computer "looks up" its address on the index and then moves the access mechanism accordingly. Thus, when records must be accessed in a random manner, indexed sequential file organization can result in a substantial amount of time saved as compared to standard sequential organization. Suppose, for example, that the manager of a company wants to retrieve information pertaining to 1,000 employees from a 75,000-employee file. The requested employee data are not sequenced. With an indexed sequential file, it is a relatively simple matter to read and extract these records randomly. Thus the term "random-access" implies that records are to be processed or accessed in some order other than the one in which they were written on the disk.

Direct File Organization. Another method of disk organization is called **direct organization.** In this type of file, records are accessed by a key field which, through some arithmetic calculations, reduces to the actual address (cylinder and track numbers) of the record, without the necessity to first seek the record and its address from an index. Suppose, for example, that the value of a specific key field, such as part number, can be multiplied by 859 and then divided by 87 to yield the cylinder number where the record is located. In addition, suppose that if that part number is divided by 63, the result is the track number. No table is required from which the actual address is searched; instead, some mathematical calculations are performed by the computer according to programmer-supplied formulas to yield the address.

Although direct organization can result in extremely fast access of specific records, in practice there are several factors that must be considered before this type of organization is adopted. More programming effort is required with direct files, since it is necessary for the programmer to supply the formula for converting the key fields into actual addresses. It should be noted that the example above used extremely simple formulas to determine the address. In reality, very complex formulas are often necessary. This is usually the case since the programmer can only use specified areas of the disk for his file; the remaining areas may be either filled with other data or "dedicated" for use later for a given function. As a consequence, the task of finding the appropriate formulas to refer to only certain available addresses can become very difficult. In addition to this difficulty, complex formulas may result in increased access time as compared to indexed sequential organization. It might require more time for the computer to perform the calculation to find the address than to look up the address in the index. Because of these considerations, direct files are not as commonly used in business applications as indexed sequential files.

Other Considerations for Efficient Disk Utilization

When a programmer establishes a disk file, he must estimate how much of the physical area should be allotted for the file on the disk pack. This factor is based on the initial number of records that will be placed on the file plus an allowance for growth. Ordinarily, when the file is created, all records will first be sorted into sequence by some key field such as employee number or account number.

You will recall that records cannot easily be added to a tape file. Since tape files are usually in an established sequence, a *new* tape file is required when additions or deletions are to be made to an existing tape. Because of the random-access ability of disks, it is not necessary to recreate a disk file each time additions must be inserted. These additions are merely placed in an **overflow area**, since they need not appear on the disk in a specified sequence. Thus, when *creating* a disk file, the file is generally established in two sections—the prime area to hold all the records necessary for establishing the file and an overflow area to hold new records that are subsequently added to the file.

The deletion of obsolete or unwanted disk records is also a relatively simple task. A special code is added to each record that is to be deleted. Periodically, the file is *rewritten*. All active records (those that are not to be deleted) from the prime and overflow areas are resorted into proper sequence, the newly organized file is temporarily stored on a work file and then rewritten onto the disk pack in the prime area, thus achieving a nonoverflow status. In this process of rewriting the file, all records that were tagged for deletion have, in fact, been deleted, since they were bypassed when the file was reorganized.

In addition to deleting obsolete records, the rewrite process saves access time for future computer runs. It is less time-consuming for the computer to access data from the prime area only, than to be required to search the overflow area as well.

Note that disk files generally have header labels similar to those discussed for magnetic tape. In addition, records on a disk can also be blocked or unblocked, with fixed or variable lengths.

Conclusion

We have seen that one of the main advantages of disk storage as compared to magnetic tape is the random-access feature. We have also seen that there are basically three types of file organization for disk—standard sequential, indexed sequential, and direct.

Disk processing is most efficient when large numbers of data records are required for processing, in a random manner. Because of the random-access feature, disks are also commonly used to store table files. **Table files** are items or records that are not part of data files but are an integral part of the processing function. Withholding tax rate tables, for example, are necessary in payroll systems to compute each employee's withholding taxes (federal, state, and local) based on his salary. Such files are often stored on disk and accessed when required.

We will now illustrate the use of a withholding tax rate

table that has been simplified for ease of discussion. Suppose, for example, that the tax bracket for each salary level is represented by 25 disk records. Each table record has a salary range and includes corresponding withholding tax percentages for federal and state taxes, as shown below.

Salary Range	Federal Withholding Tax Percentage[a]	State Withholding Tax Percentage[a]
00001–01000	14.0	2.0
01000–02000	15.0	3.0
02000–03000	16.0	3.5
03000–04000	17.0	4.0
04000–08000	19.0	5.0
•	•	•
•	•	•
•	•	•

[a]These figures are used for the purpose of illustration only.

The salary for each employee must be taxed according to its appropriate bracket. That is, each employee record must be read and its corresponding tax percentage "looked up" on the salary table.

	Input Record	Salary Range	Federal W / H	State W / H
Table	Salary = 02226	00001–01000	14.0	2.0
Look-Up		01000–02000	15.0	3.0
Procedure		02000–03000	16.0	3.5

If this salary table file is put onto tape, sequential processing of salary levels is required. That is, each time a salary figure is read in on an employee record, the tape must be read from record 1, the lowest salary level, until the appropriate salary on the tax table is found. This can result in excessive processing time. If the first employee record contains a salary of $99,000, for example, much of the table would be read before the appropriate salary is found.

If a disk is used to store the tax table with the salary as a key field, then each employee's salary can be looked up on the disk index, the appropriate record accessed directly, and the corresponding tax percentages found quickly.

In addition to tax tables for payroll, we often find price tables for stock numbers (in order to process purchasing files), and so on.

COMPARING CARDS, TAPE, AND DISK AS FILE TYPES

The systems analyst, along with the businessperson, determines the most efficient files to be used in new or revised systems. Selecting an inefficient medium would be extremely costly in the end. Thus every attempt must be made to find the appropriate file types. Table 6.1 is a summary of the major characteristics of card, tape, and disk files. This table should serve as a review of the previous sections.

The following examples will illustrate how file types are selected.

EXAMPLE 1. A payroll system servicing 75,000 employees produces weekly payroll checks in social security number sequence. Two reports are also produced, both in social security number sequence.

Since the volume is relatively large and the output must be produced as efficiently and timely as possible, card processing would not be adequate. Since records in a payroll file would generally be processed in a fixed sequence (social security number, usually), the direct-access feature of disk would not be applicable. Thus tape is the best medium for a payroll file, such as the one above.

TABLE 6.1

CHARACTERISTICS OF THE THREE MAJOR FILE TYPES

File Type	Characteristics	Advantages	Disadvantages
Punched Card	80 columns; data recorded by keypunch machine or card punch of computer	Utilized by electronic accounting machines to supplement computer use; relatively inexpensive in small-volume jobs; can be maintained by operator because data is visual	Warps easily; easily mishandled; very inefficient for large-volume jobs because of relatively slow I / O capability
Magnetic Tape	Data represented as magnetized bits on an iron-oxide coating; data recorded by computer via tape drive or a keytape converter	Efficient for large volume jobs; any size record can be stored; stores millions of characters on a single tape	Information not visible with the naked eye; strictly sequential processing; cannot easily read and write from same tape during a single operation
Direct-Access Files	Include magnetic disk, drum, and data cell; addresses of disk records may be "looked up" on an index; data recorded by computer via disk drive or key-to-disk recorders	Efficient for large-volume jobs; any size record can be stored; stores millions of characters on a single disk; random and sequential processing; can read and write from one disk during a single operation	Data usually recorded by computer only; keying devices relatively expensive; disk drives expensive; requires much software; restrictions must often be placed on number of drives in an installation

EXAMPLE 2. A small-scale company has 500 customers and wishes to maintain a single accounts receivable file that can be used by the computer to produce monthly bills and that can be used by the clerks to answer inquiries.

Since the volume is relatively small, cards would be a suitable medium. They can be entered as input to the computer and also manually read to answer inquiries.

EXAMPLE 3. A large department store has 200,000 charge customers and wishes to maintain a computerized accounts receivable file. The file is used once a month to prepare customer bills. In addition, a program has been written that would utilize inquiry cards as input, search the file, and print answers to the inquiry. Inquiries are made at the volume of 15,000 daily and are fed into the computer on cards that are entered in no specified sequence.

A direct-access file is the only viable alternative for this system. The volume of the file necessitates a high-speed device. The inquiry cards necessitate a file search in random sequence. Thus a direct-access file would be required.

EXAMPLE 4. A medium-sized company now maintains an inventory on 2,000 stock parts. The company plans to merge with another organization in the near future and maintain an inventory on all parts currently held by both companies.

Ordinarily, if only 2,000 records on parts are to be stored on a file, a card file could be least costly. But since the company expects a rapid growth shortly, a tape file would probably be a better alternative.

Regardless of which type of file is chosen for a particular application, it is necessary for the analyst to draw a layout of a typical record in that file. Figure 6.21 illustrates a sample layout for a payroll master tape. This layout is important not only for the programmer, who will need it to write the program, but also for the businessperson. The latter can review the layout to ascertain that it contains all relevant fields.

CUSTOMER INFORMATION CONTROL SYSTEMS (CICS)

One of the most important aspects of a system is the manner in which data files are constructed and employed. Almost all of the activities of a system are somehow related to its files. It is essential to the overall efficiency of a system that data be accessed in the most expeditious manner. It is not desirable to

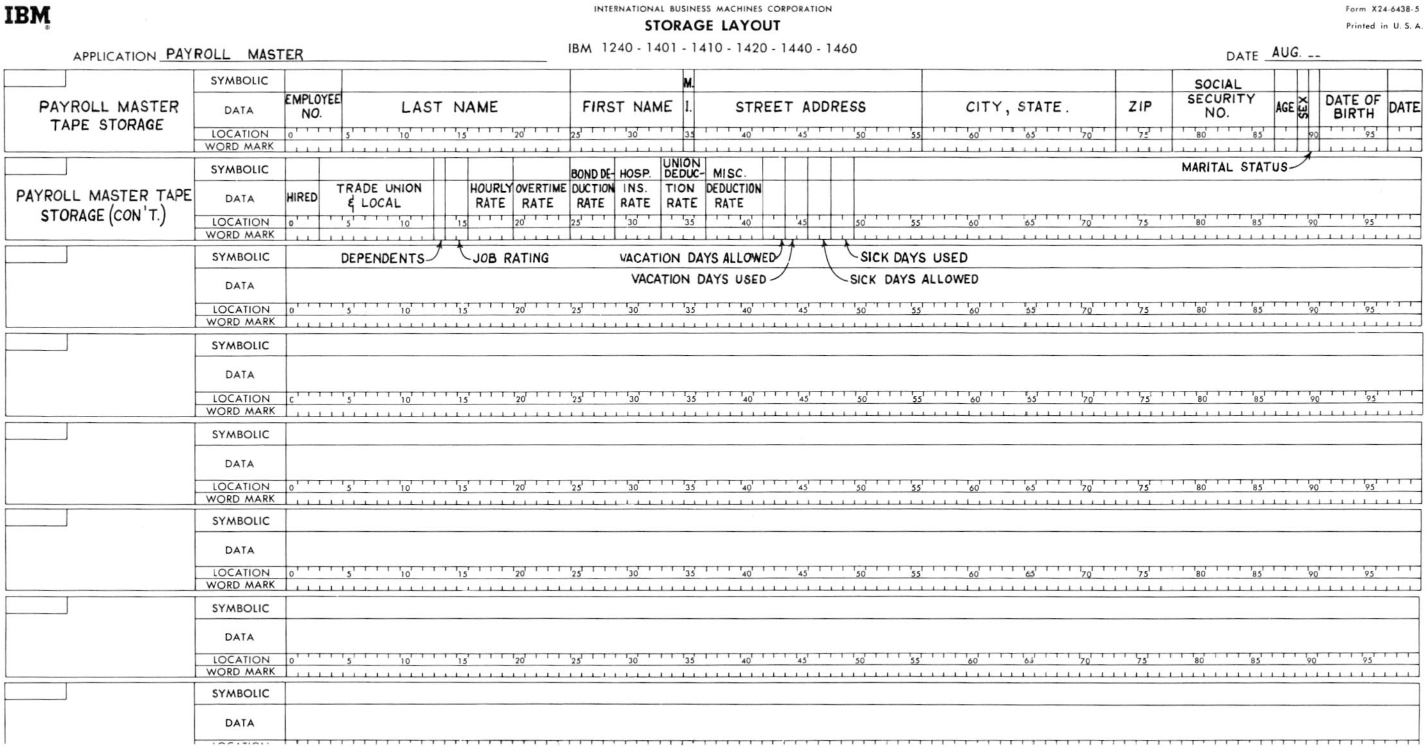

IBM

INTERNATIONAL BUSINESS MACHINES CORPORATION

STORAGE LAYOUT

IBM 1240 - 1401 - 1410 - 1420 - 1440 - 1460

Form X24-6438-5
Printed in U. S. A.

APPLICATION PAYROLL MASTER

DATE AUG. --

PAYROLL MASTER TAPE STORAGE

DATA	EMPLOYEE NO.	LAST NAME	FIRST NAME	M. I.	STREET ADDRESS	CITY, STATE.	ZIP	SOCIAL SECURITY NO.	AGE	SEX	DATE OF BIRTH	DATE
LOCATION	0	5–23	25	35	36–55	56–72	73–77	78–86			90–95	

PAYROLL MASTER TAPE STORAGE (CON'T.)

DATA	HIRED	TRADE UNION & LOCAL			HOURLY RATE	OVERTIME RATE	BOND DEDUCTION RATE	HOSP. INS. RATE	UNION DEDUCTION RATE	MISC. DEDUCTION RATE				
LOCATION	0	5, 10		15		20	25	30	35	40		45		50

MARITAL STATUS

DEPENDENTS

JOB RATING

VACATION DAYS ALLOWED

VACATION DAYS USED

SICK DAYS USED

SICK DAYS ALLOWED

SYMBOLIC / DATA / LOCATION / WORD MARK

Figure 6.21 Storage layout of payroll master tape.

have the system sit idle while precious time is lost in merely finding the desired data.

From a systems perspective, this point becomes more apparent considering the increased storage capabilities of today's computer systems. Technological advances in computer hardware necessitated and spawned the development of equally sophisticated software to accommodate use of the vast amount of data available. As data bases were developed, it became necessary to write the software required to handle them.

Many of the most recently developed systems could not exist without the support of such software. Sophisticated systems, such as real-time systems, on-line information systems, and management information systems (MIS), could not function without the support of the software developed to manipulate the vast data bases that are an integral part of each system.

Let us consider, as an illustration of an on-line information system, an airline reservations system. The amount of data required to support an airline reservations system is quite extensive when one considers the quantity of flights, passengers, cities, and times involved. Of significant interest, however, is the fact that all of this data must be readily and virtually instantaneously available. A constraint characteristic of any on-line reservations system is the necessity to service the potential passenger almost immediately. Thus, in handling passenger requests and transactions, demands are continuously being placed on the system's data files. The acceptance of a passenger's flight reservation requires that the system instantly update its files and reveal this change in flight space availability (the number of seats available on the flight).

In addition, a reservations system must be capable of handling the different and varied informational requests made against the system. Often, flight information is accessed by airport location, arriving or departing city, or time of day, not by flight number. The system must be capable of handling inquiries of this type made from on-line data terminals.

All of the prior flight-related data requests are directly dependent on some form of on-line data file or data base. Obviously, the speed, accuracy, and reliability with which any of these inquiries is handled would not be possible without the appropriate software.

The development of software to specifically control and supervise the activities related to a data file or data base has occurred over the past decade. During the 1960s and early

1970s, the IBM Corporation, for example, stepped to the forefront of this research and developed a software package specifically designed to support both data bases and data communications activities. The system developed was the **Customer Information Control System**, or **CICS**. CICS could handle all of the file manipulations required for an on-line data base and facilitate the transmission of data throughout a system by teleprocessing. CICS was specifically designed to facilitate the interface of data-based files and on-line terminals.

This factor is of considerable importance when discussing the scope of CICS-type operations. One of the original drawbacks in developing a CICS-like system was the tremendous expense and time required to write the software to support the interaction of data files and terminal devices. With a CICS system, the user is completely relieved of the need to develop any of the software that relates to the computer environment in which the system will operate. Thus the data processing staff can concentrate all of their resources on designing and developing solutions related to the commercial application under study. For example, analysts could concentrate on designing the best output forms, input cards, and so on, and programmers could write programs necessary to provide the required system outputs.

Being relieved of the necessity to write environmental software is just one of the advantages of the CICS system. Other advantages are:

1. Elimination of duplicate files of data. Since one massive data base is maintained, redundant data files are eliminated. As a result, analyst/programmers can turn their attention to other work projects.
2. Almost all data are readily accessible. All of the files constructed with a CICS are random-access files. Thus whatever data are maintained within the system are directly accessible.
3. Flexibility in satisfying user needs. Considering the speed with which the vast quantity of data stored within the system can be accessed, the analyst can potentially design and implement almost any type of systems solution. Obviously, if the data are available, any form of output is possible.

These advantages will be reflected in terms of dollar savings accruable to the computer system and data processing staff. Many man-hours will be saved by eliminating programs that will not have to be written, as well as wasted computer time and resources, and by providing a quicker implementation of the overall system.

A disadvantage to CICS is the potential cost of supporting the activities of such a system. Two facts must be considered:

1. A large CPU is required to support CICS activities.
2. Sufficient storage space must be provided within the system for further growth.

When these two consideration are coupled together, a central processing unit (CPU) of considerable size is virtually mandated. Today it is not uncommon, for example, to find CPUs of 256,000 bytes or larger. Of course, the size of the CPU selected to support any system is arrived at only after lengthy technical discussions between the data processing staff and computer manufacturers and submission of economic justification to management.

The constraint relating to the size of the CPU is only one of the factors encountered by the analyst when involved in a CICS project. During the design phase, other factors considered by the analyst are:

1. The maximum number of on-line terminals the system can support. This limitation could affect who will have terminals and where they will be located.
2. The number of terminals required to support the system under design. This is the number of terminals that the analyst has envisioned as part of the system. If the design requires more terminals than the system can support, the design must be altered or a larger computer system considered.
3. The amount of file activity required of the system. The higher the activity of the system with respect to its files, the slower the relative speed of the system. For example, if the system must access data from different files within the data base, even with the tremendous speed of computers, the performance of the system will be affected. Logically, if the system must service more people at the same time, this will also affect the performance of the system. It should be noted that all files within CICS must be random-access files.
4. The size and characteristics of files within the data base. It is important to have proper file construction. Data logically

related to a particular operation or task should be combined within one file. Poor file design will necessitate that the system search through the data base for the desired information, with a resultant loss of system efficiency.
5. Future systems growth. The analyst must consider what is currently envisioned for the system, as well as the future demands that might be placed on the system. Sufficient storage must be designed into the data base for future growth.

The incorporation of CICS within a company's data processing operation provides a powerful processing capablity. An illustration will assist in reinforcing some of the aspects of CICS.

A Savings Bank

The application of a savings bank is perfectly suited for implementation of a CICS system. Consider a large bank with branches distributed throughout one geographical area (i.e., one bank with many branches within one county or one city).

An on-line savings system (CICS), as illustrated in Figure 6.22, would make it possible for customers to complete deposits and withdrawal transactions at any of the various branches. These transactions would be entered by tellers at terminals located in any of the branch offices. The data would be transmitted to the bank's main computer. All transactions would be automatically posted against the respective customer account. The advantages resulting from this system would be:

1. Improved overall customer service.
2. Customer convenience—customers could utilize the bank's services from any branch.

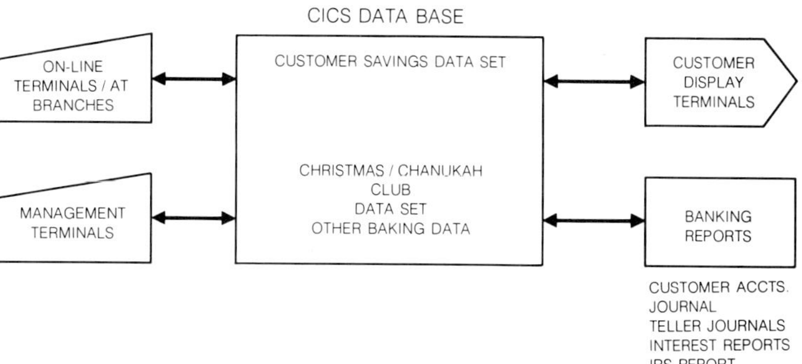

Figure 6.22 On-line savings system (CICS).

3. Standardized banking procedures at each office, resulting in improved control of banking activities.
4. More timely and accurate information relating to customer accounts.
5. Improved control of accounts to facilitate customer transactions (e.g., interest paid, transfer of funds between accounts), as well as the searching for delinquent customer accounts.
6. Providing data for advertising or marketing surveys undertaken by the bank.

Overall, the CICS system will enable the bank to service its customers quickly and accurately, and will provide a full range of banking services. The bank will have improved and tighter control over its accounts and all bank-related activities. Lastly, this system can be implemented and installed within a short time and with a minimum of disruption to the bank's normal operation.

GLOSSARY

Batch processing. Processing of data in groups or batches rather than individually.

Bit. *B*inary dig*it* machine code.

Blocking factor. Number of records in a block of data.

CICS. Customer Information Control System.

Direct access. Ability of a computing system to access particular data from a storage device without reading through or searching data that are not needed.

Direct organization. A method of disk organization whereby records are accessed by a key field that can be converted into the actual storage address of a particular record.

File protection ring. A plastic ring that fits into the groove in a reel of magnetic tape and permits data to be recorded on the tape.

Fixed-length records. Records whose lengths are of a predetermined, uniform format.

Header label. First record on a tape or disk file that identifies the file.

Key-to-tape encoder. Device used to code data from source documents onto magnetic tape.

Logical record. A set of related fields.

Master file. The main data file that holds all current information for a specific department or system.

Parity bit. An extra bit used to determine the validity of a coded character.

Physical record. Data that the computer reads or writes at one time when an I/O instruction is executed. A physical record can consist of several logical records if the data are blocked.

Retention cycle. Indication of how long a particular file should be maintained.

Sequential file. A file that is read one record at a time, in some predetermined order.

Tape density. The number of characters that can be represented in a given area of tape.

Updating. The process of making a master file of data current.

Utility program. A program, usually supplied by the computer manufacturer, to handle a specific type of processing, such as sorting a file of records.

Variable-length records. Records whose storage format is dependent on the size of the record being used. That is, records whose length varies, depending on the type and number of characters required.

QUESTIONS

1. What are the major advantages of tape processing as opposed to disk processing?
2. What are the major advantages of disk processing as opposed to tape processing?
3. What is the "identification problem" with respect to both tape and disk processing?
4. How are data recorded on tape and disk?
5. Explain the purpose of update procedures in data processing centers.
6. How are the following characters represented on magnetic tape?
   a. C
   b. 8
   c. Y
   d. ¢
   e. 6
   f. H
   g. L
   h. 0

7. What is the purpose of parity?
8. If you were assigned the task of determining the cost-effectiveness of utilizing a new magnetic tape, what questions would you ask the manufacturer?
9. If you were assigned the task of determining the cost-effectiveness of utilizing a new magnetic tape drive, what questions would you ask the manufacturer?
10. What is the purpose of IBGs, and how do they work?
11. Indicate the differences between a logical record and a physical record.
12. How would you go about determining the availability of utility programs and the needs of your company with respect to utility programs?
13. What are the differences between read/write heads on a tape drive and read/write heads on a disk drive?
14. State the differences between types of disk file organizations.
15. What are table files and how are they used in business functions?

Answer questions 16 and 17 for each of the following sample systems:

Insurance company application
Medical/hospital industry
Law enforcement/police system
Utility industry (public gas and electric company)
Import/export company

16. Can a CICS system be applied to the company or industry?
17. If a CICS system were possible:
    a. What type of data files would be created?
    b. What data might be contained within these files?
    c. What files or data would require instantaneous update?
    d. How would the consumer benefit by the implementation of a CICS system?
    e. How would management benefit?
    f. Would on-line terminals be employed? If so, what type would you recommend (visual display, hard-copy devices, remote job entry terminals, CRTs, etc.)?
    g. Compile a list of printed outputs that might be required to support this system.

CHAPTER 7

SYSTEMS FLOWCHARTS AND DECISION TABLES

In Chapter 2, we learned that the analytic phase of the systems analyst's job begins with the collection of large amounts of data. The analyst must amass all information on the system before he can undertake a meaningful analysis.

But the collection of data, itself, does not necessarily provide the analyst with a complete understanding of the system. All facts and information obtained must be arranged and organized so that a complete picture of the system evolves.

SYSTEMS FLOWCHARTS

It is no easy task to arrange and organize large amounts of data into a meaningful interpretation of the whole. A pictorial representation called a **systems flowchart** is a standardized method of simplifying the analyst's task of rearranging data and placing it in its proper perspective. That is, the systems flowchart provides a logical diagram of how the system operates.

The collection of data must yield, in a broad sense, all the elements of a system: objectives, constraints, inputs, outputs, processing, controls, and feedback. These elements are, however, amassed in no specific order. The systems flowchart serves to organize some of these elements. It defines, both clearly and concisely, and in a step-by-step fashion, all inputs and outputs, and the necessary resources and operations employed to convert one into the other. In short, the flowchart provides the analyst with a graphic representation of the system in its entirety, but in a simplified manner.

Thus the systems flowchart is a useful analytic tool to represent the present system. It is also a valuable design tool, used to represent the workings of the new or revised system.

The systems flowchart serves many individuals within the company:

1. **Analyst.** It is easier for the systems analyst to describe the functions of the present system in a diagram, as opposed to a formal narrative. The interaction between the various input

forms that produce the desired outputs can be clearly seen on a systems flowchart. Similarly, the operations and resources used to operate on data become clearer. In this way, the analyst gets a clear, concise, and logical picture of how the system operates.

It is also easier for the analyst to determine which aspects of the system need revision by studying the flowchart. That is, if he has difficulty representing an item on the flowchart or if a cumbersome diagram is the end result, then the problem areas of the system can be more easily determined. Although formal narrative will also serve to describe a system, difficulties in logic and flaws in procedures often go unnoticed in lengthy descriptions.

When the analyst begins to design alternate systems, he can easily experiment with various ideas by drawing numerous systems flowcharts, to determine how all the facets would interrelate. This technique, then, is used to formalize his thoughts.

2. Department Representative. The analyst generally shows the completed flowchart of the present system to all department representatives to make certain that a full understanding of the flow of data has been achieved. Through the use of this graphic representation, both the analyst and the interviewees build a frame of reference from which to coordinate their knowledge of the system.

Similarly, during the design phase, the analyst would show the flowchart of the new or revised system to the department representatives for their comments.

3. Management. The analyst must provide management with an analysis of the system in the form of a problem definition before the design phase can be undertaken. A summary of the current system must be illustrated prior to any analysis. The systems flowchart provides management with a logical representation of the system. Similarly, the new system design is best illustrated with a flowchart.

4. Programmer. When a new system design requires new programs to be written or existing ones to be modified, programmers are assigned to segments of the system. Before they can operate on a section of the system, they must be given a perspective of the system as a whole. The systems flowchart is the best tool to acquaint the programmer with the operations and procedures involved.

Note that there are many similarities between a systems flowchart and a program flowchart. Both are pictorial representations of the flow of data. The program flowchart illustrates the logic utilized within a program. It is usually a *detailed* diagram paralleling the set of instructions within the program. The systems flowchart is more general in nature. Keep in mind that a single system design may require numerous programs; *one* systems flowchart can frequently be utilized to represent the entire design, while individual program flowcharts are required to represent the numerous programs within the system.

Thus the systems flowchart is more *concise* than the program flowchart. The former is very often utilized by high-level employees who have neither the time nor the inclination to wade through minute detail.

EXAMPLE 1. Figure 7.1 is a sample systems flowchart summarizing the flow of data in a particular payroll system. Notice that the large number of operations and procedures used within this payroll system can be presented on a single page. Notice, also, that as in a program flowchart, a series of symbols with descriptive notes inside, connected by flowlines, make up the diagram. The symbols used in a systems flowchart are, however, different from those used in a program flowchart.

Upon analysis of the flowchart, you should be able to understand the following characteristics of the system even though you may have had no previous exposure to systems flowcharts:

1. Two source documents initiate the flow of data into the payroll system.
2. The data on new hires and position changes are keypunched and verified, and payroll cards are created.
3. The cards are sorted into social security number sequence.
4. The sorted deck and the current master payroll tape are used as input to the computer to create payroll checks, an updated master tape, and a force report.
5. The payroll cards are filed for use by the personnel department for their update procedure; the checks and the force report are produced; and the updated master will be used for the next month's run.

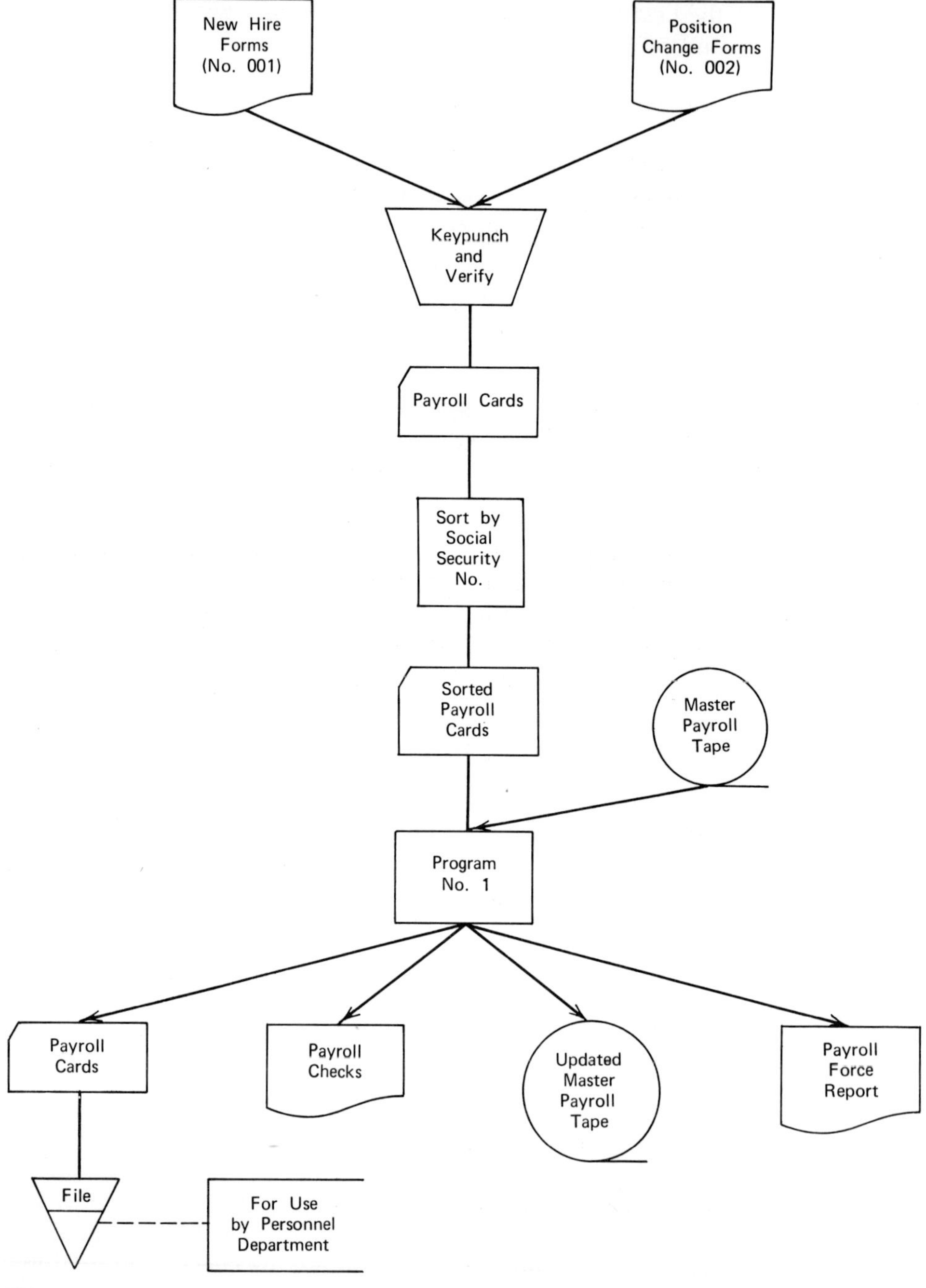

Figure 7.1 Payroll system — monthly run.

A major advantage of the flowchart should be evident. An individual with little or no experience in systems work can understand the main facets of a system by examining the flowchart. A single-page diagram can describe, clearly, concisely, and logically, the workings of this payroll system.

The systems flowchart is a *standard* diagram. That is, the symbols conform to those established by the United States of America Standards Institute (USASI), formerly the American Standards Association (ASA).

A template (Figure 7.2) is used to draw the symbols representing specified functions. This template illustrates the established standard for all flowcharting symbols, those used for systems flowcharts and those used for program flowcharts.

Let us discuss the most widely used symbols, which are illustrated in Figure 7.3

There are some other commonly used symbols that are not currently part of the USASI flowchart standards. These are shown in Figure 7.4.

Each symbol in the flowchart is connected by a flowline. Within each symbol an explanatory note is generally given that reveals the specific nature of the function to be performed. The flowchart is read from top to bottom and from left to right, unless otherwise noted.

The following examples will illustrate the interrelation among symbols in a flowchart.

EXAMPLE 2. Figure 7.5 is a graphic representation of the updating procedure of an accounts receivable system in a department store.

The flowchart in Figure 7.5 illustrates, first, that credit slips and sales slips are keypunched and verified. The cards are then sorted by account number. The sorted deck serves as input to the computer together with the accounts receivable master tape. The computer run produces an updated accounts receivable tape and a sales journal listing. The transaction cards are filed for two months and then destroyed.

EXAMPLE 3. Figure 7.6 illustrates the creation of new records on a master accounts receivable disk file.

This flowchart illustrates that the approved applications for charge accounts must be keypunched, verified, and sorted by account number. A computer run is then used to write the information onto the disk file. The cards are then stored offline for six months as backup, in case it becomes necessary to

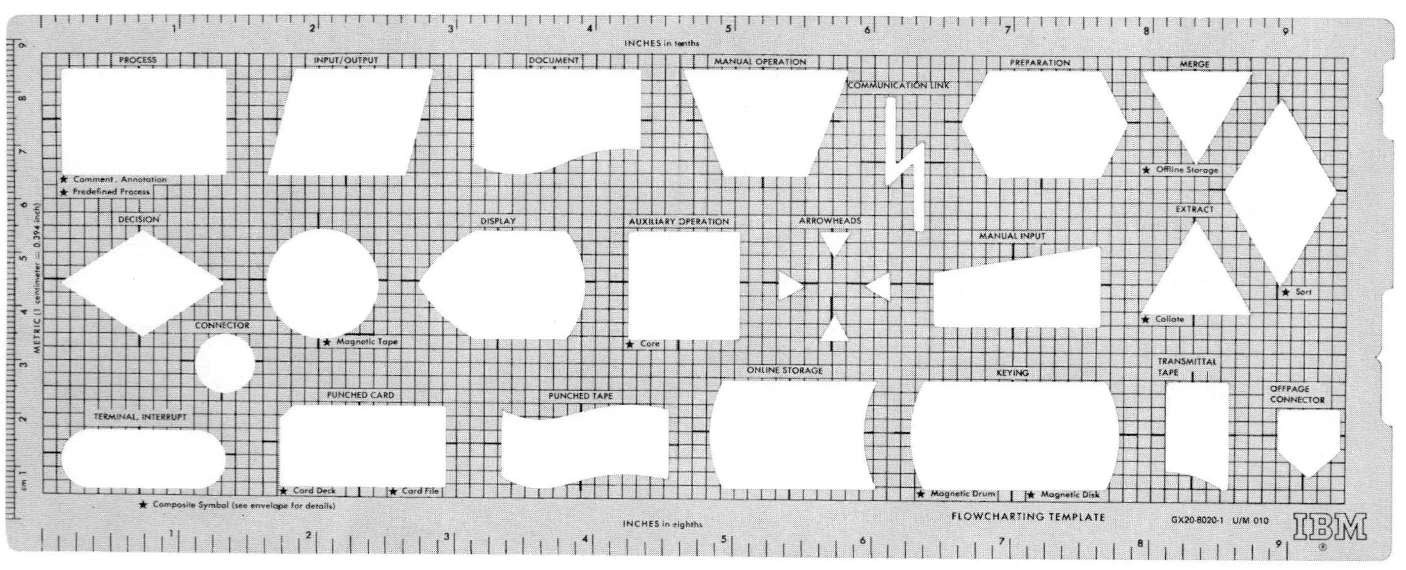

Figure 7.2 Flowcharting template.

SYMBOL	INPUT/OUTPUT SYMBOLS	
	NAME	DESCRIPTION
	INPUT/OUTPUT (I/O)	This is a generalized I/O symbol used to denote data entering the system or information that is generated as output. It is most often used when the medium of input or output is not specifically designated. i.e.  INVENTORY ERROR CORRECTIONS where such corrections may enter the system by cards, slips of paper or even telephone messages.
	PUNCHED CARD	This symbol is used when the data entered into the system or coming out of the system is in the form of a punched card.
	MAGNETIC TAPE	Magnetic tape is either the input or output medium.
	DOCUMENT	The input or output is a printed document or report.
	ONLINE STORAGE	Data is stored on all online or direct-access device such as a magnetic disk or drum.

Figure 7.3 Systems flowchart symbols.

recreate the disk file because of some mechanical or operator error.

EXAMPLE 4. Figure 7.7 illustrates the updating of accounts in an accounts payable system.

PROCESSING SYMBOLS		
SYMBOL	NAME	DESCRIPTION
	PROCESSING	This symbol represents the performing of an operation or a group of operations, generally by a computer or accounting machine, where the processing is a major function of the system. i.e. CARD TO TAPE PROGRAM; REPRODUCE INPUT CARDS
	MANUAL OPERATION	This symbol represents a manual operation or one which requires an operator. Keypunching and verifying are examples of manual operations.
	ANNOTATION	This symbol is used when explanatory notes are required to clarify another symbol. This symbol is not in the main flow of the diagram. i.e. CONSOLE SWITCH MUST BE OFF; COMPUTER RUN #107
	AUXILIARY OPERATION	Offline equipment is used to perform such functions as sorting, merging, collating, etc.
	CONNECTOR	This symbol is used to alter or terminate the flow of data. i.e. 2-B Go to page 2, symbol labelled B

Figure 7.3 Continued.

	INPUT / OUTPUT SYMBOLS	
SYMBOL	NAME	DESCRIPTION
	DISPLAY	*Output* information is displayed on console typewriters, displays, online terminals, plotters, etc.
	MANUAL INPUT	*Input* Information is supplied manually at the time of processing from an online device such as a console typewriter.
	COMMUNICATION LINK	Information is transmitted automatically from one location to another via communication lines.
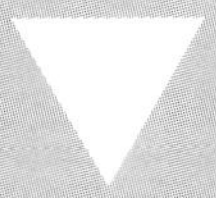	OFFLINE STORAGE	Data is stored on an offline medium; that is, data stored is not immediately accessible by the computer. An online device, such as a magnetic disk may always be available for immediate processing. A magnetic tape, however, is generally stored offline in a tape library and cannot be accessed immediately.
	PUNCHED TAPE	Data is stored on a punched paper tape as either input or output. This medium is often used as the initial data form, before conversion to magnetic tape. i.e. 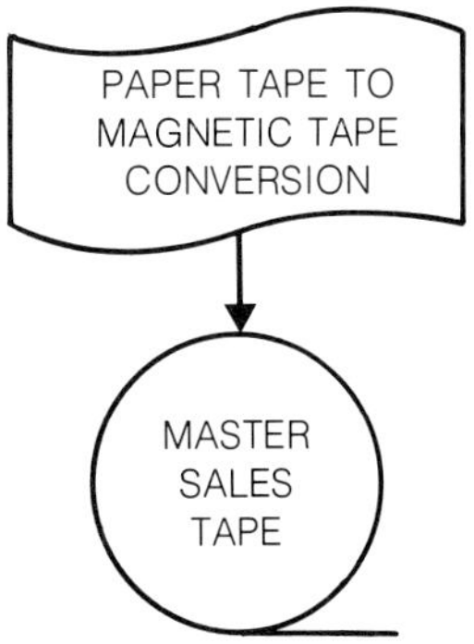 PAPER TAPE TO MAGNETIC TAPE CONVERSION → MASTER SALES TAPE

Figure 7.3 Continued.

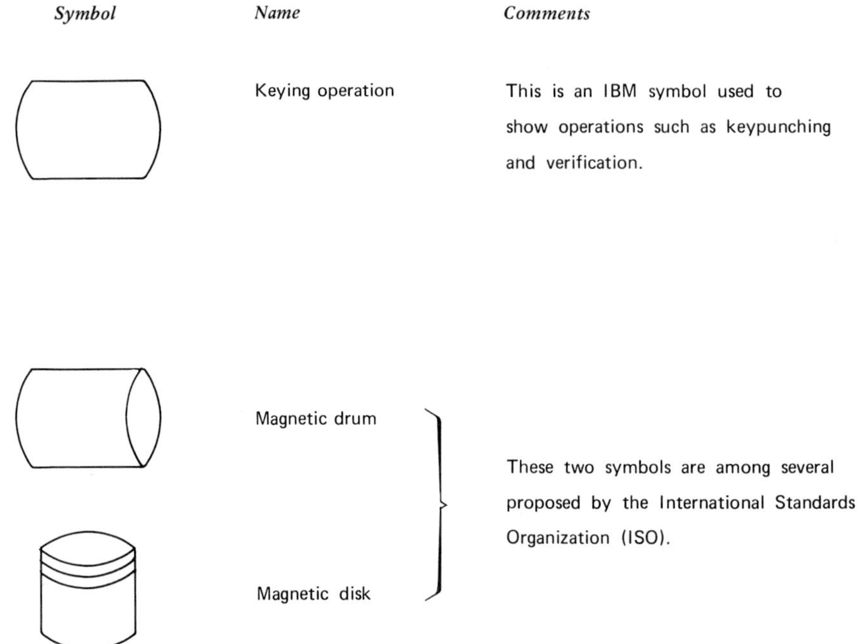

Symbol
Name
Comments
Keying operation
This is an IBM symbol used to show operations such as keypunching and verification.
Magnetic drum
Magnetic disk
These two symbols are among several proposed by the International Standards Organization (ISO).

Figure 7.4 Supplemental flowchart symbols.

This flowchart shows that cards are keypunched and verified from purchase orders, receiving reports, inspection reports, and payment reports. They are read into the computer where a card-to-tape utility program transfers the information to a tape, in an unsorted arrangement. A sort utility program is then used to sort the tape transaction records by account number. This sorted tape is used with the accounts payable master tape to create an updated accounts payable master tape and a listing of the day's accounts payable activity. Note the use of the manual input symbol to indicate that the current date of the run is read into the computer from the console typewriter.

EXAMPLE 5. Figure 7.8 illustrates the transmission of payroll information from a branch office to the centrally located computer.

This flowchart shows that the employee time sheets at office A are used to record payroll information directly onto a magnetic tape. The data are then transmitted via communication lines to the central computer, where an updated payroll tape and a payroll information report are produced.

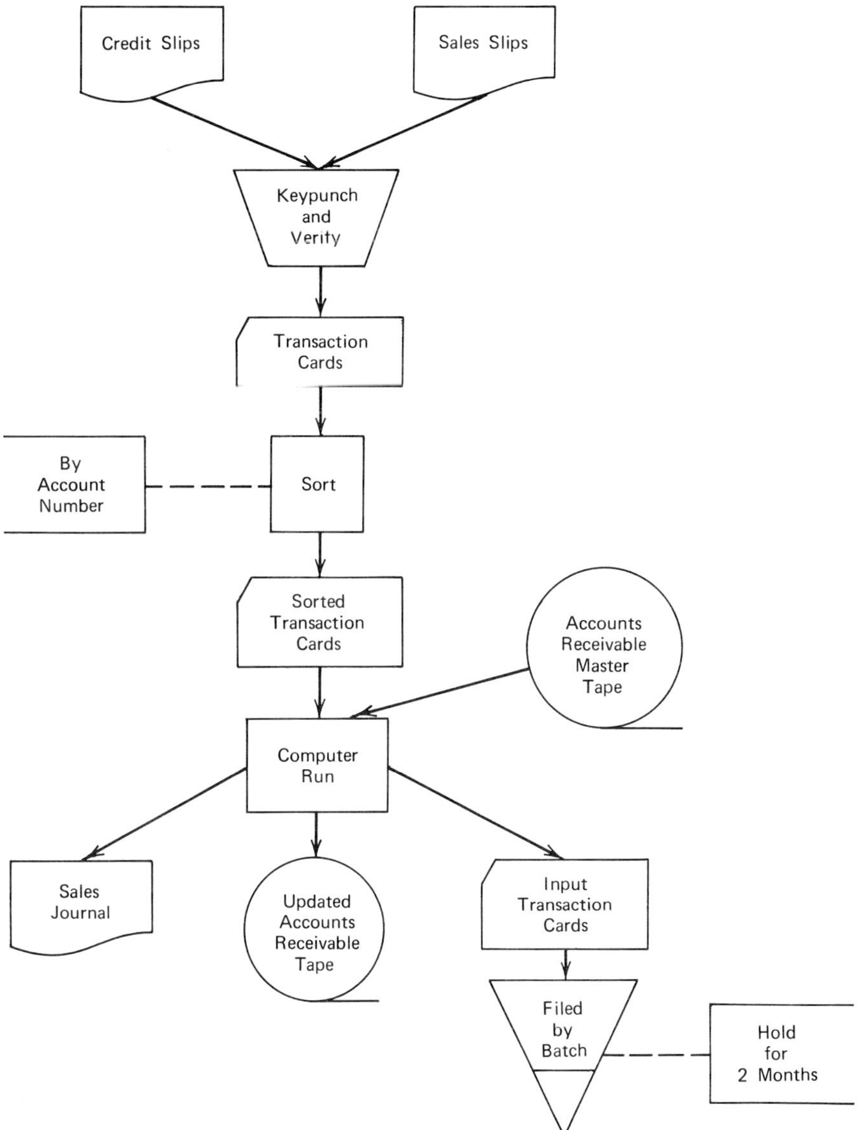

Figure 7.5 Update procedure for accounts receivable system.

Note that not all systems nor all systems flowcharts utilize a computer.

EXAMPLE 6. Figure 7.9 illustrates a personnel system that utilizes electronic accounting machines without the assistance of computers.

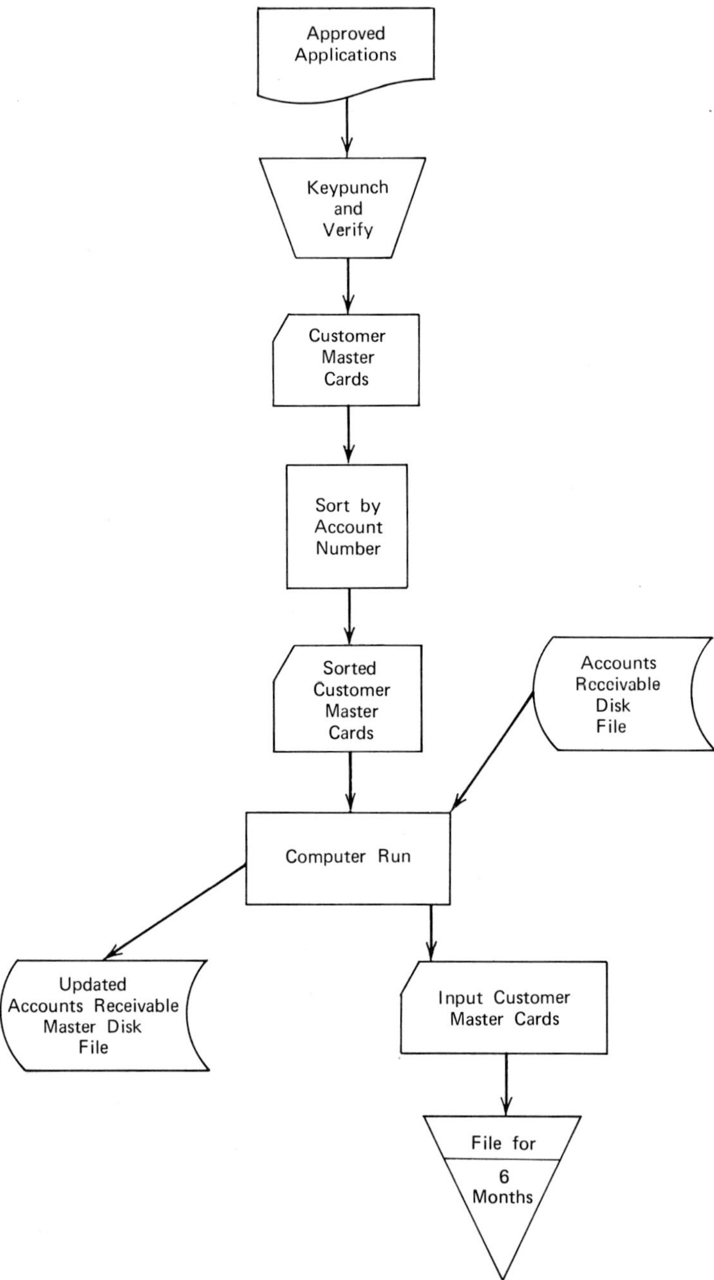

Figure 7.6 Creation of new records on accounts receivable master disk file.

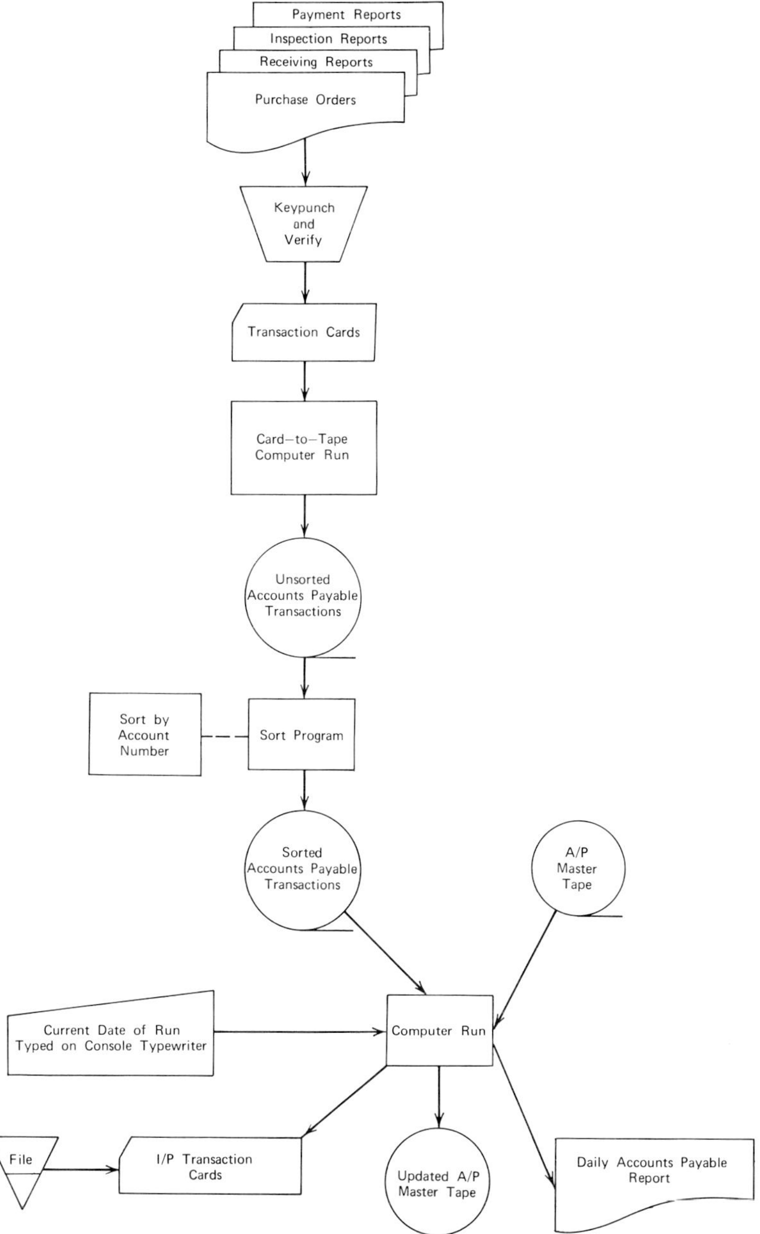

Figure 7.7 Update of accounts payable system.

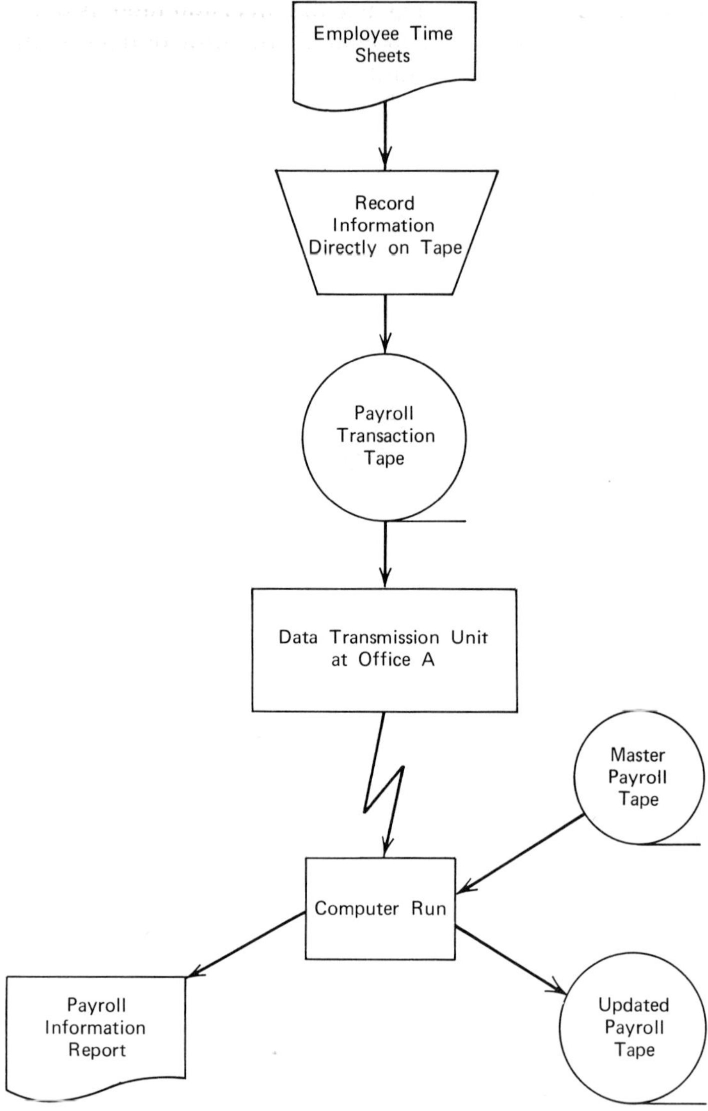

Figure 7.8 Remote transmission of payroll data.

Several of the above illustrations represent systems in their entirety. Others represent a portion of the system. Sometimes an entire flowchart is used to illustrate a segment of the system, where that segment must, for some reason, be emphasized, or when the system is so large that segmenting it becomes a necessity.

DECISION TABLES

The use of a **decision table** is one method by which an analyst can analyze the flow of data within a particular system under study. Decision tables are particularly useful for describing a

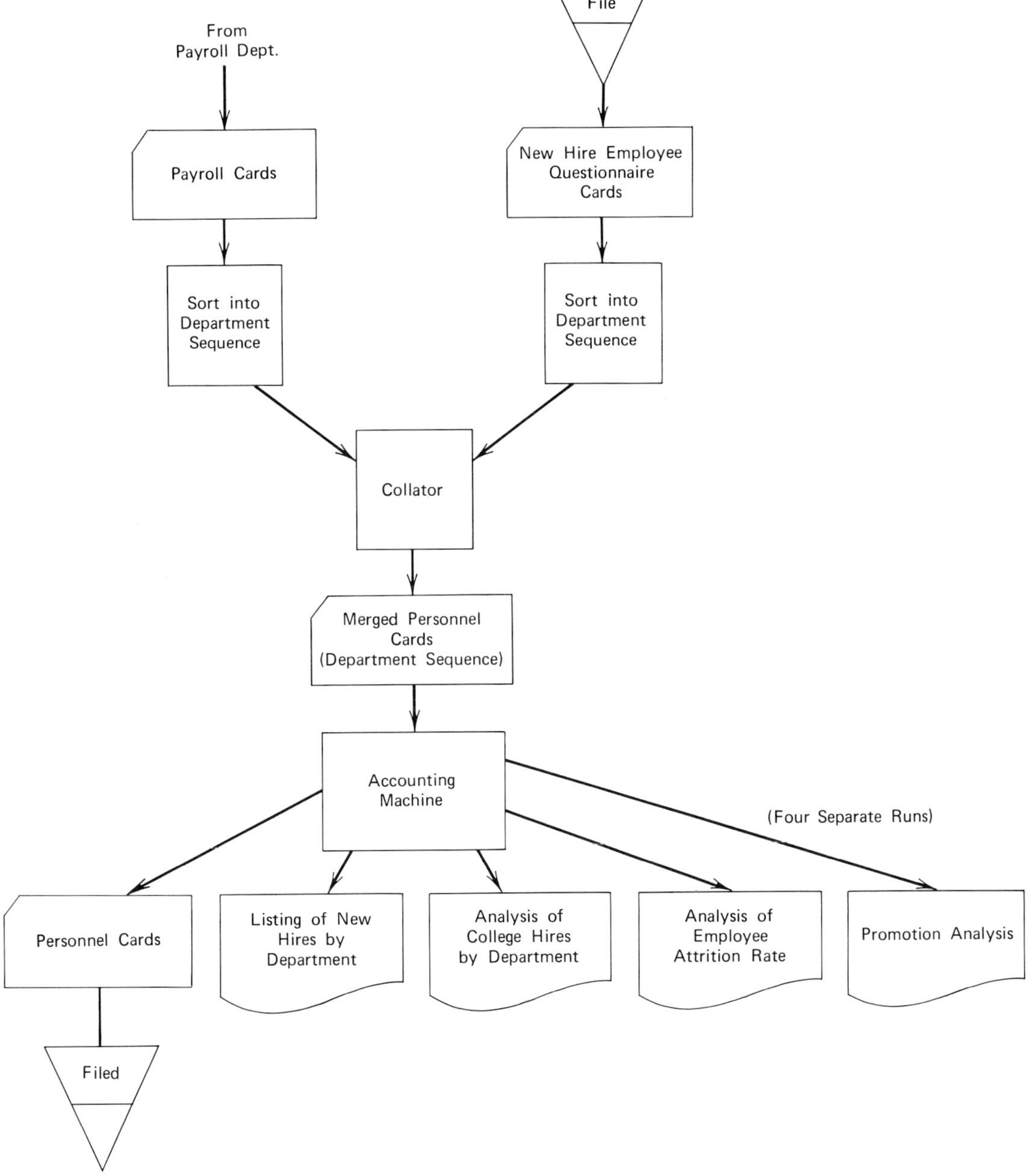

Figure 7.9 Unit-record personnel system.

system where numerous and complex conditions affect the logic flow. That is, if operations and procedures within a system are greatly affected by specific conditions with various possible outcomes, then a decision table is an extremely useful tool for describing that system. Note that in any situation involving numerous combinations, conditions, and actions, it is very easy to overlook the possible occurence of a given combination. Decision tables provide a mathematically precise method of ensuring that every possible combination is included.

Note that the decision table does not replace a systems flowchart. It is generally used to supplement the latter where complex conditions may make the flowchart cumbersome. The decision table, like the flowchart, is a graphic representation of procedures and operations. It is used as documentation, to help illustrate the understanding and analysis of the present system or to assist in describing the new or revised system.

Figure 7.10 illustrates the four basic entries within a decision table. We generally read *down* rather than across the diagram. That is, for *each* condition entry, we determine the appropriate action by reading down the chart.

Let us consider the decision table in Figure 7.11.

Notice that Y denotes yes, that the condition exists; N denotes no, that the condition does not exist; and X denotes that the corresponding action is taken. Reading from top to bottom and beginning with the first rule, we have

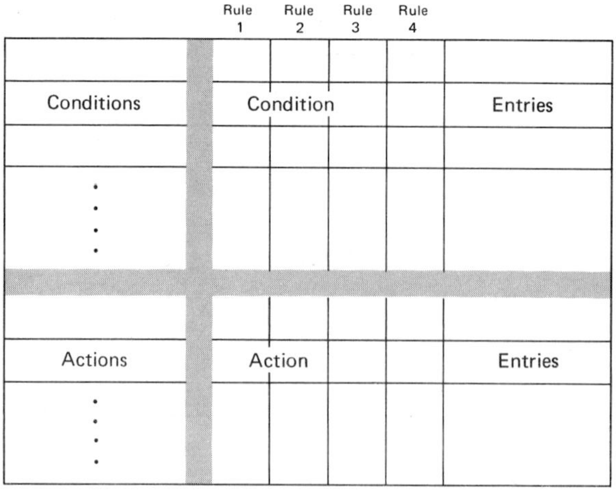

	Rule 1	Rule 2	Rule 3	Rule 4	
Conditions	Condition				Entries
⋮					
Actions	Action				Entries
⋮					

Figure 7.10 Decision table entries.

Airlines Reservation System	Rule 1	Rule 2	Rule 3	Rule 4
Request is for	First class	First class	Tourist	Tourist
First class available	Y	N		
Tourist class available			Y	N
Issue	First class		Tourist	
Place on waiting list		X		X

Figure 7.11 Decision table for simplified airline reservations system.

CONDITIONS	First class available	Y
	Tourist class available	
ACTIONS	Issue	First class
	Place on waiting list	

If first class is available (Y in condition *first class*), then issue first-class ticket (action taken).

With rule 2, we have

CONDITIONS	First class available	N
	Tourist class available	
ACTIONS	Issue	
	Place on waiting list	X

Use the following in determining the meaning of decision table entries:

If (condition), then (action).

If first class is *not* available (N for not), then place on waiting list.

With rule 3, we have

CONDITIONS	First class available	
	Tourist class available	Y
ACTIONS	Issue	Tourist
	Place on waiting list	

If (condition), then (action); that is, *if* tourist class is available, then issue tourist ticket.

With rule 4, we have

CONDITIONS	First class available	
	Tourist class available	N
ACTIONS	Issue	
	Place on waiting list	X

If tourist class is *not* available, then place on waiting list.

Note also that this is not the only method for preparing a decision table of this series of conditions. The decision table in Figure 7.12 provides for *exactly* the same conditions as above.

Let us now examine a more sophisticated airline reservations system. This system will also grant first-class tickets, if available, to those who request them and, similarly, it will grant tourist tickets, if available, to those who request them. If, however, desired class tickets are not available on request, then the reservations clerk will determine if the other class ticket is acceptable to the individual and available. If these conditions are both met, then the clerk will make out the appropriate ticket; if not, then the individual's name must be placed on the corresponding waiting list.

The above may be expressed in terms of the following criteria:

	Rule 1	Rule 2	Rule 3	Rule 4
Request is first class	Y	Y		
Request is tourist			Y	Y
First class available	Y	N		
Tourist available			Y	N
Issue first class ticket	X			
Issue tourist ticket			X	
Place on waiting list		X		X

Figure 7.12 Expanded decision table for airline reservations system.

1. If a first-class ticket is requested and available, then a first-class ticket is made out.
2. If a tourist-class ticket is requested and available, then a tourist-class ticket is issued.
3. If a first-class ticket is requested but not available, determine if tourist class is acceptable and available. If a tourist-class ticket is acceptable and available, issue a tourist-class ticket; if not, place individual's name on a first-class waiting list.
4. If a tourist-class ticket is requested and not available, determine if a first-class ticket is acceptable and available. If a first-class ticket is acceptable and available, issue a first-class ticket; if not, place the individual's name on a tourist waiting list.

The decision table in Figure 7.13 represents a schematic for the above.

GLOSSARY

Decision table. A graphic method of describing the flow of data within a system.

Flowchart. A graphic representation of the logic flow and sequence of an operation.

Figure 7.13 Complex decision table for airline reservations system.

	Rule 1	Rule 2	Rule 3	Rule 4	Rule 5	Rule 6	Rule 7	Rule 8
First class request	Y	Y	Y	Y				
Tourist request					Y	Y	Y	Y
First class open	Y	N	N	N		Y	N	
Tourist open		Y	N		Y	N	N	N
Alternate class acceptable		Y	Y	N		Y	Y	N
Issue first class ticket	X					X		
Issue tourist ticket		X			X			
Place on tourist waiting list			X				X	X
Place on first class waiting list			X	X			X	

Off-line. Any operation that utilizes equipment not in direct communication with the central processing unit of a computer system.

QUESTIONS

1. Draw a decision table of the various operations that are part of the registration procedure at your school.
2. What is a template?
3. Draw a systems flowchart on a proposed payroll system that you would like to implement.
4. What is the purpose of a decision table, and when is it used?
5. What is the purpose of a systems flowchart, and when is it used?

UNIT 

INFORMATION PROCESSING

CHAPTER **8**

HARDWARE

The systems analyst must be familiar with the basic types of devices or hardware available with the computer. He or she must be aware of the advantages, disadvantages, speed, and the approximate cost of these devices so that the needs of specific business systems can be effectively met.

It is often the task of the systems analyst to choose the most efficient devices to be utilized in an installation. At other times, he is required to work within the limits of computer hardware that already exists in the data processing center. In the latter case, the analyst must make judgments concerning what devices *within the installation* should be used for the specific system being designed.

CRITERIA FOR SELECTING HARDWARE

You will recall that computer systems consist of the following:

1. A series of input devices that accept data and transmit it to the CPU
2. A central processing unit (CPU) that processes incoming data by performing arithmetic operations, logic functions, and by otherwise manipulating data to produce output
3. A series of output devices that transmit resultant data from the CPU to an output medium, by converting it from the computer code to an acceptable output format

A very simplified computer system could function with a card reader, a central processing unit, and a printer. That is, the system utilizes card input only and produces printed reports as the sole form of output. Most computer centers, however, require more diversified equipment to handle files of data for a varied list of business applications.

Each device can handle a *form* of computer input or output. Some devices are input/output machines that can function by reading a specific form or by writing output using the same form. A card reader-punch, for example can read card input and produce card output.

Each input or output device is linked to the central processing unit by cables that operate by electronic transmission.

The medium on which data are recorded (such as cards and printed reports) is determined by the systems analyst and is a direct function of each business application. The media used must be compatible with the equipment or computer devices available at the installation. That is, cards are a feasible medium only if the company has acquired, or plans to acquire, a card reader.

The systems analyst must determine which file types for input and output will best suit the department's needs without being excessively costly for the company. In addition, however, he must determine whether the source documents should be converted to punched cards or magnetic tape or some other medium in an effort to produce the output as efficiently as possible. He must also be aware of the advantages and the limitations of the file type and its respective hardware devices so that he can formulate reasonable expectations and estimate costs for the automated procedure.

The file types selected for each application, and thus the computer devices or hardware utilized, will be discussed with respect to the following elements:

1. **Speed.** Some devices are much slower than others, thereby causing increased processing time and longer delay time.

2. **Cost.** Slower, more cumbersome devices can process data at a more reasonsble cost than high-speed, specialized equipment.

3. **Volume.** Note that the *volume* of data to be processed for a given application will directly relate to both speed and cost. Specific file types handle large volumes of data more efficiently than others. Thus the number of input and output records within the corresponding files will be a decisive factor in determining file type. High-volume files require devices that:
a. Process data very quickly
b. Store data in a neat, compact form
c. Process data cheaply

These factors undergo frequent changes and it is incumbent on the analyst to keep abreast of current literature that provides updated figures.

4. Frequency of Processing. Files that are accessed or processed daily, for example, will require different consideration than those that are processed monthly. Frequent handling necessitates files that are very durable and that are processed quickly and cheaply.

5. Nature of Source Document. Sometimes the form of the source document predetermines the input file type. A utility company bill (for example, gas bill) that is really a punched card, and a punched paper tape registering cash receipts are examples of source documents already in machine-readable form. To convert to another input form, even one that is more suitable, might be too costly. Similarly, if the source document is a printed report that must be entered into the computer flow in voluminous quantity, it might be cheaper in the end to use a device that can read printed reports, such as an optical scanner, even though this device is costly.

6. Record Size. As we have indicated, most card records are restricted to 80 characters or multiples of 80 characters, when more than one card record is used. Most other file types, as we have seen, do not have this limitation. Thus, while cards, for example, are cheap, they may not be suitable for applications that have relatively large record sizes.

7. Type of Processing. Records can be processed **sequentially**, one at a time in sequence, or **randomly**, in no specific sequence. Some devices are equipped to process records randomly while others can only process them in sequence. When files must be processed sequentially, they must be *sorted* prior to entering the data flow.

Computer systems are designed to handle data and produce information in different ways, depending on hardware and software limitations. The following represents a review of the methods that may be used to process data.

a. Batch Processing. Data are entered into the information flow in large volumes, or batches. That is, the processing by computer is performed at some time interval (weekly, monthly, etc.) when large volumes are accumulated. Daily accounts receivable tickets, for example, may be *batch processed.* Instead of processing the tickets as they are received, they are processed weekly, when a sufficient volume has been accumulated.

There are several inherent disadvantages to batch processing. The system that utilizes batch processing is not very timely, since it takes a fixed time interval before current information is added. That is, the main or master accounts receivable file, in our example, does not contain the current accounts receivable data for a full week. For this reason, a system that utilizes batch processing cannot effectively answer inquiries *between* processing intervals. The accounts receivable file in our example is only current on the day of the processing cycle; after that, current information will not be processed until the following week's run.

b. On-line Processing. Data are entered into the information flow immediately, without waiting for a fixed time interval. Similarly, inquiries may be answered by the computer system in relatively short intervals.

A bank, for example, may utilize on-line processing to maintain a transaction file. Each time a customer makes a deposit or withdrawal, it is entered into the computer flow, via an on-line device called a terminal.

On-line processing will be discussed in depth in Chapter 9.

c. Real-Time Processing. *Real-time processing* utilizes online operations in an environment that is so responsive that it produces output quickly enough to affect decision making or to serve customer's needs.

The bank, in our previous example, which utilizes on-line processing and which operates on the deposits and withdrawals quickly enough to give the customer a current status of his account, at any given time, is said to function in a real-time environment. Chapter 9 also discusses this in depth.

d. Off-line Processing. Computer processing is, without question, expensive. Thus any operation that can avoid direct utilization of computer equipment can save a company much money. *Off-line processing* is the processing of information that is not directly under the control of the CPU.

A card-to-print off-line hardware device, for example, is one that can take data from a card and print it according to a specified format, *without the use of a central processing unit of a computer.* There are numerous off-line devices that are compatible with most computer systems. These will be discussed presently.

Thus the student of systems analysis can see that the type of processing utilized can directly affect the efficiency of a computer system.

8. Equipment Available at the Installation. Usually, computer specialists will attempt to satisfy a businessperson's needs with the hardware or computer devices currently available at the center. To order new equipment because of a specific application is not a usual procedure unless the device can be justified from a cost standpoint. That is, if a very costly procedure is computerized and a specific device, not on hand, is ideally suited to it, the acquisition of the equipment might result in an eventual savings to the company. If not, the computer specialist will utilize the equipment on hand.

9. Accuracy of Records. Some devices read or write with more reliability than others. Where large numbers of records are processed and errors occur infrequently and are easily correctable, the more reliable devices may not be required.

Let us consider the file types and corresponding devices that are available for computer processing. Each will be considered with regard to the items above. Such devices will be discussed most specifically as they relate to medium-sized computers. While selection of the most frequently used devices, such as card reader-punches, magnetic tape drives, and magnetic disk drives, must be evaluated with respect to the above items, these devices have already been discussed. In short, we will assume that these devices have already been implemented, and thus the analyst needs to concern himself with more specialized equipment.

DEVICES THAT CAN READ SOURCE DOCUMENTS

Notice that cards, tapes, and disks, the media most often used as input, require *conversion from a source document.* This conversion process, using keypunch machines or key-to-tape encoders with operators, can be extremely costly and time-consuming. In addition, it requires a major control procedure. Source documents must be counted and the total number compared against the number of input records (created by the conversion) to ensure that records have not been misplaced. Manual procedures must be employed to physically transport source documents to an operations or control staff, and then to transport the machine-readable input records to the computer room.

As computer equipment becomes even faster and more sophisticated, this conversion process consumes a greater percentage of total data processing time. In many companies, where inputs are voluminous, this conversion process can require up to 35 percent of the total operation time.

In an effort to alleviate the increased cost and time allotted to conversion, manufacturers have sought to produce equipment that will accept source input without requiring extensive conversion. The major devices in use today include:

1. Magnetic ink character recognition (MICR) equipment
2. Optical character recognition (OCR) equipment
3. Punched paper tape reader-punch
4. Computer output microfilm (COM) equipment
5. Terminal devices

Terminal equipment requires special consideration because it functions in an on-line environment. Thus it will be discussed in depth in Chapter 9. Table 8.1 provides a synopsis of file types discussed in this section.

Let us now discuss the first three devices (1 to 3 above). These usually employ *batch processing* procedures. That is, they are best suited for applications that utilize large volumes of data, processed in a group, where conversion from a source document is relatively costly. The above devices perform the conversion from a source document to a machine-readable form directly, as discussed below.

Magnetic Ink Character Recognition (MICR) Equipment (Figure 8.1)

The banking industry is a specific area where the conversion of source documents, or checks, requires a massive operation. Thus, about a decade ago, the Federal Reserve System adopted a new technique whereby checks have account numbers and check amounts recorded in special type characters that are printed on the bottom of the check. These special characters are treated with a magnetic ink that can be sensed by MICR equipment. Magnetic ink character reader-sorter units interpret checks, sort them by account or bank number into pockets, and transfer the data to the CPU.

Thus blank checks are prepared by special machines that imprint account number, bank number, and other identifying data. These checks are then used by the customer for transactions. When the checks that have been transacted and signed are returned to the bank, an operator uses a machine to encode the amount of the check in magnetic ink at the bottom. Thus

TABLE 8.1 MAJOR CHARACTERISTICS OF SPECIALIZED FILE TYPES

File type	Characteristics	Advantages	Disadvantages	Major Users
MAGNETIC INK CHARACTER RECOGNITION (MICR) FILES	Data is recorded in special type characters of magnetic ink. Such data may be read and sorted by MICR devices used in conjunction with computer systems.	This file type enables the computer to read source documents imprinted with magnetic numbers without requiring a conversion process; the devices used with this file type are highly accurate even if an input document is bent or slightly mutilated; such devices can handle any size document.	MICR devices can only detect numbers.	Banking Systems utilize checks with MICR numbers imprinted on bottom as ACCOUNT NUMBER and AMOUNT (after check has been processed).
PRINTED DOCUMENTS READ BY OPTICAL CHARACTER RECOGNITION (OCR) EQUIPMENT	Data is recorded in regular type or even handwritten form; such data may be read by OCR equipment and transmitted to a computer, without requiring the conversion process from a source document to a machine-readable form; characters must be printed or typed in designated positions.	Saves considerable time and expense by eliminating the conversion process.	Rigid conformance to standard type fonts is required by devices; erasures and slight overlapping of positions cause enumerable errors in transmission; OCR devices are extremely expensive compared to other input/output devices and cannot be justified unless input to the system is considerable (e.g., 20,000 documents or more per day).	Department stores utilize OCR devices to read handwritten sales slips for charge customers. The sales slips are meticulously prepared by trained sales personnel; they are then read by OCR equipment which transmits the data to the computer which then updates the Accounts Receivable file.
PUNCHED PAPER TAPE	Tape is punched by machine (computer device, cash registers, adding machine) with holes in specified rows and columns; it	File can be represented on a continuous tape without record length restrictions; it is easier to transport and store paper tape	Paper Tape files are not as durable as card files; the punched paper tape read/punches are slower than card devices.	Punched Paper tape in the form of cash register receipts, adding machine tapes are read by computer. Communications companies can

File Type	Characteristics	Advantages	Disadvantages	Major Users
PUNCHED PAPER TAPE	then is read by a PAPER TAPE READ/PUNCH of a computer system.	than cards; there is no sequencing problem with a continuous tape.		maintain records of all telephone calls for example from a given area on paper tape.
MICROFILM	A microfilm is a photographed record in miniature—1/24 to 1/42 of its original size; there are computer devices that create microfilm records as a result of a computer run—this is called Computer Output Microfilm (COM) equipment; there are special viewers that may then be used to read the microfilm records and/or convert them to a printed report; there are computer devices that can read microfilm called Computer Input Microfilm (CIM) equipment.	The two major advantages of microfilm are the greatly reduced storage area required to maintain computer output (as opposed to the printed report which is the most common output form) and the ability of high speed microfilm readers to access this computer output speedily.	The use of microfilm as a file type requires additional computer hardware and viewers that are relatively costly.	Any firm which must store large amounts of printed information and which must be able to retrieve it speedily can benefit from the use of microfilm. Motor Vehicle Bureaus which must maintain millions of records and which also must be able to access these records fast in case of accidents, stolen cars, etc., are sometimes dependent on microfilm. Similarly, personnel records, accounting ledgers, etc., at large companies are stored on microfilm.

an MICR device may be used to sort the checks into account number or bank number sequence. Similarly, an MICR device may be used to transmit the information on the check to the CPU. In this way, the checks themselves can serve as input to a data processing installation. They need not be converted to cards or tape or disk. Deposit slips in commercial banks are also encoded in this manner.

The average speed of MICR equipment ranges from approximately 600 to 1,600 checks per minute or from 100 to 500 characters per second. The main purpose of the device is to enable the computer to read source documents that are also manually readable without requiring a conversion process.

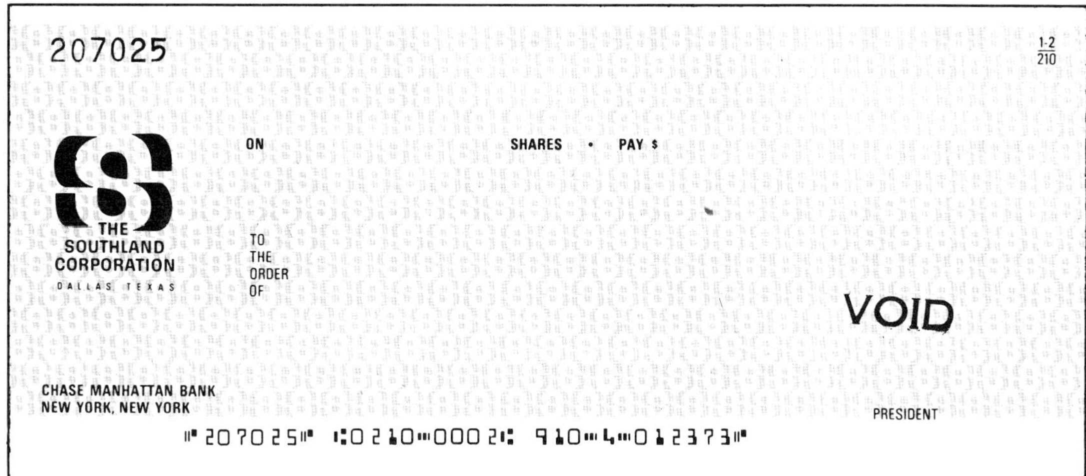
207025

1-2
210

THE SOUTHLAND CORPORATION
DALLAS TEXAS

ON SHARES • PAY $

TO THE ORDER OF

VOID

CHASE MANHATTAN BANK
NEW YORK, NEW YORK

PRESIDENT

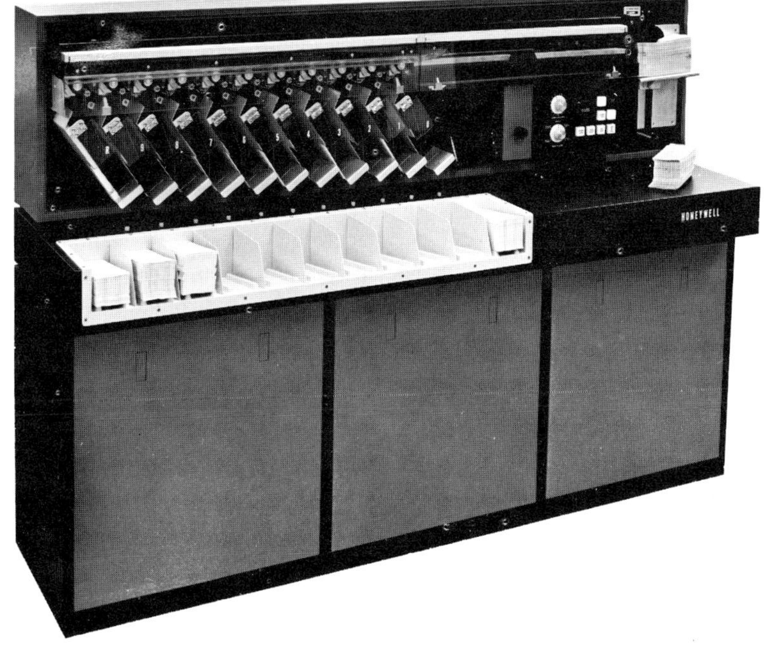

Figure 8.1 MICR reader-sorter (courtesy Honeywell). Especially for bankers — this low-cost document reader-sorter for banks is marketed by Honeywell Information Systems. This unit reads magnetic ink-encoded documents at speeds up to 600 documents per minute and sorts them into 11 different pockets (10 accept and 1 reject). Called the Type 232 MICR Reader-Sorter, the device can be operated as a free-standing unit or on-line to any Series 200 computer, including Honeywell's small-scale, low-cost 110 system.

MICR equipment can handle almost any size check or deposit slip so that an industry-wide standard check size is not required. These devices are also highly accurate; they do not missort or transmit incorrectly, even if the condition of the check is poor.

The one main disadvantage is that currently only *numbers* have been used as MICR characters, to be read by MICR equipment. Thus any application requiring the encoding of letters or special characters cannot utilize this equipment.

As indicated, MICR equipment is used as a standard in the banking industry. Any industry, however, that performs voluminous source document conversion and that uses exclusively digits as identifying characters, may employ this equipment.

Optical Character Recognition (OCR) Equipment (Figure 8.2) and Other Optical Readers

An OCR device, commonly referred to as an **optical scanner**, reads characters from printed documents. No special ink (as with MICR devices) or typing is required. (See Figure 8.3.)

The optical scanner senses typed data with the use of a photoelectric device. The printed data are read by an ultra-bright light source, which converts these characters into electrical impulses. On many devices, the printed input document must have characters or marks in designated positions in order to be properly sensed. The computer, then, must be instructed as to which positions will contain the data.

A major use of optical scanners is in conjunction with gasoline company credit card receipts. Credit card identification from a plastic plate is imprinted on the receipt along with the amount of purchase. These receipts are then read into a computer with the use of an optical scanner that senses the amount and customer account number. Another major use of optical scanners is in accounting departments of businesses that use adding machine tapes and cash register tapes that contain typed data as direct input. That is, the optical scanner can read these tapes directly.

The optical character recognition device is unquestionably a major breakthrough in computer technology. Source documents that contain regular typed printing can be read as input, directly into a computer system. (See Figure 8.4.) With some sophisticated optical scanners, handwritten material can be accepted if the characters are printed in a standard form. Many department stores train their clerks to print a sales slip total in a standard manner. These sales slips are then entered as input to a computer system with the use of an optical scan-

Figure 8.2 Optical character reader (courtesy IBM).

ner. No manual conversion is required. Consider the tremendous advantage of reducing the need for a large and costly operations staff by using the source document as machine-readable input.

OCR equipment varies in speed from approximately 50 characters per second, for devices that can read handwritten letters, to 2,400 characters per second, and from 200 to 1,200 documents per minute. Most page readers are very costly, however, ranging in price from $160,000 to $400,000 on the average, with monthly rentals from $2,500 to $6,000. Considering the savings of keying machines with operators for the typical conversion process, the expense can often be justified in a cost analysis. In one company, a systems analyst performed a cost study to determine the feasibility of acquiring

#15550

IMPORTANT: THE NUMBERS WRITTEN IN THE GREEN BOXES MUST BE HANDWRITTEN IN THIS STYLE → 1 2 3 4 5 6 7 8 9 0

FORMOST FORM-PRINT, NEW YORK, N.Y. 10001

CLIENT DISBURSEMENT CHARGE FORM
PAUL, WEISS, GOLDBERG, RIFKIND, WHARTON & GARRISON

L

HAND ENTRY [X] 013

CASE NUMBER		DISBURSEMENT	DATE			AMOUNT	
CLIENT	MATTER	CODE	MONTH	DAY	YEAR	DOLLARS	CENTS
		023					
CASE NUMBER		DISBURSEMENT	DATE			AMOUNT	

CLIENT			
MATTER			
LAWYERS NAME	DELIVER BY ☐ / PICK UP BY ☐	AM	PM
SPECIAL INSTRUCTIONS			

DO NOT CHARGE CLIENT	TRANSPORT COST	TOT. TIME FOR DEL. HOURS	MINUTES	DELIVERED BY	SIGNATURE OF MAILROOM PERSONNEL
☐	$				

ACCOUNTING DEPT. COPY

HAND DELIVERY

PAUL, WEISS, GOLDBERG, RIFKIND, WHARTON & GARRISON

Figure 8.3 Sample input (courtesy International Business Forms).

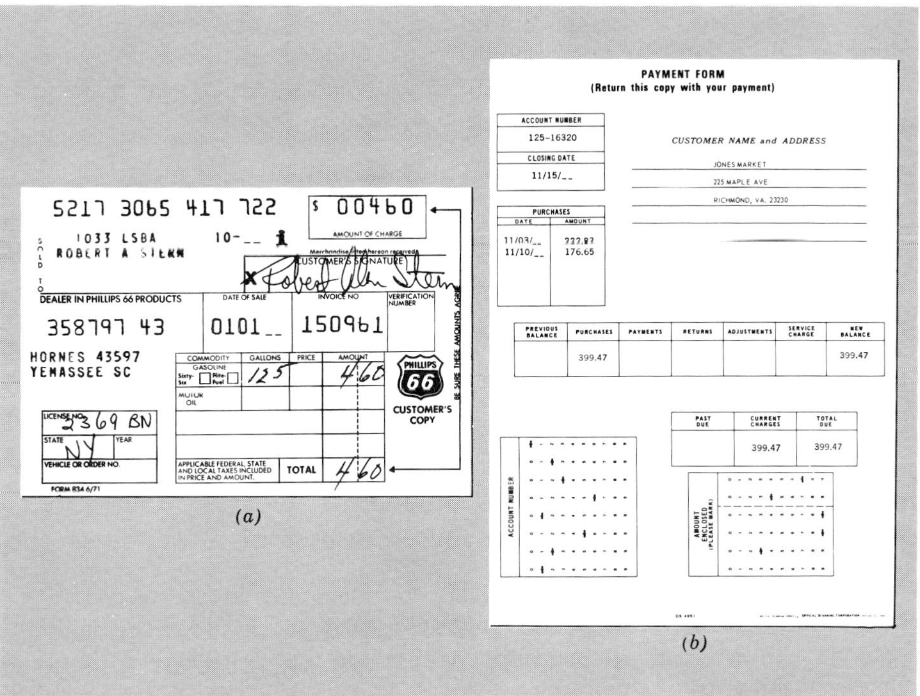

5217 3065 417 722 $ 00460
AMOUNT OF CHARGE
1033 LSBA 10-__
ROBERT A STERN
SOLD TO
CUSTOMER'S SIGNATURE
DEALER IN PHILLIPS 66 PRODUCTS | DATE OF SALE | INVOICE NO. | VERIFICATION NUMBER
358797 43 | 0101__ | 150961
HORNES 43597
YEMASSEE SC
COMMODITY | GALLONS | PRICE | AMOUNT
GASOLINE
MOTOR OIL
LICENSE NO. 2369 BN
STATE NY | YEAR
VEHICLE OR ORDER NO.
APPLICABLE FEDERAL, STATE AND LOCAL TAXES INCLUDED IN PRICE AND AMOUNT. | TOTAL
PHILLIPS 66
CUSTOMER'S COPY
BE SURE THESE AMOUNTS AGREE
FORM 834 6/71

(a)

PAYMENT FORM
(Return this copy with your payment)

ACCOUNT NUMBER
125-16320
CLOSING DATE
11/15/__

CUSTOMER NAME and ADDRESS
JONES MARKET
225 MAPLE AVE
RICHMOND, VA. 23230

PURCHASES	
DATE	AMOUNT
11/03/__	222.82
11/10/__	176.65

PREVIOUS BALANCE	PURCHASES	PAYMENTS	RETURNS	ADJUSTMENTS	SERVICE CHARGE	NEW BALANCE
	399.47					399.47

PAST DUE	CURRENT CHARGES	TOTAL DUE
	399.47	399.47

ACCOUNT NUMBER
AMOUNT ENCLOSED (PLEASE MARK)

(b)

Figure 8.4 Sample input to optical reader (courtesy Optical Scanning Corporation); (*a*) on gasoline credit slip, only imprinted data are read by the optical reader; (*b*) payment form serves as a statement to the customer, and, when returned, the account number and amount enclosed (marked at the bottom of the form) serve as input to an optical scanner.

an OCR device for a billing system. It was determined that an OCR device could only be monetarily justified where the system processed 20,000 documents per day. With fewer documents, the standard conversion process would be more economical. Thus we can see that such a device is relatively costly and is justifiable only when processing a voluminous quantity of input.

Thus far, we have discussed the optical scanner as the major type of optical reader. This optical scanner may be one of the following.

1. Hand-print reader—the printing must conform to a specified pattern
2. Single-font reader—the typed printing may be in only one type font or style
3. Multifont reader—two or more different type styles may be used

In addition to the optical scanner, the **mark reader** is considered an optical reader. Mark-sensed cards, which have been discussed in Chapter 5, may be read by a mark reader. In addition to mark-sensed cards, there are other documents that may be read by mark readers.

Optical mark reading and bar-code reading devices are optical readers, far simpler in principle than optical scanners, that may also be used for converting data from a source document into a machine-readable form. A bar-code reader can read preprinted codes on documents by detecting spots at various predetermined sections across the reading path. Bar-code readers are often employed to read amount figures on payment cards or stubs. After reading the data, they then transform the information into punched cards, magnetic tape, or some other medium.

A mark-sense reader detects the presence of pencil marks on predetermined grids. Typical documents to be mark-sensed are computer-scored test papers, where students are required to indicate the correct answer by pencilling in grid A, B, C, D, or E. Note that the mark-sensed cards discussed in Chapter 5 are examples of input documents that can be read by mark-sense readers. Here again, the data can be transformed into an input medium. Note that while these are optical readers, they have limited facility and therefore limited use. Their capability is much less than that of optical scanners, where actual handwritten or typed data can be read.

Optical readers, although a real asset to many computer installations, have several inherent disadvantages. Characters that are sensed by this device often must *rigidly* conform to the standard. Typing erasures, overlapping of positions, and so on can cause the erroneous transmission of data. In some applications, as much as 10 percent of the input data is unreadable because of such errors. In addition, optical scanners are very costly devices. In short, the promise of increased reliability and decreased cost in future years will make OCR equipment more widespread than it is today.

Punched Paper Tape Reader-Punch (Figure 8.5)

A punched paper tape (Figure 8.6) is a paper tape that, like a card, is punched with holes in specified rows and columns. A paper tape reader-punch is, like a card reader-punch, two separate units that can read from a paper tape or punch data into one.

Punched paper tape can be produced by special adding machines, accounting machines, and cash registers. With the

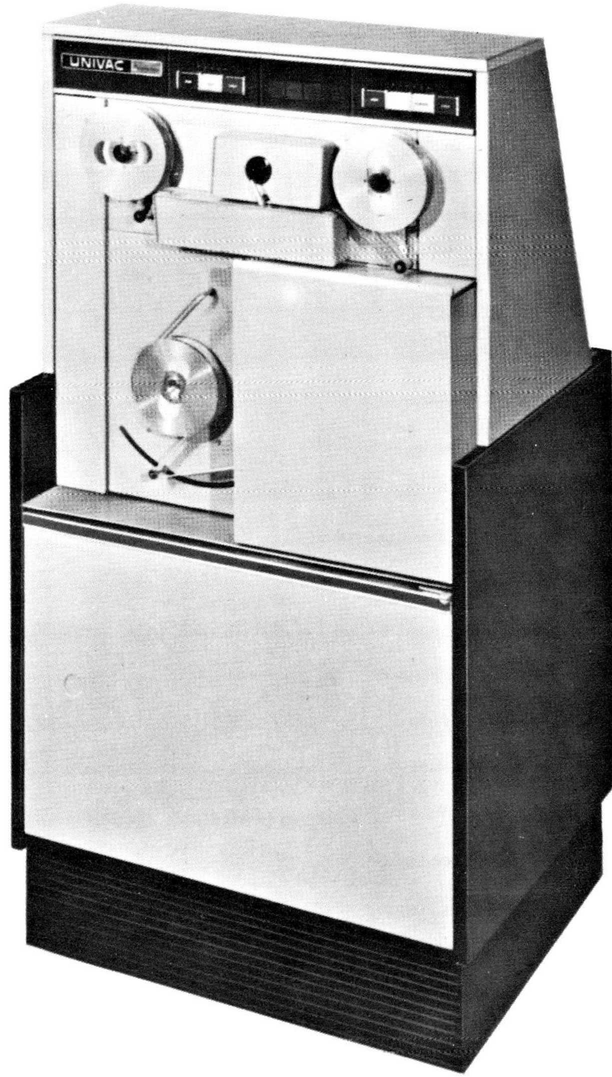

Figure 8.5 Punched paper tape reader punch (courtesy Sperry Rand).

use of the reader-punch, it can then be used, as a source document, by the computer system.

The punched paper tape has several advantages that make it more suitable for some applications than card processing. A file can be represented on a continuous tape; thus there is no limitation on record size as with punched cards. Punched paper tape equipment is less expensive than card equipment. It is easier to store and transport paper tapes than large vol-

Figure 8.6 Punched paper tape.

umes of cards. There is no problem with sequencing the tape records, since the file can be represented on one continuous tape.

There are, however, several limitations to paper tape processing. Paper tape is not as durable as cards. Paper tape devices are slower than card equipment. Typical paper tape reader-punch devices can read 300 characters per second and punch 110 characters per second. In general, only applications that use cash register or adding machine tapes or other specialized systems employ paper tape devices.

In short, there are several computer devices available that can read source documents directly without requiring a conversion to some other medium, such as cards, tape, or disk. Terminal devices are also included in this category, but because they are utilized in an on-line environment, they will be considered separately in Chapter 9.

COMPUTER OUTPUT MICROFILM (COM) DEVICES

Microfilm, as a noncomputerized storage medium, has been in existence for many years. It is a photographed record or document in miniature. Devices are required to *create* the microfilm. Because of its miniature size, devices are also required to *read* the microfilm. Many newspapers use microfilm for storing reproductions of the paper, in miniature, for a fixed number of years. An individual can locate and read a given newspaper article by accessing the film and utilizing a microfilm reader to view it.

In recent years, the computer industry has recognized the distinctive assets of mirofilm. Since storage of large numbers of cards or even printed reports has proved cumbersome, microfilm devices can be used to reproduce such records in miniature. Computer output microfilm (COM) devices (Figure 8.7) have been developed to produce human-readable microfilmed output from a computer system at relatively high speeds. Most often, magnetic tape information to be printed as a report is recorded on microfilm instead, using a computer system. In addition to high-speed output, microfilm can save about 98 percent of the storage space required for cards or reports. Typically microimage forms are from 1/24th to 1/42nd of their original size. Most often, the magnetic tape drives convert data to microfilm using special devices not under the control of a computer, since such a conversion requires much time when many records are to be created on microfilm.

Figure 8.7 Computer output microfilm (COM) recorder (courtesy Stromberg Datagraphix).

Forms of computer output microfilm include:

1. Rolled film represented on reels
2. Cards containing individual microfilm records

The film used to produce microfilm can be 16mm, 35mm, or 105mm.

Microfilm output can be created at computer speeds up to 120,000 characters per second or 21,800 lines per minute.

Thus rolled film and cards are the two forms of microfilm. There are two types of microfilm cards:

1. Microfiche cards—with rectangular holes that can store frames of microfilm. One card can typically store *many* records.
2. Aperture cards—unit records of film. Typically these are punched cards that provide an area for individual frames of microfilm—one card contains *one* record. There are microfiche viewers and hard-copy printers that can produce reports from these cards.

Figure 8.8 illustrates these cards. The microfiche viewer, for example, can hold typically 750 microfiche cards and access any one of them in approximately 3 seconds (see Figure 8.9).

Aperture cards contain punched data that serve as identification in addition to the film. In this way, standard card devices can be used to process the punched card information, while microfilm readers can be used to read the filmed portion.

Similarly, there are microfilm card reader-printers that can access an aperture or microfiche card or rolled film in seconds and print the corresponding photographed image. In this way, computer printouts can be stored on microfilm, accessed im-

Figure 8.8 (*a*) Microfiche card. Each contains dozens of microfilm images. To access an individual record, a microfiche viewer must be used. (*b*) Aperture card. Each contains punched card data with an individual microfilm image.

Figure 8.9 Remkard display unit — microfiche viewer (courtesy Remington Rand). This system can store 75,000 microfilmed pages of information on 750 microfiche cards, each with an individual index that permits fast random pushbutton selection.

mediately when they are needed, and reproduced without the use of a computer.

Computer devices can also be used to *read* microfilm. CIM (computer input microfilm) is used when data are *read* from a high-speed microfilm device and *transmitted* to the computer. To date, there are far less applications for CIM than for COM. This is because microfilm is generally used to store *output* documents that are not intended to reenter the data flow as input.

Thus the two major advantages of microfilm are in the compact storage of records and in the speedy retrieval of data. Microfilm is most often used to store the following types of data:

Engineering drawings (maps, blueprints, and so on)
Customer records
Accounting ledgers
Personnel records
Assorted computer printouts
Toll billing

Figure 8.10 provides a comparison between normal printing and microfilm operations.

OFF-LINE DEVICES

As we have seen, utilization of computer equipment in conjunction with a CPU is very costly. There are devices available that can operate on computer files or media *without requiring the CPU*. These are called **off-line devices**.

Thus far, we have been exposed to keypunch machines, key-to-tape encoders, and key-to-disk recorders, which are characterized as *off-line* equipment, since they do not require the central processing unit for their conversion processes. A keypunch machine is an off-line device that creates card output. Similarly, a key-to-tape encoder is an off-line device that creates tape records from source documents.

There are, however, numerous other off-line devices that, if utilized properly, result in substantial savings to a company. That is, rather than using hardware devices under the control of the CPU, the following may be employed off-line:

Figure 8.10 Comparison of printing operations and microfilm operations (courtesy Stromberg Datagraphix Inc.). Where volume is very great, microfilm can result in savings of computer time, paper bursting, binding, retrieval, and distribution of information. Computer output is converted

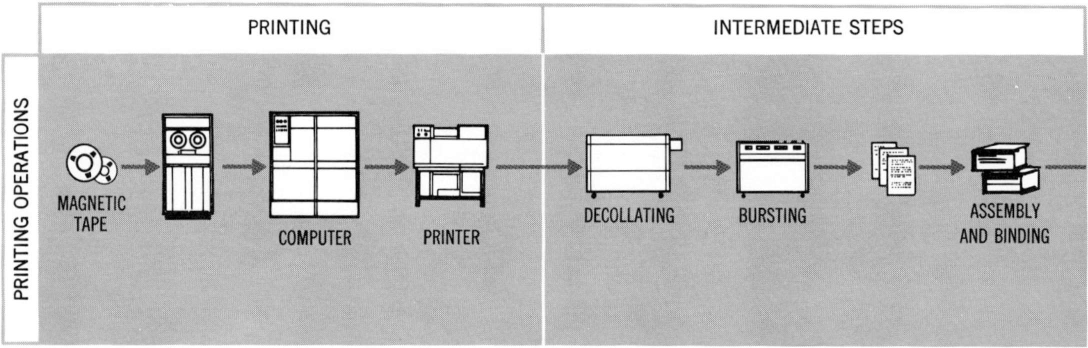

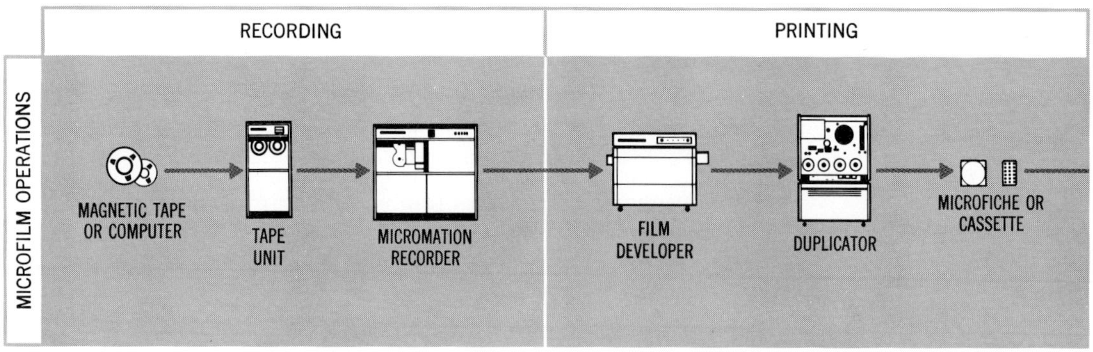

1. Pencil-marked document-to-tape devices (see Figure 8.11)
2. Tape-to-print off-line devices
3. Card-to-tape off-line devices
4. Card-to-print off-line devices
5. Punched-paper-to-magnetic-tape off-line devices
6. Tape-to-microfilm off-line devices

Note that off-line operations often utilize auxiliary **mini-computers** to perform required conversions. Although a computer is employed, this conversion is considered off-line since processing is not under the control of the *main* computer. Figure 8.12 illustrates an optical page reader used in conjunction with a minicomputer to produce a tape or disk file off-line. This utilization of minicomputers for off-line operations to relieve the load of full-size computers is becoming increasingly popular because of the monetary savings.

There are many, many more off-line devices. The essential concept of these is to take information, usually entered at different points and usually requiring a relatively slow conver-

into readable text at speeds up to 342 completely filled, standard-sized computer pages a minute. The output is printed on film that may be viewed at a micromation inquiry station or used to produce hard copies (printed reports).

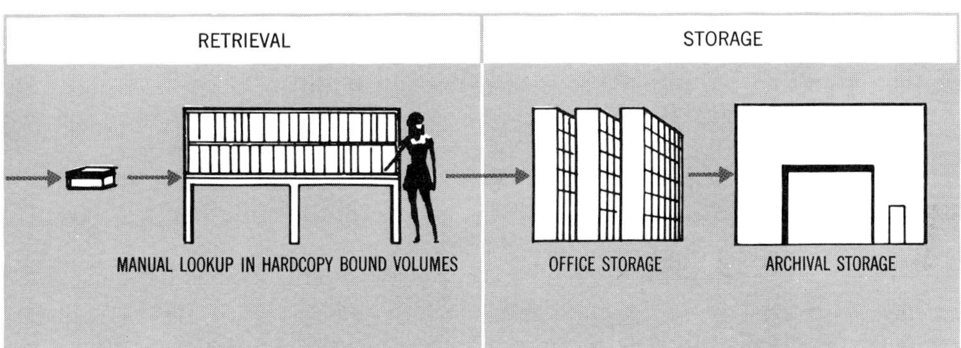

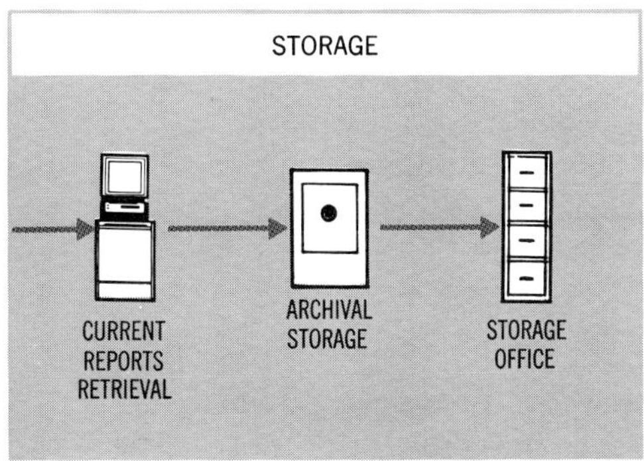

Figure 8.11 Off-line optical scanner (courtesy Optical Scanning Corp.). Pencil-marked information is optically scanned and transferred to tape at speeds up to 2,400 sheets per hour.

sion process, and produce a machine-readable form. The output then is usually some high-speed medium that can be entered as input to a CPU much faster.

In summary, we have presented the major forms of hardware (with the exception of terminal devices) that are used in most companies.

It is the responsibility of the analyst to keep abreast of new advances in technology. The systems analyst is often responsible for initiating feasibility studies to determine if newer, more sophisticated, or more suitable computer equipment should be acquired. Note, too, that the systems analyst of today is quite possibly the top-level executive of tomorrow. And top-level management is ultimately responsible for major decisions on all aspects of computer acquisition. Thus we cannot overestimate the importance of familiarity with recent advances in hardware devices.

CATEGORIES OF COMPUTERS

We have thus far discussed computer systems in general. The reader is now aware that computer systems can consist of many diversified devices and complex CPUs. The extent of diversification should be apparent. We have also seen that computer systems vary broadly in capability and cost. Let us now discuss the various classes of computer systems.

Figure 8.12 Page reader used in conjunction with minicomputers, off-line (courtesy Varian Data Machines). An office worker feeds printed information to the Farrington 3030 Page Reader. In background is the Varian 620/i minicomputer, which lets the office worker perform the task without having to access a central processing mainframe unit.

1. Minicomputers. These computers are designed to handle simple data processing functions. While medium- and large-scale computers are used to process the information flow of relatively complex systems that are then broken down into smaller aspects, minicomputers are capable of performing these independent tasks and do not lend themselves to integrated networks of systems.

Minicomputers are manufactured by Digital Equipment Co., which has a major share of the market, Varian Data Machines, and Wang Laboratories, just to name some of the larger manufacturers. These machines are generally small and often fit on a desk top. Some are punched card systems capable of reading and/or producing punched cards. Most minicomputers have the ability to print data. Some just contain a keyboard for input entries, where data is keyed in by an operator or programmer. Others can contain far more sophisticated input/output forms, but these are more costly. They are designed to be stand-alone computers, which means that they operate independently, or they can be part of a vast network or system. Many minicomputers, for example, at different locations can amass data, edit and verify, perform simple calculations, and then transmit the data to a large-scale computer for manipulation of all the elements. Minicomputers are capable of handling typical I/O forms such as those used with much larger machines. There are, however, limitations in core capacity, speed, and functions that can be performed. They have the major advantage of being relatively inexpensive—selling for $10,000 to $20,000.

Figure 8.13 illustrates a minicomputer manufactured by Wang Laboratories, Inc. This is a device to be used by insurance agents that will enable them to develop a personalized statement for each client, quickly and accurately, that explains financial benefits.

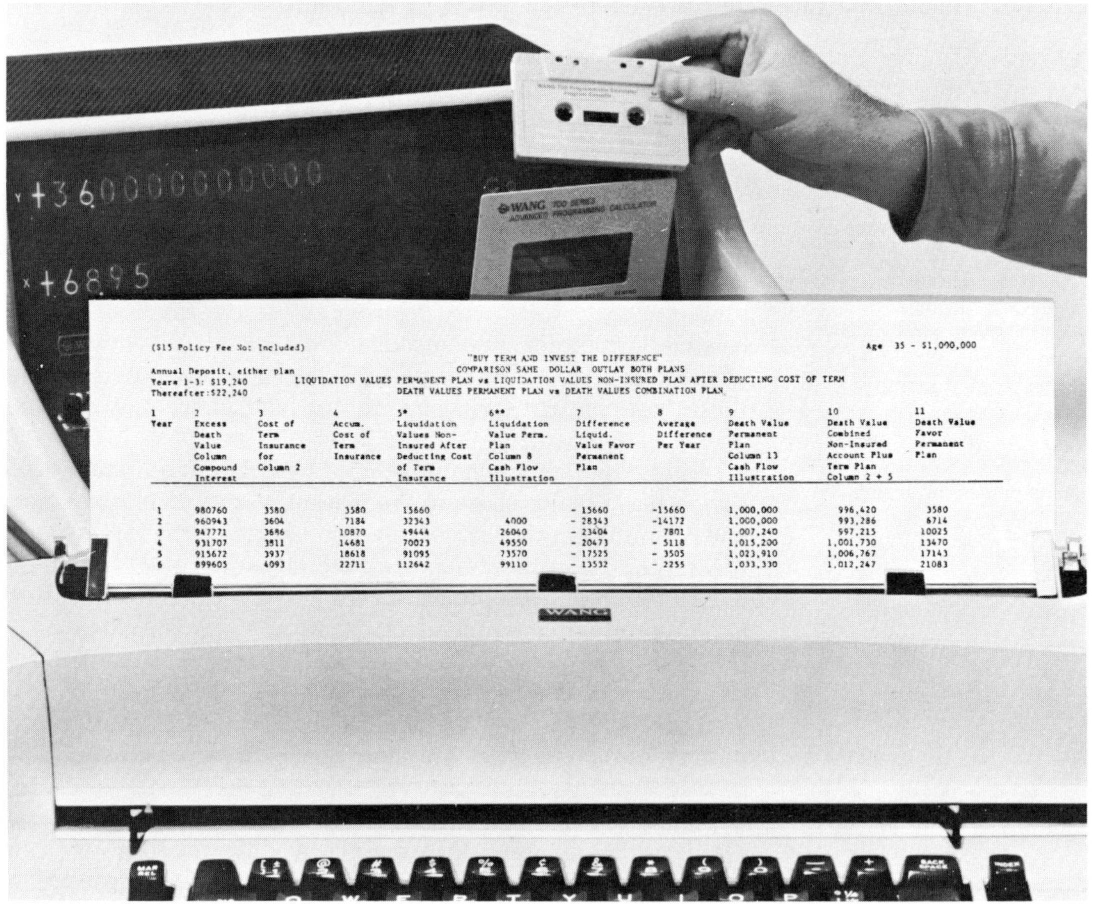

Figure 8.13 Example of a minicomputer (courtesy Wang Laboratories, Inc.).

This minicomuter consists of an electronic calculator and an output writer. It comes equipped with preprogrammed tape cassettes, on which the manufacturer-supplied programs are written.

Utilizing the system, an agent can custom design each client's exact insurance needs. Increased insurance sales result from this system indirectly, because clients are impressed by an agent who can design an insurance investment portfolio on his own computer.

Cost of the system is under $10,000. With the use of this minicomputer, agents need not submit requests for the preperation of personalized benefit statements for each client, which would then require massive clerical assistance and/or use of a large-scale computer.

Figure 8.14 illustrates a typical minicomputer manufactured by Varian Data Machines, Inc. Such a computer is used in on-line and real-time systems for the following applications.

a. Baggage-handling systems, by maintaining data on the destination of as many as 12,000 suitcases per hour in order to make sure that passengers and their luggage depart on the same flight
b. Teaching-machine systems, by providing computer-aided instruction and pupil profiles for teachers
c. Tracking systems, by supplying real-time display of information relative to airplane flights

These systems are utilizing a relatively inexpensive minicomputer to perform operations that were heretofore performed by large-scale expensive computer systems. These are but a few of the newer systems currently employing minicomputers. In short, this relatively new advance of minicomputers will undoubtedly become a very important and substantial element in succeeding years.

2. Small-Scale Computers. These include computers designed to perform unit-record functions in far less time and with greater accuracy than EAM equipment. IBM system 360/20, the IBM System/3 (Figure 8.15), NCR 50 and 100, Univac 9400, as examples, fall into this category. They utilize predominantly punched card input, and, although they have the capability of producing high-level output, they are basically used to produce printed output. The IBM System/3 uses a new 96-column card designed with 20 percent more capacity than

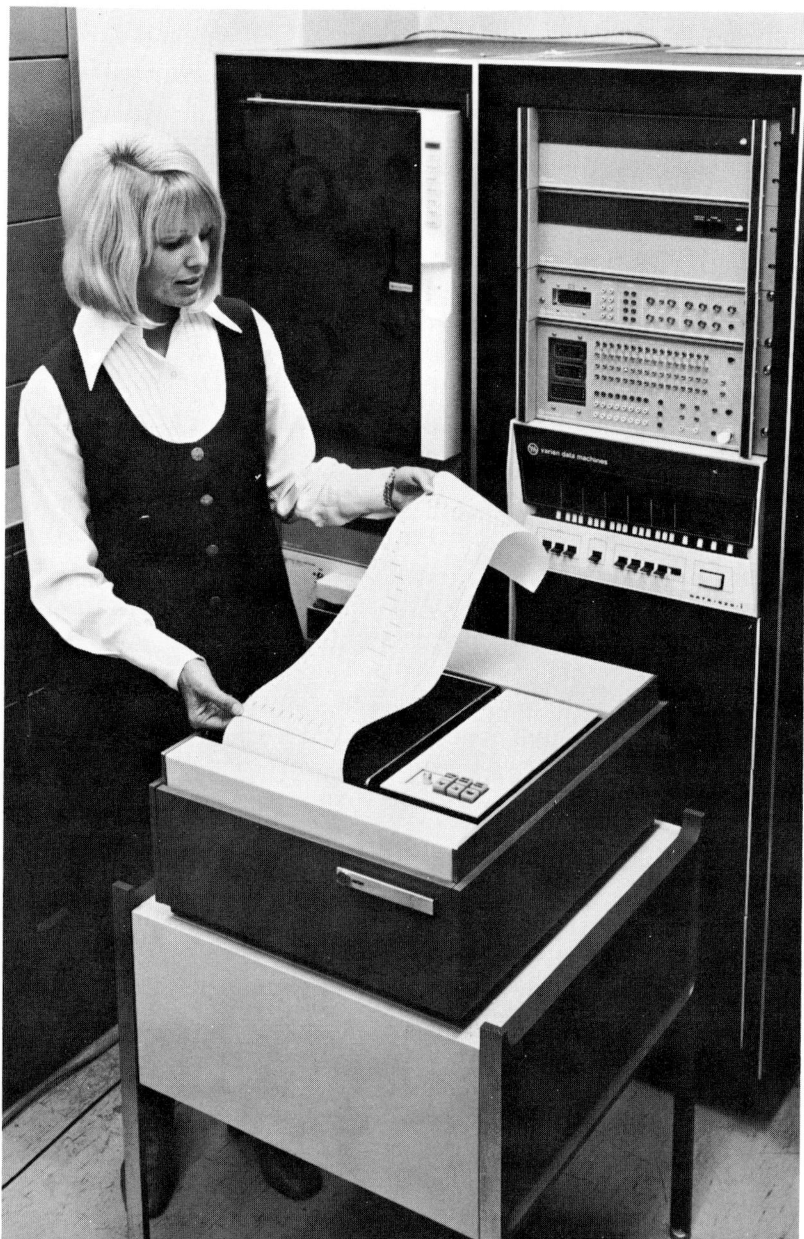

Figure 8.14 Varian 620/i minicomputer (courtesy Varian Data Machines, Inc.).

Figure 8.15 IBM System/3 (courtesy IBM).

the 80-column card.[1] The disadvantage of this card used in conjunction with the System/3 is that it cannot be used with other data processing equipment. Thus a company that rents such equipment and uses this card cannot use it with EAM devices or other computers that employ the standard 80-column card.

3. Medium-Scale Computers. The medium-scale computers are more widely used and more capable machines. These include the IBM S/360 models 30 and 40, IBM S/370 models 115 and 125, Burroughs 3500, 4500, and 5500 series, Xerox Sigma 5, and so on. These devices are most often employed at typical business organizations throughout the country. Their average rental is approximately $5,000 to $20,000 per month, and they are capable of high speed and complex operations. They can also use high-level I/O devices. They do, however, require

[1]See Chapter 5 for a discussion of the 96-column card.

some operator intervention, even though they utilize supervisors to handle many typical control procedures.

4. Large-Scale Computers. These are the really high-level machines that have storage capacities in the million-byte range and rent for about $100,000 per month. These usually contain full control systems with minimal operator intervention. They are capable of linking up with dozens of high-level I/O devices and performing operations at phenomenal rates. Such large-scale computers include the IBM S/360 model 195, IBM S/370 model 165, Burroughs 700, and others.

A word, now, is necessary about the IBM S/360 and S/370 series. You will note that model numbers range from model 20 to model 195 on the S/360, where higher model numbers mean greater capability and greater cost. The S/370 has similar series numbers. Most options on these machines have *upward compatibility*, which means that whatever can be performed on a lower-model machine can also be performed on a higher model. That is, any programs that are designed for the IBM S/360 model 30 can also be used on the 40 and all higher models. With this facility, IBM hopes to enable its users to acquire higher-level computers (higher models) without requiring a complex conversion process.

You will note that minicomputers or even medium-sized computers often work in conjunction with large-scale computers to alleviate the load of the latter. A Varian 620/i minicomputer, for example, is used in conjunction with an IBM 360/95 to provide world-wide weather information. The job of the Varian unit is to *edit* the stream of data being transmitted via satellite. Rather than expend unnecessary time of the big IBM computer, the data are fed into the Varian, which produces a magnetic tape containing only significant data. For a discussion of the diversified and rather interesting applications of computers see the workbook. Most business organizations use medium-sized commercial computers to perform daily processing.

The analyst is often called on to suggest the use of specific devices that will improve overall productivity in his company. Similarly, a system that he is designing might require the use of a specialized device.

In short, the systems analyst must always be aware of the state of the art. He must be able to make recommendations as to which devices would best serve the needs of his company.

The Appendix at the end of the text lists computer characteristics and costs for typical computer systems used in business.

GLOSSARY

Batch processing. The processing of data in groups or batches.

CIM equipment. Computer input microfilm devices that can read data from a high-speed microfilm device and transmit them to the computer.

COM equipment. Computer output microfilm devices that can produce microfilmed output from a computer system.

MICR equipment. Magnetic ink character recognition devices.

OCR equipment. Optical character recognition devices.

Off-line processing. Processing of data by devices that are not directly under the control of the central processing unit (CPU).

On-line processing. Processing of data as soon as they are generated.

Random processing. Processing of records in no specific sequence.

Sequential processing. Processing of records one at a time, in a particular sequence.

QUESTIONS

1. Prepare a list of questions you, as a systems analyst, would ask a manufacturer who wishes to supply your company with its data processing equipment.
2. Define and explain the basic types of computer processing.
3. When is it feasible for a company to utilize OCR or MICR equipment?
4. What organizations with which you are familiar utilize punched paper tape? What are the advantages and disadvantages of this medium?
5. For what types of applications is COM equipment best suited?
6. What are the major distinctions between on-line and off-line devices?

7. Prepare two hypothetical examples of the types of applications for which minicomputers are best suited.
8. How would you determine the availability of special-purpose minicomputers?
9. Prepare a list of variables that would help you determine whether your company should utilize minicomputers or small-scale computers for a particular application.
10. How important is it for a systems analyst to keep abreast of recent advances in computer hardware technology? Explain your answer.

CHAPTER **9**

DATA COMMUNICATIONS

The ultimate purpose of systems analysis and design is the creation of more efficient and effective systems. Computers can generally be used to enhance production within a system, since they greatly facilitate large-scale processing. The analyst, then, must have significant expertise in the data processing area so that he can recommend appropriate equipment for the new or revised system.

As stated previously, it is assumed that the student of systems analysis and design is familiar with basic computer methodology. This unit discusses advanced topics of computer methodology that, because of their complexity, are not usually covered in an introductory data processing course. These topics will, however, enhance the analyst's ability to more effectively employ computers in the design of specific systems.

This chapter considers data communications, a recent advance that enables a centrally located computer to be linked to remote terminals located at various points within an organization. (See Figure 9.1.)

SIGNIFICANCE OF DATA COMMUNICATIONS

We have seen that the major use of commercial computers is in the processing of vast amounts of data in relatively little time. Each new generation or model of computer has increased speed so that input data can be converted to output in even shorter time periods.

A major problem with the utilization of such equipment is not, however, the speed with which computers process data, but the time required to physically transport information into the computer room and to then transport the required output to the proper department or business area.

You will recall that there are several steps involved in obtaining required output from input. (See Figure 9.2.)

1. Incoming source documents must be transmitted from the user or requesting department to the control unit of a data

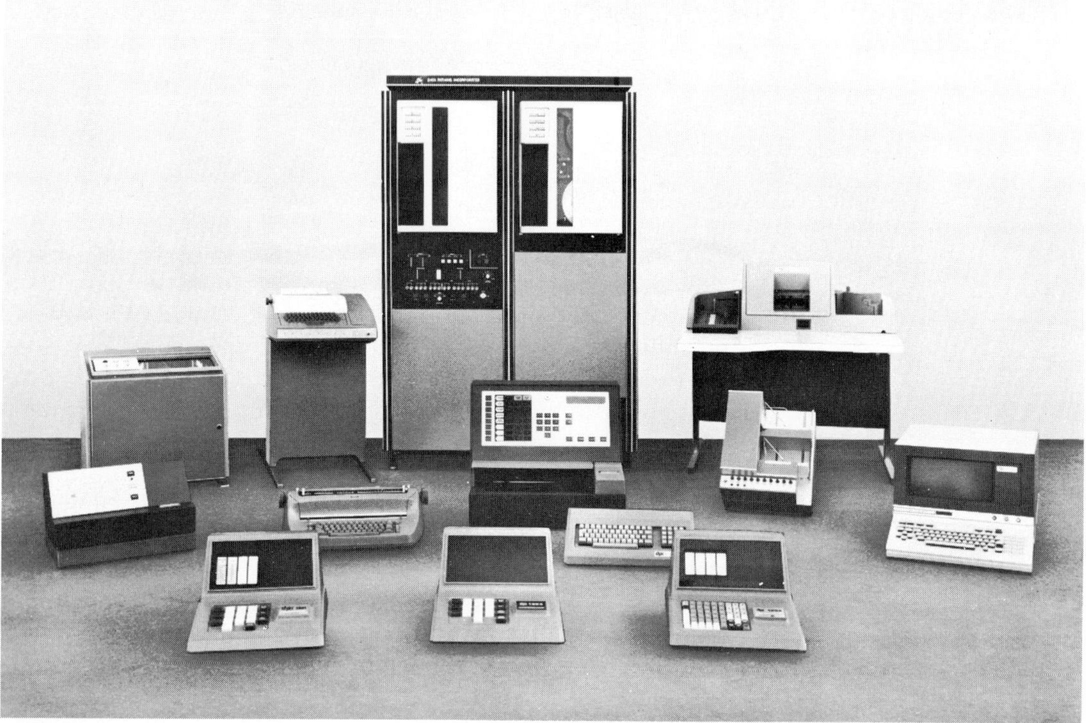

Figure 9.1 Terminal equipment (courtesy Data Pathing, Inc.).

processing installation. The control unit must check these documents to determine if they are complete and proper. A count is maintained to ensure that none are lost.

2. The source documents must generally be transmitted from the control unit to the operations staff for conversion to a machine-readable form such as cards, tape, or disk, unless the incoming documents are already in an appropriate form. If card processing is utilized, the deck often must be sorted, collated, reproduced, or in some other way operated upon by electronic accounting machine (EAM) equipment.
3. The source documents and their converted counterparts must again be sent to the control unit for tally checks to ensure that nothing has been lost.
4. The machine-readable input must then be sent to the computer room, where it often must wait hours or even days for processing because of unforeseen backlogs.
5. The output must be transmitted to the control unit for further checks.

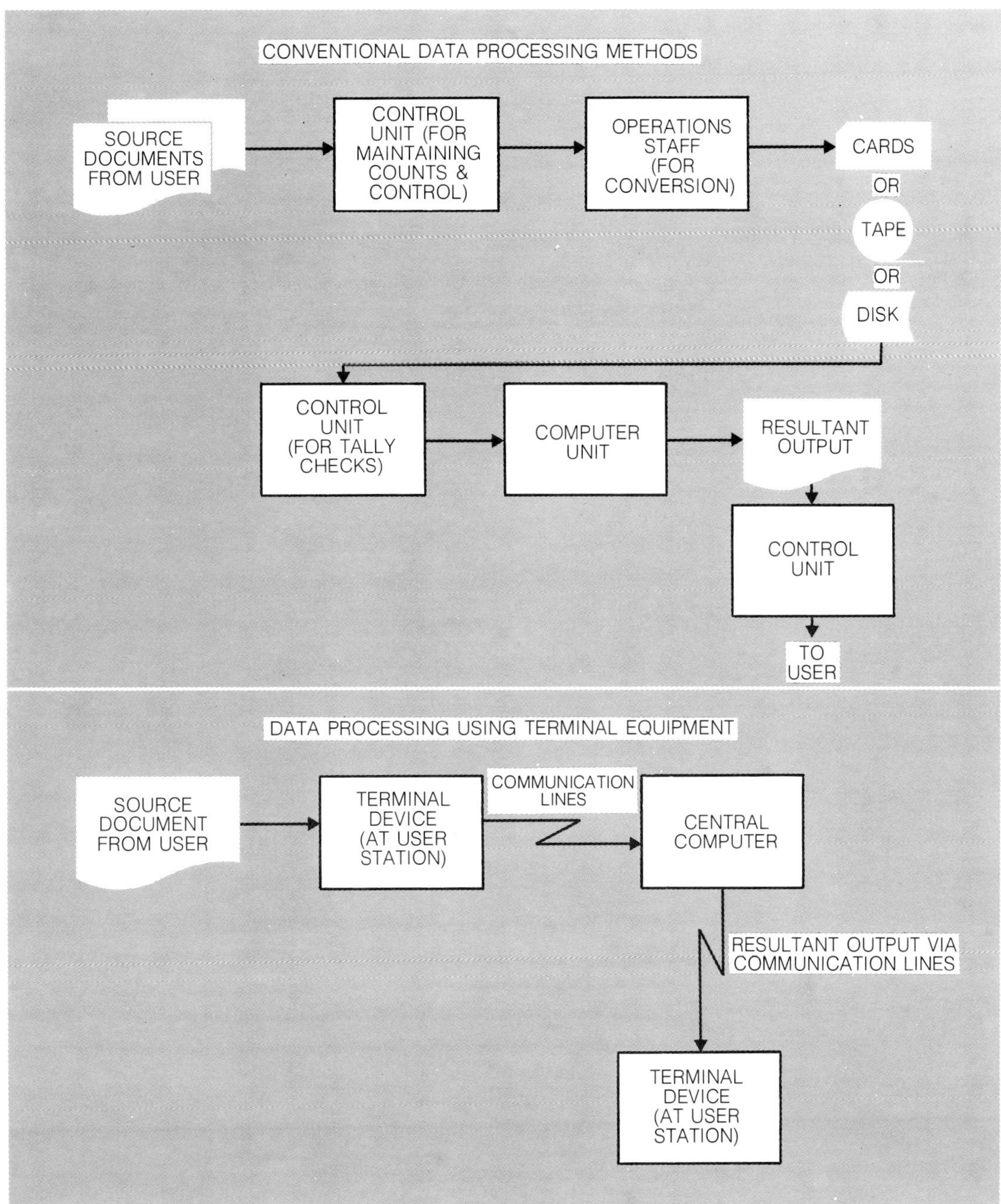

Figure 9.2 Comparison of conventional data processing methods with data processing methods using terminal equipment.

6. The output must then be sent to the user or requesting department.

Each of the above procedures relies, in large part, on *manual* operations or operators. The result can be lengthy delays or other inefficiencies. Thus, while it may require 30 minutes to operate on input and convert it to output in a computer run, it may take three or four days in total, including the transmittal of the input to the data processing center, conversion to a machine-acceptable form, and transmittal back again from the data processing center. If such input and output are transmitted via interoffice mail instead of by a special messenger, the total elapsed time may even be longer. In either case, high-speed computer processing must wait for conventional distribution methods for transmittal. Thus any systematic procedure that could reduce this elapsed time would greatly enhance the total effectiveness of computer processing.

We have thus far discussed devices that can effectively eliminate step no. 2 above, the conversion of source documents to a machine-readable form. These include magnetic ink character recognition (MICR) and optical character recognition (OCR) devices.

In this chapter we will discuss terminal equipment that:

1. Effectively eliminates the conversion of source documents to a machine-readable form.
2. Results in decreased manual intervention and thereby greatly enhances the speed with which output can be delivered to a requesting department or customer by employing on-line, or immediate, processing.

Data communications, sometimes called **teleprocessing**, is a relatively new area of data processing that facilitates the flow of data both into and out from a computer center. Input devices, called **remote terminals** are placed strategically throughout a company, often within the requesting departments themselves. These devices, using leased or public telephone lines, are linked with a central computer in a data processing center. They are called *remote* terminals since they do not appear in a data processing center side-by-side with a computer. Operators key data into the terminal, where it is automatically transmitted to the central computer. These operators need only be familiar with a typewriter keyboard in order to key in required information. This system reduces the need for the following:

1. A control unit to maintain constant checks on incoming data. Incoming data are automatically transmitted to the central computer, and thus information is not lost in transit. Similarly, data need not be manually checked for validity. The computer will automatically reject invalid information.
2. A keypunch or operations staff to convert incoming source documents to a machine-readable form. The terminal operators "feed" the data directly to the computer, thus eliminating the conversion process. In this way, purchase orders, payroll changes, customer inquiries, and so on may be keyed directly into a computer via a terminal.
3. Backlogging of computer runs, since the computer can be programmed to operate on data as they are entered, or by some established priority.
4. Messengers to physically transport input data from the requesting department to the data processing center and then to transport output data from the data processing center back to the department. The terminal is linked with the central computer thereby eliminating manual delivery. If the terminal can receive messages or accept output (some are strictly input devices), then again, manual intervention may be eliminated, since the computer can transmit the required output *directly* to the department via the terminal.

A central computer can have numerous terminals hooked up to it. These terminals may be utilized by separate *departments* employing a central computer, or by separate *companies* employing a central computer. These terminals may be located in the same building, to be used by various departments, or they may be spread out across the country if the user departments or businesses are not centrally located. (See Figure 9.3.)

Source data automation (SDA) is the term now used for data processing systems where the conversion of data to machine-readable form is performed at the point where it originates instead of at some centralized location. High-level SDA systems today usually involve several departments; thus top management must be cognizant of the options available so that major company-wide decisions may be reached that will gain cooperation from all or most departments.

The recent rise of terminals in businesses today signals a major advance in computer technology. With the use of terminals in business areas throughout companies, the gap between data processing personnel and businesspeople is

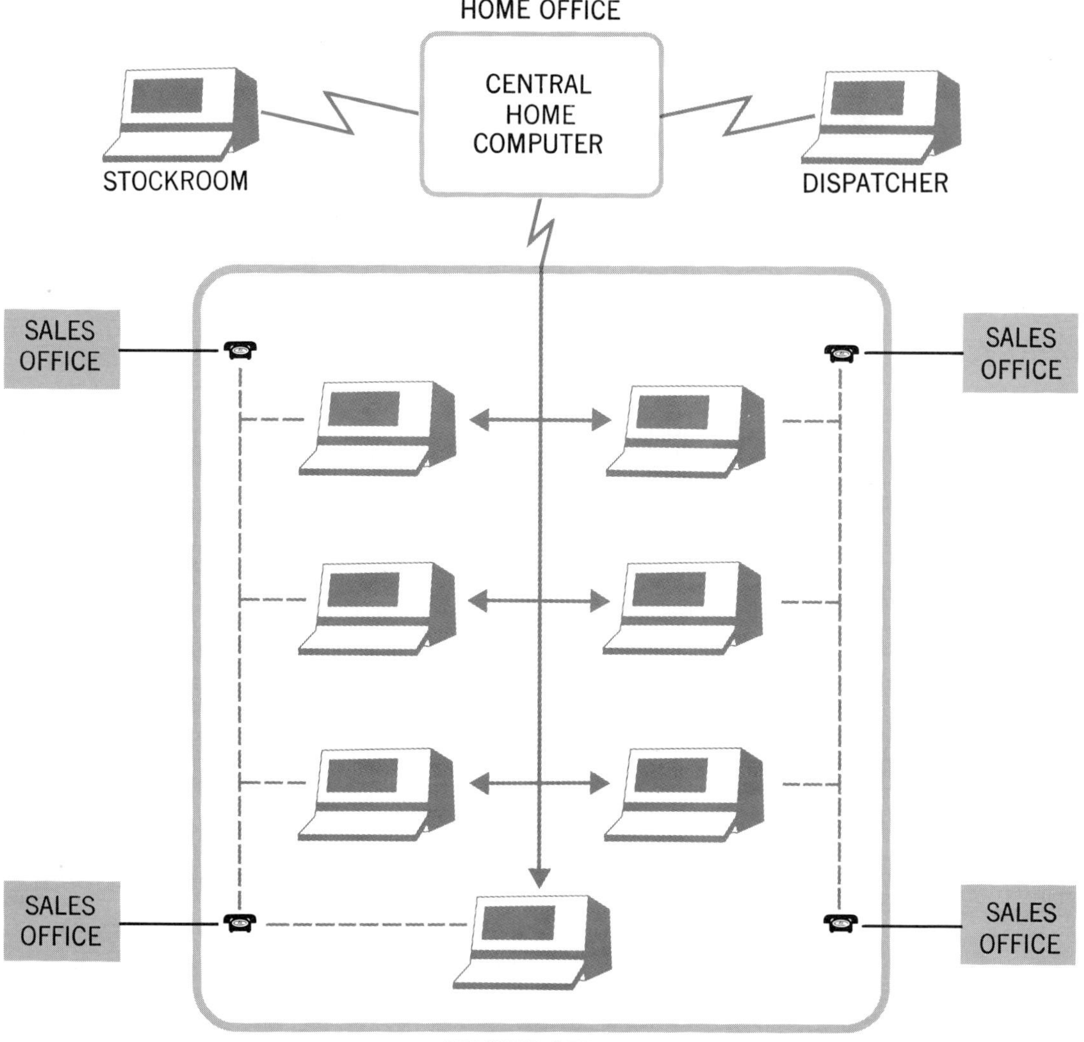

Figure 9.3 Terminals remotely linked to a central computer (courtesy UNIVAC).

greatly reduced. The *direct* transmittal of data from departments to the data processing center minimizes inefficiencies and communication errors. Thus it is imperative for systems analysts to be cognizant of how these devices can enhance operations within specific business areas.

This chapter will attempt to enlighten students of systems analysis as to the potential of terminals in business, and will indicate how to effectively utilize and understand terminal processing.

DATA COMMUNICATIONS CONCEPTS

There are four major areas in which terminal technology is most often employed. Let us discuss each in detail.

Remote Accumulation of Data

As we have noted, numerous terminals, spaced remotely in key locations, may have access to a central computer for the purpose of entering input. These terminals may be placed in different departments, such as payroll, accounts receivable, inventory, accounts payable, and so on. In this way, the accounts receivable department, for example, can enter billing data into the computer via its terminal and the payroll department can similarly enter salary changes via its terminal. Both departments, then, have direct access to one central computer that is capable of processing all the data.

Several terminals may also be used within a *single* department. Suppose, for example, that the inventory department has several warehouses throughout the United States. To computerize inventory procedures *without* the use of data communications, these warehouses would be required to prepare inventory statements and send them to the data processing center, where they would be verified and then converted to a machine-acceptable form, prior to computer processing. The transmittal of data would be performed manually and, therefore, could become very inefficient. With the use of data communications, however, remote terminals can be placed at each of these warehouses. The inventory data can then be transmitted speedily and *directly* to the computer via the terminal without conversion or rigid manual controls. The computer can then accumulate all warehouse data efficiently and effectively by minimizing manual intervention.

Figure 9.4 represents typical terminal usage for an inventory system with branch offices throughout the country. There may be two order points, as shown, or many more. A request for an item is made at an order point. If the item is available, the warehouse is notified, by computer, and the item is shipped. If the number of such items at the warehouse reaches a prescribed minimum number, then the manufacturing facility is notified, by computer, to produce more.

Thus terminals may be used in many different business areas for the remote accumulation of data. Let us consider how the computer can operate on this data.

On-line Processing. When input data are entered from a terminal for the purpose of *immediately* altering the contents of records on a file, an *on-line* operation is required. That is, the

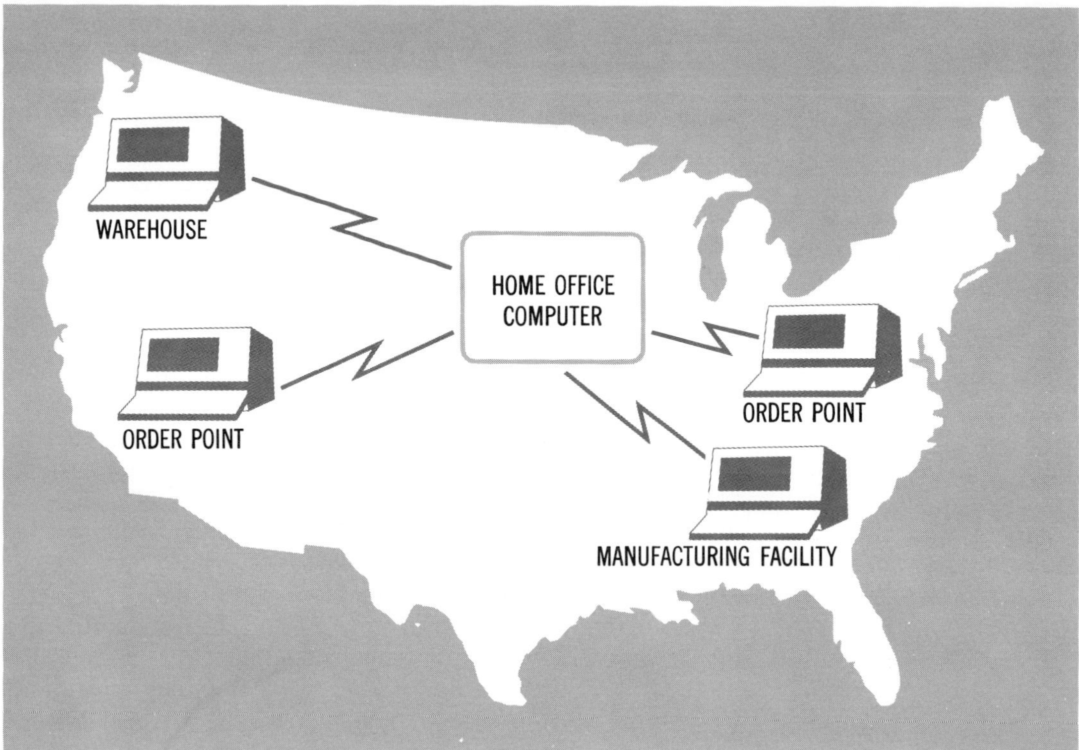

Figure 9.4 Use of data communications for an inventory system (courtesy UNIVAC).

computer processes the input data as they are entered and alters or *updates* the required files immediately. Terminals are utilized to enter data for on-line operations, since they provide immediate and direct input to the data processing flow, eliminating the need for manual transmittal. Magnetic disks are most often utilized for storing files when data are to be updated on-line, since they provide the ability to access records via terminals directly and, therefore, rapidly.

An inventory disk file, for example, may be altered or updated by an on-line operation at the precise time that changes in stock items are keyed into the computer via a terminal. In this way, all inventory data on the disk are current and may be used to answer inquiries or to produce printouts, with relative accuracy, at any time. Without the use of on-line processing, data files would only be current immediately after a periodic (weekly, semimonthly, monthly) update procedure. At all other times, these files would not contain changes that have occurred during the current period or cycle.

In short, where terminals are used for on-line operations, *immediate* updating of files is considered a necessity.

Off-line Processing. An analyst may design a system where terminals are used mainly to eliminate manual controls. That is, terminals are used where on-line or immediate computer processing is *not* required. In this case, terminal data to be entered into the computer can be initially *stored* until other terminal data are received. That is, terminal data are first converted to a separate medium such as punched cards, punched paper tape, magnetic tape, magnetic disk, in an *off-line* operation. When all such terminal data have been entered, the resultant medium (punched cards, punched paper tape, magnetic tape, or magnetic disk) is then used to transmit the data to the computer via communication lines in a *batch processing* mode. In this way, the computer can process the data more efficiently. Thus the terminal serves a twofold purpose:

1. It is used to enter source data, which are then converted to a medium that can be more quickly processed by the computer. This is performed *off-line*.
2. It is used to then transmit the data from this converted form to the computer in a batch processing mode, that is, when the data have been collected in a large quantity.

The terminal can contain a keyboard, for example, to enter the data, and a high-speed device, such as a punched paper tape drive or a magnetic tape drive, to store the data. The latter unit of the terminal is then used to transmit the data to the computer via telephone or teletypewriter lines.

A payroll system, for example, may utilize a terminal to:

1. Read payroll data from timecards and convert the information to a magnetic tape in an *off-line* operation.
2. Transmit the grouped payroll data from magnetic tape to the computer in a batch processing operation, from a remote location.

Figure 9.5 serves as a similar illustration of the utilization of terminals off-line.

In summary, when a terminal is used for converting data to a more efficient medium using specialized equipment *not directly under the control of the computer,* we call this an off-line operation. Off-line conversions and then the batch processing of data from high-speed devices can result in substantial savings of computer time, where on-line processing is not required.

Inquiry

A central computer with files of data stored on a medium such as a disk may be accessed by a terminal for the purpose of requesting information. That is, the terminal at a remote location is *not* used to update or alter a file, but to make inquiries concerning the data on that file.

Consider a terminal in the accounts receivable department of a large company. Because of the large clientele, it may not be feasible for the department itself to maintain, within its manual records, billing information on each of its customers. This information can be stored, instead, at a computer center on a magnetic disk. When a customer requests information pertaining to a bill, a terminal device linked to a central computer can extract the appropriate information. The terminal

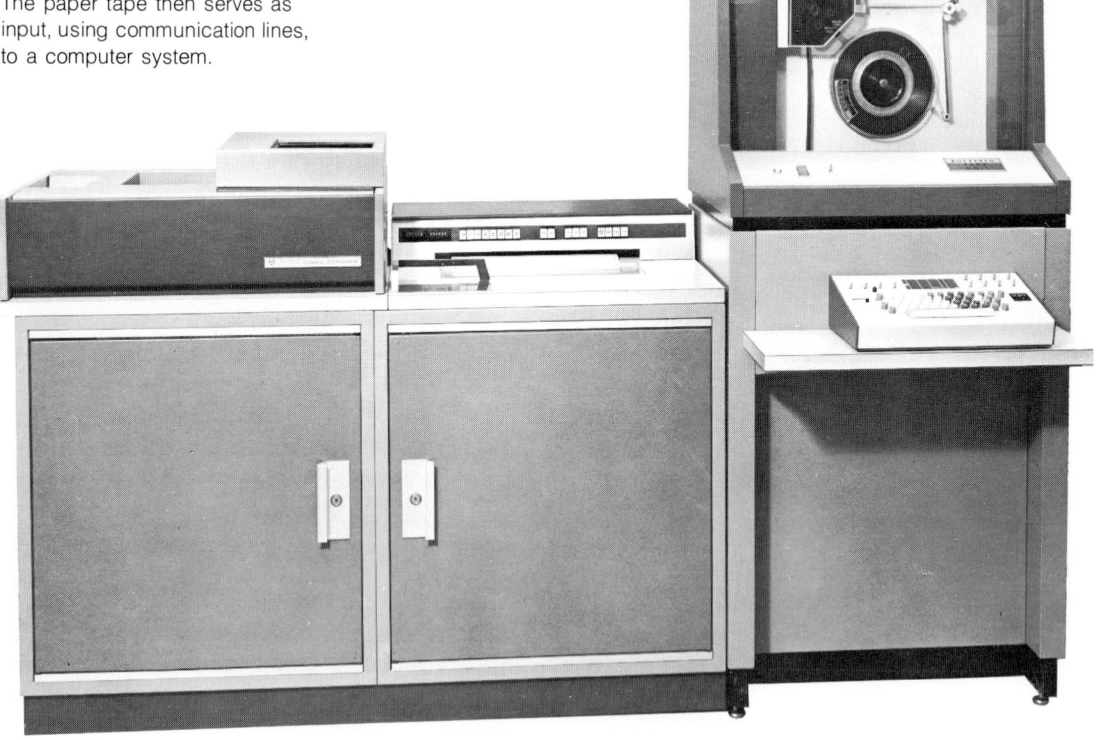

Figure 9.5 CODE (computer-oriented data entry) scanner (courtesy Addressograph Multigraph Corp.). This is a terminal device that reads data from embossed plastic cards utilizing an optical scanning unit and converts the data, off-line, to either a punched paper tape or a magnetic tape. The paper tape then serves as input, using communication lines, to a computer system.

must be capable of entering the request and also of receiving a reply. That is, the terminal must be an input/output device.

The terminal is a beneficial method of access or inquiry only when information must be extracted from a file *immediately*. When a request can be delayed, or answered at a later date, then the expense of utilizing terminals may be unjustified.

Usually *direct-access* files are used to store the data, since these increase access speed. In most cases the files themselves are updated *on-line*, since the inquiries require records with *current* information.

Various businesses find terminal devices for inquiry purposes a necessity. Brokerage firms, for example, rely on such devices for quoting stock prices to their customers. A direct-access file is maintained with stock prices. It is updated on-line as new prices become available.

This file is accessed by the stock broker via an input/output terminal at his desk. To obtain a price, he keys in the stock code; the computer receives this information immediately, accesses the price from the file, and transmits the data back to the terminal. In this way, any stock price can be quoted within seconds. The computer itself must be preprogrammed to accept any inquiry, seek the appropriate information, and transmit it to the user.

Terminals are generally used for inquiry purposes where:

1. Customers need immediate replies to inquiries.
2. Business representatives or managers need information for decision-making purposes.

Figure 9.6 illustrates the use of terminals for *both* the remote accumulation of data and for inquiries. The stockroom, for example, has a terminal for accumulation of data, while the executive offices use a terminal for inquiry on stock levels about which company-wide decisions are made. Chapter 10 discusses the recent advances in point-of-entry systems.

Real-time systems

A **real-time system** is one that has the capability of accessing and updating computer files using terminal equipment quickly enough to affect decision making. A typical example of such a system is an airline reservations system. This is a real-time application, where customers can request airline information and receive responses quickly enough to make a decision concerning the reservation of an airplane seat.

A customer can inquire about a specific flight or about

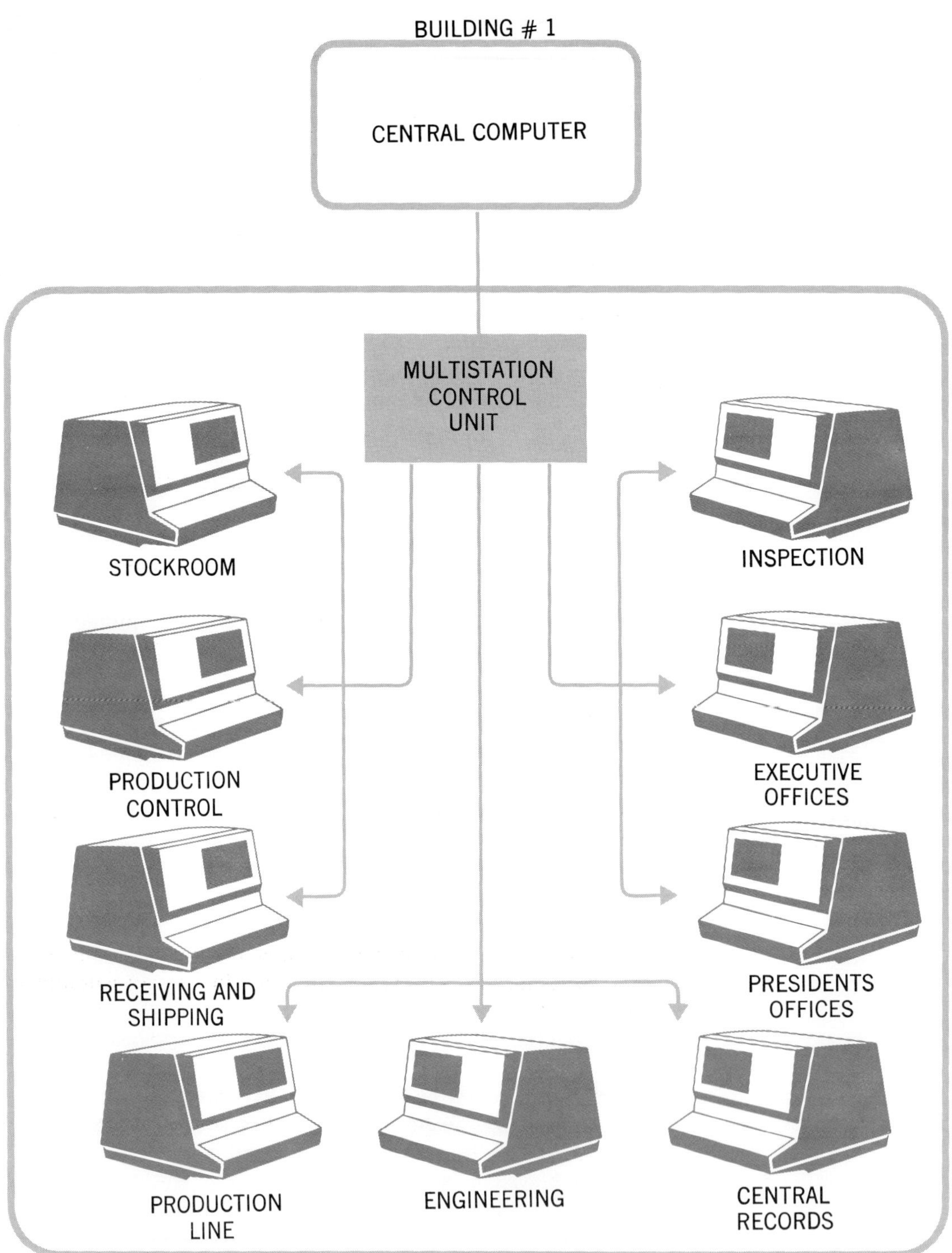

Figure 9.6 Use of terminals for inventory and sales systems (courtesy UNIVAC).

flights leaving for a specific location on a given day. The airline representative keys the inquiry into a terminal. The terminal is hooked up to a central computer, which immediately accesses the data and prints the requested information on the terminal (flight number, date of departure, time, destination, arrival time, number of seats available). If the customer wishes to make a reservation, the airline representative can enter the appropriate information into the terminal. The data will be used to immediately *update* the main file, which would then indicate one less space on the specific flight. Similarly, cancellations can be keyed into the terminal that would update the file so that it reflects one more space. These terminals may be placed in hundreds of airline offices throughout the country.

Thus real-time systems are *on-line* systems with the facility of *accessing and updating* files using terminal equipment, *quickly enough to affect decision making*. This type of processing is utilized by other reservations systems, such as hotels. Banks frequently use real-time systems to update accounts and to answer inquiries concerning specific transactions. Betting facilities use terminals in a real-time environment to key in betting statistics. The computer can then instantaneously print the existing odds.

Real-time systems may also be employed to process the internal operations of a company in an integrated manner. In this way, management can make quick and effective decisions based on inquiries made to the computer via terminal equipment. That is, profits and losses, assets and liabilities, profit ratios, and so on, may be maintained accurately and precisely through real-time processing, and may be accessed, at any time, by management for the purpose of making executive-level decisions.

Real-time systems utilize perhaps the most sophisticated programming and systems techniques in data processing today. They can generally be employed only in large-scale companies that can afford the vast equipment required. Real-time systems require large expenditures for sophisticated equipment and for enormous programming effort. Although they do not initially result in savings to a company because of their great expense, the intangible benefits (to the customers served, or to management, which can employ real-time systems for its decision making) can produce huge profits.

Time-Sharing

Small-scale companies often need data processing equipment but find the cost of acquisition and maintenance prohibitive. Such companies can rent or lease computer time from leasing firms that profit from buying a large-scale computer and then renting time on it. The small-scale organizations, in effect, *share* the computer's use. This concept is called **time-sharing**. Most often, time-sharing is achieved by the establishment of terminals at a specific location in each company that wants to share a computer's use. These terminals are often employed by the user to transmit a program, or set of instructions, followed by the corresponding input to be processed. Similarly, the user can transmit input data to be processed by a program that has already been stored in the computer.

Terminals may also be used for time-sharing where a large company has one central computer and permits user departments or branch offices to access it via terminals for the purpose of entering programs and/or data to be processed.

Note that in the previous three applications of terminal equipment, the terminal devices were used for input or input/output. The program to accept and transmit this data must be previously stored in the computer. That is, an airline reservations clerk who keys an inquiry into the computer will not receive a reply unless the computer has been programmed to accept the input. Similarly, the terminals at warehouses throughout the country may not be used to key in inventory information in an on-line environment unless the centralized computer has a stored program that instructs it to *accept* the data. With terminals used for time-sharing, however, these devices can be used to key in *programs* first. These programs are generally simplified, since the terminal, as a manual device, is not a very efficient method for entering large-scale programs. Most often, these programs are coded in BASIC, a programming language specifically suited for condensed or efficient coding. Once the program has been transmitted to the CPU via the terminal, any required data can then be entered.

An engineering company would find great benefit in using a central computer with terminals in various engineering offices for time-sharing. In this way, engineers with equations to solve can utilize a terminal in conjunction with a computer to obtain a solution. They are spared tedious hours solving mathematical problems that the computer can do accurately and efficiently in seconds. The engineers might, for example, write the equations in the BASIC language and obtain their answers, usually within seconds.

Time-sharing, using terminals linked to a central computer, has recently become highly effective in educational institutions for teaching programming. Some schools cannot justify the cost of a computer system. Many of these collectively lease centralized equipment, with terminals at each campus. The students then learn the BASIC language and can write simplified programs. They can then use the computer to solve required problems. Similarly, large schools with numerous campuses can employ a central computer with terminals at each campus hooked up to it, in a time-sharing environment. In this way, there is only one expense for the central computer.

From the above, we can see that data communications holds a key position in the present and future of computer technology. Its concepts may be used in high-level, expensive real-time systems or in small companies requiring minimum access to a computer. In short, where immediate communication with a computer is needed for (1) inquiry or (2) updating of files, or where (3) remote terminals can efficiently save manual intervention and extensive control of documents, or where (4) a central computer may be shared by several offices, data communications equipment is employed. (See Figure 9.7.)

EQUIPMENT

There are three major facets of a data communications system:

1. Terminal devices
2. Communication lines
3. Computer system

Terminal Devices

As we have indicated, terminal devices are located wherever large amounts of input data are anticipated. That is, it is important to space remote terminals at strategic points where the information flow is the greatest.

Terminals that we will be considering may be classified as:

1. Input to the computer (transmit only)
2. Output from the computer (receive only)
3. Sample combination input/output (transmit-only and receive-only units)

The vast majority of terminals in use today include both a receive-only unit (output terminal) and a transmit-only unit (input terminal). Terminals that can transmit only are rarely in use, since the computer usually needs some way to communicate with the terminal, even if only to provide error signals or wait impulses. The input or transmit-only terminals discussed

Order Processing and Inventory Control
A company may have a number of warehouse and distribution points. By tying each of these locations to a computer through a terminal, one can transmit orders daily to the computer for processing. Almost immediately, the computer will determine which items are to be shipped from each location, and transmit shipping data to the appropriate terminal. The terminal, in turn, will print bills-of-lading, invoices and up-dated inventory listings, and also punch summary cards.

Now one can recognize and correct problem areas much sooner than by any previous method; warehouse space and shipping expenses are significantly reduced; and one can quickly revise and more accurately forecast sales and market trends.

Payroll and Accounting
With a terminal, at all or selected key locations, daily transmission of local data on payroll, purchasing, billing, etc. can be processed at a central computer site the same day it is generated—no more misunderstandings or delays due to mailing, loss or damage. Weekly financial reports are now ready on Monday morning instead of Wednesday afternoon—in fact, daily reports are possible now.

Optimum Scheduling of production, manpower, equipment and maintenance, as well as the routing and delivery of products to and from many widely separated points.
Information Retrieval of personnel or student records, medical data on patients, high-volume statistical data, etc., in industrial organizations, school systems, hospitals, and other large or decentralized operations.

Programming from a location other than a computer site. Programs in Basic or other source languages can be written locally and quickly transmitted by a terminal to the central computer. Almost immediately the results are returned to the terminal, saving valuable time between need and the reponse.
Management Reports summarizing current status of both headquarter and outlying operations, including trend analysis and product trade information.

Plus . . .
Accounts receivable, accounts payable, credit ratings, market research, operations research, customer inquiries . . . or any application in which one would normally use a computer.

Figure 9.7 How terminal equipment may typically be used (courtesy UNIVAC).

below, then, are generally part of input/output terminals. The receive-only or output terminals, however, can be used independently.

Input Terminal Units. Transmit-only terminals are used to enter data from remote locations directly into a computer system. If a terminal were needed to enter data for an on-line or an off-line operation and no inquiries were necessary, then an input or transmit-only terminal could be used independently, although it rarely is employed as a stand-alone device. As indicated above, input units are used almost exclusively in conjunction with output (transmit-only) units as combination input/output terminals. The typical input units include:

1. Card Reader (where input is a punched card). Many payroll systems utilize card readers at remote locations where employees are given timecards with which to check in and out. These readers read the data punched into each employee's timecard.

2. Magnetic Tape Drive. When magnetic tape drive serves as an input unit of a terminal, the data recorded on the tape have usually been entered in some off-line operation. Such tape data may be on typical reels of tape, or cassettes or cartridges.

3. Optical Character Reader or Optical Scanner. Where documents such as invoices, purchase orders, and bills are entered as input in large volume, from various locations, optical scanners can serve as remote input terminals.

Optical scanners may be located, for example, at various points on each sales floor of a large department store for the purpose of transmitting sales information directly into the computer. In this way, the accounts receivable file can be maintained with greater accuracy and precision, so that customer inquiries may be answered based on the most current information. Similarly, management can make inquiries on sales patterns, at any given time, for decision-making purposes.

4. Paper Tape Reader. These are often used to enter cash register tapes or accounting machine tapes from remote locations.

Note that there are numerous other input terminals, but the above represent the most frequently used. Note also that these input terminals are sometimes used in off-line processing prior to entering the computer flow. That is, a card reader at a remote location may be linked, off-line, to a magnetic tape drive. In this way, card data are read by the reader and immediately placed on tape. The tape is then used, at a later date, as input to the computer, remotely, in a batch processing mode. Thus we may have terminal systems at remote locations with several devices that are integrated for off-line processing prior to transmitting data to a central computer.

Output Terminal Units. When remote locations require output from a computer with minimum delay and maximum efficiency, then an output terminal is most appropriate. Note, however, that strict output terminals may *not* be used at remote locations when operator communication with the CPU is required. That is, a receive-only or output terminal displays information and cannot transmit requests back to the CPU. There is often a need for receive-only terminals, but most receive-only units are used in conjunction with an input unit.

Frequently used output units include:

1. **Line Printer.** Suppose, for example, a large company has numerous branch offices throughout the United States. Payroll checks may be printed directly at these branch offices utilizing one central computer and a line printer at each branch office. In this way, duplicate files need not be maintained at the various locations, and only minimum control is required to see that checks are properly received.

2. **Card Punch.** Devices that punch output cards may also be used to transmit central information to various locations. See Figure 9.8 for an illustration of several of these devices in an integrated network.

3. **Paper tape punch.** The above three output units can operate as transmit-only output units if desired. The cathode ray tube, audio response unit, and graph plotter must be used in conjunction with an input device, and thus will not be discussed here.

Sample Combination Input/Output Terminals. For most on-line teleprocessing applications, where requests are keyed in at

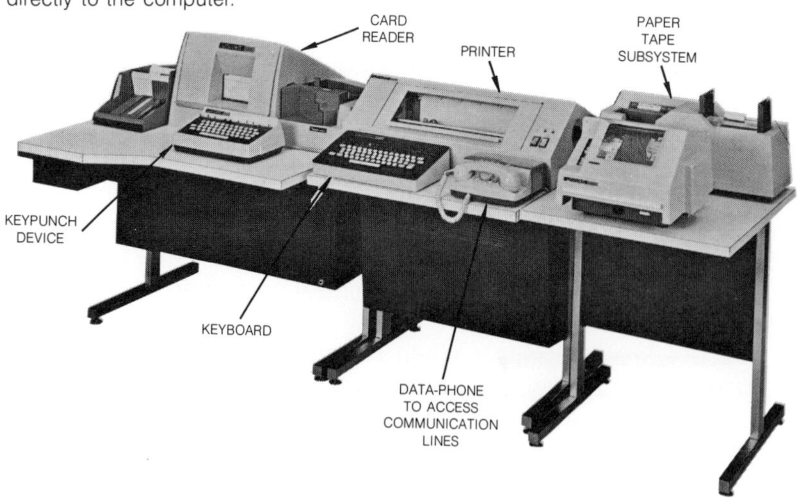

Figure 9.8 Integrated data communications terminal set-up (courtesy UNIVAC). It can be used to operate on-line or to batch process off-line prior to communication with the computer. That is, card data may be read by the card reader and converted, off-line, to a punched paper tape, or transmitted directly to the computer.

remote locations and the central computer transmits responses, input/output terminals are used. That is, most terminals have the capability of both transmitting to and receiving messages from a computer. Any combination input/output keyboard is available but the most commonly used I/O terminals include:

1. **Terminal Typewriter or Keyboard (Figure 9.9).** This is the most widely used input/output terminal. The device is not unlike a typewriter. When input is entered, an operator keys the data by depressing the various keys in much the same way as data are typed on a typewriter. Depending on the data to be processed at the specific terminal, the keyboard may be strictly numeric, strictly alphabetic, or standard alphanumeric, where all characters are included. There is a typed *hard-copy* printout of all data entered. A **hard-copy printout** is one that may be maintained for future reference, as opposed to data displayed on a screen, for example, which are not avail-

Figure 9.9 Keyboard terminal (courtesy IBM).

able after they are viewed. When the computer communicates with the operator, the typewriter is activated by the CPU, and the required information is printed on the typed sheet.

As indicated, this is the most widely used I/O terminal. Operators may key in as input, stock receipts, purchase orders, payroll changes, and so on. In addition, these operators can make requests of the computer via the terminal and receive immediate responses. (See Figure 9.10.)

2. Cathode Ray Tube with Keyboard or Light Pen (Figure 9.11). The keyboard is the standard input medium. An operator keys in data or makes inquiries using this typewriter-like unit.

The cathode ray tube (CRT) is a visual display device similar to a television screen. This output unit instantaneously displays data from the computer on the screen. This is a high-speed device, since data are *not* transmitted to a typed page using a relatively slow print device. Instead, large amounts of information can be displayed instantly.

As indicated, the keyboard is a standard *input* unit for the CRT. A light pen can also serve as an input tool, to be used for making graphic corrections or additions to the visual display on the cathode ray tube. An operator simply uses the pen to

Figure 9.10 Computer on wheels: a four-wheeled cart keeps up with quality at American Motors. A computer terminal on wheels is helping American Motors' production specialists assure the performance and safety of its cars. This IBM communications terminal, mounted on a four-wheeled cart and connected to an IBM computer by cable, lets an industrial engineer quickly spot any recurring problems on the AM assembly line. After singling out a car for computer review, the engineer uses his traveling computer terminal to tell a centrally located IBM computer everything that has been listed on the car's inspection log as it is indexed along the assembly line. Any recurring problems are quickly spotted, and immediate action is taken to alleviate the condition. (courtesy IBM)

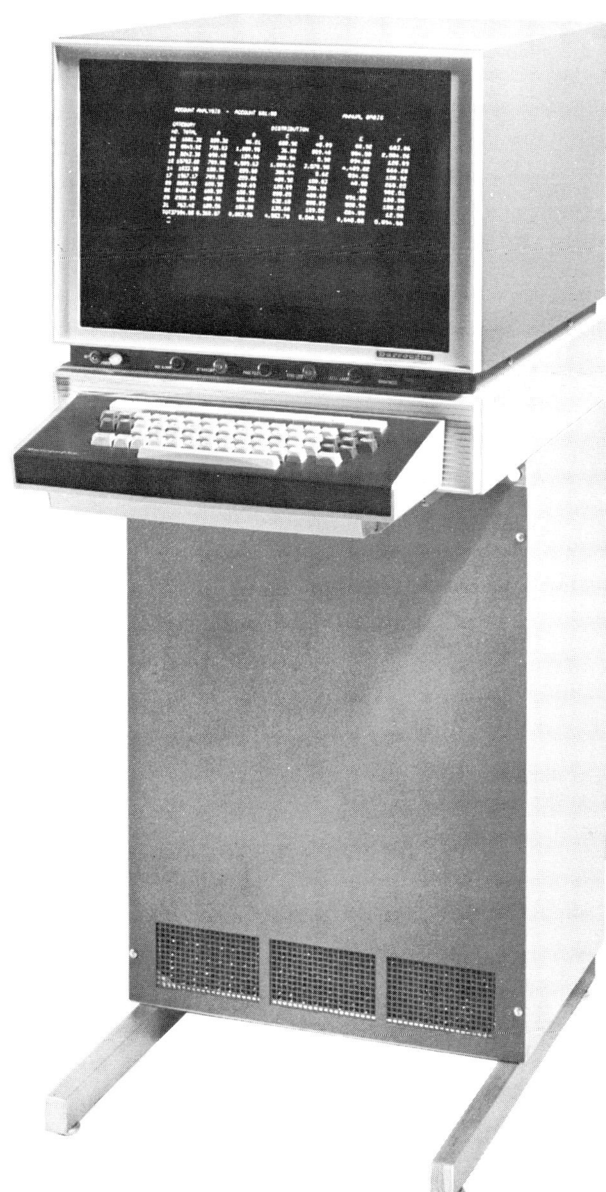

Figure 9.11 Cathode ray tube (CRT) with keyboard (courtesy Burroughs Corporation).

modify data on the screen. These modifications are then transmitted to the CPU. (See Figure 9.12.)

CRT devices are extremely beneficial where output from a computer is desired at remote locations very quickly. Airline

Figure 9.12 Cathode ray tube terminal with keyboard (courtesy IBM). The operator can make modifications to the displayed data using a light pen. Drawings, diagrams, charts, words, and numbers displayed on the screen can be modified by the user with an electronic light pen. When the "copy" button is pushed on the display copier, shown at left, a photocopy is produced in 15 to 38 seconds, depending upon the complexity of the image. That is, the display copier produces a hard-copy version of the visual display on the CRT.

terminals, for example, use cathode ray tubes to display flight information. Changes to the data displayed on the screen are instantaneously added. Similarly, stock brokerage firms use CRTs in conjunction with a keyboard for requesting the latest stock quotations. The computer responses are displayed on the screen. (See Figure 9.13.) Such CRT output provides **soft copy**, a visual display with no permanent record.

For high-speed output, CRT devices are extremely beneficial. They are, however, more costly than other terminals. If hard-copy versions of the output are necessary, then CRT devices must be equipped with additional features. (See Figure 9.12.) Costs of these CRTs range from a purchase price of approximately \$1,000 or a rental of \$50 per month to a purchase price of \$200,000 with no rental available.

3. Graph Plotter. A graph plotter is often used with a keyboard for input/output teleprocessing. The keyboard is used for making inquiries. The plotter produces an output graph that is transmitted from the CPU. This is a very useful terminal for management, to be used for decision making, and

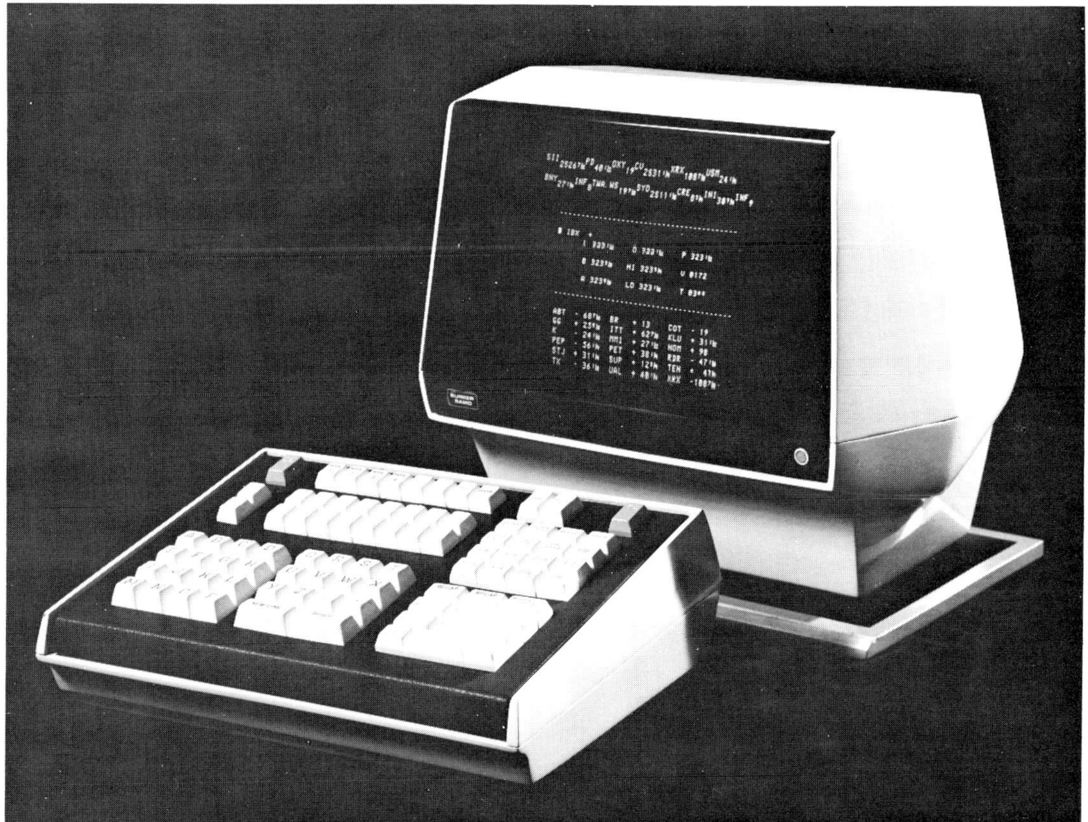

Figure 9.13 Bunker Ramo Market Decision System 7 provides brokers with simultaneous displays of data from three different sources, including tickers, newswires, computer and stock market data bases containing a variety of information on stocks, commodities, and averages. In addition, these units perform all the functions of a programmable computer terminal, enabling the user to perform trading computations, to transmit buy and sell orders, and to switch circuits at will to any of the many services to which the unit may be connected. (courtesy Bunker Ramo Corporation)

for engineers and mathematicians, who require charts and graphs that display specific activities.

4. Audio Response Device. The input unit may be a keyboard, where requests are typed. Or, the input unit may be telephone equipment, where the dialing of appropriate digits or codes or the depressing of keys with touchtone equipment, results in a computer inquiry. The computer-generated output or response is a verbal one instead of a printed one. The computer can be equipped with various prerecorded key phrases or words that are extracted, as required, for the purpose of answering a specific request, and are transmitted via an audio response unit.

Many banking establishments use telephone equipment as audio response units. A customer wishes to cash a check at a branch office. The touchtone digits are used to key in the customer's account number and the amount of the check. The computer then determines if the account has sufficient funds on hand. The appropriate response is then transmitted to the teller via the telephone (an audio response unit). The teller will then either cash the check or politely refuse, depending on the computer's response. (See Figure 9.14.)

5. Voice Input to Control Station (Figure 9.15). A recent advance in data communications is a speaker recognition system that currently utilizes a Varian minicomputer. The computer stores distinctive accoustical features of a person speaking his own name in its core memory. Companies or agencies requiring strict security systems or otherwise tightly selected admittance can use the minicomputer's memory to screen personnel or visitors. The comparison of the speaker's voice, transmitted via a telephone as an input terminal, takes only milliseconds

Figure 9.14 Audio response unit (courtesy Bell System Data Communications Service): (*a*) In addition to its primary use as a telephone, the Touch-Tone® telephone can also function as an efficient data input device. Today, business and professional people use Touch-Tone telephones to transmit billing information to a central billing and service organization to control inventories, purchasing, and shipping, and for a variety of other business activities. (*b*) Here, a bank teller uses a Touch-Tone telephone to call a distant computer and request the status of an account. After tapping out the account number and a code for the information she wants, the teller receives a voice response.

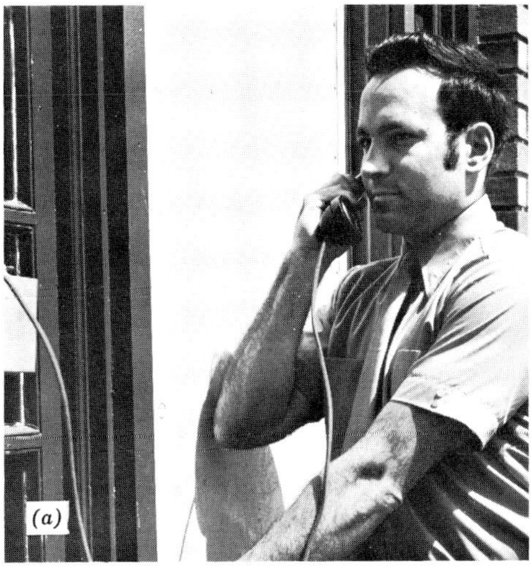

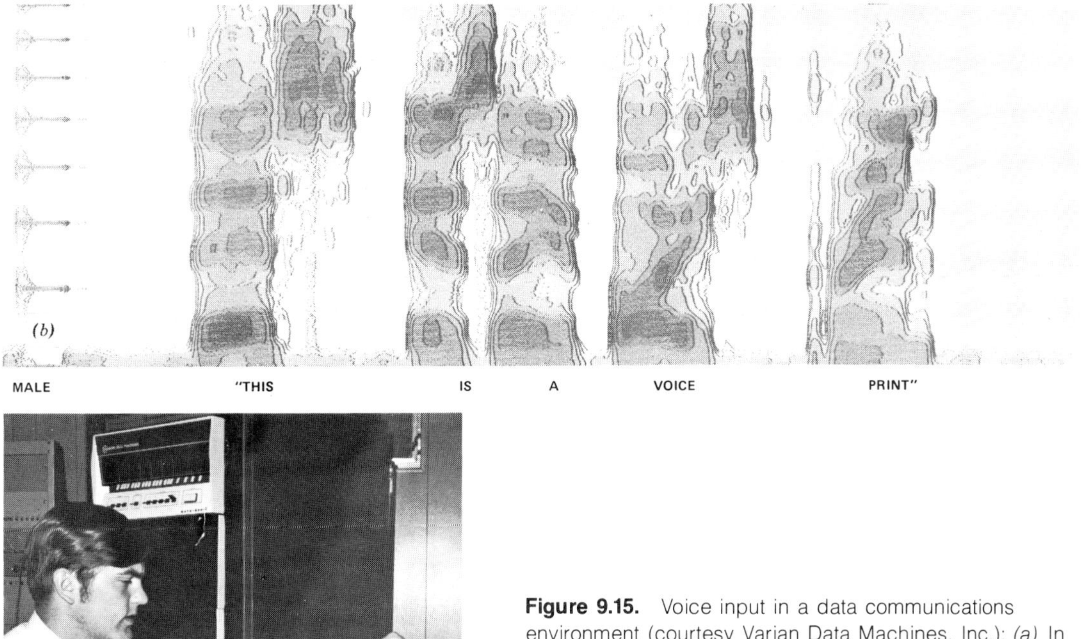

MALE "THIS IS A VOICE PRINT"

Figure 9.15. Voice input in a data communications environment (courtesy Varian Data Machines, Inc.): *(a)* In this three-photo sequence, a person requesting entrance into a secured area uses telephone portion of the speaker recognition system for voice input to control station. This could be the person's name or other code word or number. *(b)* A hard-copy version of a typical male print showing the acoustical energy concentrations called "formants." *(c)* A technician calls up the voiceprint from a Varian 620/i minicomputer's core memory, using Teletype for verification of the matched voiceprints.

after the person speaks. This data communications technique will eventually be used for credit card holder verification.

Selecting Terminal Equipment. The analyst must consider several factors in determining the most suitable terminal equipment for a given application. The following represents a partial list:

1. **Computer and Communication Lines (to be discussed in the next section).** The computer and the communication lines must be compatible with the terminals under consideration. You will see that some terminals require high-speed lines and highly complex computer equipment.

2. **Functions To Be Performed by the Terminal.** It is obviously inefficient to select an input/output terminal if a strict output one would serve the purpose. That is, an input/output device should only be selected if computer response to the remote station is a requirement or if the systems analyst thinks it may be a requirement in the future.

3. **Cost**

4. **Speed.** The speed of transmission will normally vary directly with the cost of the device. Slow-speed terminals transmit approximately 20 characters per second, while high-speed devices can transmit as many as several thousand characters per second. There are numerous speeds available between these limits. A device must be selected that is fast enough to serve the needs of the company within budgetary limitations.

5. **Human Adaptability.** In most cases, input to the terminal is provided by an operator who keys in the appropriate data. Unless the device selected is easy to operate, training time may be excessive. One reason for the popularity of the keyboard device is that it is very similar to a typewriter, and special training is therefore unnecessary. When establishing the type of data to be entered as input to the terminal, human adaptability must be considered. A **conversational code**, for example, is generally easier for an operator to transmit than, perhaps, a **digital code**. The former consists of words and phrases that are more meaningful to an operator than a series of digits. In most cases, there is less error when transmitting conversational codes.

6. **Sizes and Type of Display.** If the analyst determines that large amounts of data are required as ouput on a single printed line, then the size of the output display must be considered. That is, if 100 characters must be displayed on a single line, then the typewriter terminal is not appropriate, since generally a maximum of 72 characters can be displayed on that device. Since the various output units differ widely in their characteristics, we will not list them all. Notice, however, that size is a key factor when determining the terminal device to employ.

The type of output is generally classified as soft copy or hard copy. A hard copy is one that can be stored for future reference. A punched card and a printed sheet of paper are hard-copy items. Soft copy is output that can be seen or heard but that is not retained. Visual display units and audio response devices can produce soft copy, since the output can be indicated with no written copy maintained for reference. Soft copy is used when an operator is required to receive responses that are needed at very frequent intervals and for which no document need be kept. Stockbrokers, for example, who are required to quote prices very often need output that can be displayed or heard quickly and for which no future reference is needed. When a permanent document must be maintained, such as an airline or hotel reservation, then hard copy may be necessary instead of, or in addition to, soft copy.

Keep in mind that for most operations, several terminals are linked to the same central computer. Where many terminals make requests or inquiries during a single time interval, it is not always feasible for the computer to handle them all within a matter of seconds. That is, some terminals may be required to wait for the computer to complete other operations.

For some systems, a priority arrangement should be established. That is, if one terminal's requests or input messages are more important to the system than another, this terminal must have priority.

If no schedule or priority is deemed necessary, each terminal message is processed in the order in which it is received. In this case, all terminal operations are considered independent, with none being more important than any other, and thus they are processed in a "first come, first served" manner.

Note that large third-generation computer systems have the ability to process several problems at one time. Thus a computer can handle several terminal requests at the same time.

When too many terminals require the use of the computer at the same time, a queue or "waiting line" may develop. This is the case when the computer has reached its capacity and the succeeding messages must wait in line. If, after a system has been implemented, queues are frequent and extend over long intervals, systems work is often required to enhance the flow of data. The use of additional terminals, for example, may be a method for alleviating the problem, or more off-line processing may be required, or a greater-capacity and faster central computer may be necessary.

Some terminals, however, require **scheduling**, or the establishment of priorities. Suppose, for example, that data from terminal A is required before data from terminal B can be processed. This requires a master station to control the transmission of messages. This master station must *invite* appropriate remote terminals to send messages according to an established sequence. This operation is called **polling**. Where an inventory system, for example, requires data to be *transmitted* from various locations according to a specified sequence then polling is required. This can be handled by sophisticated programming techniques.

Where messages must be transmitted from the computer to a terminal according to a given schedule, a master station must again be utilized to invite a remote terminal to *receive* a message. This operation is called **addressing**. Where payroll offices, for example, are required to *receive* output checks from terminal devices according to a specified sequence, then addressing is required. Keep in mind that both polling and addressing are utilized only when terminals are required to either transmit or to receive according to an established priority.

Notice that there is additional programming effort required when terminals are employed. Programming packages or software support may be obtained from the major computer manufacturers or software houses. These packages can greatly facilitate the programmer's task. They can, for example, establish priorities and also provide for polling and addressing. Extensive programming effort can be saved with the use of this software.

Communication Lines

Most data communications systems utilize telephone or teletypewriter lines for the transmission of data. Teletypewriter lines are the least costly and the slowest. Voice-grade telephone lines may be used with high-speed terminal equipment, but they were not designed for the degree of noise-free transmission and reliability required. Thus, although these lines provide fast transmission, the error rate is frequently unacceptable. Leased private telephone lines, while generally expensive, eliminate noise and interference. These are, however, slower than voice-grade lines. All three facilities are in frequent use today.

Note that two or more terminals may be hooked up to a central computer by a single communication line, not unlike the old telephone party line. This is often done to save expense. This operation is called a **multidrop facility**. Its major advantage is monetary savings, and its major disadvantage is increased contention for the line. One terminal hooked up to a multidrop facility may, for example, tie up the line for an extended transmission. In such a case, the other terminals must wait in line.

In general, when selecting either teletypewriter lines, voice-grade telephone lines, or leased private telephone lines, the major considerations are cost, speed, and the degree of noisefree transmission that is deemed acceptable.

In addition to communication lines, **modems** are required for data communication systems. Since terminals transmit data in digital form and telephone lines transmit in another form (analog), a converter called a modem (*mo*dulator-*dem*odulator) is required. (See Figure 9.16.) The modulator is

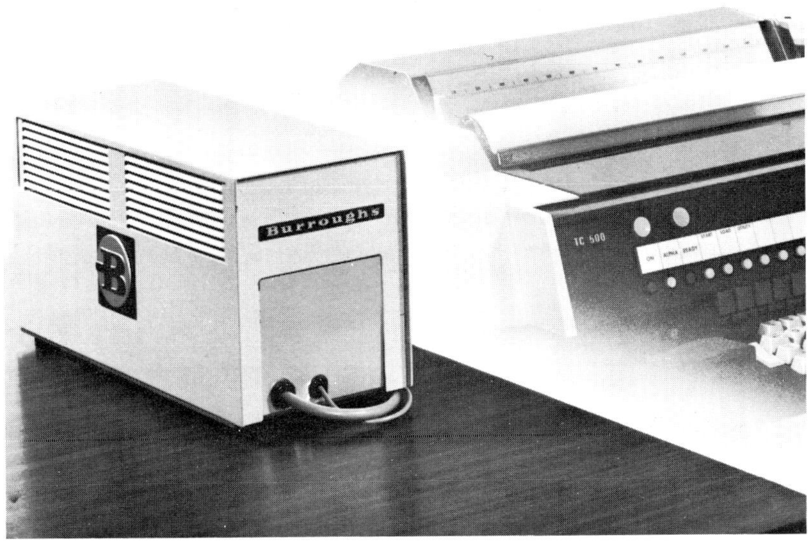

Figure 9.16 Modem (courtesy Burroughs Corporation).

that part of a modem that converts terminal data into a pattern that will be transmitted across the telephone lines, while the demodulator is that part of the modem that converts the telephone line's analog form back into digital form for transmission to a computer device.

Computer Requirements

A computer used in conjunction with teleprocessing equipment generally requires the following:

1. A large core storage capacity. This is necessary so that it can hold incoming and outgoing messages in case of busy lines. That is, when queues occur, the computer must possess enough *buffer* areas to store messages.
2. Complex control. A highly sophisticated control system is required to effectively process data with numerous entry points.
3. Interrupt ability. Because of priority schedules, the computer is often required to interrupt a given task so that it may execute a more urgent one. It must possess the ability to then complete the previous one. This condition is often compounded by several operations that may require the use of a given device at the same time. In such cases, the interrupts must proceed from job to job.
4. Multiprogramming facility. The ability to partition core storage so that several programs may be executed at the same time is called **multiprogramming**.

OTHER ELEMENTS OF DATA COMMUNICATIONS

Errors

The three common types of teleprocessing errors result from operator mistakes, malfunction of communication lines (noisy lines, external disturbances such as lightning, etc.), and malfunction of the terminal equipment itself. These three factors generally result in a fairly high error rate. It has been estimated that an average of one error in 10,000 characters can result from equipment malfunctions alone. This is a much higher error ratio than when other hardware devices are integrated in a computer system.

The most effective method for determining if an error has occurred is to have the computer read back or retransmit all messages that it receives. This, however, is time-consuming and, therefore, very expensive. For these reasons, it is often not done. Most errors can be prevented or checked by:

1. Using a start-of-message indicator and an end-of-message indicator. These indicators will be garbled if equipment failure has occurred. Thus they are effective to check against terminal and line malfunctions. In such cases, the computer would request retransmission.
2. Properly trained operators and the use of a conversational keying mode.
3. Automatic checking of data. This includes a *redundancy* check, similar to a parity or validity check, which is performed by the program to determine if the proper coding of data has been achieved.

Scheduling

The analyst who designs a data communications system must often establish priorities and must provide techniques for handling queues, when the computer is tied up, and busy signals, when the lines are functioning at capacity. Keep in mind that a company ultimately loses business if customers are made to wait for a response to an inquiry. Proper systems analysis eliminates extensive queues by providing the proper number of terminals at appropriate locations.

Security

It is generally necessary to protect a data communications system from unauthorized use. It is important, for example, to classify a payroll system that utilizes terminals so that only key personnel can access the files. Most employees would consider it a serious invasion of their privacy if any colleague could inquire about their salary history. If proper steps are not taken to prevent this occurrence, a company may find itself with an employee morale problem.

Passwords known only by a select few are sometimes required before a master file may be accessed. Where the terminals themselves are to be used by a select few, codes are sometimes required before the terminals can be employed.

Note that this chapter was designed to present the student of systems analysis with a fundamental introduction to the uses of data communications. Where an analyst is called on to create systems employing data communications equipment, a more extensive investigation with regard to the specific system would usually be required.

GLOSSARY

Addressing. Invitation rendered by the master station that permits remote stations to receive data from it.

Conversational code. A code of communication between a terminal user and a computer, composed of English-type phrases.

Data communications. A recent advance that enables a centrally located computer to be linked to remote terminals located at various points within an organization.

Digital code. A code of communication between a terminal user and a computer, composed of numbers.

Hard copy. A term used to denote computer outputs that are in a readable format and that can be stored or filed.

Modem. A device (modulator-demodulator) that converts terminal data into a form suitable for transmission and also converts data transmitted into a form suitable for a computer device.

Multidrop facility. Combined usage of one telephone line to service two or more terminals.

Multiprogramming. Ability of a computing system to process two or more programs at one time.

Polling. Invitation to remote terminal stations to transmit, to the master station, by the established sequence.

Real-time system. System that has the capability of accessing and updating computer files quickly enough to affect decision making.

Scheduling. Establishment of priorities within a data communications system.

Soft copy. A term used to denote those outputs, usually visual, that are not retained after usage.

Source data automation. Data processing system where the conversion of data to machine-readable form is performed at the point where data originate.

Teleprocessing. Transmission of data from a remote terminal, through some type of communication line or facility, to the main computing center.

Time-sharing. A system for supplying computer facilities to multiple users simultaneously and for providing rapid responses to each of the users.

QUESTIONS

1. What are the major advantages of data communications systems?
2. What type of communication lines may be used with data communications systems?
3. Prepare a list of questions you would need to ask if your assignment was to determine the feasibility of utilizing data communications equipment.
4. Describe the four major areas in which terminal technology is most often employed and provide examples, from your own experience, of how terminals are utilized in these applications.
5. What are the differences between real-time processing and on-line processing? What criteria would you use for determining the feasibility of an on-line system?
6. Prepare a list of questions you would ask terminal manufacturers in determining the type of equipment your company should lease.
7. What are the security problems most often encountered with data communications systems, and how are they generally handled?
8. What are the most frequent sources of error in data communications systems, and what are the techniques employed to minimize them?
9. What are the two ways in which the term "time-sharing" is most often used?
10. The use of data communications equipment often necessitates special features of the main computer. What are some of these requirements?

CHAPTER **10**

MANAGEMENT INFORMATION SYSTEMS

Thus far, we have centered our discussions about the analysis and design of individual systems that satisfy the specific informational requirements of one department. An accounts payable system provides information specifically prepared for the accounts payable department. If departments were treated as independent entities and not as integrated parts of the whole, a most unfavorable situation would result, where all systems were highly specialized and noninteracting. We could agree that each individual system was functioning properly and providing management with meaningful data. However, the interrelation of separate and individual systems would be virtually nonexistent. This condition would eventually result in an excessive duplication of effort and undoubtedly in increased operating costs. The situation would be akin to "the right hand's not knowing what the left hand is doing."

The development of a **management information system (MIS)** is a solution to the above problem. The MIS concept was developed within the computer industry and designed to provide management with a totally integrated computer system. This all-encompassing system would provide management with all of the data required for its decision-making processes, enable improved control over each of the individual systems, and permit efficient interaction among these systems.

The MIS concept is applicable to any type, size, or form of business. In the majority of instances, the MIS concept is applied to companies that are experiencing continued growth or radical increases in the informational demands on their computer systems. Because of expansion, greater quantities of work are placed on the company's computer center and related systems. As each of the component systems becomes overtaxed, the necessity and rationale for redesign become more evident. To redesign a company's internal business system with no thought of interrelating the informational resources of each of these systems would be highly inefficient and eventually prove very costly. Management information systems strive to eliminate a piecemeal effort and effect a totally integrated system.

BASIC CONCEPT

The concept on which a management information system is developed is the total integration of all systems utilized within a company. That is, each system should interrelate, with the capability of data being transferred between all systems. The result of compiling data is an output that will enable management to effectively control and administer company policy. This concept may become clearer after considering an example.

EXAMPLE. A retailing company has contained within its operation the business systems depicted in Figure 10.1. Each system is functionally independent and has the following objectives:

1. *Accounts receivable.* To maintain a status on all customer charge accounts, credit limits, and time payments.
2. *Payroll.* To prepare and issue a weekly payroll and to maintain a status on all pay records.
3. *Personnel.* To document, administer, and effect all changes within the personnel records.
4. *Inventory.* To update, correct, and purchase items to keep satisfactory inventory stock levels.
5. *Sales.* To project sales forecasts and to maintain an accounting of daily sales figures.

Each system operates with its own resources. Data are available from one system to another only in the form of output. Inputs for each system are established with only the respective system considered. Little or no thought is given to the requirements of other systems, even if they are directly affected. The resultant effects are, for example:

Figure 10.1 Business elements within a retailing company.

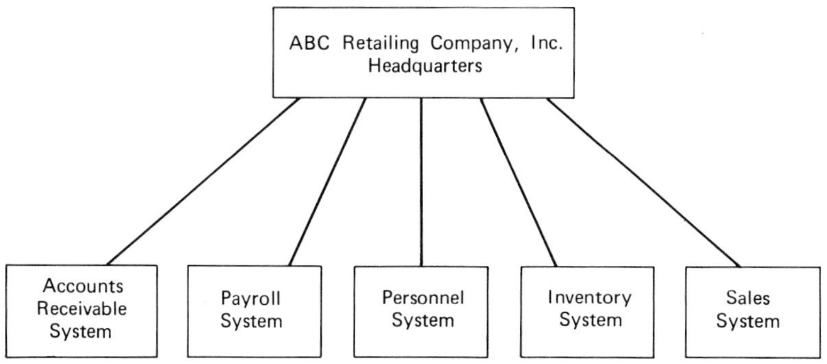

1. The payroll system must create its own personnel file—a duplicate of the existing personnel file.
2. The inventory system must generate its own sales records to monitor changes within company inventory and to issue purchase orders to replenish stock.
3. The accounts receivable system reflects only charges to customers and no changes in stock levels or sales levels.

These are a few of the shortcomings that evolved as the company grew. Here, systems that were effective when the company was smaller, and communications easier, became unwieldy. The volume of data handled, frequency of usage, and processing time required made the systems unworkable.

Of equal importance, though, is management's inability to render policy decisions using the data available. Management could not answer, with the data on hand, the following questions:

1. Does the company have and project a favorable cash flow?
2. Do our cash and accounts receivable positions necessitate a change in our credit limits?
3. Do sales projections and market forecasts require purchases of stock today?
4. Which new lines and what stock levels should be maintained, or which old items should be dropped for optimum profits?

The existing systems cannot provide sufficient data for management. As greater demands are placed on them, they will operate more inefficiently and eventually prove unprofitable for the company.

Let us now take the same systems and reestablish their operating parameters. Each system must interrelate with all others. A vast, common storage base is established to maintain data related to all systems. Thus the systems may be depicted as functioning in the manner shown in Figure 10.2. This diagram provides an overview of the system relationships.

Within this overall system framework, all smaller systems become subsystems and interrelate with the *total system,* or total company. This interrelationship, through a common data base, is exemplified by the following aspects:

1. The personnel and payroll systems use the same personnel file.

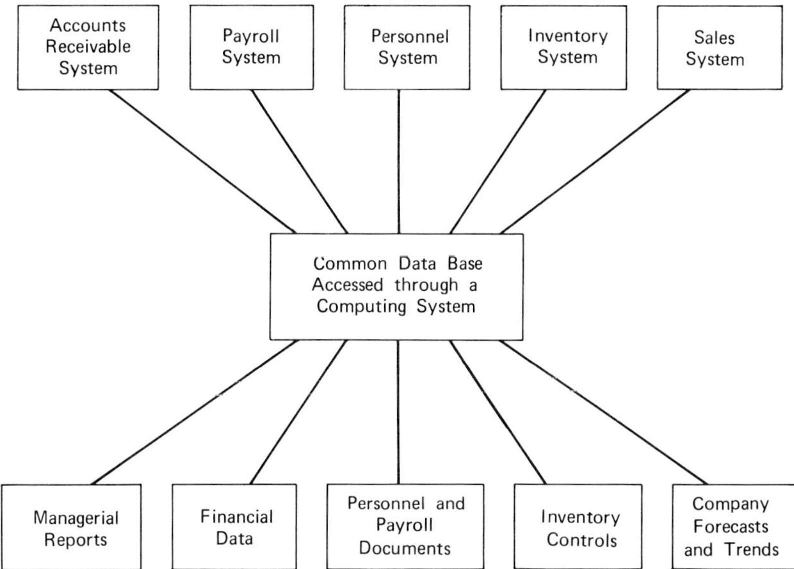

Figure 10.2 Relationships among systems in a company.

2. All sales, cash or credit, utilize the same format. Any sale or transaction will generate an update in the inventory, sales, payroll (commission), and possibly, the accounts receivable systems.
3. Money received through cash sales, customer credit payments, or credit returns will effect a change in the cash flow status and other management-type reports.
4. Purchase requests will be generated when (a) an inventory level falls below a prescribed level, (b) through attrition, the predefined economic order time period has elapsed, or (c) a sales projection indicates that a significant market trend is forthcoming.
5. Individual managerial reports can reflect information from several different departments. That is, a report may indicate *total company assets* by compiling data from many departments.

This example illustrates the purpose of an MIS concept. That is, to totally relate the functional aspects of all subsystems and to provide management with meaningful data on which decisions may be based. Because fewer repetitive, detailed tasks are required, managerial personnel are freer to exercise decision-making powers, to provide more attentive supervision, and to assimilate greater quantities of data.

COMMON CHARACTERISTICS

Although the detailed purpose of a management information system may vary, each system will have certain characteristics in common. These features result from a desire to reduce duplication, to improve data communication, and to speed the processing of data. The following characteristics may be considered:

1. Common Data Base. Instead of each separate system having its own specialized data file or group of files, all of the subsystems within a management information system will access data from the same vast **data base**. This data base will contain data required by each of the individual subsystems. Employing this manner of storage, the savings to the entire system is considerable. For example:

a. Separate data files do not have to be created and duplicated, thereby eliminating the redundancy evident when duplicate files are created for individual subsystems.

b. File maintenance is more readily performed, since the data base is updated in one pass. Here, cost is decreased when a saving in machine time is realized. Also, fewer programs have to be written, freeing the programmers and analysts for other tasks.

c. The space required for storing data is reduced. Since data are available at one central area, the total cost of the system can be reduced accordingly.

d. The data available for decision-making purposes are uniformly current, since most of the data are updated at the same time. Overall, management has more efficient, up-to-date information to work with and employ when formulating decisions.

2. Systems Integration. The interrelation of subsystems will improve the overall efficiency of the system, as subsystems will rely on each other for data and will share items of data. The data produced by one system could be accessed by another subsystem or become input to another system's processing. For example, the output of an inventory control system might be information relating to items with quantity-on-hand levels that have fallen below a specific number. These data, output from the inventory control system, would be input to the purchasing system and trigger the production of a series of purchase orders for those specific inventory parts.

3. Real-Time Capability. An MIS system is an on-line system and must have the capability of updating its data files on an immediate basis. Moreover, the MIS system must make data immediately available to management for its decision-making function. Consider a stock brokerage firm attempting to transact business on the stock exchange with quotes on stocks that are, at best, a few hours old, when all other brokerage houses have the most current information. The former brokerage firm could not remain competitive and would soon be in financial straits.

4. Data Communications. In an effort to process data more rapidly, data communications equipment will be used. Data gathered at a remote installation normally require shipment to the company's main computer center for processing. Thus a delay in processing results. Data communications devices using telephone lines, for example, can transmit data instantaneously to the main computer center. Thus a considerable saving in time is gained. The company can process the data sooner and make them available to management more rapidly. Chapter 9 reviewed many of the data communications devices currently available.

5. Vast Central Processing Unit. To adequately process the quantity of data under discussion, a CPU of considerable size is required. A large supervisor is necessary for (a) control of the many facets of the system, (b) multiprocessing facility, (c) accepting data from terminal equipment, and (d) multiprogramming functions. When considering a CPU, a unit with a capacity of at least one hundred thousand bytes is required.

6. Time. When considering an MIS project, an allotment for time is imperative. A project to implement a system of such magnitude involves an elapsed time of more than two years. The majority of the time is expended in designing the systems interface, that is, the specific interrelation of each subsystem and its joint relationship to the whole system.

7. Cost. The cost of a management information system is quite extensive. Because of the number of people required (analysts, programmers, etc.), the computing equipment necessary, and the time involved, these projects are not undertaken by every company. The expense involved may run into the millions of dollars. This is generally a limiting factor. In the light of economic conditions, most companies must have adequate capital to embark on a venture of this size. Thus there must be a real need for such a system.

Let us examine two cases where the justification for an MIS and its related costs were quite diverse.

EXAMPLE. A nation-wide railway company recently instituted an MIS system. The system is designed to control and maintain the status on all freight and cargo moved through its nation-wide railway system. The high cost of the MIS system was justified by citing improved control over shipments, reduced losses in cargo, reapportionments in manpower usage, improved rail schedules, increases in revenues resulting from improved and faster deliveries. Here, the management of the rail company justified the costs by citing future advantages. They reasoned that, for economic reasons, they would eventually have to embark on a similar course of action. The company's present financial status was strong, and the cost of a project could be adequately handled at this time. The management felt they were dealing from a position of strength and were in control of the situation. It was wiser, they reasoned, to bear the cost of such a system in a period of economic strength rather than one of economic decline.

EXAMPLE. In the late 1960s, the stock market in New York City experienced a potentially serious phenomenon—a majority of the brokerage houses found that they were incapable of handling the volume of paperwork being created by the increased daily sales volume. In effect, these brokerage houses were literally being choked by their paperwork. It became evident to the leaders on Wall Street that, if they did not implement some form of MIS system that was capable of handling the current and future sales volume, serious financial losses would be incurred. The choice of alternatives was quite clear. A project to computerize all of the Wall Street brokerage houses was undertaken immediately. The major portion of the project, designed to relieve the backlog of in-house paperwork, was completed in less than two years.

In this example, alternatives to an MIS system were nonexistent. The existing and future financial circumstances virtually dictated the implementation of a management information system. Only an MIS system could have provided the management of the brokerage houses with:

1. The total volume of sales for the day.
2. A breakdown of the sales by common stocks, bonds, commodities, etc.

3. An instantaneous update of customer accounts, so that customers' invoices could be sent out the next day. This feature of the system is vital, since stock transactions must be completed within five working days.
4. The maintaining of a status on all customer accounts that are open and those that have not paid for stocks, bonds, etc., bought.
5. The daily issuance of checks to accounts that have sold stocks and are awaiting their money.
6. A breakdown of the day's cash flow.
7. The monitoring of the activities of the various stock exchanges and the capability to provide the prices of all stocks that are trading as well as a history of each stock's performance. These data would be available via CRT-like terminals.
8. The ability to provide a current status and history of any customer account.

All of the above features require a vast quantity of data, as well as the ability to instantaneously process the millions of transactions that occur each day. An MIS system is perfectly suited for this type of activity.

DESIGN ALTERNATIVES

In the design of the complete management information system, two alternative techniques are available to the systems staff. Each represents a markedly different approach. The alternative methods are:

1. Total system development
2. Subsystem development

Total systems development requires that the entire system be developed before the system is made operational. This essentially means that all interfaces are developed "en masse," with the design effort lasting years. There is virtually no design effort required after the system is "on-the-air."

The advantage associated with this effort is that when this system is operational, all facets of the system are functional. The disadvantages, though, are the extreme cost and the elapsed time required before completion. Although the design effort is continuing, the system is not accruing any savings.

Subsystem development is the design approach preferred by most analysts. This approach selects one subsystem as the lead design element. It is completely developed, and all subsequent subsystems are interfaced with it. One could consider it the prototype of the system.

The advantage of this alternative is that, in a short time period, a portion of the system is operating and effecting some savings. This approach is easier to sell to management because they can readily observe some type of effective design and monetary savings. Problem areas are encountered on a gradual basis. The drawback lies in the fact that the system is undergoing continuing change. This continual change creates some difficulty within the area of documentation.

RETAIL MIS

Let us examine an illustration of a management information system that could be applied to a retail establishment. This example should assist the student in conceptually understanding the vastness, complexity, and scope of an MIS system.

Requirements of the System

Prior to our discussion of the MIS system, we should develop a sense of the type of information required by a retail operation. Suppose that you were the president of a retail store; what data items might you require for effective decision making?

Let us consider the following information that the president of a retail store might require at the completion of a day's operation.

1. Total volume of sales
2. Total cash sales
3. Total value of charge sales
4. Breakdown of refunds, returns, etc.
5. Net change in the value of inventory
6. Net change in cash flow

All of the data in the above list are of a summary nature and would normally take a considerable length of time and effort to prepare. Considering the average retail outlet, what is the probability of having the above information available one half-hour after the closing of the store? Obviously, the compilation of such data would be impossible without the assistance of a computer. Moreover, the computer system employed must contain a closely integrated group of subsystems and data files. Here is a case where a management information system is a logical solution to these problems and the only system capable of providing the required information. We will discuss some major points of a retail management information system, then introduce an existing retail system—the NCR 280 Retail System.

Hypothetical System

If we examine our original list of data desired by the company president, we can note that all of that information is somehow related to the sale of merchandise. Likewise, the majority of information entering the system is generated by sales. It seems logical to have some form of computerized method of entering data at the point where the sale is transacted. Employing a form of computerized data entry will reduce the possibility that incorrect data will be input to the computer and will improve the quality and reliability of the data that the system will employ in preparing its outputs for management. The operational solution applied to the retail system would be to computerize the cash register. That is, alter the cash register so that it could be employed as a traditional cash register and also function as a data entry station for the store's computer system. Thus, as a sales transaction is completed, the data relating to that transaction are fed directly to the computer.

A system that collects its data in this fashion is referred to as a **point-of-sale (POS) system**, since data are collected at the point where the sale is completed. The specially designed cash registers are called point-of-sale retail terminals, an example of which is shown in Figure 10.3.

The point-of-sale terminal is essential to the success of any retail MIS system, as it is an integral part of the system. Let us discuss how the POS terminal is employed and the resultant effect upon the system.

The retail terminal will record all sales, cash or charge. Data relating to either type of sale will be transmitted, via the retail terminal, directly to the computer system. Let us initially turn our attention to handling a cash transaction.

The cash purchase of an item is the simplest form of transaction. The customer pays cash and receives the goods. In addition, a sales slip is produced by the retail terminal. Data relating to the sale of each item purchased are instantaneously relayed to the computer in an on-line system. Recorded via the terminal are the following items of data: cost of item purchased, the number of items bought, the inventory number of that item, style number, today's date, the number of the retail terminal completing the sale, sales taxes, and total cost of the sale. All of the data will be transmitted directly to the system's data base and posted against the appropriate file records.

Figure 10.3 Point-of-sale terminal (courtesy National Cash Register). This terminal serves as a data entry terminal for the system, as well as a cash register for the sales clerk.

For example, the number of items on inventory (of the item purchased) will be reduced by the number of units sold. The inventory number and quantity of items bought were required for this update. Likewise, the sales tax, cost of the item, and total sales price will be posted against the daily sales records. These data will be employed at the end of the day to compile daily sales summaries for that register and for the entire store.

The above sales data will be recorded for each sale, whether it is a charge or cash transaction. Prior to processing of a charge sale, however, an additional step is involved. A check on the customer's credit and charge account must be performed before the transaction is entered. The customer's charge account number is input to the system, using the retail terminal. The computer will access the customer's record, examine the account, and determine the status of the account. The status of the account may be either satisfactory or suspended because of nonpayment or because the customer's charge has exceeded an approved credit limit. In either case, the account status will be transmitted to the sales clerk at the counter, via the terminal. If the account is suspended, the charge transaction will not be accepted and the sales clerk will seek assistance from the floor manager. A valid account status will cause the transaction to be completed automatically. All of the information relating to that charge will be posted against the appropriate records, in a manner similar to that of a cash sale. The customer's charge account will also be updated. The status of that charge account will reveal a new charge balance, an update on the credit available to the customer, and a record of the items purchased.

The updating of the company's inventory records occurs in a somewhat similar manner. After a sale (cash or charge), the records relating to the item sold are accessed and updated. The number of items sold is subtracted from the quantity on hand. Note that if this number falls below a predetermined level, the system will automatically produce a purchase order to buy more of that item. This action would also involve data drawn from the various vendor records, which would be part of the system's data base.

The massive data base required for a retail MIS system would contain data relating to all of the store's activities. The list that follows includes the major files that would compose a retail data base:

1. Customer charge accounts
2. Credit information for customer and vendor
3. Inventory levels for all goods
4. Purchasing statistics and statuses
5. Vendor files
6. Forecasting/marketing data

As noted, the majority of data would be entered via the retail terminal. However, some of the above data do not originate at the sales counter (e.g., customer refunds or returns, posting new items into inventory, credit checks made by phone from the sales floor). For these types of inquiries, online terminal devices capable of searching the files would be employed. Each of these terminal devices would have an interactive capability and could access all information contained within the system. These terminals would be distributed throughout the company.

The MIS system, in addition to supporting all of this online activity, must be capable of supporting all forms of normal DP operations. The system must handle all personnel actions, process a payroll for all employees, print checks for vendors, provide inventory listings, support marketing surveys, print all of the mailing labels required for sales surveys and advertising, customer statements, etc. Obviously, the scope, type and nature of processing required of the system we have discussed is only possible with a management information system. Only an MIS system would be capable of providing the president of a retail company with the information contained on our original list of data. Figure 10.4 is a flowchart of the retail MIS system we have discussed.

NCR 280 Retail System

We have discussed a hypothetical retail MIS system. Let us now review an actual retail system that could operate as a retail MIS system. The system in question is the National Cash Register 280 Retail System. A portion of the overall operation of this system is depicted in Figure 10.5.

The NCR 280 Retail System employs the point-of-sale retail terminal to record sales transactions for the system. The retail terminals in the 280 system are equipped with a special data entry feature—a magnetic wand reader.

The wand reader has a magnetic tip that can read data off the specially prepared magnetic tags attached to every sales item in the store. The special tag contains data about the item (unit cost, stock number, color, type of style, store location, etc.). These data are read by the wand and transmitted directly to the computer's data files. The data are employed to update inventory and sales records. The use of the wand reader eliminates the necessity of having the sales clerk key information into the system and thereby improves the quality of data by reducing error.

Charge sales are handled at the retail terminal also. A credit check on the customer's account may be performed at the terminal. The terminal will receive the numbers of the credit card and transmit them to the credit accounts file. After accessing the individual customer account, the state of the account will be indicated at the retail terminal. If the account is valid, the wand is passed over the sales tag and the transaction is completed. Similarly, if a bad credit rating is indicated, the sales transaction could not be entered and processed. Customer returns and refunds would not be handled at the sales counter. This type of transaction would be processed at a separate counter, via a different form of on-line terminal tied directly into the system. All changes in customer accounts would be facilitated through this terminal. The terminal used to process customer inquiries would not need to be a point-of-sale retail terminal. It should be a visual display terminal for ease of reading. This terminal's primary purpose is accessing customer information, not collecting money. As such, an

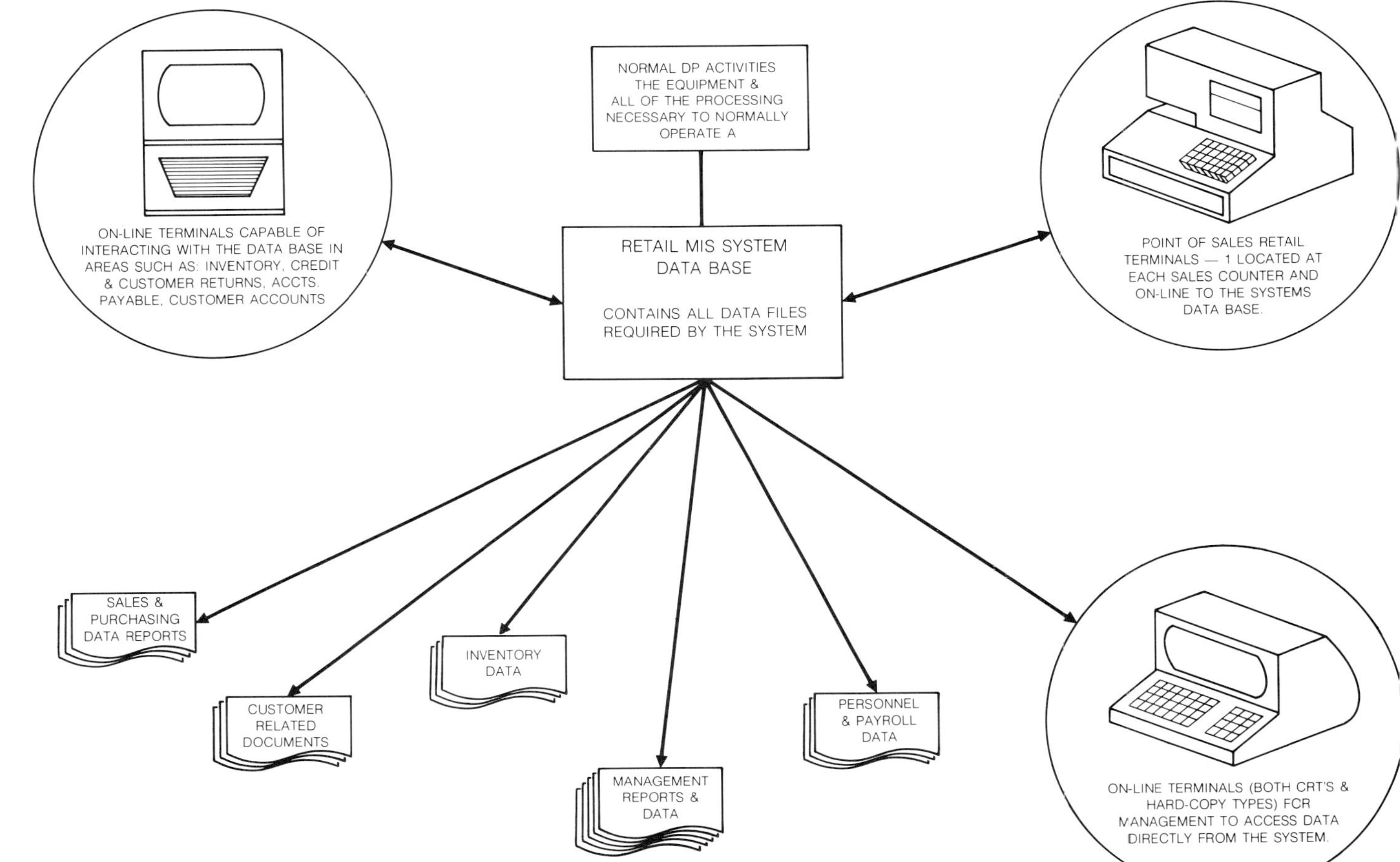

Figure 10.4 Some of the activities that can occur within a retail management information system.

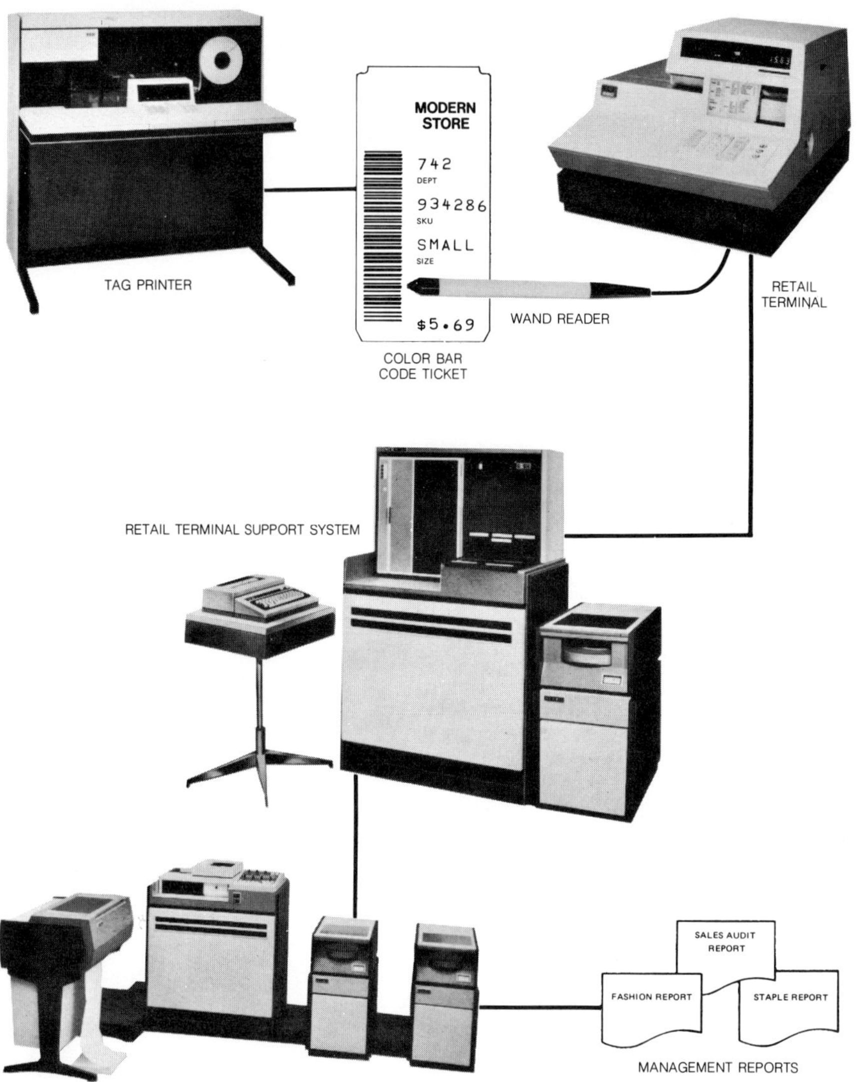

Figure 10.5 NCR 280 Retail System (courtesy National Cash Register).

on-line terminal capable of interacting with the computer system would be sufficient.

As you may surmise, the retail system is designed to provide real-time support for the sales clerk and make possible the instantaneous entry of data from the sales counter. We must not overlook the capabilities of the 280 system to process information in conventional DP terms. The 280 system is capable of operating in a batch processing environment.

For example, additions and deletions to inventory would be processed daily in one group or batch. Checks to vendors would be produced biweekly, in one group. Personnel action forms, noting changes in addresses, names, dependents, etc., would be batched and processed once a month (quite often this approach to processing is chosen because of economic alternatives). A company may elect to support selected DP activities on a real-time basis, and relegate all other processing to a batch processing mode. In this instance, real-time support was applied to the collection of sales data, where the company felt it would be beneficial and economically justifiable.

The NCR 280 Retail System can perform all of the other data processing activities required by the retail company. As a result, for example, payroll and personnel files are updated regularly; payroll checks are processed on schedule (weekly, semimonthly, or monthly); refund checks are regularly issued to customers; vendors are paid on a biweekly basis for services and goods delivered; the normal batching of managerial reports and listings occurs on a weekly or monthly basis; and all of the sales-oriented reports and inventory reports are processed without any complications. In essence, the 280 system is capable of handling any form of processing required—both of an on-line and batch processing nature.

LIMITATIONS OF MIS

Management information systems have extensive potential and capability for the decision- and policy-makers in a large company. Note, however, that not all MIS projects undertaken have met with success.

Some of the reasons for failure of MIS projects to provide management with the type of information it requires follow.

1. The task of planning, designing, and implementing an information system to be used by management was left to the computer specialist, a technician often not skilled in the area of management and thus poorly equipped to guess at the requirements of such a system.

As one expert states:[1]

> Many companies rushed to obtain the new generation computer equipment, justifying the cost with vague notions of the potential services it would provide. How much of this was a result of effec-

[1] "Why Management Information Systems Fail," by John R. Gale, *Financial Executive*, August 1968.

tive computer selling, the data processing manager's enthusiasm, or management's pride in having the biggest and the newest, could easily be the subject of many books. Computer hardware and software expenditures mounted, and companies suddenly discovered that they had large investments in equipment whose overall use had never been defined. They had a horse, but no wagon for it to pull. They had complex, costly, and sophisticated data processing equipment, but no idea of how to use its data output.

Management then asked: How can we use this equipment? Answers to this question had to revolve around the computer, and a computer-oriented management information system developed. This approach usually allowed the computer technicians to set the goals for the information system. The technicians' goals, however, were frequently geared to maximum computer operating efficiency rather than to the usefulness of its output. Since computers are very efficient by human standards—particularly in terms of the speed with which they can manipulate data—the effort would have been better spent by restricting information input and output to that necessary to manage the business.

More appropriate questions would have been: What information do we require to control and manage our business, and what is the most economical way of getting it? To answer these questions, the users' information needs must be determined, evaluated, and if feasible, used as the objectives of the system. Only after determining users' needs should the company consider what sort of computer equipment to procure.

2. The task of planning, designing, and implementing this vast and complex system was often underestimated. Management was often inaccurately briefed as to the time and cost estimates of such a system by computer specialists who were very enthusiastic to undertake such a project.

Here, again, management has not been properly trained to make evaluations on data processing functions:

> Because of the difficulties encountered during implementation phases, few management information systems are now functioning as originally conceived. This results from failure to realize that the systems are complex and require the same—if not more—top-management involvement as any other major company effort.[2]

3. It was difficult to establish priorities so that the most critical departments' executives, who are the prime users of the system, obtain information first. With a priority schedule, critical factors can be decided upon by the major departments.

[2]*Ibid.*

Unfortunately, when priorities are to be established, power politics becomes a major factor. Thus it is often the most powerful executive, and not the prime user, who has the priorities within the system.

> The successful management information system has a clearly defined set of priorities and related implementation objectives. For example, a company operating in a highly competitive low-margin consumer market should give top priority to elements of marketing and distribution information, with production and financial information to follow.[3]

4. Company personnel have often been inadequately trained as to the nature and purpose of the system. Thus personnel are too eager to satisfy their own immediate needs, often sacrificing the total company's requirements.

In short:

> A management information system should be a continually changing and evolving activity as long as the company exists. To compete in today's market place, a company must have available information for planning, decision, and control. The company that obtains effective data upon which to base decisions, at a reasonable cost, will be better able to compete and improve profits.[4]

TYPICAL COMPANIES USING MIS[5]

Westinghouse Electric Corporation

Westinghouse chose to implement a management information system in a middle-management area that dealt with large amounts of data and required judgment and computation in decision making. This area is monthly sales forecasting and production scheduling for one of their major appliance products—the laundry division. In the Westinghouse application, for example, all parameters of the problem are initially presented to the manager in the form of a light-pen menu. By pointing the light pen at the information on a cathode ray tube, the manager can choose the information content and form he wants displayed. The display data can be manipulated by light pen and keyboard, and in this way, the manager conveniently moves back and forth within the data base, ask-

[3]*Ibid.*
[4]*Ibid.*
[5]Information in this section is supplied through the courtesy of Information Displays, Inc.

ing, "What if?" and making decisions. Although the data are computer-generated, they are presented in a form with which the manager is intimately familiar. He need not learn a new language in order to communicate with the computer. And the response from the computer is fast enough so that he does not forget the original "What if?" question.

The market managers can access any report. The user selects information desired with a light pen by pointing to the appropriate places on the cathode ray tube and indicating (1) whether he wants the plot to be compensated for seasonal variation, (4) the month and year over which he wants to start the plot, and (5) the month and year over which he wants to end the plot.

This results in a plot like that shown in Figure 10.6, which includes both numeric and graphic data describing the condi-

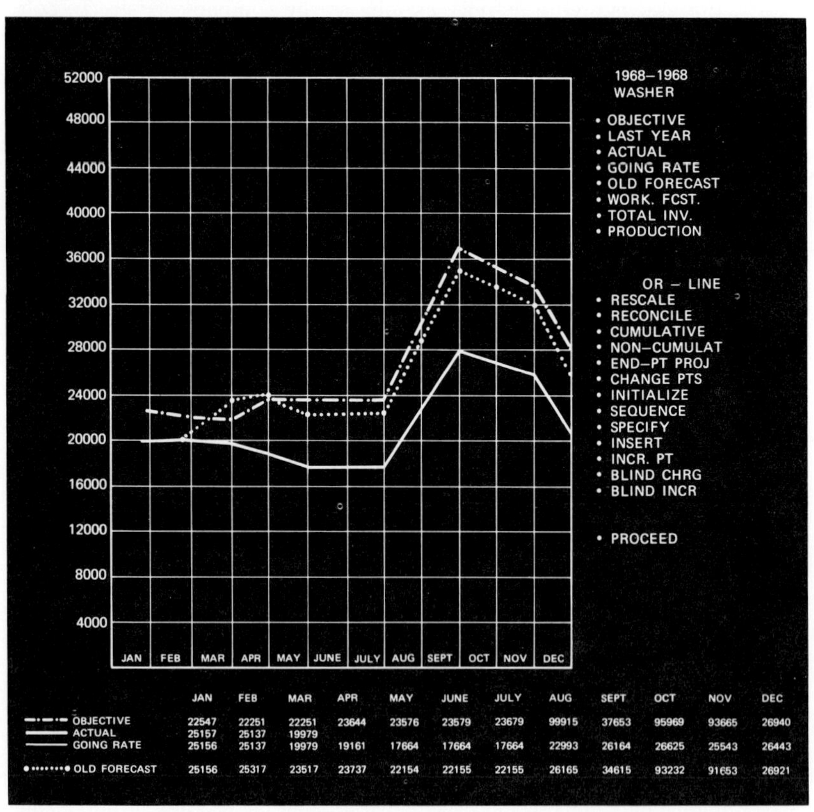

Figure 10.6 Sample light-pen menu (courtesy Information Displays, Inc.). By placing light pen on desired items at right, the appropriate graph is produced.

tions the operator selected. Notice that to the right of the presentation are additional light-pen functions so the manager can continue to interact with his data base.

In the Westinghouse application, the planners move through approximately 20 presentations in order to complete their monthly schedule. Westinghouse concludes that the system is a practical tool and the prototype of future manager-computer interactive systems for planning and control activities.

Boeing Company

In conjunction with the SCRAM missile program, Boeing Company was required by their customer (the Air Force) to maintain an MIS that would give their customer access to the same planning data that Boeing was using to make decisions. Boeing chose to implement this requirement by establishing a computer-based MIS in which all of the appropriate information describing program status was kept in a central file and could be retrieved by Boeing managers through a series of light-pen interrogated displays. In all, about 8,000 different reports and presentations could be reviewed. In order to satisfy the customer's requirement for access to the same data base, the central computer was connected by telephone line to an identical installation at the customer's facility in Dayton, Ohio, and the customer had the same information retrieval capability as did Boeing.

Chemical Bank of New York

Chemical Bank of New York requires a way for money managers to jointly view timely economic information. Chemical Bank of New York has just contracted for a display system that automatically presents computer-generated data in four colors on screens up to theater size. Chemical Bank's initial use of the system will be to produce economic charts on a 5-foot by 6-foot screen. The bank will be able to call up computer-stored data and have it displayed within seconds on a large four-color chart. Initially, Chemical Bank will tie into a cooperative economic data bank shared by several large New York companies and financial institutions. The output of the computer will produce graphs of economic international time series. Later, as part of the bank's information system, data can also be quickly relayed from computers to a display projector in the bank's main office. Closed-circuit television could then relay the information to several remote offices.

GLOSSARY

Data base. An integrated system technique whereby all subsystems access data from the same vast storage area.

Management information system (MIS). A recent advance in computer technology designed to provide management with an integrated, all-encompassing approach to the total company, in order to facilitate the decision-making process.

Point-of-sale system. Retail system where as a sales transaction is completed, the data relating to that transaction are fed directly to the computer.

QUESTIONS

1. Compile a list of activities that you feel would potentially be served by an MIS-type system.
2. Of the following list, check those choices you think could support or warrant an MIS system. On those you check, explain how that choice would benefit from an MIS system, and what data would be gained from the outputs of such a system.
   a. Race track
   b. Import/export agency
   c. Police/summons court
   d. Savings bank
   e. College registration system
   f. Homeowner
2. Compile a list of data items and their related field sizes that you would incorporate in a data base for the following systems:
   a. Retail sales operation (similar to the example introduced in the chapter)
   b. A student master registration system (to include data relating to past grades and courses taken)
4. If you were designing an MIS system, what features would you incorporate in your design to provide security for the system so that unauthorized people could not gain access to your data files?
5. Do you think that customer accounts within a retail MIS system require protection? How about student school records?

UNIT 

PROJECT CONTROLS AND MANAGEMENT

CHAPTER **11**

CONTROLS AND FEEDBACK

CONTROLS

Perhaps the most critical elements of a system are the methods used to control or check errors. When the analyst is analyzing the current system in operation, it is essential that he or she identify controls that are already in use. With knowledge of these controls, he can then incorporate them in the proposed system, and perhaps suggest some additional controls to the businessman or woman. When something goes wrong in a system, it is common for those not knowledgeable of data processing to think that the computer has made a mistake. This is usually not the case. It is most often the fault of the systems analyst, the programmer, or of someone submitting invalid, unverified data for processing. For example, how many times have we heard of an individual receiving a paycheck for $300,000 or a bill for $57,000? These errors are most often the result of a programming or verification error instead of a machine failure.

The following examples of controls are presented to give the analyst an idea of what he should consider when analyzing a system and proposing one or more alternatives.

EDITING DATA

Types of Edit Programs

An **edit procedure** is the process of validating a file of data to ensure that records do not contain obvious omissions, inconsistencies, or errors. Errors in files are relatively common because of (a) source document errors made by departmental employees and (b) conversion errors made by operations personnel in keypunching data onto cards, keying data onto tape, keying data into a terminal, and so on.

The common edit procedures are performed during the phases illustrated in Figure 11.1.

Edits Prior to Master File Creation (Step 1 in Figure 11.1). When a new system is designed, a master file that will contain all pertinent data and will be used for all output operations must be created. This is a one-shot program. That is, once the program

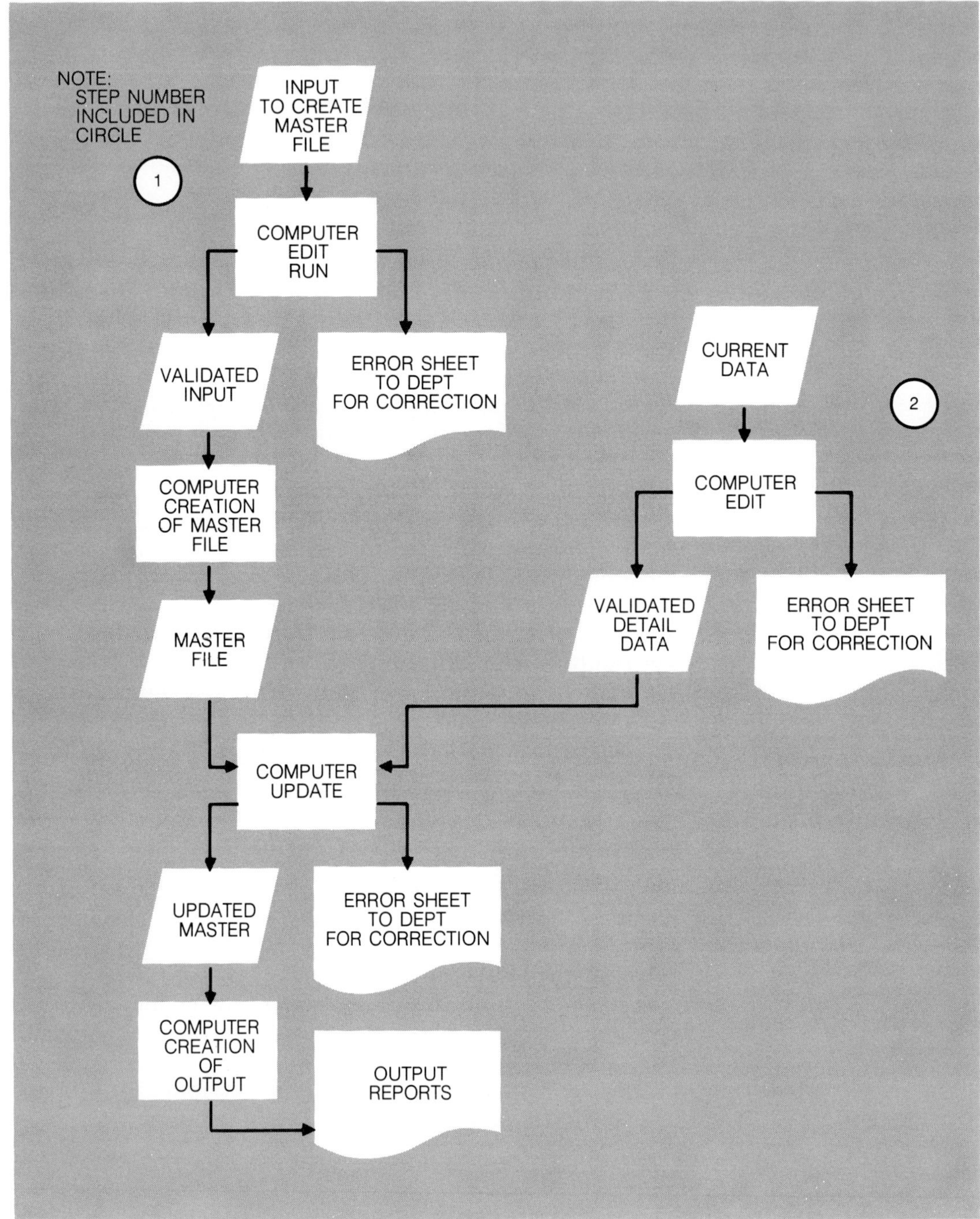

Figure 11.1 Systems flowchart of typical business procedures.

successfully creates a master file, it need not be used again. The master file is then maintained and updated using file maintenance routines. Such a master file creation is usually performed by a utility program (card-to-tape, card-to-disk, etc.).

Since the master file is usually the most important file in a system, it must be created with as few errors as possible. Thus an edit operation is generally required prior to master file creation to ensure relatively accurate recording.

Edits Prior to Updates or File Maintenance Routines (Step 2 in Figure 11.1). We revise a master file with **update** or **file maintenance routines**. Before altering a master file, however, we must attempt to ensure that the *change* or *detail records* contain as few errors as possible. Thus an edit operation is generally required prior to updating a master file, to ensure that the data used to alter the master file are relatively accurate.

Outputs from an Edit Program

Outputs from an edit program to be discussed are: (1) a validated file and (2) an error listing.

Validated File. This file will contain as few errors as possible. Any clearly erroneous data will either be rejected or corrected, if possible, depending on the system's requirements. Note that a validated file may simply be all input records minus the erroneous ones. This is the typical procedure with card data. For other types of files, a validated file may be a newly created one containing all valid input records and some erroneous records with incorrect fields zero-filled or blank-filled. Similarly, an edit procedure may utilize card input, for example, and create a validated tape as output.

Note that it is not possible to validate *all* data. Without additional information, for example, it would not be possible to determine if an employee record with a birth date of 08/50 is valid or not. However, we can determine if such a date falls within proper limits. That is, the month is a valid number if it is between 01 and 12; and the year is valid if it is greater than 11 (there are no employees older than 65 and we are assuming a present year of 76: 76 − 11 = 65) but less than 58 (there are no employees younger than 18).

To validate a file, it is sometimes necessary to utilize another file, such as a table file, to compare against input data and to ensure relative accuracy.

For example, a payroll record may contain a job classification code together with an annual salary. It may be necessary to read a table file with job codes and their corresponding salary ranges. Thus, in the edit procedures, we can test to determine if the payroll record contains an annual salary that is within the established range for the given job code (see Figure 11.2).

Table files are often used in conjunction with edit programs to assist in validating input information.

Error List. This is sent to the corresponding department so that errors may be subsequently corrected. This error list should clearly and concisely specify every error condition and the corresponding action taken. It should also indicate totals so that the percentage of errors or error rate can be determined.

Types of Edit Tests

Keep in mind that the specific edit procedures required for an application are supplied by the programmer or analyst and are verified by the businessperson. Typical edit procedures include the tests indicated in Figure 11.3.

Field Test. A **field test** is used to determine if specific data fields have valid formats, with regard to:

1. Class—numeric or alphabetic
2. Sign (if numeric)—positive or negative

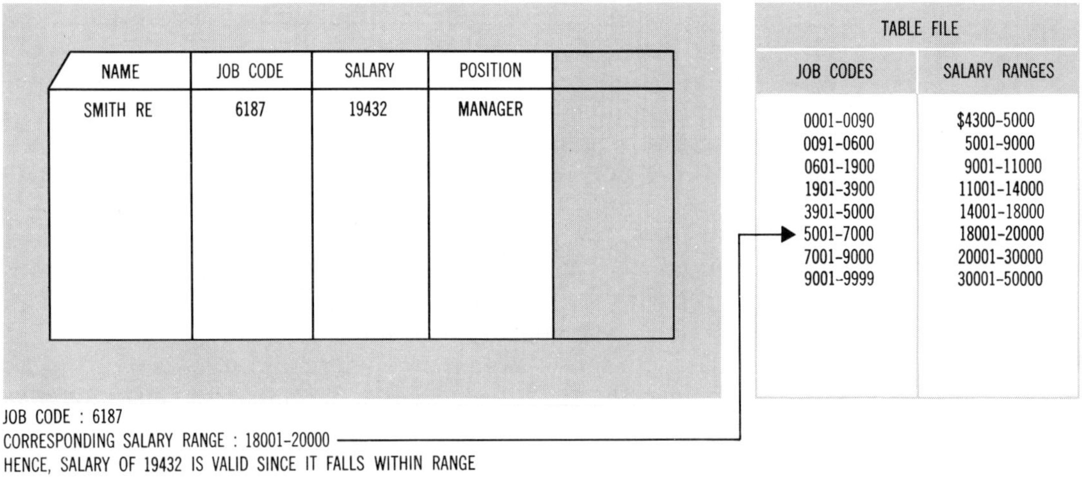

Figure 11.2 Validating routine to determine if salary on card is consistent with job code.

NAME	JOB CODE	SALARY	POSITION	
SMITH RE	6187	19432	MANAGER	

TABLE FILE

JOB CODES	SALARY RANGES
0001-0090	$4300-5000
0091-0600	5001-9000
0601-1900	9001-11000
1901-3900	11001-14000
3901-5000	14001-18000
5001-7000	18001-20000
7001-9000	20001-30000
9001-9999	30001-50000

JOB CODE : 6187
CORRESPONDING SALARY RANGE : 18001-20000
HENCE, SALARY OF 19432 IS VALID SINCE IT FALLS WITHIN RANGE

FIELD TEST—Determine if specific fields have valid class (numeric, alphabetic), valid sign (if numeric), valid format.
CODE TEST—Determine if code in field is valid.
SEQUENCE TEST—Determine if data is in proper sequence.
MISSING DATA TEST—Determine if key fields contain necessary data.
CHECK DIGIT TEST—Determine if coded check digits within a field are valid.
LIMIT TEST—Ascertain that specific fields do not exceed reasonable limits.

Figure 11.3 Common types of edit tests.

An amount field, for example, on an input record must be numeric. If it is not, then an error on input has occurred, and unless the field is corrected or omitted, erroneous processing will occur. In some programming languages, an arithmetic operation performed on numeric fields that erroneously contain nonnumeric data will cause a program interrupt.

All numeric fields in an input record should be checked to determine if, in fact, they contain strictly numeric data. Erroneous coding of source documents or encoding (keypunching) can produce errors. A blank, for example, is not usually valid in a numeric field. The validity depends on the programming language being used. In FORTRAN, for example, blanks in numeric fields are automatically converted by the computer into zeros. In COBOL, on the other hand, blanks in numeric fields can cause data exception interrupts if those fields are being used in calculations.

Depending on the nature of the numeric field, we may *reject* an erroneously coded numeric field or we may simply fill it with zeros on the validated file (if the validated file is an output form from the edit procedure). If, for example, an ACCOUNT NUMBER field contains nonnumeric data and this is the key field on the master file, then we must reject the record.

Similarly, some fields such as NAME, DESCRIPTION, CITY should contain only alphabetic data. The edit routine should check to determine that they do, in fact, contain strictly alphabetic data. Here again, we may reject records with erroneously coded alphabetic fields or we may simply fill the field with spaces. If the edit procedure does not create a new output file, then error records must be rejected.

Some numeric fields may contain a sign, while others require strictly unsigned data. This must also be tested.

You will recall that a sign is usually placed in the lower-order or units position of a numeric field, together with the low-order digit. An AMOUNT field, for example, may contain a sign, but a QUANTITY field generally does not.

In short, the format of input records must be edited to ensure accuracy. The programmer and the businessperson work closely to determine what constitutes an error. Where an input record contains an erroneous format, the record may be rejected or, if possible, appropriate revisions may be made. For example, invalid numeric fields may be replaced with zeros *when such fields are not absolutely critical for processing.* If a numeric field such as AMOUNT or QUANTITY or EMPLOYEE NUMBER is not coded with numeric data, then the entire record would generally be rejected since such fields are usually required for any significant processing.

Code Test. A code test is used to determine if a coded field is valid; it can sometimes be performed with no other inputs required. Sometimes, however, it necessitates the use of a table file for comparison purposes.

EXAMPLE 1. Suppose we have a sales record with the format indicated in Figure 11.4.

Suppose, too, that there are currently five branch offices, coded 1 to 5. An edit program should incorporate a routine to determine if the field called BRANCH contains a number from 1 to 5. If it does not, an error condition must be noted. Either the record will be rejected because branch office is a key field, or the field will be flagged as erroneous, so that a future correction can be made.

EXAMPLE 2. Suppose we wish to validate ACCOUNT NUMBER on an accounts receivable file. Each customer is assigned an account number by the accounts receivable department. There are currently 980 accounts within the company, numbered 0001 to 0980.

We could write a procedure to ensure that ACCOUNT NUMBER is between 0001 and 0980. This would require no additional input. However, it would not be a reliable or advisable test, since the program would require revision as soon as more accounts were added to the accounts receivable file.

Instead, a routine could be coded in the program to deter-

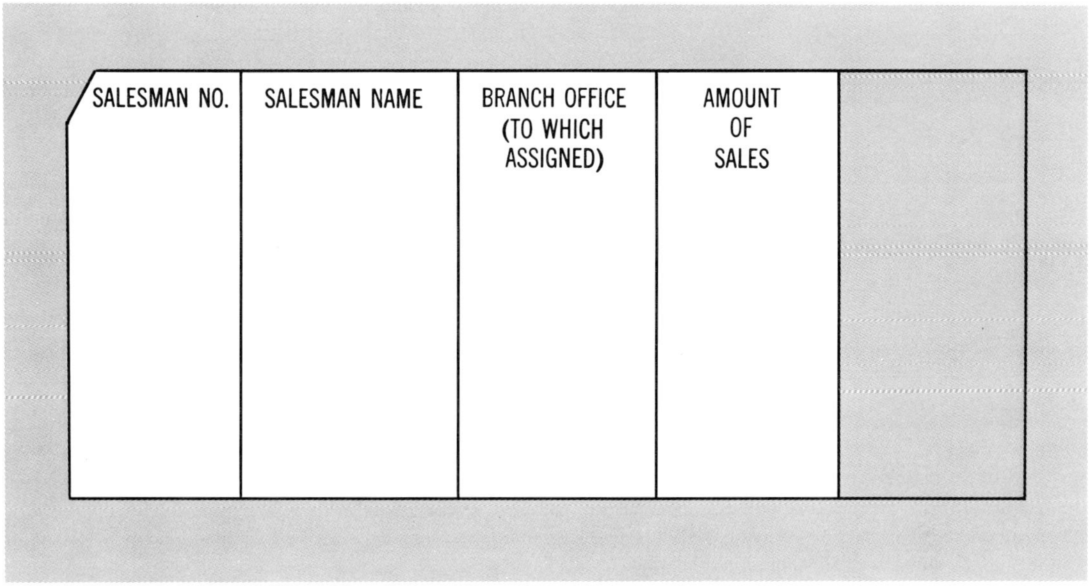

SALESMAN NO.	SALESMAN NAME	BRANCH OFFICE (TO WHICH ASSIGNED)	AMOUNT OF SALES	

Figure 11.4 Format of sales record.

mine, for example, if the assigned account number is valid for a specific branch. Suppose the accounts receivable department has assigned account numbers to branch offices according to Table 11.1.

Two possibilities exist here:

a. The table remains constant. That is, the ranges of account numbers remain the same for each branch office. This is possible only if the accounts receivable department periodically deactivates specific customers and assigns the corresponding account number to a new customer. If, for example, account number 0102 has not transacted any

TABLE 11.1

Account Number	Branch
0001–0106	1
0107–0198	2
0199–0275	3
0276–0392	4
0393–0487	5
0488–0610	6
0611–0724	7
0725–0842	8
0843–	9

business in three years, this may be sufficient grounds for deactivating that account and reassigning the number to a new customer in branch office 2. In this way, the range of account numbers and their corresponding branch offices remain constant.

If the table remains constant, then the corresponding figures may be used *within the program itself*, as constants.

We first test to ensure that ACCOUNT NUMBER is numeric and positive. If not, then it has been erroneously coded and an error condition must be indicated. Then we test ACCOUNT NUMBER for the proper ranges for each branch.

b. *The table varies.* When changes to a table occur frequently, it is better programming form to read in the table each time as part of the program and provide a routine to determine if the input ACCOUNT NUMBER and BRANCH are consistent, using the *variable entries* in the table as a comparison.

This routine would require a *table look-up*, a procedure whereby a table is read into storage and used for comparison to determine if a specific condition is met.

EXAMPLE 3. Suppose we have an accounts payable record with the format indicated in Figure 11.5.

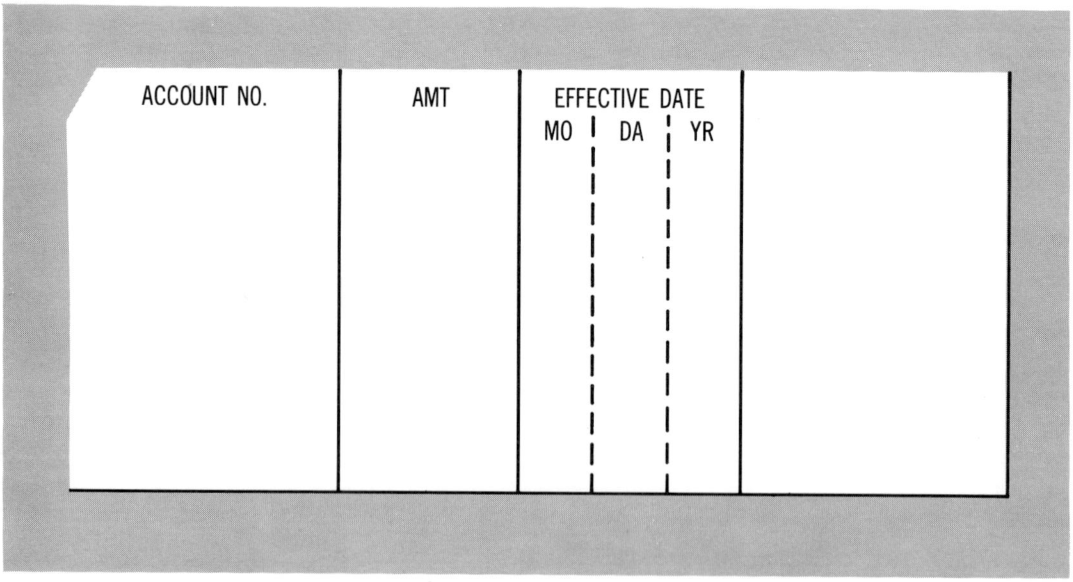

Figure 11.5 Accounts payable record.

ACCOUNT NO.	AMT	EFFECTIVE DATE MO / DA / YR	

When the company receives merchandise, the invoice data are keyed into the record described. EFFECTIVE DATE is the date on which the merchandise was received.

Each week we run an edit to determine if EFFECTIVE DATE contains a valid month, day, and year. This field in an accounts payable system is critical, since it is used to determine whether a discount can be taken if the company pays the bill within a specific period of time.

Often the edit routine incorporates a procedure for determining, for example, if EFFECTIVE DATE is relatively current. That is, we can determine if EFFECTIVE DATE is within one month of the run date. If EFFECTIVE DATE is not relatively current, this may denote an error; that is, the field may have been erroneously coded as 12/01/70 instead of 12/01/76.

The computer operator prepares a card with the month, date, and year of the current run. If EFFECTIVE DATE is any date *more recent than the previous month* (month before RUN MONTH), but not any date beyond the present month, it is considered valid. That is, if current run date is 12/30/76, then any date more recent than 11/30/76 is considered valid.

Figure 11.6 illustrates the use of an edit routine to check on the validity of an EFFECTIVE DATE.

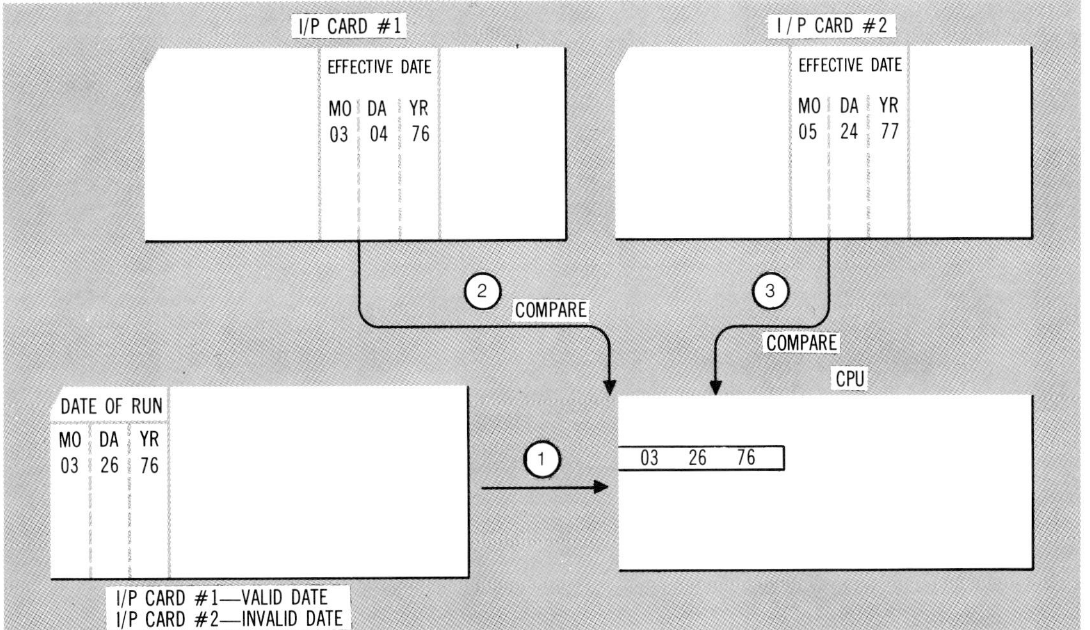

Figure 11.6 Use of an edit routine to determine if a date is relatively current.

If the year of EFFECTIVE DATE is the same as the year of CURRENT RUN DATE, then a test can be made on the month. If the month on both dates is the same, then we can proceed with our logic. If the year on both dates is not the same (e.g., EFFECTIVE DATE is 12/01/76 and CURRENT RUN DATE is 01/01/77), then a more complex logic operation is required.

Sequence Test. In many cases it is imperative that data be entered into a system in a specific sequence. In the case where *detail cards*, for example, will be used to update a *master tape*, the cards must be in a specific sequence, since tape updates require sequential processing.

If a sequence error is found, we can:

1. Reject the record in error. Rejected data will be entered in the data flow for the next cycle, where it must be sorted again.
2. Reject the record in error, but if a predetermined number of errors occurs, the run will be terminated. We can reject out-of-sequence data, but if the data have been missorted, we can conceivably have more rejected records than correct ones. Thus, to ensure that only a small number of out-of-sequence records exists, we can incorporate a routine where each time an out-of-sequence condition occurs, we add one to a counter; if the counter should exceed a predetermined number, then the run will be aborted and reexecuted after the data have been resorted.
3. Abort the run if any sequence errors occur. The data are initially arranged in a specified sequence. Therefore *no* errors should occur. Rather than reject any record, it is sometimes more advisable to stop the run, resequence the erroneous records, and ensure that the remainder of the file is in correct order.

Missing Data Test. For most records, key data fields are required for processing. For example, a payroll record *must* contain a social security number and annual salary. If either of these fields is missing, then the record must be rejected since it would not be serviceable in any payroll file maintenance. Similarly, an accounts receivable record with a missing ACCOUNT NUMBER or AMOUNT is equally useless.

If a key field is missing data, then the edit program usually rejects the entire record. For data fields that are not critical, missing information may be merely noted or else filled with some compensating data. For example, an EFFECTIVE DATE field on a card that is erroneously blank may be filled with the date of the run, as supplied by the computer operator. Again, changes to an input file are only made if a validated file is created as output. If the input file is merely checked, then errors can only be rejected and not corrected.

Check Digit Test. Many numbers such as charge account numbers, inventory numbers, and identification numbers can easily cause errors in file maintenance routines if they are incorrectly written or keypunched. For example, if a customer buys an item on credit and his account number is written on the sales slip or keypunched on a card as 123 456 instead of 123 546, this can result in the wrong customer getting billed. The most common type of numeric error is in transposition of digits, as above. One way to minimize this type of error is to incorporate an extra digit called the **check digit**, in the number. A typical procedure is as follows:

1. Assign the number, such as 123 546.
2. Beginning with the first digit, take every other digit and multiply by two:

$1 \times 2 = 2$
$3 \times 2 = 6$
$4 \times 2 = 8$

3. Add these numbers together and then add the digits that have not been multiplied by 2, obtaining a single total:

$(2 + 6 + 8) + (2 + 5 + 6) = 29$

4. Subtract the low-order or units digit of this sum from 10:

$10 - 9 = 1$

The low-order digit that results is the *check digit*, which is then added onto the original number (see Figure 11.7). Usually, although not necessarily, the check digit is tacked on at the right of the number. (Note that when the sum obtained in step 3 is a multiple of 10 the check digit is zero: $10 - 0 = 0$). Therefore, for the above example, the full account number assigned is 123 546 1.

Thus the account number is originally assigned to the customer *with* the included check digit. The edit program must include a routine with the above arithmetic operations to de-

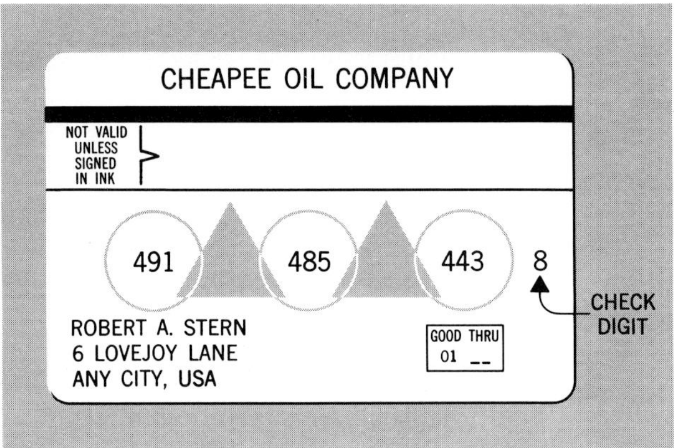

Figure 11.7 Credit card with check digit.

termine if the account number on a card punched from a charge slip is valid; that is, if the digit calculated by the computer is the same as that in the input then the charge account number is considered valid. If not, then the input number probably contains a transposition of digits and the record must be rejected. If the number were entered as 123 456 1 instead of 123 546 1, this would be detected as an error. When the computer performs the calculations to produce the check digit, a digit of zero would result. When this digit is compared against the check digit of 1 that was entered as input, an error condition would be noted.

Note that this technique is not foolproof, since 123 645 1 could be an incorrectly coded version of 123 546 1 and yet the check digit routine would *not* indicate an error. In general, where a *single* transposition of digits in coding occurs, a check digit routine is extremely useful. Where more than one transposition exists, which is not as likely, then the error may not be recognized until the incorrectly billed customer complains. Note also that the above check digit routine is not the *only* one commonly used.

At this point, you should be cognizant of the overwhelming need for precise and thorough edit routines on input data to ensure, where possible, that errors do not appear in the record. Errors in key data fields of input can cause serious problems in file maintenance routines resulting in inaccuracies in the master file, erroneous reports, and so on.

Remember that the above edits represent only a few of the possible tests. The number of edit tests performed is directly proportional to the input form. If input is on tape or cards, for example, it may require more editing than if it is on source documents entered on an optical scanner. The cards or tape data may have two types of errors: original errors on source documents and encoding (keypunching or key-to-tape) errors. The source documents used as input to an optical scanner may contain only the former type and thus, theoretically, are not as prone to inaccuracies, assuming that the optical scanner itself does not make errors in transmission.

In general, terminal data require the most precise edit control for several reasons: (1) source documents may be coded improperly; (2) the terminal keying may be inaccurate; (3) there is no verification (other than visual) of terminal typing as there is with card or tape encoding; (4) the equipment itself is prone to transmission problems because of the distance the data must travel.

OTHER TYPES OF CONTROLS

In addition to the editing of input data, there are other controls that can be used to check the accuracy of data. Keypunch verification, for example, has already been discussed in Chapter 5. Other controls include the following:

1. **Batch Total (Figure 11.8).** If a group of inputs is to be processed, a total figure is taken of a specific input field prior to processing. After processing, this **batch total** is compared to the input total to confirm that all input was, in fact, processed. For example, suppose that in a department store at the end of each day, each sales clerk takes all of the charge slips from his department and adds up the total of charge sales for that day. He sends the slips to the accounts receivable department, where posting is made to each customer's account and various reports are prepared. After all posting is done for that day, a

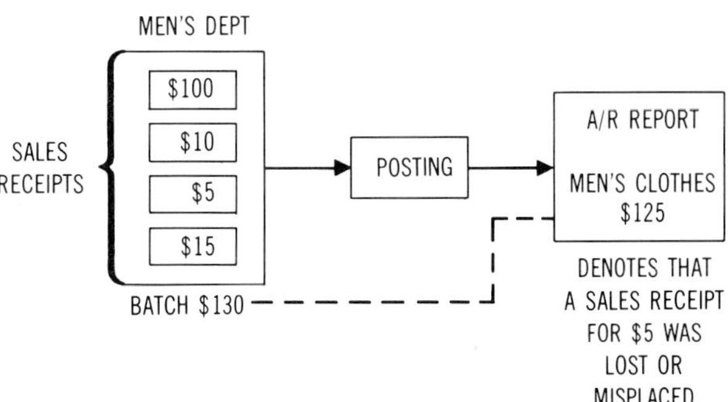

Figure 11.8 Use of a batch total.

report is prepared that shows the total of the charge sales that were posted from each department. If one of these totals disagrees with the batch total obtained by a particular sales clerk, then that information has been incorrectly processed. Appropriate measures must then be taken to ascertain the reason for the discrepancy and then to take corrective action.

2. Item Count. In addition to using a batch total, another control is to count the number of items both before and after processing. In this manner, if any items are lost during processing, an error in the **item count** will occur.

3. Limit Test. During processing, a test of reasonableness can be made to check for errors. As an example, in a payroll system for workers paid on an hourly basis, a **limit test** might be employed as follows. The highest hourly rate is $10 per hour, and the most hours worked is usually 60 hours per week. Overtime starts after 40 hours. Therefore, a limit check of $700 per week for gross pay is reasonable, calculating overtime at time and one-half. If, during processing, gross pay for an individual turned out to be $900, we would not process that check until further investigation was made.

4. Trial Balances. A **trial balance** is a report that is prepared to ensure the accuracy of all posting to account ledgers. If the transactions for the specific time period are properly posted, the total of debits shown on the report will equal the total of credits, as shown in Figure 11.9.

FEEDBACK

It must be borne in mind that the mere existence of certain controls in a system does not *guarantee* that errors will not occur. It may be that a particular condition that occurs very infrequently was overlooked (intentionally or unintentionally) when the new system was designed.

Suppose, for example, that we have incorporated a check digit in the account number of a credit card. We saw previously that a typical check digit test will detect transpositions of adjacent numbers but will not pick up an error where the transposition is of nonadjacent numbers (e.g., 1257 instead of 1752).

In addition to getting feedback from customers, employees, and other recipients of computer-produced reports that there are errors, the analyst may also get feedback of a different nature. Management, for example, may want certain reports

ACCOUNTS RECEIVABLE TRIAL BALANCE

AS OF 9-30-__

ACCOUNT NO.	DEBITS	CREDITS
01025	50.25	
01026	27.65	
01030	35.10	
01035		27.15
01037	26.07	
01038		
TOTALS	557,233.10	385,957.15
DEBITS–CREDITS	171,275.95	

Figure 11.9 Trial balance.

changed in format. It is wise to bear in mind the adage that states that anything conceivable that can go wrong with a system when it is first established will almost certainly go wrong. The analyst must be prepared for these contingencies, and he or she must therefore build into the new system a mechanism for obtaining and processing feedback. Forms and procedures must be incorporated to handle errors that are found in paychecks, customer statements, sales reports, and so on. In this connection, the analyst must realize that there may be constraints on the way feedback is handled in a particular system. In an accounts receivable system, for example, the Federal Truth in Lending Act dictates the procedures that must be followed by both the customer who complains about an incorrect bill and by the company that has billed him. A typical set of procedures that is sent to credit card holders is shown in Figure 11.10.

In summary, we observe that the analysis of a current system and the design of a new one require consideration of (1) management's objectives, (2) the constraints imposed on the system, (3) the relationship of output, processing, and input, *and* (4) the need for and use of controls and feedback procedures.

FEDERAL LAW DISCLOSURE NOTICE CONCERNING BILLING INQUIRIES

In Case of Errors or Inquiries About Your Bill

The Federal Truth in Lending Act requires prompt correction of billing mistakes.

1. If you want to preserve your rights under the Act, here's what to do if you think your bill is wrong or if you need more information about an item on your bill:
   a. Do not write on the bill. On a separate sheet of paper write (you may telephone your inquiry but doing so will not preserve your rights under this law) the following:
      i. Your name and account number.
      ii. A description of the error and an explanation (to the extent you can explain) why you believe it is an error.

         If you only need more information, explain the item you are not sure about and, if you wish, ask for evidence of the charge such as a copy of the charge slip. Do not send in your copy of a sales slip or other document unless you have a duplicate copy for your records.
      iii. The dollar amount of the suspected error.
      iv. Any other information (such as your address) which you think will help us to identify you or the reason for your complaint or inquiry.
   b. Send your billing error notice to the address on your bill which is listed after the words: "Direct written inquiries concerning this statement to".

      Mail it as soon as you can, but in any case, early enough to reach us within 60 days after the bill was mailed to you.
2. We must acknowledge all letters pointing out possible errors within 30 days of receipt, unless we are able to correct your bill during that 30 days. Within 90 days after receiving your letter, we must either correct the error or explain why we believe the bill was correct. Once we have explained the bill, we have no further obligation to you even though you still believe that there is an error, except as provided in paragraph 5 below.
3. After we have been notified, neither we nor an attorney nor a collection agency may send you collection letters or take other collection action with respect to the amount in dispute; but periodic statements may be sent to you, and the disputed amount can be applied against your credit limit. You cannot be threatened with damage to your credit rating or sued for the amount in question, nor can the disputed amount be reported to a credit bureau or to other creditors as delinquent until we have answered your inquiry. However, you remain obligated to pay the parts of your bill not in dispute.
4. If it is determined that we have made a mistake on your bill, you will not have to pay any **finance charges** on any disputed amount. If it turns out that we have not made an error, you may have to pay **finance charges** on the amount in dispute, and you will have to make up any missed minimum or required payments on the disputed amount. Unless you have agreed that your bill was correct, we must send you a written notification of what you owe; and if it is determined that we did make a mistake in billing the disputed amount, you must be given the time to pay which you normally are given to pay undisputed amounts before any more **finance charges** or late payment charges on the disputed amount can be charged to you.

Figure 11.10 Procedures to be followed in case of errors or inquiries about a bill.

5. If our explanation does not satisfy you and you notify us in writing within 10 days after you receive our explanation that you still refuse to pay the disputed amount, we may report you to credit bureaus and other creditors and may pursue regular collection procedures. But we must also report that you think you do not owe the money, and we must let you know to whom such reports were made. Once the matter has been settled between you and us, we must notify those to whom we reported you as delinquent of the subsequent resolution.

6. If we do not follow these rules, we are not allowed to collect the first $50 of the disputed amount and **finance charges,** even if the bill turns out to be correct.

7. If you have a problem with property or services purchased with a credit card, you may have the right not to pay the remaining amount due on them, if you first try in good faith to return them or give the merchant a chance to correct the problem. There are two limitations on this right:
   a. You must have bought them in your home state or if not within your home state within 100 miles of your current mailing address; and
   b. The purchase price must have been more than $50.

   However, these limitations do not apply if the merchant is owned or operated by us, or if we mailed you the advertisement for the property or services.

Figure 11.10 Continued.

GLOSSARY

Batch total. A total figure of a specific field in a group of inputs to be processed.

Check digit. An extra digit incorporated into an account number, part number, etc., that is used to test for the transposition of digits.

Detail record. A record, consisting of a transaction, that will be used to update a master file.

Edit procedure. The process of validating a file of data.

Field test. Used to determine if specific data fields have valid formats with regard to class (numeric or alphabetic) or sign (positive or negative).

File maintenance routine. A set of instructions to update a master file.

Item count. A count of the number of items of input to be processed.

Limit test. A check for reasonableness of a particular field.

Sequence test. Used to determine if input records are in the correct sequence prior to processing.

QUESTIONS

1. Prepare a sample of a typical payroll record and indicate the type of editing you think would be necessary to ensure its accuracy.
2. Prepare a sample of a typical inventory record and indicate the type of editing you think would be necessary to ensure its accuracy.
3. What are the various types of controls that are often utilized to ensure the accuracy of card data?
4. What are the various types of controls that are often utilized to ensure the accuracy of magnetic tape data?
5. Suppose your company wants to establish a control unit as part of the data processing facility. What would you envision as some of the tasks of this control unit?
6. Provide a list of the liaison responsibilities of a control unit.
7. What are some of the feedback procedures that a company might employ for its payroll system?
8. What are some of the feedback procedures that a company might employ for its accounts receivable system?
9. Do you think that data processing errors would be minimized or increased when data communications equipment is utilized? Explain your answer.
10. What is a limit test, and how is it used in a data processing environment?

CHAPTER **12**

ANALYSIS OF SYSTEMS COSTS

Thus far, we have discussed the basic elements of a system, how data are collected, and the pictorial illustrations used to place them in proper perspective. From all of the prior chapters, then, the analyst should be able to gather information on a system and to formulate a meaningful interpretation and understanding of it.

Once the system elements have been placed in proper perspective, the analyst will generally have some ideas on the basic problem areas. There is no clear-cut method for determining these areas, but most objective, logical, and business-oriented individuals can observe a system in its entirety and then discover significant problems within it.

This chapter will discuss cost, a factor in analysis that can be used to determine major problems. Cost analysis is used to determine costs associated with a system and, from them, to determine the monetary problem areas within it.

Note that the most convincing arguments either for or against a system must be substantiated with monetary factors. Management determines that an existing system is operating improperly generally because it is costing too much in relation to the output obtained. Similarly, no decision to implement a new design will be forthcoming unless a favorable economic justification is presented. Here, indications of monetary savings or benefits would be presented.

Costs, then, are extremely significant factors in analysis. Each system must be evaluated from a cost standpoint. Note, however, that costly systems are not necessarily inefficient ones. The analyst must not arbitrarily reject a system because it is expensive. Costly systems may well be the best ones within a company if they achieve their stated objectives with minimum error and if they serve to increase income. A real-time system, for example, is very expensive, yet its potential for serving customer needs and thus for attracting greater numbers of clients, makes it an extremely valuable asset.

Many systems, however, have subsystems that are disproportionately expensive. The analyst must determine when costly operations are inefficient or when they should be maintained.

The analysis of current system costs will attempt to illustrate how the analyst can discover how well the present system is:

1. Satisfying objectives
2. Capable of adapting to future requirements
3. Maintaining costs within budgetary guidelines

Before considering the analysis of any particular system, it is necessary to introduce terms and concepts relating to types of costs. These concepts, applicable to any analysis, will assist in our understanding of costs.

TANGIBLE AND INTANGIBLE COSTS

All costs may be placed within two categories—tangible and intangible costs. A **tangible cost** is one with which a dollar figure can be readily associated. When a company purchases $1,000 of office equipment, one may physically assess the exact number of desks, tables, and cabinets. It is possible to directly associate the materials received with the dollars expended.

An **intangible cost** presents a different type of problem. A dollar value cannot be readily associated with it. Consider the case where an erroneous inventory report is produced each month, causing the company to accept some customer orders when, in fact, the product is not on hand. This causes an intangible cost, a loss of business and goodwill that cannot be measured. Intangible benefits or savings are as difficult to analyze. It is not possible, for example, to assess the monetary savings derived from the ability to (1) better control one's employees, or (2) have data that are more accurate, or (3) make a decision one hour sooner. While increased accuracy will undoubtedly improve the efficiency of the system, the actual amount of savings cannot adequately be measured in dollars. Whenever a dollar figure is given to an intangible cost, it is an estimate. To an analyst, this type of cost is of great value. Many systems are designed to improve data communication and accuracy. The analyst should, therefore, include these points in his analysis and justification. He must be careful not to reject costly operations if they have intangible benefits. However, it remains difficult to assess these benefits. They can only be mentioned in a cost justification.

When preparing an estimate of costs, we should first consider tangible costs. These costs may be separated into recurring and nonrecurring costs. **Nonrecurring costs** are defined as one-time costs. That is, costs that, once accrued, will not occur again. This type of cost is associated with proposed systems changes or redesign. Since it is a **sunk cost**, money that cannot be recouped, it may not be applied to an analysis of an existing system unless there is a change impending. Consider the need for larger facilities, for an existing system, as a nonrecurring cost. Generally, this type of expense was incurred when the system was installed and cannot be included in its cost analysis. The nonrecurring cost is a critical factor in the design of any new system.

Recurring costs are incurred on a regular basis. Usually on a monthly basis, this expense will be maintained for the life of the system's operation. This type of cost is applicable in the analysis of any system (Table 12.1).

System A is an established system. System B is a new system.

By examining Table 12.1, we find a one-time cost for facilities, in System B. Here, the cost might be incurred to construct a specially air-conditioned room, with power supplies, to house the computer. Once this facility is completed, this cost would not arise again. Notice that, for the existing system, A, there is no one-time cost. Since programmer/analysts would be regularly employed, this expense is listed for both systems under recurring costs.

All costs in Table 12.1 were compiled on an annual basis. The analyst must make an effort to compare like values (that is, annual dollars versus annual dollars). In this manner, the

TABLE 12.1

	System A	**System B**
Nonrecurring Costs		
Facilities		$ 12,000
Systems studies		18,000
Total nonrecurring costs		30,000
Recurring Costs		
Programmer/analysts	$ 45,000	40,000
Operations	35,000	28,000
Supplies	20,000	20,000
Rental (equipment)	100,000	85,000
TOTAL ANNUAL COSTS	$200,000	$173,000

establishment of a valid base for judgment is assured. This fact is of paramount importance when subsequent comparisons, between alternative systems, must be made.

ANALYSIS OF CURRENT COSTS

An analysis of current costs may be performed on the total system or any of the various **components** that contribute to its operation. When costs are compiled for a subsystem, we can sometimes observe its relationship to the entire system. This cost figure could be valuable to the analyst by highlighting unwarranted overexpenditures and by marking this area for future investigation. Again, note that management costs do not always imply inefficiencies, but they may provide cause for analysis.

Thus each subsystem must be analyzed from a cost standpoint. In addition, the analyst should compare the system costs to previous years. In this way, he can determine how well growth factors have been accommodated in the system.

As an example, we may find that the payroll section has had its cost of operation rise from $500 per week to $800 per week, over the past year. During this period, the average increase in operating costs within the accounting department has been 10 percent. The analyst, observing the increase of 60 percent in operating costs in the payroll section, would initiate a survey to determine the cause of this rise. Relationships between the cost of operating the total system and each subsystem may be found in this manner. Cost trends may be established by utilizing these expense figures. These trends can be used in planning future systems efforts and budget estimates.

The estimates of total systems costs are of great interest to top management. Since management is more concerned with the total overview, the entire system must be functional. They are not as concerned with the interrelationships of each subsystem. Management simply does not want the total system's cost to exceed its budgeted amount. When this condition occurs, more often than department managers like to admit, the shrewd analyst is directed to discover what areas are contributing to the inefficiency.

The analyst utilizes the total cost figure as a measure of a system's effectiveness. Is the system providing the required outputs, within the cost constraints imposed? Will the system be extended past its capabilities and at what cost? When should redesign be attempted? From the cost figures derived in the analysis of an existing system, these questions may be answered.

There are four types of recurring costs that must be considered when analyzing each subsystem or operational component.

1. Labor Rate. For each operation, the analyst must determine the labor or personnel cost. The salary of each person associated with the operation must be obtained from the department manager.

This includes departmental employees and any data processing employees utilized for specific functions. If cards must be punched, for example, then the cost of using keypunch operators must be evaluated. The data processing manager has available the cost factors of data processing staff members.

2. Equipment Expenses. All typewriters, adding machines, or any other manual devices must be assessed. Also, any data processing equipment must also be included. If a system utilizes two hours of computer time each month, its cost must be included.

3. Materials and Supplies. Printed forms, punched cards, stationery, etc., are included here.

4. Overhead. This includes the cost of facilities, electricity, and heating. Also the cost of vice-presidents or department heads, who maintain responsibility for several systems, is entered here. A vice-president may spend one-fifth of his time on a given system, and thus this cost factor must be prorated.

Let us consider some examples that may further assist in the analysis of an existing system. We shall compute cost figures to demonstrate approaches and offer appropriate comments.

EXAMPLE 1. The flowchart in Figure 12.1 describes procedures used in the preparation of a sales invoice. Compute the monthly cost of operation for this system, using a 20-day work month. There are, on the average, 300 transactions per day. One card is punched and verified for each transaction. Invoices are prepared for each customer (Figure 12.1).

Computing the costs for this report's preparation, we have:

a. Sales invoice. Each preprinted customer invoice cost $.10.

300 invoice/day × 20 day/month × .10/invoice = $600 per month

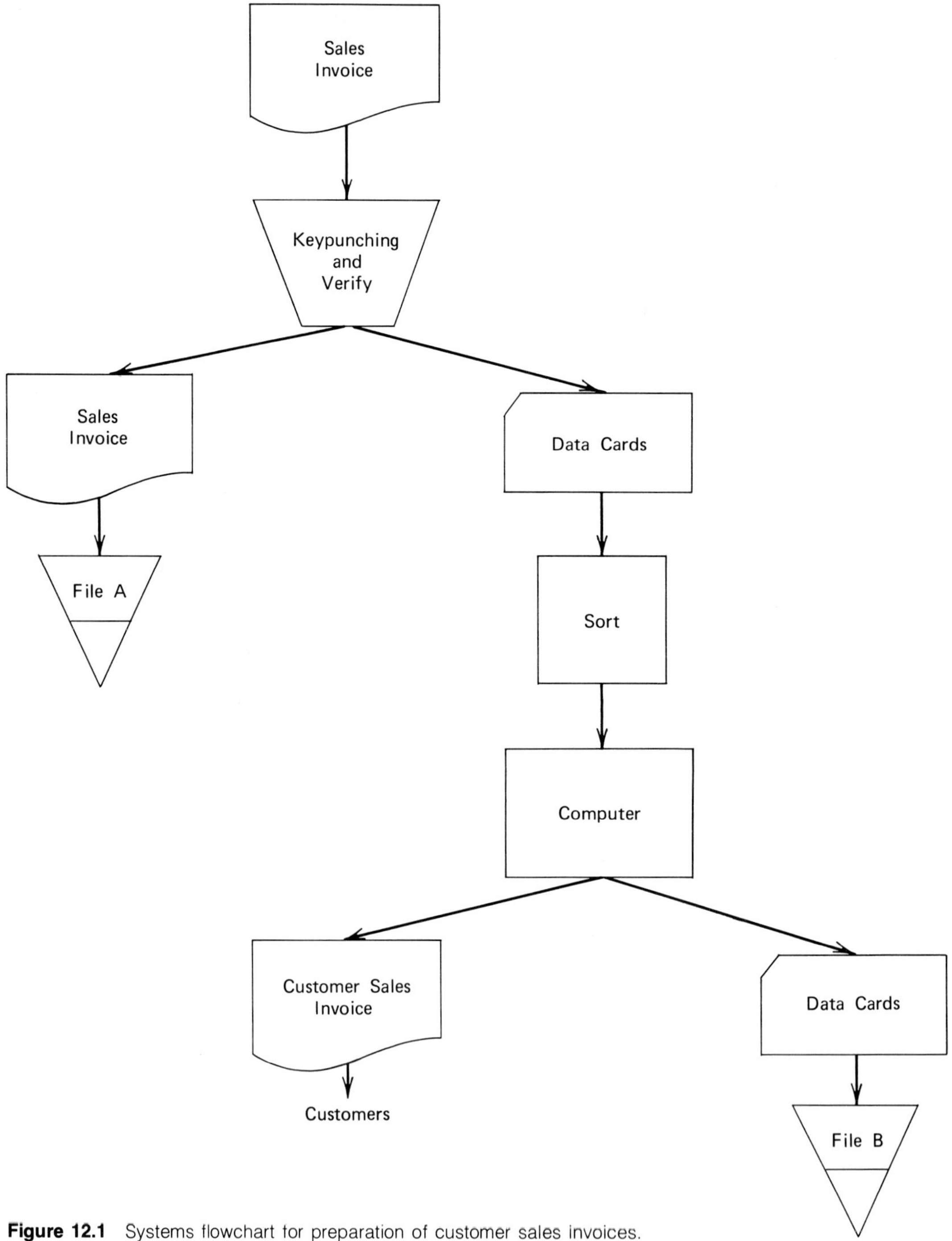

Figure 12.1 Systems flowchart for preparation of customer sales invoices.

b. *Storage file A.* The company prorates document storage at \$.01 per invoice.

300 × 20 × .01/invoice = \$60 per month

c. *Keypunching and verification.* The speed for keypunchng and verification is 2 cards per minute, for this type of card. Rental for these machines is prorated at \$.02 per card. Operators are paid a labor rate of \$2.00 per hour. Cost of cards is \$2.50 per 1,000.

Rental = 300 × 20 × .02/card = \$120 per month

Operators = 300 × 20 × .50 minute/card × 1 hour/60 minute × 2.00/hour = \$100 per month

Cost of Cards = 300 × 20/1000 × \$2.50 = \$15 per month

d. *Sort time.* A four-digit field is the key for sorting. A handling factor, the efficiency of handling cards and operating the sorter, of 25 percent is assumed. An IBM 083 sorter is used with a speed of 1,000 cards per minute. The formulas required are:

Machine Time = volume × field size/machine speed

Handling Time = handling factor × machine time

Total Sort Time = machine time + handling time

Using these formulas, we obtain:

Machine Time = 300 × 20 × 4/1000 = 24 minutes

Handling Time = 24 × .25 = 6 minutes

Total Sort Time = machine time + handling time = 24 + 6 = 30 minutes = .50 hours per month

The rental cost of the sorter is prorated at \$.01 per card.

Rental = 300 × 20 × .01/Card = \$60 per month

Operators = .50 hour/month × 2.00/hour = \$1 per month

e. *Computer rental.* The computer is maintained, including overhead, at a cost of \$400 per hour. The total time used by this run on a computer is .10 hour per day.

20 × .10 hour/day × 400/hour = \$800 per month

f. *Printed invoices.* The company uses an average of 50 invoices per day. The cost of the invoices is \$.012 per invoice.

50 invoices/day × 20 days/month × 0.12/inoivce = $12 per month

g. *Storage file B.* Card storage is prorated at $.005 per card.

300 × 20 × .005/card = $30 per month

The costs for this system are summarized in Table 12.2.

This company has a monthly operating cost of $1,798 for this system. All costs included within this cost scheme were considered to be part of the system. When constructing a system's cost statement, an effort must be made to remain within the guidelines established by the company. The attempt is to ensure uniformity between costing methods and the resulting cost analyses.

By using any method available to him, the analyst may construct a cost analysis for the system under study. When computation of the total systems cost is completed, the cost of all subsystems will be included within that total figure. Each individual subsystem would not be separately shown. All costs would be grouped to represent general, total system categories. An example will demonstrate these points more clearly.

EXAMPLE 2. The accounting department has requested its data processing section to prepare a cost statement of its existing operation. Consideration is being given, by management, to

TABLE 12.2 DATA PROCESSING SYSTEM—SALES INVOICE

	Monthly Costs	
Rentals		
Keypunch/verifiers	$120	
Sorter	60	
Computer—360 series	800	$ 980
Operator Costs		
Keypunch/verifier	100	
Sorting	1	101
Supplies		
Sales-invoices	600	
Cards	15	
Preprinted customer invoices	12	627
Storage		
File A	60	
File B	30	90
TOTAL MONTHLY COST		$1798
TOTAL ANNUAL COST		$21576

updating the existing computer system. The data processing section lists the following items.

Data processing manager	$2000/mo.
Programmer/analyst	1200/mo.—3 ea.
Secretaries	600/mo.—3 ea.
Operators	500/mo.—6 ea.
Keypunch operators	450/mo.—6 ea.
Computer rental	6600/mo.
Rental—Keypunches	240/mo.
Verifiers	200/mo.
Sorter	320/mo.
Interpreter	440/mo.
Reproducer	500/mo.
Supplies	2100/mo.

From these listed costs, an annual total cost could be prepared, as follows:

Data Processing Section	
Programmer/analysts/manager	$67,200
Operators	36,000
Secretaries/keypunch operators	54,000
Rental—Computer	79,200
Unit-record equipment	20,400
Supplies	25,200
TOTAL ANNUAL COST	$282,000

All costs have been converted to their yearly equivalents. The costs listed are recurring costs. There are no one-time costs shown, since the system is existent and no initial costs are required. The dollar figure associated with supplies is composed of all cards, forms, or printouts required within the system. No intangible costs have been defined. Computation of this total cost is similar to the preparation of a budget estimate. The total system's cost is a summation of all expenses related to it.

In example 2, a simple listing was used to represent the summation of total costs. A formalized approach toward listing system costs, preferred by some analysts, involves the use of a **resource sheet**. Data are recorded on the resource sheet in a manner similar to a bank statement. Major groupings are defined, and each item within that group is listed with its respective cost. Intermediate subtotals and a grand total are taken. The resource sheet provides the systems staff with a uniform method of documentation. Within each specific company, however, a unique but similar method of documentation may exist. This type of technique, using a resource sheet, is presented in an example in Chapter 15.

SOURCES OF DATA

It is sufficient to discuss costs, but what are the sources of these data? Data may be taken from time sheets, budgets, existing contractual agreements, payroll records, vendor estimates, supply records, purchase orders, or the like. Since the majority of the data sought refer to money, often the accounting department or business office is a fine source at which to begin your search. After extrapolation from the source document, the data must be manipulated to the desired format. Data, when found in a raw state, must often be evaluated and analyzed before they become meaningful.

Analysts often tend to overlook an area where information abounds, their own systems department. Their fellow analysts represent many areas of expertise and years of practical experience on which to draw. Associates who have worked previously within an area may suggest sources of data or provide guidelines of operation. Analysts who have studied a particular company area previously can offer an insight into problem areas. It is sometimes good practice to peruse previous systems studies. These studies can provide the historical backup data necessary and all the previously proposed alternative solutions that were not considered feasible at that time. Many hours of tedious bookwork may be eliminated by examining previously completed systems projects.

The analyst must learn to use every available source of data during analysis. He must establish the facts that are required in his analysis and must be capable of recognizing problem areas when they appear.

EXAMPLES OF PROBLEM AREAS

In this section, we consider examples of how the various factors might be used in an analysis.

PROBLEM 1 System's Growth. As greater demands are placed on a system, the set of procedures used to handle the data will become cumbersome. The system will become inefficient if no change is instituted. If a $6,000-per-year clerk must be hired every year to meet this growing demand, perhaps the installation of a computer system should be considered, replacing the existing manual system.

Here, the $6,000-per-year figure and the increased inefficiency of the manual system have alerted the analyst that an undesirable condition was developing. The analyst must begin considering a system that will handle the growth of the data requirements and that will more efficiently facilitate the manipulation and transmission of data.

PROBLEM 2 Job Evaluation. During an evaluation of a system, we examine the responsibility of each employee and recommend, where applicable, changes. The individual might need a change of responsibility, an addition of duties, or a redefinition of the job. A $24,000-per-year systems manager has two clerks working for him; yet the operating expense is $2,000 per year. A reevaluation of the manager's job should be considered, possibly increasing his control over another system. By increasing his control responsibilities to two systems, he will free someone. This person can probably be reassigned to other more important duties.

Here, the very low operating expense indicated to the analyst that these clerks were not being used to their fullest extent. This slack could be more profitably used by giving them and their manager additional responsibilities. This type of recommendation is both equitable and responsible.

PROBLEM 3 Lack of Data. Often many extra expenses are incurred when items are not available, and special orders must be initiated. An analyst has noted that the company has exceeded the figure budgeted for special orders by $8,000 per month. He also has noticed that on each order the quantity asked for is less than ten.

Here, the $8,000 figure and the low order quantity alerted the analyst. Evidently, the order quantity used by the purchasing department is not sufficient to carry the inventory through order cycles. Another consideration might be that these items are being used more frequently in production, and supply personnel have not been notified of this increase. The lack of communication with the purchasing department, coupled with incorrect ordering procedures, has caused this problem to arise.

PROBLEM 4 Systems Procedures. Because of increased growth, the accounts payable department pays its bills late but usually without incurring a service charge. On investigation, it is learned that if the payment procedures were streamlined and bills paid within ten days of their receipt, 40 percent of the bills could receive discounts amounting to $10,000 per year. This becomes a viable reason for computerizing the accounts payable operation to speed up the processing of bills and thereby gain the discounts offered.

GLOSSARY

Component. One of the elements, or subsystems, that comprises a system.

Intangible cost. A cost with which a dollar value cannot be readily associated. A loss of business goodwill, for example, is an intangible cost.

Nonrecurring costs. Costs that, once accrued, will not occur again.

Overhead. Recurring company-wide costs that must be prorated to individual departments. They include heating, electricity, and the like.

Recurring costs. Costs incurred on a regular basis.

Resource sheet. A form available to the analyst that may be used in the preparation and documentation of a cost statement.

Savings. The result achieved when income derived from a system exceeds the expense of operating the system.

Sunk cost. An expense that, when paid, can never be recovered.

Tangible cost. A cost incurred where it is possible to directly associate the materials received and the dollars expended. The purchase of office equipment, for example, is a tangible cost.

Vendor estimates. Quotes received from vendors on items the company is pricing for possible purchase.

QUESTIONS

1. Consider the problem incurred when you must take out a loan through the bank. Go to some of the banks in your community and gather a few of the advertisements that describe their loan arrangements. For a $3,000 loan, should you:
   a. Pay the whole loan off in 36 months? At what rate of interest and cost of interest? What would the total cost of the loan be?
   b. Save $1,000 and take a loan for $2,000 for 24 months. How much do you save on interest charges? How much does the extra year of payments, for the first loan, cost in interest?

   Discuss the advantages and disadvantages of each alternative.
2. Examine the cost of your own or your parents' checking account. Many banks today are offering special checking

accounts with no service charge if you maintain a certain level of money in your savings account. How much money would you save, monthly and annually, if you used one of these checking plans? Employ the following data in your computations:

a. No service or check charges if you hold a minimum of $500 in a savings account, at 5¼ percent interest, compounded quarterly (on the lowest balance in the account for that quarter).

b. No savings required. A $2.00 monthly service fee and a cost of $.20 per check. You write, on the average, 15 checks per month.

3. Prepare a budget of your own personal expenses and income. How well do you adhere to it? How do you know when you have exceeded your budget? What do you do if you need money? Can you stop spending in other areas to conserve your money?

Could a business potentially operate on the principles you enforce on yourself? When it needs money, where does a company go for short-term loans? What interest rate must be paid? Are short-term loan rates higher than long-term loan rates?

CHAPTER **13**

FEASIBILITY STUDIES

Many companies do not have their own computer facility. They process information in one of the following ways: (1) manually, (2) by electronic accounting machines, usually in conjunction with manual operations, or (3) through the use of **service bureaus**, which are companies that design computer systems and then program and operate them for a fixed fee.

When company processing expands greatly, the management will generally request that a study be conducted to determine if a data processing facility could be justified; that is, a group is appointed to determine if it is feasible to acquire, maintain, and profit from a computer system. This type of study is called a **feasibility study**.

A special committee within the company is generally formed with the authority to conduct the feasibility study. The typical committee consists of the following employees:

1. One member of each department in the company, who can best convey the department's need for a computer
2. A member of the executive committee of the company, who is most concerned with the company's policies and monetary limitations
3. Senior systems analysts, who are most suited, because of training and background, to determine a company's need for a computer
4. An outside consultant who is considered an expert in designing alternative computer systems

The importance of each of these members is discussed below.

1. It is important to have each department represented on the committee for several reasons. Each representative is aware of the particular needs within his area. He can often indicate any special requirements that could be handled by a computer sys-

tem. In addition, once management decides to obtain a computer, it needs the operational support of all departments within the company. Since each department takes part in computer selection through its representative on the feasibility committee, the possibility of resistance to the computer from independent areas is reduced.

2. A member of the executive committee of the company is needed on the feasibility committee to act as chairman. Since a feasibility study involves much time and effort and extensive paperwork, a chairman is required to coordinate the committee's efforts. In addition to serving as chairman, this member's high position in management lends great prestige and support to the committee. It is always advantageous for a committee of this kind to have management's explicit support so that any barriers to its endeavors can be easily handled. For example, the committee generally spends much time in collecting information, interviewing employees, and meeting in conferences. These disruptions in normal daily activities are more readily tolerated by department managers when a committee has the explicit endorsement of the management. An executive is an added advantage on this committee because of his familiarity with company policies and monetary limitations. He can save the committee much time and effort by channeling its proposals to assure future acceptance.

3. Senior systems analysts are needed on the committee because of their expertise in computer hardware and software. By synthesizing and analyzing the requirements of all departments in the company, the analyst can determine the size and specifications of the computer system that should be installed. He can also determine the type of system that would be most suitable. For example, he might suggest that a computer system incorporating data communications through a terminal network be adopted. Or, he might recommend a much smaller system that would be adequate. The analyst, then, must possess specific knowledge of various computer configurations so that he can assist management in determining the most practical one for the company.

4. An outside consultant is often needed to act as a kind of catalyst on this committee. Note that, like the senior systems analysts, he has specialized knowledge in computer hardware and software. Unlike the analysts, however, he can be completely objective, since his responsibilities are independent of any company or department ties. An analyst who reports to the comptroller of the company may recommend computer

systems that are most conducive to handling accounting procedures, since this is the area with which he is most familiar. A consultant, however, can maintain objectivity and can often make valid recommendations.

The basic functions of the feasibility committee can be segmented into several phases:

1. Analyze the current operations of the company.
2. Determine if the implementation of a computer system can be justified. It is possible that an overhaul of the current operations might eliminate the need for a computer installation. If not, a further investigation would be required.
3. Assuming that a computer system is still feasible, it would now be necessary to devise a list of requirements and criteria to be fulfilled by the prospective computer. This list of specifications would then be submitted to several computer manufacturers. They would evaluate the data and make bids to supply specific computer configurations to fulfill the requirements.
4. Evaluate carefully the bids received by the feasibility committee. The computer manufacturer that can best meet the company's needs is then recommended to management.
5. Devise a plan for the company to prepare for the installation of the computer system, if management gives its approval.

The above steps are not unlike the systems analyst's tasks in analysis and design. All areas must be scrutinized carefully, a design recommended and, if approved, a plan must be indicated for implementing the system.

It is important to examine each of the above functions in more depth so that the scope of a feasibility study can be fully appreciated.

ANALYZE CURRENT COMPANY OPERATIONS

This is generally regarded as a major systems analysis, where the company itself is evaluated in depth. Each department must be individually considered, as well as their relations to each other. Documents must be evaluated, and costs must be compiled. Each department is *not* evaluated with regard to its flaws but, instead, with regard to how a computer system could improve its productivity.

DETERMINE JUSTIFICATION FOR COMPUTER

It is conceivable that, after analysis of the company's operations, a computer installation may not be justifiable from a cost standpoint. Perhaps a redesign effort of various forms and procedures can lead to a more efficient utilization of the company's manpower. Even with this type of redesign effort, the feasibility committee may feel that a computer is still warranted.

Note, however, that a computer installation must pay for itself in the end in order to be considered profitable. This implies that the cost of acquiring and of maintaining a computer system must be approximated at this time to determine if further investigation should be conducted. These costs would include the following items:

1. Cost of designing computerized systems
2. Cost of programming effort
3. Rental and/or purchase costs of computer hardware and software
4. Cost of training company personnel to use computer inputs and outputs
5. Cost of supplies
6. Costs of operating a computer facility
7. Cost associated with "housing" the computer, that is, the construction of an air-conditioned room for the computer

The current cost of processing information must be compiled and then compared to the projected computer costs. Note that often it is necessary to project present costs into the future to determine what the costs would be under the present system, but with normal growth trends. Very often, a present system, if continued indefinitely, would require extensive revision anyway. These revision costs should be included in present system costs so that a fair comparison to a computerized system can be made.

If, after cost comparison is completed, there appears to be a savings in the end, by installing a computer, then the company can proceed to derive a list of requirements and criteria to be fulfilled by a computer system. Observe that the savings need not be in the near future. Sometimes the savings obtained by installing a computer system takes many years to be realized.

If a computer system cannot be justified, the committee may recommend a redesign of forms or procedures. Or, a service bureau that can perform company operations on a computer for a fee could be investigated. The distinct advantage of contracting a service bureau is that the initial cost is greatly reduced. Note, however, that the company would have no computer systems of its own; everything is owned and operated by the service bureau. If the company decides to install a computer at a future date, it must buy or rent the programs and procedures from the service bureau, or must develop them on its own.

DERIVE A LIST OF REQUIREMENTS AND CRITERIA FOR THE PROSPECTIVE COMPUTER

The next step is to prepare the set of specifications of what is desired from the computer. The various computer manufacturers will use this as a basis for preparing bids to supply specific computer configurations. The type of information required would be as folows:

1. Review of the company's objectives and goals
2. Sample input and output forms currently used and the frequency with which they are generated
3. Descriptions of the type of processing done, including types of arithmetic operations performed
4. Statements of the major controls currently used
5. Description of the information that is on file, including the length of time it is maintained
6. List of any special capabilities desired under a computer system, such as terminal inputs, specific processing requirements, etc.
7. Description of the company's physical structure, including locations of branch offices, warehouses, etc.

ANALYZE BIDS FROM COMPUTER MANUFACTURERS

Once the bids are received from the manufacturers, they must be carefully evaluated by the feasibility committee. The cost of operating each computer system proposed is the most important factor in rating competitive bids. However, intangible benefits must be considered as well. The following items must be considered prior to rendering any decision:

1. Cost of renting the computer system
2. Programming languages available with the system
3. Multiprogramming and data communications capability
4. Ability to expand storage as required at a later date
5. Specifications of input/output devices included in the configuration

6. Availability of educational materials and their corresponding charges
7. Availability and cost of service in case of computer malfunction
8. Compatibility with larger models in case a future conversion is deemed necessary

Once the committee has reviewed all the bids, it should make its recommendation to management, in writing. The recommendation should highlight the reasons that this particular system was chosen over the others considered.

DEVISE A PLAN TO PREPARE FOR THE COMPUTER

When a company finally signs a contract with a computer manufacturer, it may have to wait a year or longer before delivery is made. The feasibility committee should map out a plan that will ensure a smooth transition from current operations to a computer system. A typical plan includes these items:

1. Establish a data processing department. This necessitates the hiring of computer and keypunch operators, programmers, systems analysts, and managers. Some members may be transferred from other departments and may be trained for new positions in the data processing department.
2. Design systems for the new computer.
3. Program the new systems. Even though the computer has not yet arrived, it is possible to write programs and have them tested. Often a computer manufacturer has test centers available for running programs, for a company whose computer has not yet been installed. If this is not available, programs can usually be tested by renting computer time from other companies. If systems work and programming effort for specified systems is completed when a new computer arrives, there need be no delay before the implementation occurs. Often, these phases are not even begun until the computer is delivered and, as a result, the equipment is rarely used for many months.
4. Test the new system. It is possible to have people simulate their projected tasks when the computer comes, by using sample forms and data. In this manner, "bugs" in the system can often be detected. In addition, the personnel who are required to use the system will become familiar with its operations and procedures.

From the foregoing discussion, one can easily realize why feasibility studies sometimes take two or more man-years to complete. These studies are the foundation for tremendous change within a company.

GLOSSARY

Bids. Formal vendor quotes to provide services to the company based on company-prepared specifications.

Bugs. Errors or inconsistencies found within the existing system.

Feasibility study. A formal company effort that determines whether or not a computer system may effectively be used, or is required, by the company.

Service bureau. An outside consultant concern that will provide computer services to any company desiring assistance.

QUESTIONS

1. Typically, who should be on the committee that performs a feasibility study and why?
2. Suppose your company has a computer facility and wishes to determine the feasibility of utilizing optical scanners. Prepare a list of cost factors you consider most important in determining feasibility.
3. Suppose your company has decided to implement an optical scanning system. What are some of the critical factors that must be determined before deciding whether the system should be purchased or leased?
4. What are some of the major problems that often occur in transition from a manual to a computer system? How can these be minimized?

CHAPTER **14**

PLANNING TOOLS

CPM AND PERT CHARTS

We saw in the previous chapter how a feasibility committee determines if it is feasible for a company to acquire, maintain, and profit from a computer system. After a feasibility committee recommends to management that they acquire a computer system, much planning is required if the computer is approved. There are numerous activities that must be scheduled so that the computer can be efficiently used as soon as it is set up and operational in the company.

There are several very useful aides that can be used to keep management apprised of the progress of its plans. One of these aides, the Gantt chart, will be discussed later in this chapter. There are two other types of charts that are generally used. They are the **CPM (critical path method)** chart and the **PERT (program evaluation and review technique)** chart. These two charts are similar in construction. They basically show the relationships among activities, and they indicate where critical problems may occur.

A general discussion of a CPM chart will highlight the basic concepts. The major differences between a CPM chart and a PERT chart can then be appreciated more easily. Suppose that there are nine activities that must be accomplished before a particular objective can be achieved. The relationships among these activities must be clearly understood. For example, perhaps activity 2 can be performed at the same time as activity 3, and both activities must be completed before activity 4 can commence. In addition to establishing these relationships, an estimate of the time required to perform each activity must be determined. This estimate is a reasonable guess as to how long it will take to accomplish each part of the project, based on the anticipated availability of resources. Resources include items such as manpower, material, and money.

After the list of activities is made, and time estimates and relationships are clearly understood, a chart is drawn to reflect this information. Consider the chart in Figure 14.1. The dashed line indicates that the next activity connected by this line cannot be started until the previous activity has been com-

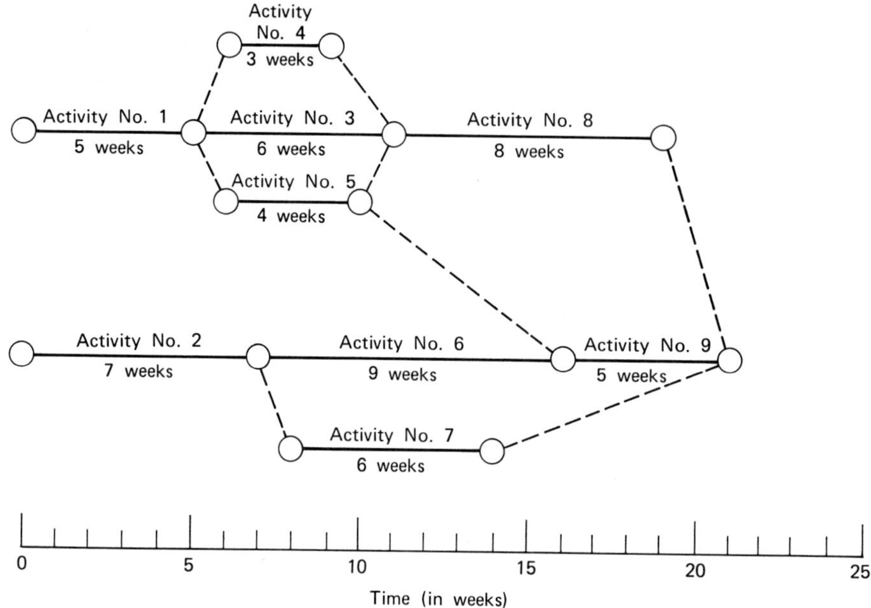

Figure 14.1 Critical path method (CPM) chart.

pleted. For example, activity 4 cannot commence until activity 1 has finished, and activity 8 cannot start until activities 4, 3, and 5 have all been completed.

It is useful for management to recognize which series of events will take the longest, since that **critical path** will determine when the project can be completed. Observe that it is possible for a CPM chart to have more than one critical path. The critical path is usually indicated on the chart by a heavy line running parallel to the activities that comprise this path. The determination of the longest path for the above illustration is shown in Table 14.1.

TABLE 14.1

Path Number	Activities That Comprise the Path	Total Time for Completion of Path
1	1, 4, 8	5 + 3 + 8 = 16 weeks
2	1, 3, 8	5 + 6 + 8 = 19 weeks
3	1, 5, 8	5 + 4 + 8 = 17 weeks
4	1, 5, 9	5 + 4 + 5 = 14 weeks
5	2, 6, 9	7 + 9 + 5 = 21 weeks
6	2, 7	7 + 6 = 13 weeks

Path 5 is thus the critical path, requiring 21 weeks for completion. Knowing this fact, management may decide to reallocate its resources in order to achieve its goal in a shorter time period.

The plans that result from a feasibility study often involve dozens of activities. A CPM chart drawn at the outset of a project alerts management immediately to the magnitude of the job ahead. Once the project has begun, the chart is updated periodically to reflect the progress to date. It may become evident, for example, that some of the original time estimates were incorrect. A reevaluation of all of the paths at this time may produce new critical paths.

The process of updating a CPM chart involves the following:

1. Observe which activities have been completed since the last time that the chart was updated. This can be accomplished by crosshatching the circle at the end of the activity.
2. Reevaluate the times required to finish each activity currently in progress. Previous times should be crossed out, not erased, and the new times should be added to the chart.
3. Reevaluate the estimated times for activities not yet started, and correct them as required.
4. Add or delete activities from the chart if there has been a change in the approach to achieving the particular goal.

It should be noted that it sometimes becomes desirable to use a computer to generate and to maintain CPM charts. This is especially true when a given goal has several hundred activities, and the chart is to be updated on a weekly basis. The determination of critical paths in this situation becomes rather tedious.

A PERT (program evaluation and review technique) chart is similar in construction to the CPM chart. However, three time estimates are associated with each activity, as described below.

1. A *most likely time* for completion of the activity is determined
2. The earliest expected time for completion, or an *optimistic estimate,* for the activity is derived
3. The latest expected time for completion, or a *pessimistic estimate* for the activity, is also determined

The "most likely time" is the best guess as to the duration of the activity under normal operating conditions. The "optimistic estimate" is the best possible time for completion of the activity. This would occur if ideal conditions existed and if all resources were operating at an optimum level. The "pessimistic estimate" indicates the time required under the worst possible circumstances. With these three estimates for each activity, it is then possible to determine three corresponding times for the overall completion of the project. These times would be the most likely time for completion, an optimistic time, and a pessimistic time. Management can then review these results to determine how it might want to reallocate its resources and, perhaps, to restructure its priorities.

GANTT CHARTS

It is essential that the systems analyst provide management with a broad idea of the amount of time that he thinks will be needed to design a new system.

The type of chart in Figure 14.2 is often used to represent an anticipated time schedule for all functions that must be performed by the analyst, assuming, as always, that management gives its OK to a new design. The illustration shown in Figure 14.2 is called a **Gantt chart.**

Note that the functions and time factors will depend on the specific system. This Gantt chart will be updated weekly and submitted to management. The analyst shades in that phase of the work already completed so that management gets a graph of progress.

Figure 14.2 Gantt chart.

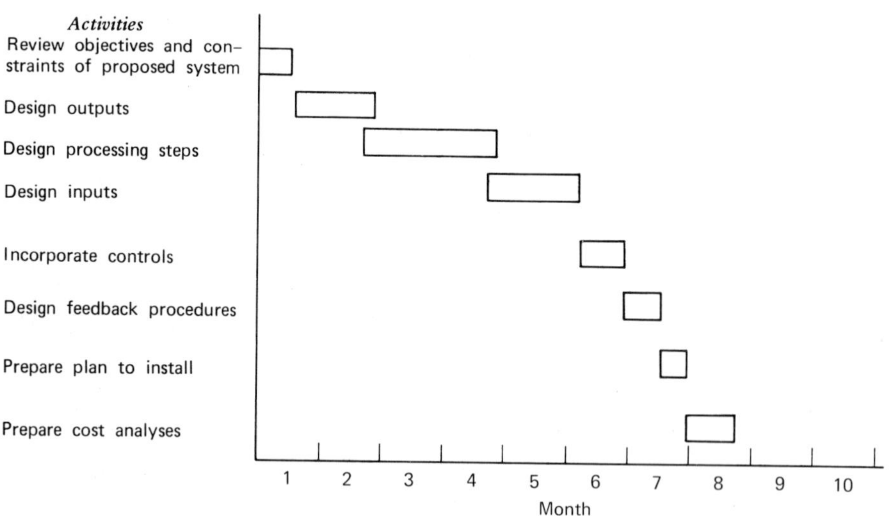

When the design phase begins, the analyst can submit his progress on this chart each week. Observe that the figures presented on a Gantt chart are merely estimates, since the analyst has no absolute method for determining just how long given phases of the design will take.

HIPO/IPO

One of the overriding critical considerations in any systems project is the factor of time. Each analyst working on a systems project is always keenly aware of the project's completion date. The questions that are repeatedly asked of the analyst are: How far are you along on your work? Does it look like you'll finish on time? Normally, as a systems project approaches its scheduled completion date, the intensity of work performed literally rises to a feverish pitch. This tremendous outpouring of effort has one obvious purpose, to reach or meet the project deadline on time.

The set of circumstances described above is indicative of a problem frequently encountered by analysts and project managers alike: to adequately maintain a status on the progress of the project. What occurs quite often, to the embarrassment of the people concerned, is that by the time that they have discovered that the project has fallen behind, it is too late to rectify the situation.

Naturally, there have been many solutions proferred in an attempt to correct or curtail this problem (e.g., PERT, CPM). Each approach has met with varying degrees of success largely dependent upon the personnel and type of project involved. No one technique has proven a panacea to controlling and supervising systems efforts.

One of the most recent developments in the area of project control is the concept of **modular**, or **structured design.**[1] The modular approach to design was initially developed for applications within the programming area. In the past few years, the concept has been applied to the area of analysis and design with considerable success.

An integral part of the modular design approach is the use of HIPO-oriented concepts. The term **HIPO** is derived from the

[1]The authors have chosen to use the term "modular design" throughout this discussion. Our investigations revealed a plethora of terms describing the same technique. The terms "composite design," "structured programming," "structured programming design," "modular programming," "composite analysis," and "design" are just a few examples that we uncovered. The term we have selected to use is a fair representation of these labels.

terms "hierarchy," "input," "processing," and "output." Originally developed to provide documentational assistance for programmer/analysts, HIPO was successfully used as a systems tool and is now recognized as an accepted tool within the analysis and design field.

The major concept upon which HIPO is based is the highly structured modular design. The HIPO documentation employs a structure that is similar to an organization chart. This type of structure permits the enforcement of major principles to HIPO, a top-to-bottom approach to design. The emphasis here is on forcing the flow of data down through the system, not in the opposite direction. Let us elaborate on this idea.

The purpose behind this top-to-bottom approach is the elimination of "output-oriented" systems solutions. An output-oriented system is concerned with providing output and often ignores many of the sound principles of systems design. In essence, an output-oriented system often gets the job done, as quickly as possible. Unfortunately, many data processing organizations, for a variety of reasons, employ this type of rationale in their systems designs. Output-oriented systems are often fragmentary or incomplete, with large gaps evident in the logic and flow of data throughout the system. Programs written for this type of system often duplicate each other in part. The net effect is that more programs are written, with a resultant loss of manpower and time.

The HIPO concept, with its highly ordered structure and top-to-bottom approach, attempts to eliminate piecemeal systems design, which results in duplicate programming efforts, and to assist systems managers in controlling their projects. Let us examine a general HIPO structure, as illustrated in Figure 14.3.

As you can observe, the HIPO structure is quite similar to that of a manager's organizational chart. The numbers employed on the HIPO chart provide a means of identifying each of the sublevels and component blocks on the chart. The rationale of subdividing and identifying the component blocks within a HIPO design is extremely important. Applying this concept, the analyst is capable of defining and completely laying out the overall structure of the entire system under study. The HIPO approach is specifically designed to accommodate the development of a system.

In employing a HIPO chart, the analyst must first determine what specifically the system will do. The definition of the system is written into block 0 and sets the tone of the en-

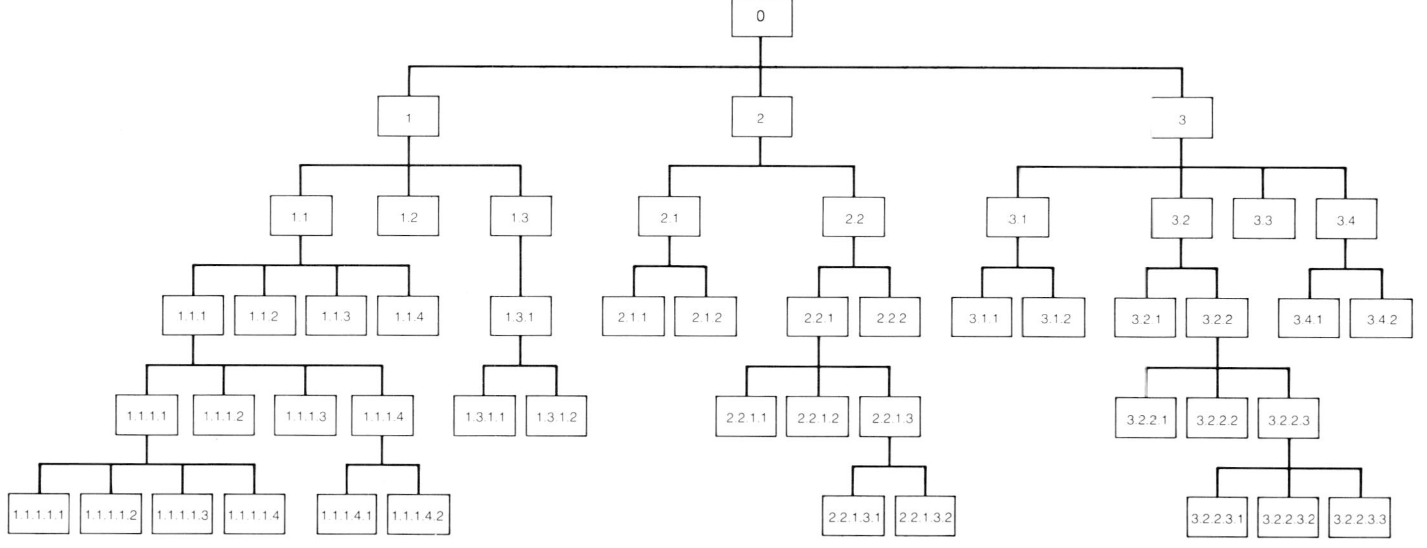

Figure 14.3 Structure of a HIPO chart, identifying all of the components within the chart by number at each of the sublevels.

tire design. After determining the specific purpose of the system, the analyst must next break down the system into its major activities and define them at the level beneath block 0 (blocks 1, 2, and 3).

Each of the major components defined in blocks 1, 2, and 3 must be carefully analyzed. Only after the analyst is secure in the knowledge that they are the correct components (at level 1) can he commence design at level 2. At level 2, each of the blocks 1, 2, and 3 are subdivided by their major components. It is at this point that the numbering convention employed within a HIPO chart becomes vital. It provides an easy method for identifying each component block, within the appropriate levels of the design, as well as the branches of the design.

Figure 14.4 depicts an excerpt of a HIPO design relating to a program. Here, the activities of the program are broken down into the most basic tasks required of the program.

The top-to-bottom approach forces the analyst to completely analyze each component at each level before continuing downward within the HIPO structure. It is felt that this type of diagnostic approach permits tighter control over a project, while ensuring a more efficient design. Approval to continue to another block is given only after analysis of the component under study is complete. This procedure ensures that:

1. The component (block) is completely analyzed and/or designed, and further work is not required
2. All of the requirements and resources necessary for that component are totally defined

Thus defining the requirements of the system is subsequently easier.

At the completion of a HIPO design effort, the entire structure of a system is defined. It is because of this detailed structure that modifications are easily handled. With the requirements of each block detailed, only the block, or blocks, affected by the modifications will be altered. The savings here come from knowing exactly what components must be changed and the extent of the change.

The modular structure also assists in clearly defining the interfaces of all of the components (blocks) within a system. Normally, this is one of the most difficult tasks facing the analyst. Since the HIPO structure requires the definition of requirements for each component within the system, interfaces

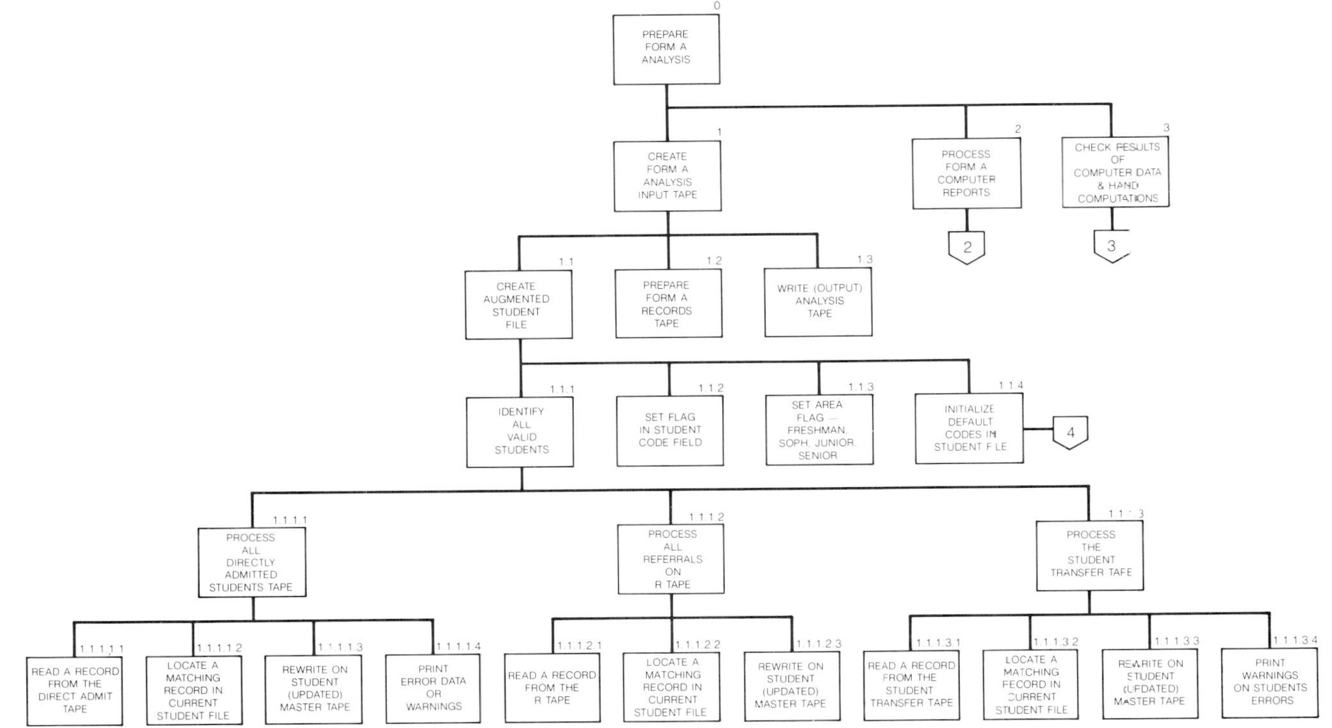

Figure 14.4 Excerpt from a HIPO chart in which level 1 is subdivided into its lowest components. Each lower level details and defines the level immediately above it.

are methodically detailed as the analyst proceeds *down* the chart. This feature represents another advantage of HIPO design as opposed to a bottom-to-top approach. All interfaces are designed well before systems implementation; the specifications for programs can be clearly detailed, so that the programs are written once. No programs are started before the system is totally laid out, thereby reducing the reprogramming effort. Reprogramming is a common occurrence with bottom-to-top systems designs.

When the analyst has completed what he considers the final design with HIPO, it must be translated into exacting operational terms. Here, each of the component blocks within the HIPO chart is scrutinized and delineated into specific input, output, processing, and file requirements. The form employed for this purpose is illustrated in Figure 14.5, and referred to as an **IPO form**.

The IPO form is employed to:

1. Identify the component block
2. Detail all inputs by reference number, tape number, file number, type, data file, card, etc.
3. Describe the processing within that block
4. Detail all outputs by firm name and number, file number, card type, etc.

Figure 14.5 IPO form. An IPO form must be completed for every block on a HIPO chart. It details all of the inputs, processing, outputs related to that component block. Notes are added to assist in understanding codes employed, special terms, labels, restraints, or problems observed.

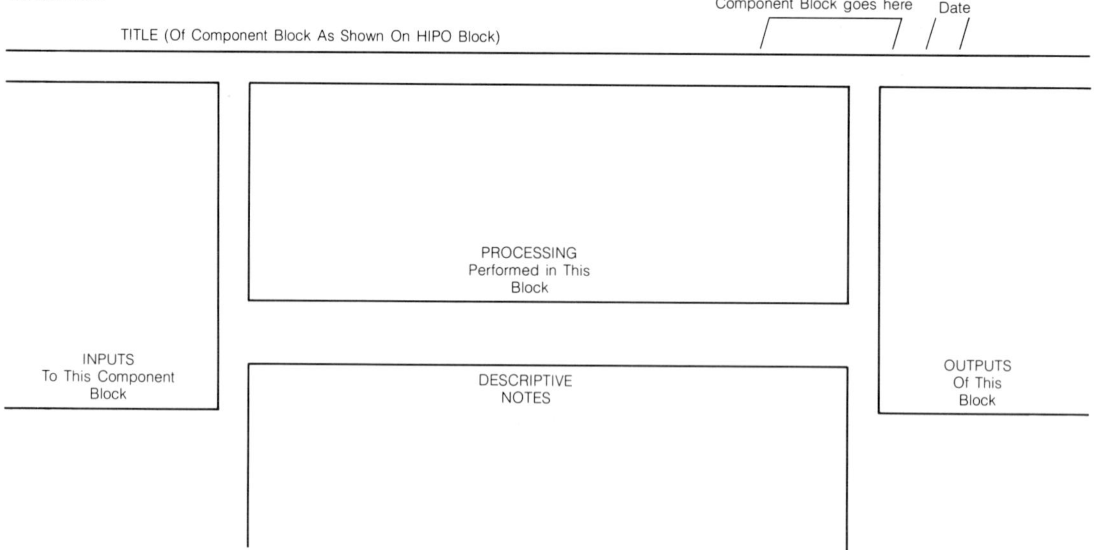

5. Provide any notes that will enable a clearer understanding of the processing being performed.

For each component block within a HIPO chart, an IPO form must be completed. Figure 14.6 illustrates some completed IPO forms that relate to the HIPO chart depicted in Figure 14.4. The numbers above the blocks on the IPO forms relate directly to the numbers used in the HIPO chart.

After the completion of the HIPO chart and accompanying IPO forms, the analyst is ready to present the design to the systems group. This presentation will enable the systems group to collectively learn about the system and examine it for potential flaws in the design. Prior to this meeting, members of the systems group must be provided with copies of the HIPO and IPO forms.

At the presentation, referred to as a structured walk-through, the participants will discuss the entire design and attempt to find weak spots within the system. The analyst defends the rationale of the proposal and notes recommendations that improve the design. The walk-through is invaluable, as it serves to inform the systems group about the system under study and provides the analyst with a sounding board for ideas.

Normally, structured walk-throughs are scheduled for per-

Figure 14.6 Completed IPO forms.

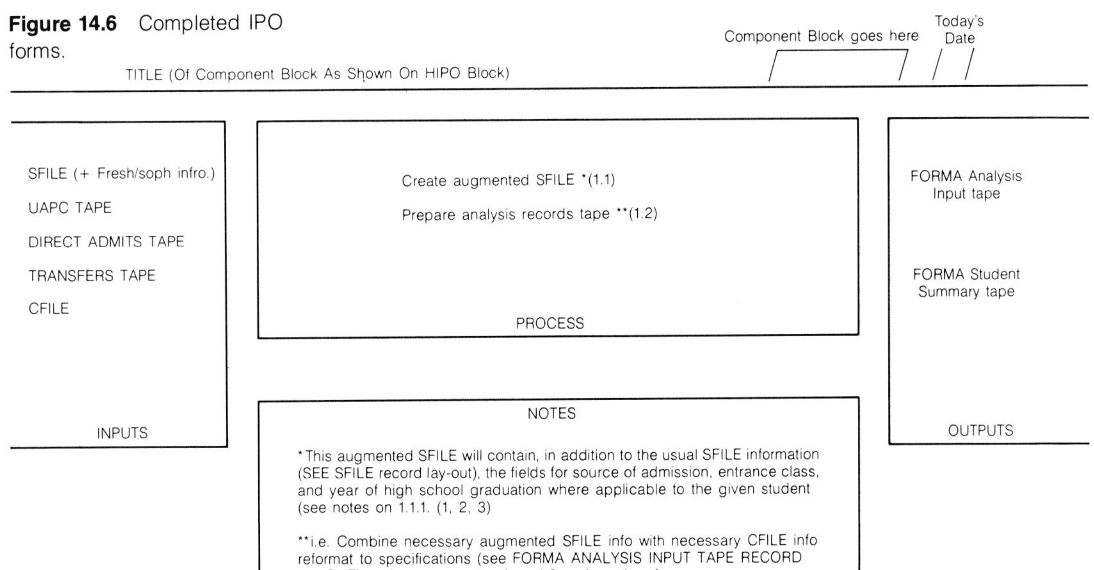
TITLE (Of Component Block As Shown On HIPO Block)

Component Block goes here

Today's Date

SFILE (+ Fresh/soph infro.)
UAPC TAPE
DIRECT ADMITS TAPE
TRANSFERS TAPE
CFILE

INPUTS

Create augmented SFILE *(1.1)
Prepare analysis records tape **(1.2)

PROCESS

FORMA Analysis Input tape

FORMA Student Summary tape

OUTPUTS

NOTES

*This augmented SFILE will contain, in addition to the usual SFILE information (SEE SFILE record lay-out), the fields for source of admission, entrance class, and year of high school graduation where applicable to the given student (see notes on 1.1.1. (1, 2, 3)

**i.e. Combine necessary augmented SFILE info with necessary CFILE info reformat to specifications (see FORMA ANALYSIS INPUT TAPE RECORD LAYOUT) and output to tape (see 1.2 and on down)

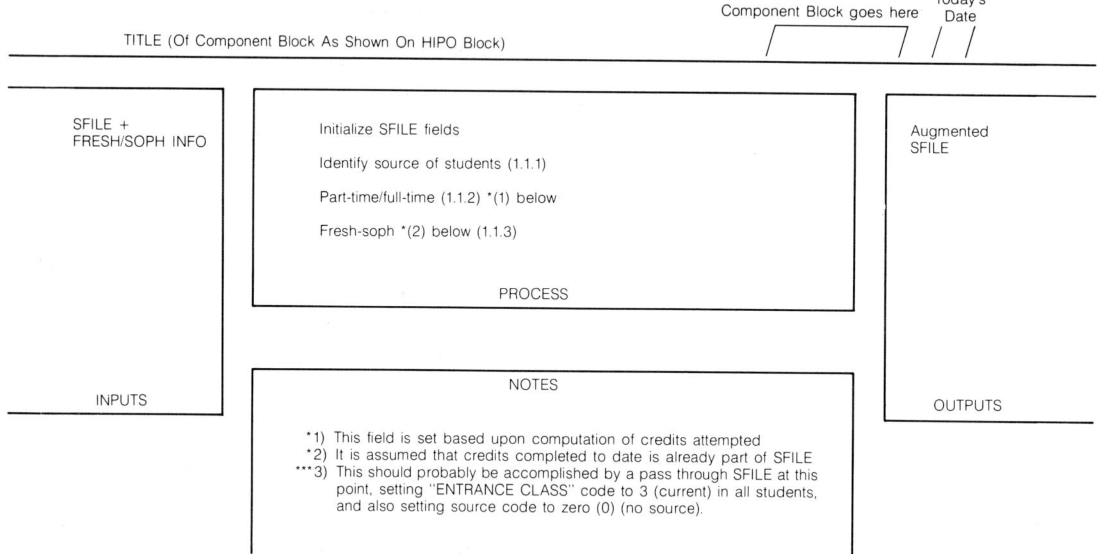

TITLE (Of Component Block As Shown On HIPO Block)
Component Block goes here
Today's Date
*Student file (SFILE)
Transfer tape
SFILE +
FRESH/SOPH INFO
INPUTS
process UAPC tape (1.1.1.2)
process transfer tape (1.1.1.3)
Initialize SFILE fields
Identify source of students (1.1.1)
Part-time/full-time (1.1.2) *(1) below
Fresh-soph *(2) below (1.1.3)
PROCESS
*SFILE as given
Augmented SFILE
OUTPUTS
NOTES
*SFILE may already be slightly "enlarged" upon entry to this routine i.e. this routine should only modify those fields which it is required to—all other fields must be preserved as read.
Note: Errors will be noted if a student has multiple sources of admissions, i.e. if he appears on both, for example, the Transfer and UAPC tapes. Merely test in each routine for non-zero entry, if so, overwrite, print error msg. and continue.
*1) This field is set based upon computation of credits attempted
*2) It is assumed that credits completed to date is already part of SFILE
***3) This should probably be accomplished by a pass through SFILE at this point, setting "ENTRANCE CLASS" code to 3 (current) in all students, and also setting source code to zero (0) (no source).

Figure 14.6 Continued.

iods of one hour. These sessions are quite intense and tend to be rather exhausting. Breaks within each one-hour session are required to permit the participants to relax.

The HIPO/IPO technique is slowly developing a following in the field as more DP people become acquainted with its concepts. This section is designed to acquaint the reader with

Figure 14.6 Continued.

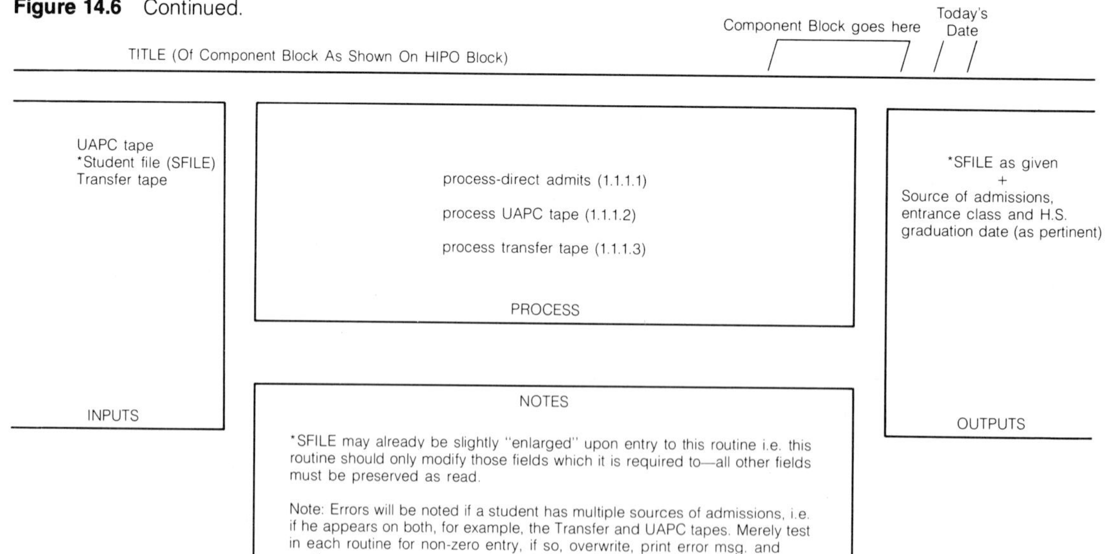

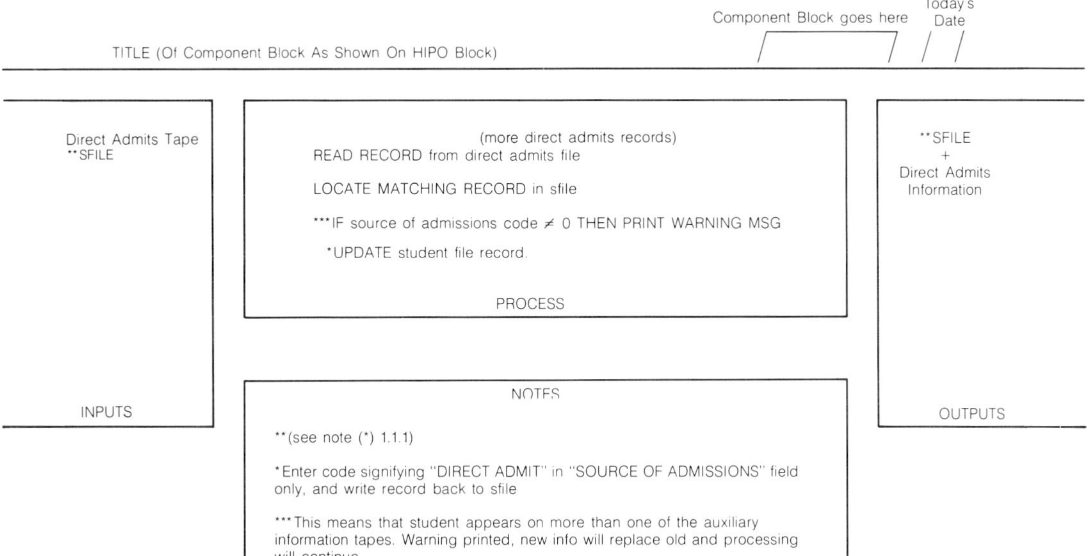

Figure 14.6 Continued.

the existence of HIPO/IPO and briefly describe its concept. It is suggested that the reader further research this subject if a more comprehensive understanding of the technique is required.

SIMULATION

Basic Concepts

Simulation is an operations research[2] technique that uses a representation or model of a system that can be manipulated and studied in order to understand the behavior of the actual system itself.

There are, in essence, two basic kinds of models used. There is the **physical model**, such as a model airplane flown in a wind tunnel to simulate actual flight conditions. The other kind of model is the one of primary interest to the businessperson, the conceptual or **mathematical model**, which can be described by an analyst and then programmed by a programmer.

The technique of simulation affords the manager the opportunity to ask the computer, What would happen if I were to do this? He can test the effectiveness of decisions without actually implementing them. In this manner, the computer can

[2]Operations research (OR) basically refers to the use of mathematics to solve business problems.

simulate the conditions the manager *intends* to impose on a system and can then project the corresponding results. Listed below are some typical applications to which simulation can be applied for the businessperson.

1. How much should the sales force in a department store be increased in order to adequately handle customer demands at peak times?
2. By how much will the addition of a specific number of new machines in a manufacturing plant alleviate production backlogs?
3. How will a specific change in policy of the inventory control department reduce inventory investment and, at the same time, maintain adequate availability of merchandise to meet consumer demands?
4. How will the company's profit picture be affected by specific proposed capital expenditures?
5. How will a change in the store's policy affect sales?
6. How will the addition of a new branch office affect the company's total profits?

Simulation is an extremely powerful technique that is becoming more widespread for several reasons:

1. It uses the computer to *simulate* time so that the effect is the representation of time, in minutes on a computer, of events that would take an actual time span of days, months, or years. Thus a manager can see immediately what the effects of a particular policy might be over an extended period of time.
2. It is often prohibitively costly, especially in terms of financial risk, time spent, and manpower, for management to implement a particular decision on the gamble that it *may* be successful. The use of simulation can increase the likelihood that a simulated decision that is found to be successful will, in actual practice, be a wise one.
3. In many business structures, the interrelationships among the various systems are extremely complex. As a result, it is not possible to determine simple relationships.

   If management varies some facet of one system, for example, the effects on all other systems may not be precisely known. Thus, using simulation, the possible effect of a major policy decision can be more precisely defined.
4. Special high-level programming languages have been developed specifically to facilitate the programmer's task of writ-

ing a program to perform simulation experiments. These languages, to mention a few of the more common ones, include:

a. GPSS—General Purpose Systems Simulator

b. DYNAMO

c. GASP—General Activity Simulation Program

d. SIMSCRIPT

With the use of these programming tools, the programmer or analyst need only supply a series of system specifications in order for the machine to perform a simulation. Thus simulation, today, has become more widespread because of software assistance.

5. Simulation is used in many companies as a training tool for management, to enable them to enhance their decision-making skills. Managers can thus participate in **management games**, a technique whereby business leaders can experiment with a hypothetical company to see if they can pinpoint problem areas and to see whether the various decisions made by them to alleviate the problems would be effective if implemented. With the use of management games, it is hoped that these business leaders would become more effective in their decision-making role.

Example of a Management Game

As was mentioned above, management games are used in many companies as a training aid for management. There have been many management games developed for this purpose. We will now briefly describe how one of these, the IBM Management Decision-Making Game, operates. The following illustration has been simplified in order to present the major concepts of the game, without dwelling on the intricate details.

Let us assume that there are three hypothetical firms in a particular marketing area that produce just one product for sale. At the beginning of the game, all firms start with the same cash, inventory, and plant facilities. The net worth of each firm, in this game, is equal to the total assets of the firm, since none of the firms is allowed to incur debts.

Management personnel are asked to make executive-level decisions for each of these hypothetical firms. In this way, the business leaders can observe the effects of any decisions and, depending on which firm produces the greatest profit, the best decision-maker for this specific type of firm can be determined.

At the beginning of each operating period, each of the firms makes its own decisions regarding:

1. Price
2. Marketing expenditures
3. Plant improvement expenditures
4. Production expenditures
5. Research and development expenditures

The decisions are punched into cards and fed into a computer. The computer then simulates the behavior of each firm and produces reports, as shown in Figures 14.7 and 14.8 showing the results of the activity in the period. This process can be repeated as many times as desired in order for the manager to see the results of his decisions and what kind of improvement he is making.

LINEAR PROGRAMMING

Linear programming, like simulation, is an operations research tool that can be used to find the best way of performing a particular activity. That is, linear programming determines the optimal method for performing a task. The term "programming," in this case, refers to the planning of economic activities rather than to the activity of a computer programmer. The term "linear" refers to the fact that this mathematical techniquc is applicable only if the economic activities being investigated are related in a straight line, or in a linear way. That is, if it costs $1 to produce one item, a linear relationship exists if it costs approximately $2 to produce two items, $4 to produce four items, and so on.

Linear programming problems are most often solved by a computer. A program, often supplied by the computer manufacturer, is used to incorporate the appropriate mathematics.

Fortunately, many business activities that can be analyzed using linear programming usually have a reasonably close linear relationship. The two main types of linear programming problems concern: (1) the allocation of resources, and (2) the transportation problem, as discussed below.

The **allocation of resources** involves a situation where there are numerous activities that can be performed in many ways, but since the necessary resources are limited, not all activities can be carried out in the best way at the same time. The basic idea of the linear programming technique is to allocate the available resources in such a way as to optimize some objective, such as maximization of profits, or minimization of costs, depending on the nature of the problem. As an example, management might want to dctcrmine the best way of assigning

FIRM 1 REPORT

SALES ANALYSIS

Orders	253
Sales	253
Unit price	$40
Sales revenue	$10,119
Marketing expenses	$600

PRODUCTION

	Inventory	Plant Capacity	Current Production
Quantity	9	260	216
Unit cost	$35.49	$34.44	$35.49
Total cost	$304	$8,955	$7,650

PROFIT and LOSS STATEMENT

Total Revenue		$10,119
Cost of goods sold	$8,881	
Marketing	$600	
Research and development	$100	
Depreciation	$104	
Total expenses		$9,685
Profit before taxes		$434
Taxes		$217
Net profit		$217

CASH STATEMENT

Old balance		$8,500
Total revenue		$10,119
Production cost	$7,650	
Marketing	$600	
Research and development	$100	
Plant Improvement	$104	
Taxes	$217	
Total outlay		$8,671
New cash balance		$9,948

BALANCE SHEET

Cash balance		$9,948
Current Inventory		$304
Old Plant	$5,200	
Depreciation	$104	
Plant Improvement	$104	
New plant		$5,200
Total assets		$15,452
Net worth		$15,452

Figure 14.7 Simulation model.

INDUSTRY REPORT

Firm 1 Balance Sheet	
Cash	$9,948
Inventory	304
Plant	5,200
Total assets	$15,452
Firm 2 Balance Sheet	
Cash	$9,948
Inventory	304
Plant	5,200
Total assets	$15,452
Firm 3 Balance Sheet	
Cash	$9,948
Inventory	304
Plant	5,200
Total assets	$15,452
Total Market Survey	
Total orders	759
Total sales	759
Total marketing expenditure	$1,800
Firm 1 price	$40
Firm 2 price	$40
Firm 3 price	$40

Figure 14.8 Simulation of economic systems.

work to its employees in a factory or the best way of scheduling jobs on machines. Management might also want to determine the best way to allocate corporate financial resources. Since there are so many variables, a simple problem-solving set of equations cannot be used. Instead, the computer is employed to maximize the desired result. In this way, necessary changes to the variables are listed by the computer to effect maximization of profits, for example.

The **transportation problem** is a common type of problem solved by the linear programming technique. As an example, a company may have several warehouses located throughout the country that supply various items of merchandise to different stores. The question arises as to the best way to stock merchandise in the warehouses so as to minimize the cost of distribution. Here again, the use of linear programming can help the manager to determine the best decision to make.

GLOSSARY

Critical path. The series of events that will take the longest period of time to complete.

CPM chart. Critical path method chart.

Gantt chart. A form of bar chart used to represent an anticipated time schedule for all functions to be performed by the analyst in analyzing and/or designing a system.

HIPO chart. Hierarchy, input, processing, and output chart.

Linear programming. An operations research tool used to find the best way of performing a particular activity.

Optimistic estimate. Earliest expected time for completion of a particular activity.

PERT chart. Program evaluation and review technique chart.

Pessimistic estimate. Latest expected time for completion of a particular activity.

Simulation. An operations research technique that uses a representation or model of a system that can be manipulated and studied in order to understand the behavior of the actual system itself.

QUESTIONS

1. What is a CPM chart, and how is it used?
2. What is a PERT chart, and how is it used?
3. What is a Gantt chart, and how is it used?
4. What sorts of problems might best be handled by simulation techniques?
5. How are management games utilized? Illustrate.
6. What is the purpose of linear programming, and how is it used in a business environment?
7. What is meant by a HIPO structure?

UNIT **V**

THE SYSTEMS PACKAGE

CHAPTER **15**

PROBLEM DEFINITION AND SYSTEMS DOCUMENTATION

PROBLEM DEFINITION

Defining the Problem

We have seen that before new systems can be designed, the current systems and procedures must be evaluated in depth. More revised systems are inadequate because of a poor evaluation of the present system than for any other reason. Thus a thorough description of the current system and a detailed analysis of its problems are fundamental functions of the analyst.

Recall that the ultimate objective of this analytic phase is to determine:

1. The goals and objectives of the system
2. How the system strives to meet these goals and objectives
3. What aspects of the present system hamper the fulfillment of these goals and objectives

The goals and objectives of a system, as well as the manner in which the system effectively meets these criteria, are learned from the facts obtained from procedures manuals, the evaluation of documents, and the interviewing of departmental representatives.

An evaluation of policies will provide a fundamental analysis of the objectives and constraints established by management. It will also enable the analyst to view the system as it relates to the entire organization. We discuss outputs in the form of report documents, since they are the most frequently used media. Thus our discussion on analysis is subdivided into five major problem areas: policies, forms, processing, inputs, and controls and feedback.

Policies. The analyst must evaluate all amassed data on the system before making judgments concerning its problem areas. He should initially view the system as a whole, in the macrocosm. He must analyze the overall performance of the system before considering its basic components. The executive policies and directives of the company insofar as they affect the system must be evaluated in depth. Too often, these policies are treated as sacred cows, too holy to be questioned. A systems analyst must, however, strive to improve all areas within a company. If he determines that specific company policies require revision, he must be prepared to indicate this decisively, but tactfully.

Let us consider the following checklist of policies that are generally analyzed when investigating a system. Note that such a list cannot be all-encompassing because of major differences among business organizations.

1. *Is the leadership of the department in which the system functions overburdened?* Perhaps a separation of the system into two or more divisions might enhance the achievement of the company's goals and objectives. A large company, for example, might do well to divide its purchasing and receiving department into a purchasing unit and a materials handling unit.
2. *Is the leadership of the system divided between two or more individuals to the detriment of the company?* Too often, a dichotomy in leadership makes for ambiguous lines of responsibility.
3. *Is the system self-sufficient, or would it best be served by combining it with some existing group?* Perhaps, in a small organization, the personnel department could become a subdivision of the payroll department at a monetary savings to the company.
4. *Does any company policy adversely affect the performance of the system?* Let us suppose that management has the prerogative of requesting reports from a department, giving only 48-hour notice. This practice requires specific employees to delay their own assignments in favor of preparing these reports. If the management documents are not, in fact, urgently required, it might be more efficient to request that executive personnel follow normal procedures when a report is desired.
5. *Is responsibility clearly defined, and if so, is it properly delegated?*
6. *Are there any unnecessary subdivisions of departmental responsibilities?* Some departments maintain assistant managers whose assignments have become obsolete.
7. *Is the work flow adversely affected by the necessity to coordinate operations with other systems?*

8. *Is the budget constraint for the system a realistic one?* Perhaps the system is stifled by being forced to work within an inflexible budget.

If many policy changes are required for a specific system, then a major revision of the present system would be appropriate.

Forms. The preparation of forms is often the result of numerous operations and activities. These documents represent the finalized output that is to be scrutinized and evaluated by management. For this reason, its efficient preparation is a requisite of any good system.

The following checklist has been previously presented, although in a slightly different form:

1. Can the data on this report be gotten from any other source? If such is the case, then the report might possibly be eliminated.
2. Is the report easy to read and use?
3. Are there any unnecessary items of data on the report?
4. Can several reports be combined into one major report?
5. Is the frequency of receipt of the document optimal?
6. Will a change in distribution of the form optimize its use?

Processing. The processing of data requires employees and activities or operations.

EMPLOYEE WORK FORCE. Once the analyst has considered the system in its entirety, he can then begin to view the various elements that form the system. He may begin by evaluating the employee work force to determine if changes in personnel are required or if changes in the system are needed to meet growing dissatisfaction or resistance on the part of the staff.

Let us consider the following checklist:

1. Are highly skilled personnel properly placed? Too often, skilled personnel are used to perform routine clerical functions.
2. Is overstaffing or understaffing in evidence?
3. Are there many clerical operations that might be more economically and efficiently performed by data processing equipment?
4. Do conditions exist that are causing morale problems?

5. Is there enough flexibility so that employees in different groups are properly trained to be called on to handle peak loads?

ACTIVITIES. At this juncture, the analyst must segment the system into its various activities, operations, and procedures to determine the aspects of the system that need revision.

Even though the analyst must segment the system, he should keep in mind its entire structural organization. That is, he must not sacrifice the forest for the trees. Note that a basic flaw in one activity might have its fundamental cause, or be manifested in, another. Consider the following example.

EXAMPLE. Ten employees working within an accounts receivable system find that they need a particular document for a certain phase of their job. They do not normally receive this document. It may appear, on an initial observation, that ten additional copies of this form ought to be prepared. On further investigation, however, it may prove to be more advantageous to assign *one* employee to perform the duties of the ten that require the form. Thus, while reviewing each activity, keep in mind its relation to the system as a whole.

The following represents a checklist of items to be considered when evaluating the activities within a system:

1. Can a monetary savings be realized by revising the activity? Perhaps a computerized system would better serve the fulfillment of goals and objectives.
2. Does the present activity utilize excessive time and effort on the part of the employees?
3. Does inaccurate or late reporting result in duplication of effort?
4. Is the output from the activity reliable enough for the department to have faith in it?
5. Is the present activity so rigid and inflexible that minor changes would require major revamping?
6. Can the present system handle larger volumes that would result from normal growth?
7. Does the activity meet with any major resistance?

Inputs. Cumbersome or inefficient input documents can make processing difficult and the resultant output inadequate. Therefore it is necessary for the analyst to analyze the input forms after he has determined any problem areas in both output and processing.

This is a checklist of items that may be considered when evaluating input:

1. Are the input data considered reliable and accurate? Sometimes input data must be completely edited and even revised before they are considered acceptable.
2. Do the input data enter the system on time? Sometimes late input reporting substantially thwarts productivity.
3. Are the input data readable? Sometimes the sixth carbon copy that enters the system is too blurred to be useful.
4. Is the input document really necessary at all? Sometimes a department can obtain the same data from another input document.

In utilizing this checklist, the analyst must determine how input documents can be improved on to provide a better quality of output.

Controls and Feedback. An analysis of the controls of the system gives the analyst a general idea of the reliability and accuracy of the system as a whole. That is, if the system maintains adequate controls, then the output data will probably be considered reliable and normally will contain few errors. Sometimes, however, the growth of the system has made previous controls inadequate and even unworkable.

Similarly, feedback is a protective measure originally established to assure management that its goals and objectives would be achieved. If a problem area originally existed, the feedback of information would reveal it. In actuality, however, the feedback procedure is usually not followed once a system has been effectively established.

Both controls and feedback on the present system can help the analyst to discover problem areas. Major difficulties in a system become evident when controls and/or feedback is implemented.

The above areas represent the ones with which the analyst must be concerned in the analytic phase of his job. When this is completed, the analyst must *formalize* his impressions, ideas, and criticisms of the system.

The **problem definition** is the formal document, prepared by the analyst, that defines in detail all aspects of the system and their basic inadequacies. It contains, in effect, the analysis of the present system. It ferrets out the fundamental problem areas in the system that impede the achievement of its objectives and requirements.

This problem definition is generally presented to management for review prior to the design of a new system. Management must determine whether a new system design is justified and feasible. The problem definition is the chief tool used for such a determination. Along with detailed descriptions of present activities, it contains the analyst's projections of the time it will take to design a new system.

Management representatives then discuss this document with the department head to determine if a new system should be designed and implemented at that time.

It should be noted that, barring unforeseen complications, management generally approves the problem definition and gives its OK to a new system design. The analyst was initially assigned to a system because a new design was deemed necessary. Therefore, unless a new system will simply cost too much, or the analyst does not think a new design is justified, or conditions within the company have substantially altered its policies, management will give its approval to a new design.

Basic Format

The problem definition must be a detailed, formalized document. When an analyst is called on to study a system, it is generally because the system has basic, inherent problem areas. Very often, the department in which the system functions cannot localize these flaws. It is imperative, then, that the analyst formalize, clearly and concisely, those aspects of the system that he will improve, once he receives the OK from management for a new design.

Thus the problem definition will specify the problems that will be corrected by the revised system. Similarly, it will discuss the goals of the present system that are not effectively met.

To achieve these ends, the analyst must first describe in detail his understanding of the system as it presently exists. Then, step by step, he must indicate its flaws.

The analyst should usually show the completed problem definition to the department representatives whom he has interviewed. They might have some pertinent suggestions or comments on items overlooked or misrepresented in the document. There is, however, a more subtle reason for showing the problem definition to the department. The chance that a document will be approved by management is far greater if it has the support of the department. Sometimes, however, employees will resist changes in their system. The analyst generally becomes aware of this attitude during the interview. In such a case, it is best not to show the problem definition and, thus, avoid any confrontation with department representatives until support is gathered.

Language structure is very important when preparing the problem definition. The analyst must keep in mind that the document is to be reviewed by executive- or managerial-level personnel who have neither the time nor the inclination to wade through pages of unnecessary detail. The language of the problem definition, then, must be clear and concise, emphasizing the major activities within the system that need revamping. The information must be presented in a manner that will be meaningful to management. If the problem definition fails in this respect, it is entirely conceivable that a new system design will not be approved.

The language of the report must be clear and concise for another reason. Once management has approved the problem definition, the analyst can begin his new design based on the problems therein presented. During the design phase, it often happens that department representatives become unsatisfied with the proposed changes. They then claim that they did not understand the problems presented in the definition or that they totally disagree with the analyst's interpretation of the significance of these problems. If a *clear* problem definition is written, such a claim cannot be effectively substantiated. Thus a precise and explicit definition will minimize the possibility of semantic difficulties during the design phase.

In preparing a problem definition, the present system should be described explicitly. Do not assume that management is familiar with the internal structure of the system. High-level employees usually need a clear picture of the organization within the system to "refresh" their memories.

The document should, where feasible, segment the problems defined into their smallest possible components. That is, *each* activity that warrants revision should be discussed in terms of its basic segments and fundamental problems. When describing a problem in the system, indicate how it relates to each activity. In this way, any activity that management decides to maintain in its entirety will not mean a major reevaluation or revamping of the analyst's thinking.

There are still other justifications for segmenting the problems into their basic components. Sometimes, a new system design will be assigned to several analysts even though an individual analyst prepares the original problem definition. If the activities within the system and their basic problem areas have been segmented into their fundamental components, several analysts could simply be assigned to different parts.

The formulation of the problem areas in terms of their smallest components also contributes to a clearer understanding of the system. Very often, in attempting to localize a problem, the analyst realizes that he does not, in fact, understand some aspect of the system. Similarly, it occasionally happens that the segmenting of problems leads to the discovery of additional inefficiencies.

There are basic diagramming techniques that can assist the analyst in describing the system and its problems in terms of its individual activities. Figure 15.1 is an *activity requirements model* that defines each activity in depth. It serves to illustrate how an activity can be clearly described and segmented by a diagram.

EXAMPLE. Let us consider the following facet of a purchasing system. The activity described is the ordering of parts.

Ordering of parts. Each department has the facility to order parts. The department representative completes a requisition order. He files one copy and transmits a duplicate to the purchasing department. The latter then issues the actual purchase order. One copy of the purchase order is filed, one copy is sent to the vendor, and one copy is sent to the requisitioning department. The original department representative

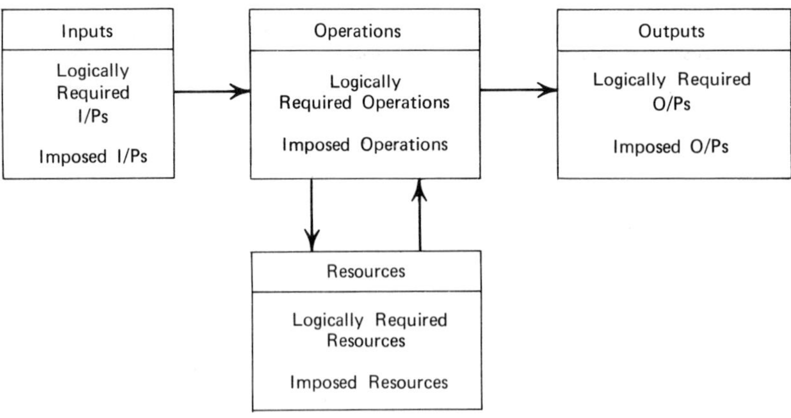

Figure 15.1 Activity requirements model (courtesy IBM). Imposed categories are those necessary for supplemental operations or outputs.

then must extract his requisition order from the file and must compare the data on it with the data on the purchase order. If there are no discrepancies, the representative throws away his requisition order and files the current purchase order. He then makes a manual entry on an account sheet indicating how much his department has spent for the item. This is necessary since each department is given a budget that it must not exceed. If there is, however, a discrepancy between the original requisition order and the final purchase order, a request for a change to the purchase order must be transmitted to the purchasing department. Note how these activities could be described by a variation of the activity requirements model (Figure 15.2).

An analysis and evaluation of the above activities should yield one point that would be evident in any good problem definition. The procedures required to purchase an item may be far too complex. The accuracy of the purchase order may be doubtful when so many steps are required before it is filed, and such a procedure can be too rigid and inflexible. Steps should be taken in the new design to facilitate the ordering of parts. Perhaps the department requesting the parts could complete the final purchase order. The departments would then be supplied with the prices of all items. This purchase order could then be sent to the purchasing department for transmit-

Figure 15.2 Activity requirements model for the ordering of parts.

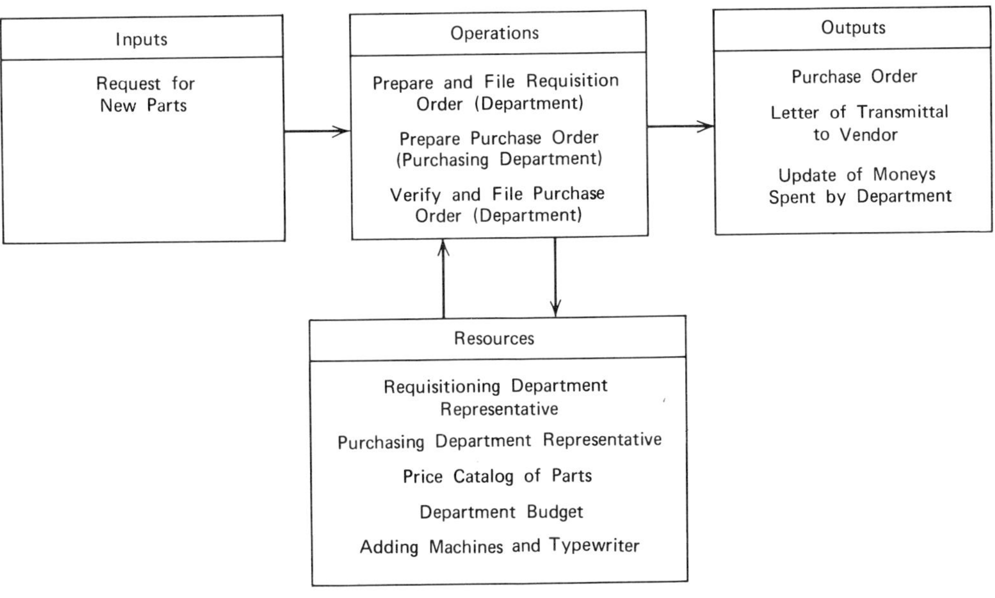

tal to the appropriate vendor. This is an initial idea for new design and would have to be formulated in detail in the design phase.

There is no industry-wide standard for the preparation of problem definitions. The analyst must prepare his document in a manner that will best describe the specific system. For some systems, simple descriptions, or narratives, will be the major item in the definition. For more complex systems, outlines that cross-reference segmented narratives might be necessary to tie together the material presented. For the majority of systems, however, diagrams are most helpful in place of, or as a supplement to, narratives.

Although no standardized format exists for problem definitions, the following items are generally included:

1. Statement of goals and objectives
2. Systems flowcharts

They will describe, in pictorial form, the flow of documents within the system. This type of diagram is of great importance, since it provides management with a quick and comprehensive understanding of the system as it presently exists.

3. Narrative

This is a clear, concise, and well-documented summary of the analyst's understanding of the system. The narrative encompasses and places in perspective all data that the analyst has obtained from procedures manuals, forms analysis, and interviews. It will consist of two basic parts: (a) a general discussion of the system, and (b) a structural discussion.

The general discussion will note the industrial relationship between the system and the rest of the company. A discussion of the major policies utilized within the system is generally included. But the major function of the general discussion is to cite the objectives and requirements of the system and to indicate how effectively they are met.

The structural discussion describes, in detail, the materials, personnel, products, and facilities utilized within the system. Cost factors associated with present equipment and personnel needs must also be included so that any cost savings in a new system can be evaluated in terms of present resources.

In the structural phase of the narrative, the system is generally segmented into its basic activities. If activity requirements models have been prepared, they will accompany this phase of the narrative.

Any diagrams, in fact, that will eliminate the need for complex discussion often accompany the narrative. Consider the resource sheet of Figure 15.3, which indicates all of the personnel utilized for a single activity.

Consider also the resource sheet shown in Figure 15.4, which defines the equipment utilized for the same activity.

Note that these diagrams relate to a *single* activity. Additional diagrams are required for the remaining activities.

Notice also that the analyst must prepare diagrams that best serve the specific system's needs. There are many standard diagrams that exist in the area of systems analysis but, ultimately, the analyst will find that it is often easier to prepare

Figure 15.3 Resource sheet (courtesy IBM).

Resoure Sheet

Name and description	Amount	Cost (In Dollars)	Notes
Manager	1	12,000 per year	Main office
Secretary	1	4,200 per year	
Underwriters	5	42,000 per year	
Typists	2	7,600 per year	
Agents	2	Commission	Sales office
Receptionists and typists	27	92,600 per year	
Doctor (uses his own office)	1	10,000 per year	

11/21/__	N. Stern	Life policy	Life insurance	1
Date	Analyst	Activity	Study	Page

Resource Sheet			
Name and description	Amount	Cost	Notes
Typewriters	30	600 per month	
Teletype	(1)	175 per month	(1) 5 units
			1 sending
			4 receiving
			Each is 3 ft. X 3 ft.
Main office — 161 Front Street	44 ft. X 37 ft.	200 per month	
Sales offices	4 offices	880 per month	
73 Clover Street	Each 24 ft. X 58 ft.		
7476 Jones Avenue			
35 Myrtle Street			
1 River Street			
Sales records, monthly for last 10 years	1200	15 per year	Monthly sales report includes 8 fields
			Repeated 120 times plus totals
Stock certificates	850	.25 per unit	Each certificate is registered and insured

11/21/__	N. Stern	Life policy	Life insurance	2
Date	Analyst	Activity	Study	Page

Figure 15.4 Resource sheet (courtesy IBM).

his own diagram than to research those that exist to find an appropriate one.

4. Description of input and output files

Each input and output file used within the system must be described in detail with regard to the following:

a. Identification (This includes serial number, file number, and any other identifying data.)
b. Formal name of the file
c. Where file is stored

d. On what media it is stored
e. Access requirements (Note here if the file is always processed sequentially, for example, or if random access is required.)
f. Sequence within the system
g. Department representatives responsible for maintenance of the file
h. Retention cycle of the file
i. Labels used to identify file
j. Actual contents of the records within the file
k. Volumes of data on the file and the frequency with which it is used
l. Priorities and schedules utilizing the file.
m. Additional remarks

Any proposed ideas for new files or for the combining of existing files in a new design could be suggested here. Suggestions for new files, although only broadly outlined, will provide management with a basic idea of the analyst's probable approach for a new system.

Keep in mind that a description of each file is not sufficient for describing the flow of data within a system. The interaction of files is an important consideration in understanding the system in its entirety. The analyst must note, in report or diagram form, how the inputs and outputs relate to one another. Although a systems flowchart is often sufficient for describing the interaction of files, more complex systems require additional diagrams.

5. Problem areas within the system that will be corrected in a new design
6. Estimates of the cost for a new systems design

It is essential that the systems analyst provide management with a broad idea of the amount of time that he thinks will be needed for the new design.

SYSTEMS DOCUMENTATION

Purpose

Documentation is defined as the formalized, detailed record containing the design of the new system. It outlines the techniques and methods utilized to correct the problem areas in the existing system, as they are described in the problem definition. It illustrates both technically and economically how a new system would better serve the objectives and goals of the company. It describes how the files and forms designed by the analyst will be integrated to form a new system.

The documentation of the new system serves many functions within a company:

1. *It is chiefly a management tool.* You will recall that a new system design is not undertaken until the problem definition on the current system has been approved by management. That is, the formalized report on the analysis of the current system is a tool utilized by management to determine if a new or revised design is necessary and feasible.

Similarly, the documentation on the new system is a tool utilized by management to determine if the new design satisfies the objectives of the company within the established constraints and if it is justifiable from a cost standpoint. That is, the documentation provides a record from which the new design can be assessed.

2. *It provides a communication link necessary in a data processing environment.* The importance of presenting a clear and detailed picture of the new system to all personnel who are affected by it cannot be overestimated. The new design must be fully described to every employee who will be required to implement it. More design work is rendered unproductive because of poor communication in depicting the system than for any other reason.

There is no better method for the analyst to establish proper communication about the new system than by preparing a formalized and precise document that will serve as a standard reference. All personnel connected with the new system will acquire the same perspective. There is little room for misunderstanding and doubt when every aspect of the new design is carefully presented in written form.

The department in which the system will function needs formalized procedures by which its employees can be guided. Similarly, the programming staff assigned to implement the new design will need a standard from which an understanding of the system as a whole can be derived and from which a detailed picture of the program specifications can be obtained.

3. *It provides a reference on the new system, once it is implemented.* Future modifications will be greatly facilitated with a written standard providing a formalized and thorough picture of the integrated system and its components.

Similarly, the training of new personnel can draw heavily on documentation, utilizing it as a standard.

In short, documentation serves as a focal point from which the analyst's design can be assessed, and as a standard to be utilized as a reference once the system is implemented.

Too often, documentation is lightly glossed over if, indeed, it is written at all. The days of documentation written on matchbook covers are, unfortunately, not over. When an analyst is required to adhere to a schedule, often too rigidly, he "cuts corners" by eliminating extensive documentation. Although this will have an adverse effect in the future, it will initially save much time.

In the end, however, such savings will work to the detriment of the system and, perhaps, even contribute to its downfall. There *must* be a formalized standard on the new design that will serve everyone; otherwise, varying misconceptions and illusions will make it extremely difficult to implement and operate. The analyst will be plagued constantly with questions and inquiries well after the system is implemented unless he provides a written record.

Contents

You will recall that the analyst designs several alternatives rather than a single system. Often, the choice is between a costly, comprehensive, "perfect" system and a more economical, less comprehensive alternative or, perhaps, a compromise between the two.

The documentation will contain a detailed design of the one system that the analyst deems most suitable and beneficial. Also included in the documentation, however, must be all alternatives, but only briefly described. In this way, management can make a realistic choice. Most often, management will adopt the analyst's formal proposal, but sometimes a change in company policy requires the selection of an alternative.

In short, the documentation contains a detailed systems design with brief descriptions of alternatives. If management approves the formal documentation, programming will commence, after which the system is tested and then implemented.

There are, as yet, no universal documentation standards, since systems vary greatly in form, content, and requirements. The format of each documentation package will be based on the following:

1. *Characteristics of the system.* Some designs require extensive narrative; others can be best illustrated by diagrams, and documents utilized within the company.
2. *Management's attitude toward documentation.* The analyst must prepare the documentation package within the limitations established by management. If management is firmly committed to formalized and comprehensive standards, the analyst is free to prepare the best documentation possible. If, however, management desires a "rush job," documentation will undoubtedly suffer.
3. *Equipment restraints.* A company with a vastly integrated computer system within a teleprocessing environment will require more formalized and technical documentation than a company with a more conservative and less extensive computer system. Similarly, a design attempting to justify new equipment that is not currently utilized by the company will require more detailed writing.

Let us now consider the elements that comprise a documentation package.

Cover Letter. The cover letter is a correspondence, primarily to management, that describes the benefits of the new design and that, generally, attempts to "sell" the system. Keep in mind that unless the documentation is approved, the new system will never be implemented and the analyst's work will have been in vain. Thus the analyst must strive to convince management that the new design presented, or one of its alternatives, is both feasible and appropriate.

The cover letter will briefly describe:

1. The purpose and function of the new system. It illustrates how the problems presented in the problem definition will be eliminated.
2. An evaluation of the files that will be maintained and of those that will be altered.
3. A simplified, one-page flowchart of the entire new design with cross-references, if necessary, to more detailed flowcharts of the subsystems appearing in the body of the report. This is sometimes referred to as an "executive flowchart," since its chief function is to give management a concise overview of the system as a whole.

The cover letter should be written in concise language to facilitate executive understanding, without requiring complete familiarity with the intricacies of the system.

Table of Contents. The inclusion of a table of contents is an absolute necessity. Pages in the documentation package must be numbered and cross-referenced in this table of contents. In this way, employees affected by specific aspects of the new design can quickly refer to the areas that concern them.

Narrative. With the narrative, we begin the detailed formulation of the new system. The first items to be included are the revised objectives and constraints of the new system.

EXAMPLE. The basic objectives of an accounts receivable system are as follows:

OBJECTIVES

1. To establish and maintain records of all charge account customers
2. To send monthly statements to each customer for payment
3. To suspend charge accounts for customers who are delinquent in payment for more than three months
4. To provide management with accurate reports for decision making and planning

The stated objectives of the revised accounts receivable system may be as follows:

The objectives of the revised system include the above with the addition of:

5. To incorporate finance charges for delinquent accounts
6. To minimize excessive errors in processing

Similarly, the constraints of the existing accounts receivable system may be as follows:

CONSTRAINTS.

Management will allow one man-year to analyze the current system and to design a new one.

The constraints in the revised system include the above and:

Additional constraint. The analyst must utilize the equipment currently on order in the company, which includes:

Central processing unit with storage capacity of approximately 256,000 characters
4 tape drives
2 disk drives
1 printer
1 card reader-punch
1 console typewriter

Every aspect of the new system should then be described and supplemented with diagrams when possible. The narrative should include an answer to each of the following:

1. Can each input be processed independently or must they be batch processed?
2. Will the system be best served by sequential or random processing?
3. How much editing is required, and should edits be performed manually or by computer?
4. Is a real-time system a requirement?
5. Is complex logic required (and if it is, it must be properly described)?
6. Is there a need for constant monitoring or operator intervention?
7. Do errors require immediate attention, or can they be corrected at a later date?
8. Can several systems elements be combined?

The above questions will serve to structure the analyst's design. The elements included are generally a major part of all systems.

The formal narrative will also include specifications on equipment requirements.

Here again, the design that is considered most suitable by the analyst is described in complete detail. All alternatives are briefly summarized. Most alternatives vary in equipment requirements, and this variation results in the major cost variations among them. Thus the equipment necessary for each design alternative is the only entry that should be stated in detail.

In short, the narrative on the formal design should explain the integrated system. In later sections, specific elements of the system are described. The emphasis here is on the integration of all components so that an understanding of the total is evolved. In addition, brief descriptions of alternative designs are indicated.

Flowcharts. Each subsystem within the analyst's one formal design should be detailed in a flowchart. Update procedures within an accounts receivable system, for example, would constitute a subsystem and thus should be described in a single flowchart. Edit routines may also require a single flowchart.

All flowcharts presented here can be interrelated by referencing the major (or executive) flowchart included in the cover letter.

File Specifications. Each file within the formal design must be described with regard to:

1. Purpose
2. Programs that will utilize the file
3. Volume
4. Frequency of use
5. Source from which the file is obtained
6. Description of fields
7. Layout and samples

Although layout and samples are almost always represented in a diagram, the other elements can be described in either narrative form or by a diagram designed by the analyst.

Program Specifications. At this point, the analyst must segment the new design so that each unit will basically be controlled by a single program, assuming that the design itself is approved by management. Usually, the elements contained within each flowchart on a subsystem will be handled by a separate program. Sometimes, however, two or more simplified flowcharts can be the basis for a single program. Similarly, a single flowchart might be too complex for one program.

One or more programs are generally written for each of the following aspects of most systems:

1. *Creation of master files.* This is usually a one-shot program (or programs), used only during implementation to

create the system files. Once the master files are created, they are revised by standard update procedures.

2. *Edits.* Most systems require editing or the validating of data, to be performed by a computer. In the new system, data processing personnel are used to handle inputs and outputs heretofore handled exclusively by departmental employees familiar with their contents. This change requires more extensive editing than is generally being performed in the existing system.

Sometimes, editing of several inputs can be performed by a single program. When more rigorous editing of input is required, one program will satisfy each edit. When editing is minimal, the routines can often be included in an update program.

3. *Updates of each master file.* After input data have been edited, they are used to update a master file. Generally, a single program is needed for each update that produces an updated master file and, sometimes, an error list and summary report.

4. *Creation of outputs.* All outputs, if they are simple and not too numerous, can be created by a single program. If, however, complex analysis of input files is required as output, then individual programs will be used to produce each output form.

5. *File clean-ups or revisions.* A file clean-up is usually performed once or twice a year by a program that will eliminate all unused records. Examples of unnecessary or unused records include separations from a company in a payroll file, inactive accounts in an accounts receivable file, and the like. Such a program generally validates existing records also and ascertains their accuracy within established limits.

6. *Utility programs.* Utility programs are prewritten programs, usually supplied by the computer manufacturer, that perform specialized tasks required of most systems. They include sorting of files by computer, merging of files, card-to-tape functions, and card-to-disk functions. These programs are already written and require only a set of parameters indicating sort fields or merge fields or card specifications, depending upon the specific utility. These utility programs save much programming effort and should be employed where possible. The creation of master files from cards, for example, is often performed by utility programs.

The above list defines typical programs that are required to supplement most systems. Many designs need some variation of the above and may even require additional programs. Keep in mind that the analyst should limit each program to the handling of relatively simple tasks, since complex programming effort is difficult to debug and therefore very costly.

Each program utilized within the system must be described with regard to the following:

1. Input specifications
2. Output specifications
3. Functions required to convert the input to output
4. Relation to other programs
5. Decision tables—if complex logic is required
6. Error specifications and recovery procedures
7. Edit specifications
8. Special tables, if necessary
9. Parameters for utility programs

The above specifications will be utilized by the programmers assigned to the specific program, once the design is approved. If documentation is good, the analyst will not be plagued by numerous phone calls from the programming staff to clarify aspects of programs.

Note that the programmer will be required to provide a program documentation for each program within the system. This describes every facet of the program to ensure that no complications occur during implementation.

Cost of the Proposed System and of Its Alternatives. The data necessary to evaluate proposed costs were discussed in Chapter 12. Once costs are determined, they must be included as part of documentation.

Test Procedures. The analyst should outline the operations and procedures that will be employed to test the new system, once it is approved. This section of the documentation will include:

1. *Data that will be used in the test run.* It is not feasible to use all input to test a system. Control is extremely difficult when large volumes of data are used in an initial run. Thus selected data representing all input forms will be used.

The analyst must provide both management and the department with the specific data to be used in a test so that an evaluation may be made to determine the validity of the test. If test data are good, all aspects of the system will be verified and minor flaws corrected; thus major problems will not occur during implementation.

A single sheet selected randomly from each batch of source documents is an example of test data for a relatively simple system.

2. *Test schedule.* It is imperative that the analyst indicate to management how testing will progress and when it will be completed. An example of a test schedule is the following:

WEEK 1

Jan. 5	(Test) master data transmitted for keypunching
Jan. 6	Keypunched data are verified
Jan. 7	Keypunched data transmitted to control unit
Jan. 8	Control unit transmits punched cards to computer room
Jan. 9	(Test) master file will be created

WEEK 2

Jan. 12	(Test) detail data transmitted to keypunch
Jan. 13	(Test) detail cards are verified
Jan. 14	(Test) detail cards transmitted to control unit
Jan. 15	Control transmits (test) detail cards to computer room
Jan. 16	Edit run and update run (programs 101 and 102) are executed—error lists and summary reports are transmitted to accounts receivable department

Note that a control unit is often established as part of the data processing department, to maintain control of documents and data handled by the computer.

Once the test is completed and the system is implemented, the above schedule can be revised to incorporate a standard schedule for the system.

3. *Performance criteria.* In selling the new design, the analyst must attempt to convince management that the output from the system will be at least as valid and accurate as in the current system.

A test of the new system is performed in parallel with the existing system. The results are then compared. Gross differences in output between the two systems indicate major difficulties in the new system that must be corrected before implementation can begin. This type of parallel run can only be performed if the existing system produces output that is relatively free from error.

The performance criteria will indicate the acceptable limits within which errors can occur, since some degree of error will always exist, particularly in a test run.

Appendix. An appendix should include major memos illustrating specific approvals by the department, or user, of the analyst's analysis and design.

Once the documentation is approved, the analyst works closely with the programmers who will program segments of the system. The analyst then must test the system according to the criteria specified in the documentation.

The testing will usually pinpoint deficient areas that must be revised prior to implementation.

Keep in mind that the analyst's job is not finished when implementation begins. He must obtain periodic feedback, or lines of communication between himself and the department, to indicate how well the system is performing. During periodic feedback, minor problems may become apparent. They are generally easy to correct if they are handled immediately. If, however, the analyst does not attempt to receive proper feedback, these minor flaws can snowball into major problems. Thus the analyst must build into his system enough flexibility to handle minor revisions without requiring extensive redesign.

GLOSSARY

Documentation. Formalized, detailed package containing the design of the new system.

File clean-up. An operation performed once or twice a year that will eliminate all unused records from a file.

Problem definition. Formal document prepared by the analyst that defines all aspects and inadequacies of the present system.

QUESTIONS

1. What are some of the problems avoided by an effective problem definition?
2. Who prepares the problem definition, and who else must be consulted?
3. What does a problem definition consist of, and when, ideally, is it prepared?

4. What are some of the general questions that the analyst should ask concerning forms preparation in the present system?
5. Should the problem definition be considered a formal document, or can it be prepared informally? Why?
6. Who in the organization should be given a copy of the problem definition? Why?
7. What is the difference between a problem definition and systems documentation?
8. What is the purpose of the cover letter in a systems documentation package?
9. What are some types of programs that are required to handle typical systems requirements?
10. What are some of the problems that may be avoided with adequate testing procedures? Who supervises a systems test, and what are some of the considerations necessary to ensure proper systems turnover?

CHAPTER **16**

CASE STUDY—PERSONNEL

This chapter will develop the design of a personnel system emphasizing an integrated approach to systems analysis. The company under discussion is newly formed under the name of Calzone Agents, Inc. They are a personnel placement agency operating in Southern California, currently with five district offices. The directors of Calzone Agents are attempting to institute new and aggressive approaches in the area of personnel management. It is this management's feeling that a computer-oriented personnel system will be of great assistance in determining an applicant's aptitude, placing an applicant, and enhancing the company's prospects for future expansion.

The analyst's approach will be:

1. Analyze management's objectives and goals
2. Prepare a problem definition
3. Design the new system

ANALYSIS OF CURRENT SYSTEM

Since there is no existing system, an analysis of a current system is not possible. Management's objectives establish the framework for the new system. We must examine these objectives and then formulate a problem definition.

Management's goals for this personnel system are:

1. A current up-to-date status on all applicants
2. An updated file on employment opportunities
3. Reports indicating significant trends (which job areas require the most applicants, which job areas require the least, the most desirable jobs, the company hiring the most applicants, the average time required to find a job for an applicant, etc.)
4. A computing system that provides terminal support for each of the five district offices
5. A system that matches an applicant's profile with employment opportunities, utilizing a computer

PROBLEM DEFINITION

The analysis of management's objectives reveals the following:

1. The system must have a growth capability, since the company desires to expand its number of branches in the future.
2. The projected number of applicants on file will average 1,500 per week, when the system is operational. A weekly turnover of 150 people is estimated.
3. Applicants will be removed from the active file after 180 days if no employment positions are found or if the applicant no longer seeks employment.
4. Automatically prepared invoices are to be sent to the hiring company or the applicant, depending on the prior contractual arrangement. In either case, the fee paid will be 100 percent of the applicant's monthly starting salary.

DESIGN OF NEW SYSTEM

Objectives

The objectives of this personnel system are the ones stated by management and discussed previously.

The objectives of this system are easily noted by the examination of a flowchart depicting the proposed system's activities. In Figure 16.1, we show the overall system's inputs and outputs.

Constraints

1. Management will allow an elapsed time of six months for the system to become operational.
2. The configuration available to the company includes:
   a. A central processing unit with a storage capacity of approximately 64,000 characters
   b. 2 tape drives
   c. 2 disk drives
   d. 1 printer
   e. 1 card reader-punch
   f. 1 console typewriter

Each of the five district offices will have a terminal tied to the main computer by a voice-grade telephone line. Any subsequent offices will be similarly equipped.

Outputs

The basic outputs of the new system are:

1. *Applicant status report.* This report will list new applicants, their job specialties, pertinent personal data, and possi-

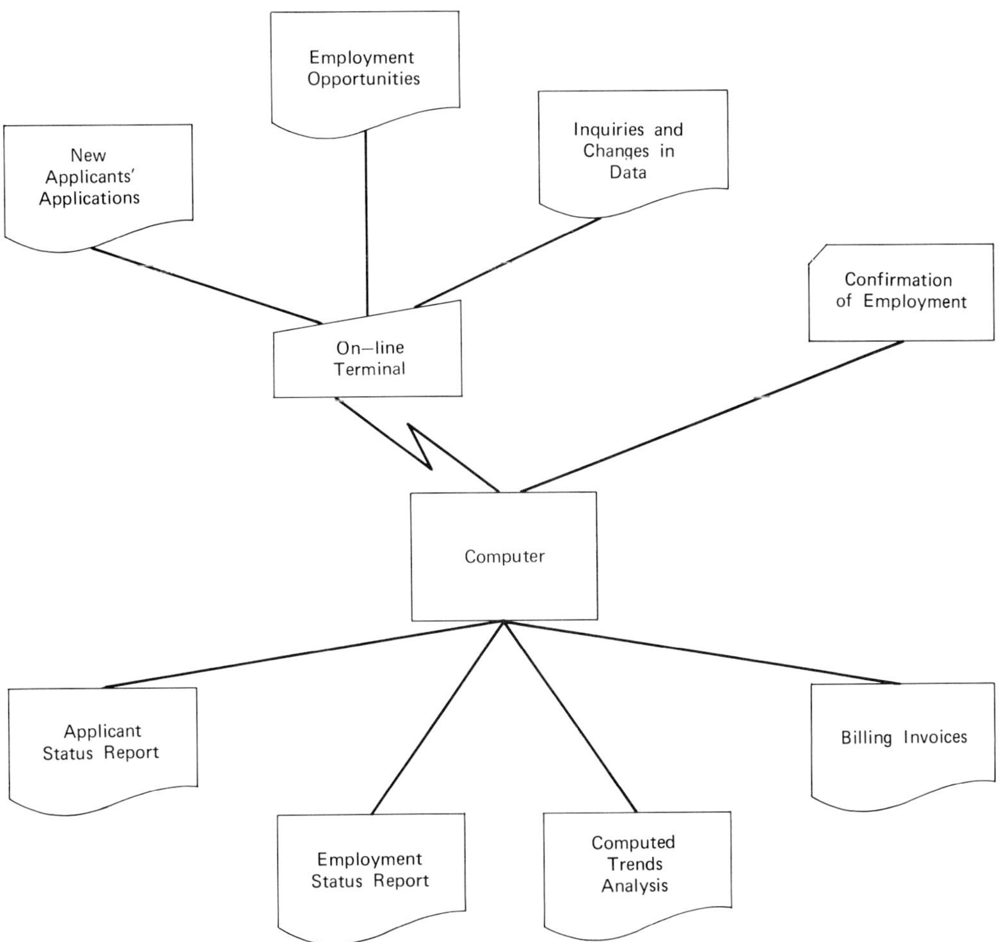

Figure 16.1 Overview of the total system's inputs and outputs.

ble employment opportunities. This listing will include those applicants who have been dropped, as of this reporting period, from the active file. Figure 16.2 illustrates this report's format.

The office branch codes used are:

Pismo Beach	PB
Whittier	WH
Los Angeles	LA
Cucamonga	CC
Anaheim	AN

2. *Employment status report.* This report will list newly hired applicants and companies that have opened new em-

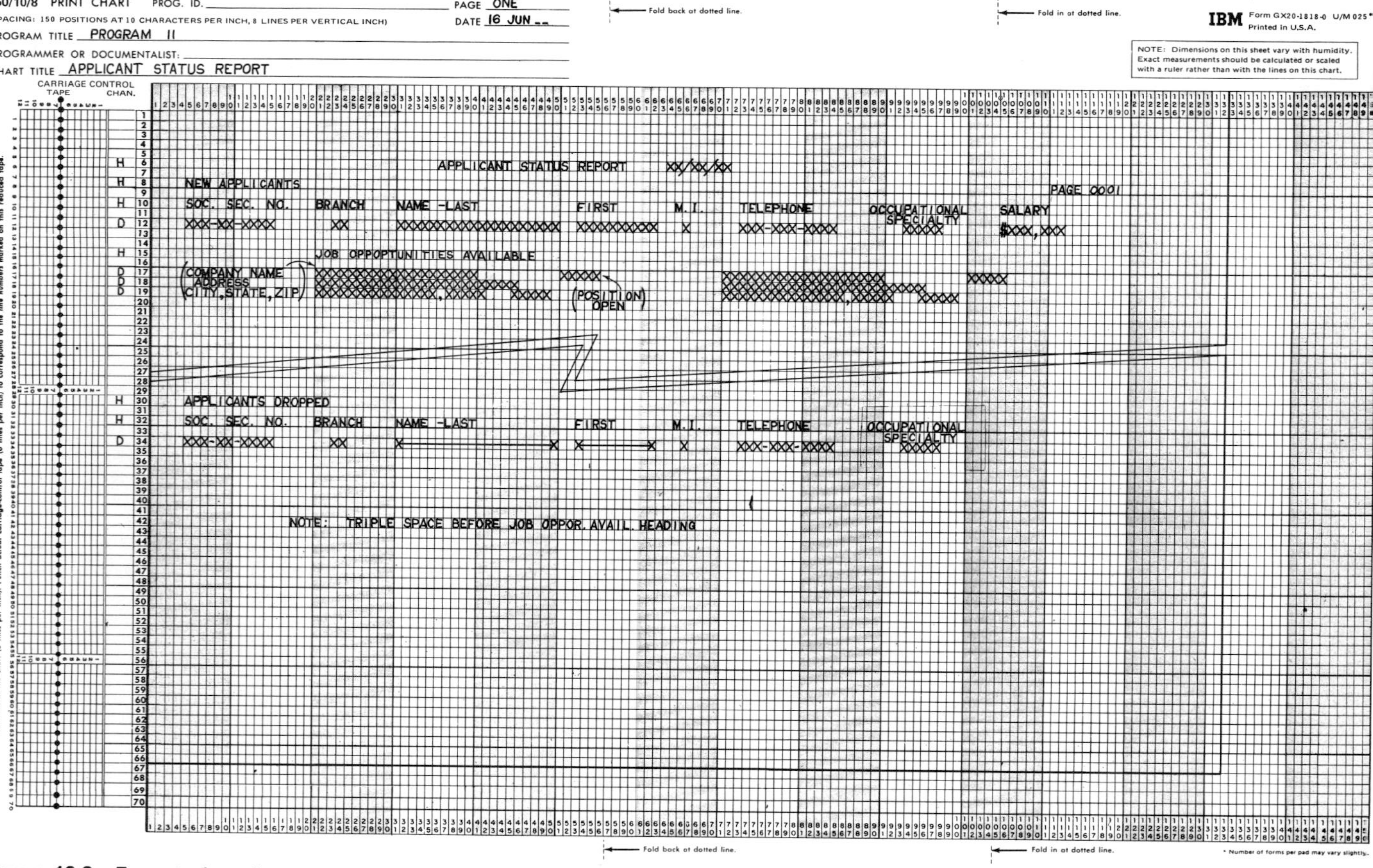

Figure 16.2 Format of applicant status report.

ployment opportunities. In this manner, companies have a method of updating their respective personnel files. In Figure 16.3, this form is shown. The company ID code is a five-digit number assigned to every company seeking this concern's assistance. The code enables easy classifying and identification of all companies (e.g., 01597, Bell Manufacturing Company).

3. *Computed trends analysis.* This output will note the results of the analyses performed on data for management. It is envisioned that significant trends, favorable or not, may be highlighted. These data are useful to management when policy decisions must be made. Figure 16.4 illustrates this form. The last category, Remaining Job Areas, is an alphabetic listing of all remaining occupational specialties. For the % Change column, an asterisk will denote negative change.

4. *Invoices for customers.* Automatically prepared invoices will be sent to the hiring company or applicant, depending on the prior contractual arrangement. This is a customized, three-part form. Copy 1 is sent to, and kept by, the company or applicant; copy 2 is sent to Calzone's accounting department; and copy 3 is returned with payment. In Figure 16.5, this specially prepared form is illustrated.

Processing

The following systems flowcharts depict the recommended processing operations under the proposed system.

1. *Creation of the master disk file and backup tape.* This task will be performed at the system's inception. The file will be created from existing data. Figure 16.6 illustrates this flowchart.

2. *Weekly update of the master disk.* This operation will be scheduled to run during the weekend shift (Friday night to Monday morning). In this manner, any data accessed will be current. All inquiries or terminal input of data for the week will have been completed prior to the processing of this job. During this processing, all files will be checked and reordered, where necessary. This is to ensure that all entries have been processed and each file is in the correct ascending, numerical order. A file of expired employment situations and 180-day droppages will be established and maintained. Figure 16.7 charts this task.

3. *Program inquiries or additions to the disk files.* From any terminal, an inquiry can be made to the computer concerning any applicant or employment opportunity. All applicants are entered onto the master disk in this manner. The

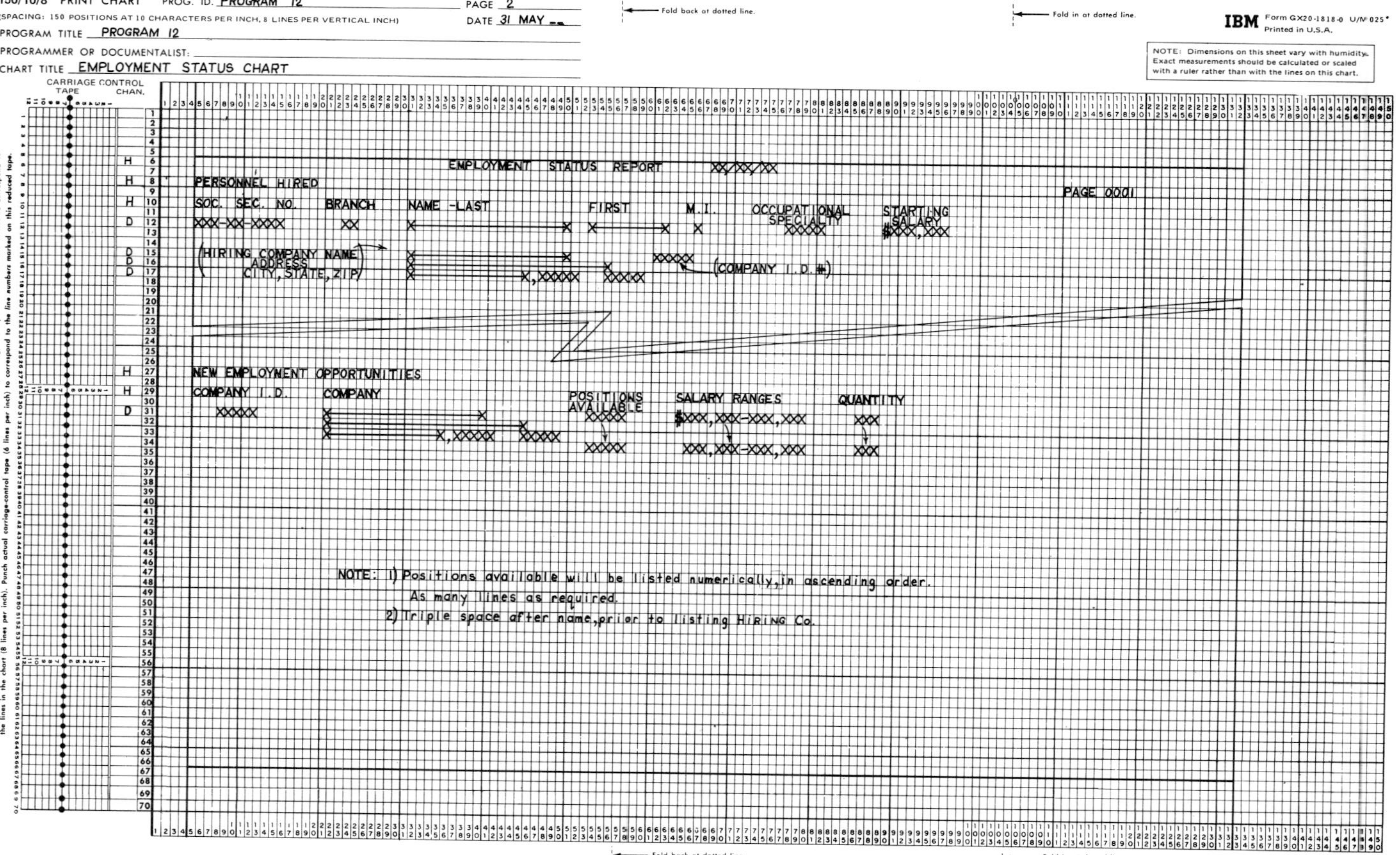

Figure 16.3 Format of employment status report.

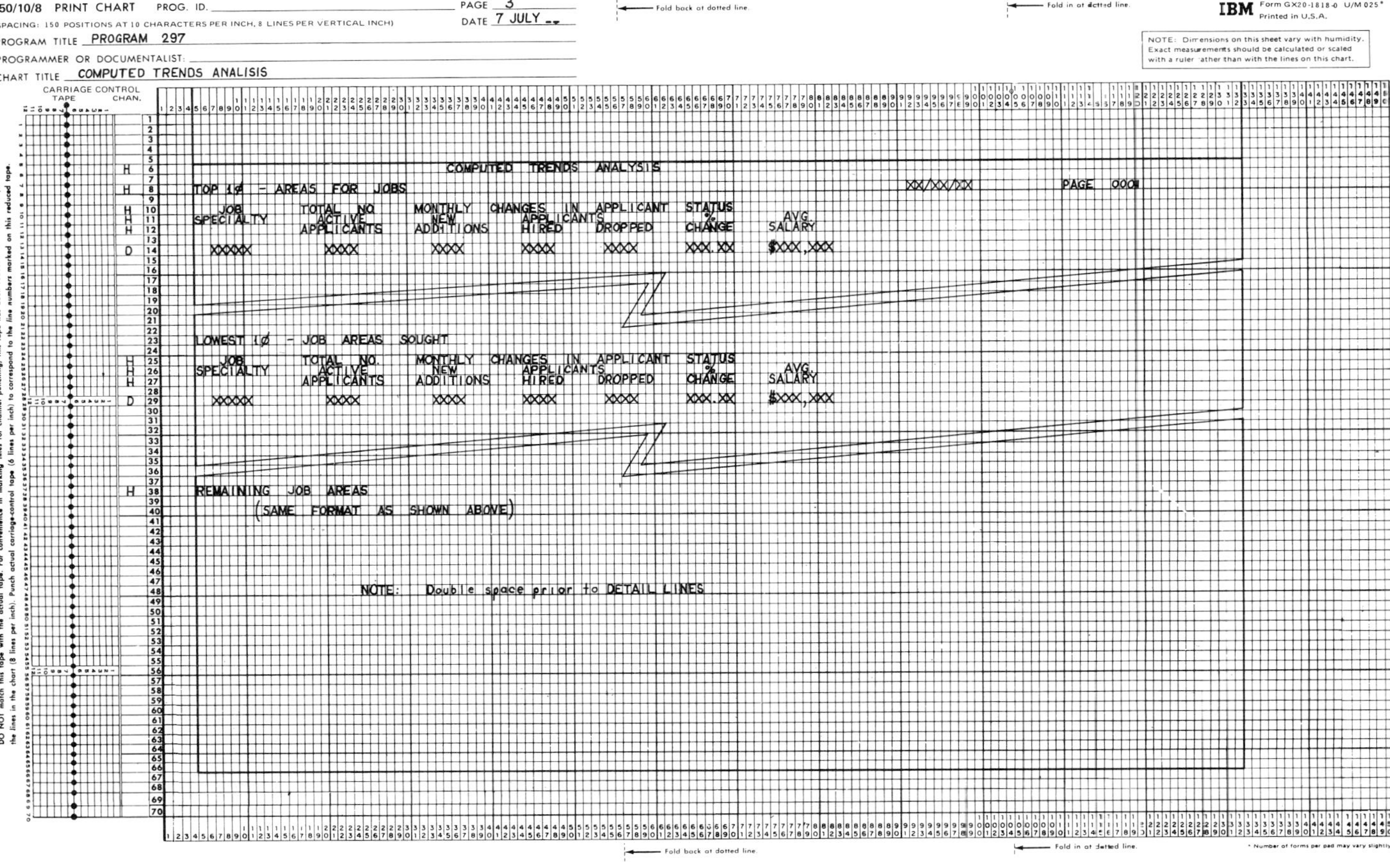

Figure 16.4 Computed trends analysis format.

To:

AGENTS

Invoice

Occupational Specialty	Applicant	Salary	Fees

Branches: Pismo Beach
Cuccamonga
Whittier
Anaheim
Los Angeles

Total due

Figure 16.5 Customized monthly billing statement.

response to an inquiry on an applicant will be similar in format to the applicant status report. Responses on employers will be similar, in format, to the employment status report. The use of a terminal permits keying in an applicant's name and obtaining, from the computer, a listing of appropriate job opportunities. Similarly, if we key in a specific job specialty, the response will list the applicants who meet those requirements. Employment opportunities will not be initially placed into the master disk from the terminal. These opportunities must be cleared through the company's main office. Figure 16.8 flowcharts this process.

4. *Match-up program.* This job is run after the weekly updating of the applicant/employment master disk. When an inquiry is made on a specific applicant, the job match-ups possible are listed with him. Figure 16.9 depicts this process.

5. *Employment status report and applicant status report.* These reports will be run each Monday. Program 11 is used to prepare the applicant status report, and program 12 is used for the employment status report. Figure 16.10 follows with this flowchart.

6. *Computed trends analysis report.* The analysis report will be run at the end of each month; Figure 16.11 illustrates the run.

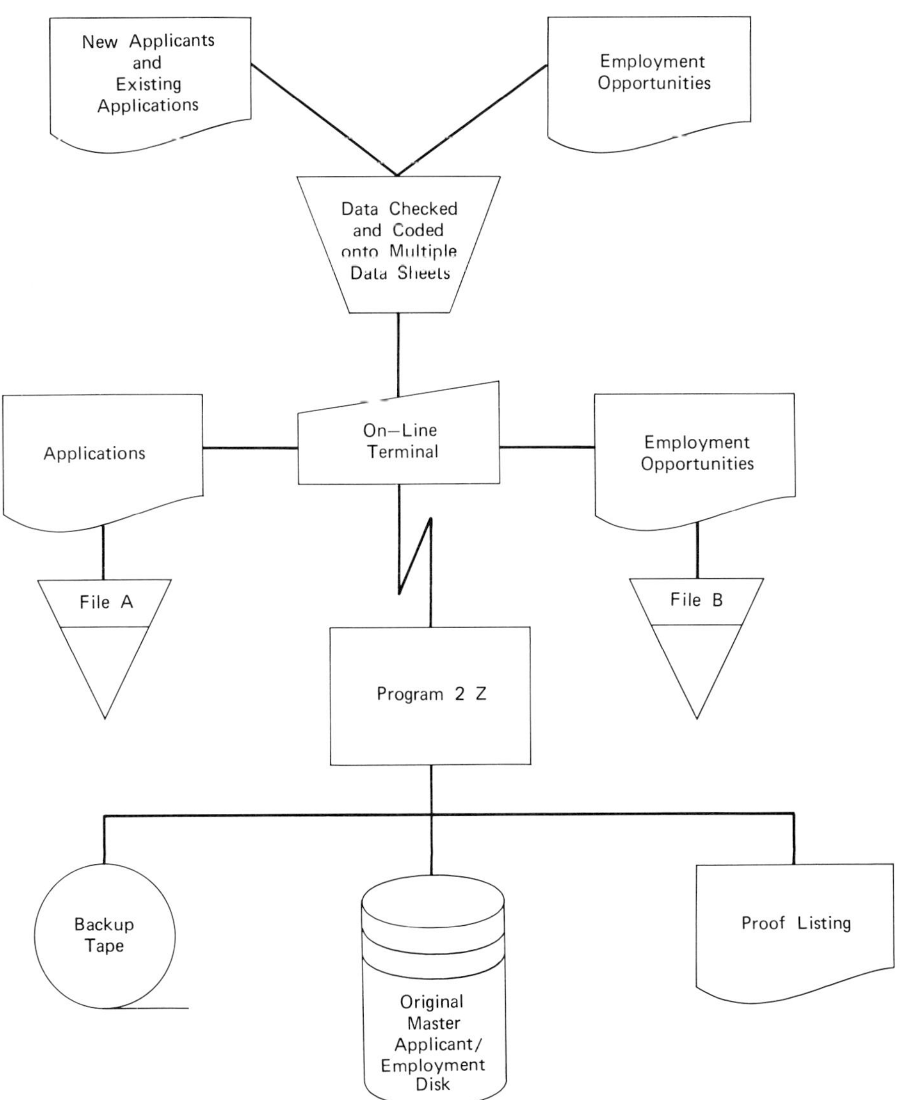

Figure 16.6 Processing required to create master disk and backup tape.

7. *Automatic invoice processing.* The billing will be done on the 20th of every month. Invoices will be posted by the 25th of the month. The process is illustrated in Figure 16.12.

Inputs

The following inputs will be required within the depicted system.

1. *Application form.* The applicant, when applying for any position, must complete this form. The application is depicted

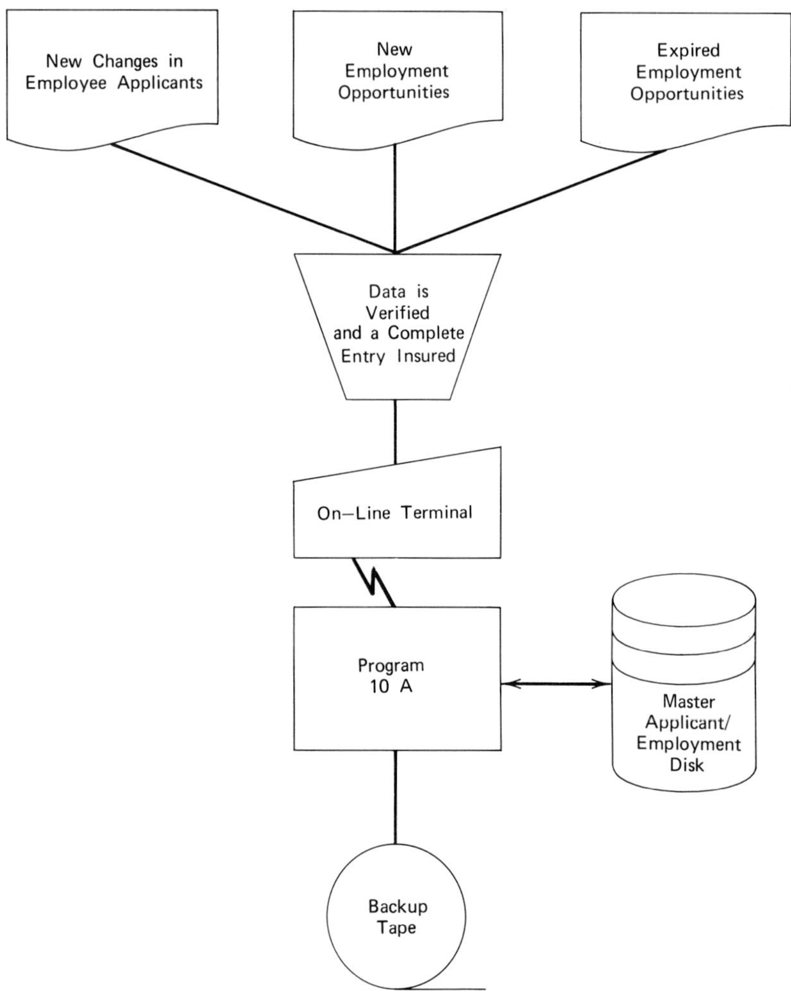

Figure 16.7 Process used for weekly update of master applicant/employment disk.

in Figure 16.13. The form will be completed prior to the actual interview.

A post-interview form must be completed, by the interviewer, for each applicant. This evaluation assists in placing the applicant in a position with favorable results. This evaluatory form is illustrated in Figure 16.14.

2. *Coding sheets.* After accepting the applicant, data from the application form are checked and verified. Data are taken from the application and coded onto a multiple keypunch layout form. This will enable the operator to easily key data on the terminal keyboard. The application is filed. The data in

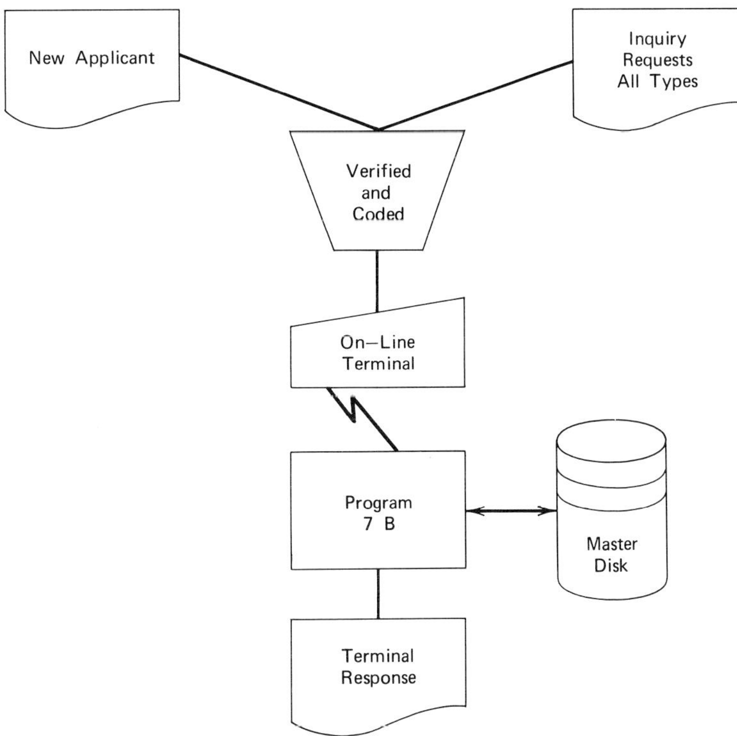

Figure 16.8 Processing to handle terminal inquiries and responses.

Figure 16.15 on the storage layout sheet represent the data format, as it would appear in storage, for the applicant and employment records.

The coding sheet, containing the appropriate fields, is illustrated in Figure 16.16, for the application form. The format

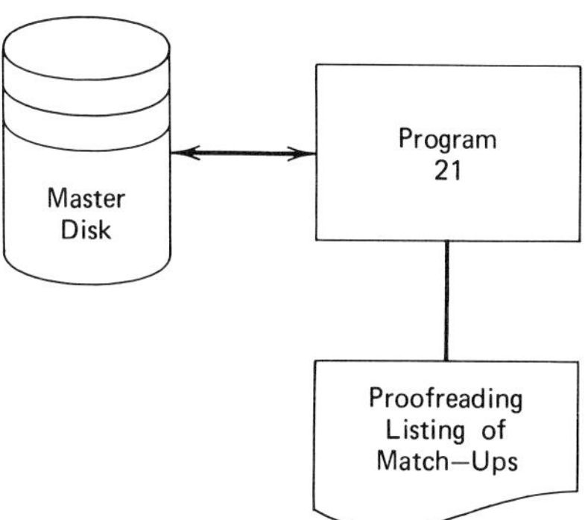

Figure 16.9 Processing of match-up program.

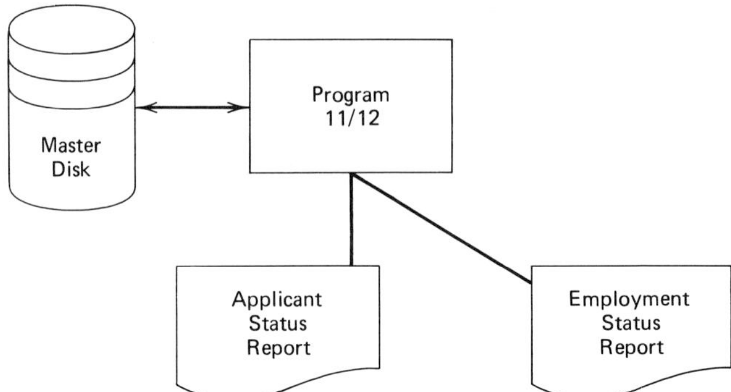

Figure 16.10 Processing of applicant status and employment reports.

used for the employment opportunities form is shown in Figure 16.17.

For each inquiry, a three-digit code will precede any transmitted data. This code will identify the purpose of the inquiry. The codes to be used are:

INA	Input of an applicant into the master disk
INJ	Input of an employment opportunity
OPA	Inquiry response on one applicant
OPJ	Inquiry response on one company's available jobs
MAT	Match-up scan for an applicant's possible jobs

The codes used for employment positions are shown in Table 16.1. If an applicant's record is desired, the inquiry statement would appear as follows:

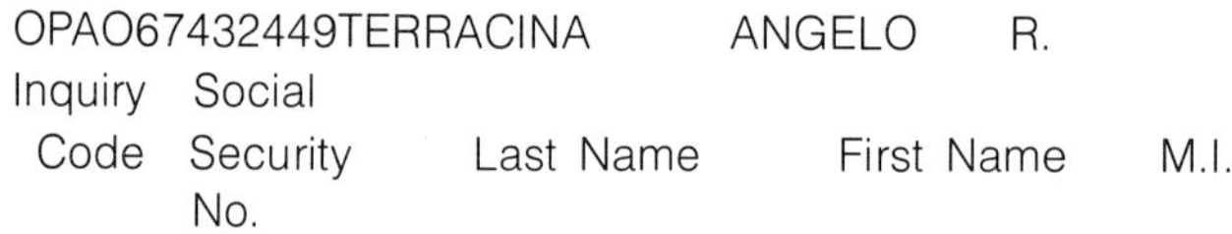

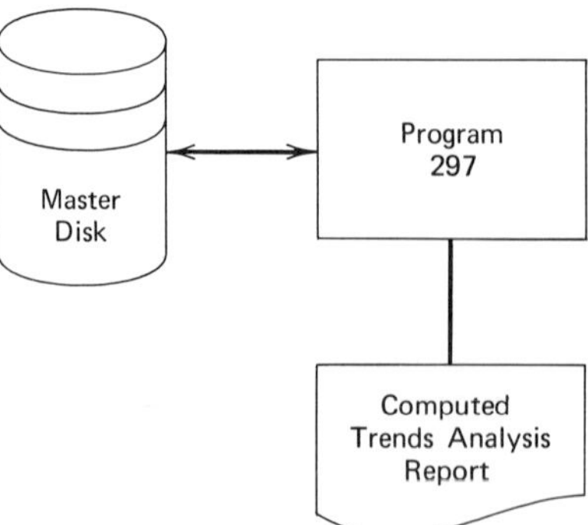

Figure 16.11 Processing to compute trends for computed trends analysis report.

TABLE 16.1 CODES FOR EMPLOYMENT PREFERENCE LIST

Accounting	10000	X-ray technician	60002
Corporate	10001	Physical therapist	60003
Small firm	10002	Dietician	60004
Bookkeeping	10003	EKG technician	60005
Other	10004	Other	60006
Architecture	20000	*Communication*	70000
Apprentice	20001	Radio	70001
Draftsman	20002	Announcing	70011
Other	20003	Sound control	70021
Art	30000	Other	70031
Commercial publications	30001	Television	70002
Industrial designing	30002	Sound technician	70012
Other	30003	Camera technician	70022
		Other	70032
Business	40000	Newspaper	70003
Advertising	40001	Telephone	70004
Sales	40002	*Computer Science*	80000
Marketing	40003	Programming	80001
Administrative	40004	FORTRAN	80011
Other	40005	COBOL	80021
Engineering	50000	BAL	80031
Structural	50001	RPG	80041
Mechanical	50002	Clerical	80051
Electrical	50003	Operations	80002
Architectural	50004	Computer	80012
Sanitation	50005	Keypunch	80022
Industrial	50006	Collator	80032
Work simplification	50016	Sorter	80042
Quality control	50026	Reproducer	80052
Time-and-motion study	50036	Interpreter	80062
Performance measurements	50046	Accounting machines	80072
Medical Technology	60000	Clerical	80082
Laboratory technician	60001		

If a company is sought, with all available jobs listed, the following inquiry would be used:

OPJ06743.
Inquiry Code — Company ID No.

If specific job areas were available, they would be individually listed after the company's ID code number, as follows:

OPJ067438002170031.

The response to the employment queries would list the company's name, address, city, state, zip, job ID, salary range, and quantity. This would be similar to the format in storage.

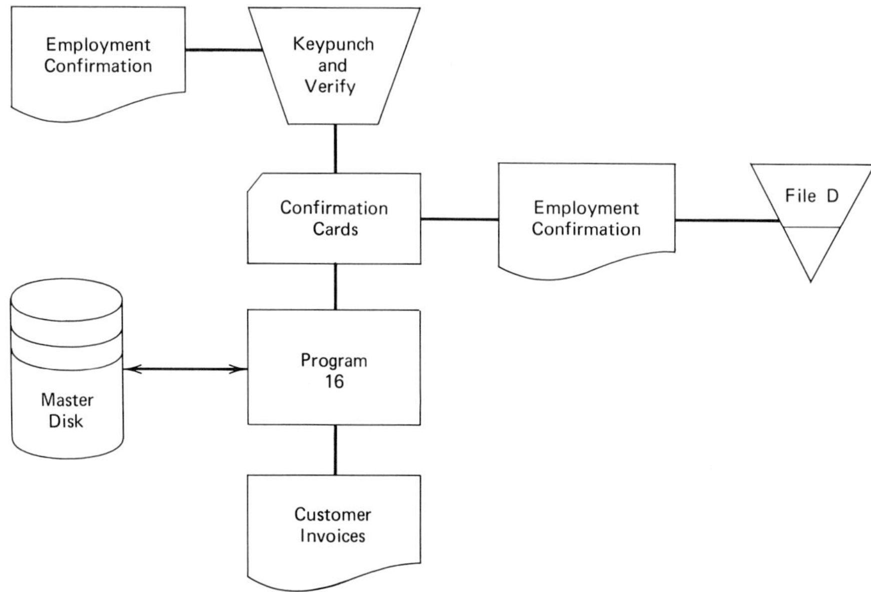

Figure 16.12 Monthly processing of custom invoices.

A match-up scan would be initiated, as follows:

MAT	50036.
Inquiry Code	Code No. of Position Desired

The response to this inquiry would list each company selected by its assigned ID number. Each company would be subsequently queried for the specifics.

3. *Employment confirmation.* This form is used as the input for the automatic billing of a customer. The appropriate data are punched into a card, and all cards are batched together. The card format is illustrated in Figure 16.18.

Controls

The system will create appropriate backup tapes and disks to permit generation of any part of the system. All data must be checked and verified before they are keyed into any terminal.

Feedback

During the testing and implementation of the system, any alteration to the system will be noted and made. After the system has been operational for three months, an evaluation of the entire system will commence. The investigation will research any "bugs" found by the analyst or operating personnel within

Branch number

Applicant number

Calzone Agents – Application Form

Date: ____________________
Month Day Year

Mr.
Mrs.
Miss. ____________________
Last First Middle

Home phone number ____________________

Present address ____________________

Permanent address ____________________

Social Security number ____________________

Age ______ Date of birth ____________________ Weight ______ Height ______
Month Day Year

Are you a citizen of the U.S.? Yes ______ No ______

Single ______ Married ______ Separated ______ Widowed ______ Engaged ______

Are you handicapped? Yes ______ No ______

If yes, please explain. ____________________

Please put down the type of work you prefer from the attached list.

1. ____________ 2. ____________

Are you willing to work? Full–time ______
Day ______
Evening ______

Hours preferred ____________________

Salary desired ____________________

Date available ____________________
Month Day Year

Are you willing to transfer? Yes ____ No ____

Education

	Years attended	Name and address	Major field of study	Degree
Grade school				
High school				
College or university				
Corres. bus. Grade, evening school				

Did you take any special courses? Yes ______ No ______

If yes, please explain. ____________________

Did you get any academic honors? Yes ______ No ______

If yes, please list them. ____________________

Are you taking any courses at present? Yes ______ No ______

If yes, give courses and name of school. ____________________

Military service

Branch of service ____________________

Years in from ____________________ to ____________________
Month Day Year Month Day Year

Type of discharge ____________________

Current status ____________________

Business experience

Please list your last employer first, and then the next 10 years.

Company name and address	Dates Month Year	Position	Salary	Phone number of company

Figure 16.13 Application form completed by all prospective applicants.

Branch number
Applicant number
Date: ____/____/____
Month Day Year

Calzone Agents – Application Form

Company name and address	Dates Month Year	Position	Salary	Phone number of company

Which business machines can you operate proficiently? ____________________

Shorthand speed ______ Method ______ Typing speed ______ Manual ______ Electric ______

If any changes come about, please notify your branch office.

____
Signature of applicant

Do not write below this point

Comments:

Hired ________ Position ________ Department ________
Salary ________ Starting date ________

Figure 16.13 Continued.

the system. A request for systems investigation will be the vehicle for company personnel to seek help for the system. Any correspondence received should be retained within a permanent file for that area.

During the reevaluation effort, any changes within the system's configuration will be made. A request for systems investigation will alert the systems staff to subsequently uncovered problem areas.

COSTS ANALYSIS

Management will be presented with two alternative solutions by the systems analysts. Each solution represents a significantly different approach. Alternative 1 is based upon a card-oriented system. Alternative 2 is the system chosen and is the system that was previously discussed.

Alternative 1 is a card system. It utilizes a weekly batching

Name Calzone Agents
Social Security Number

Interview Evaluation Date / /

This form is completed immediately after conclusion of the Applicant's interview. This sheet is attached and filed with the completed application form.

Fill in the appropriate evaluation.

	Superior	Above average	Average	Poor	Unsatisfactory
1. First impression of applicant					
2. Confidence within job knowledge					
3. Technical knowledge					
4. Interest in job					
5. Composure during interview					
6. Overall self–confidence					
7. Manner of speech					
8. Command of the language					
9. General appearance					
10. Ambitious attitude					
11. Maturity					

Final impression:

Comments:

Interviewer ______________ Date ______________

Figure 16.14 Post-interview evaluation form to be completed by interviewer.

scheme. Data are received at the main office from the branch offices, by mail. The system provides adequately for existing facilities and some limited growth. This system could handle the personnel system adequately, but no extensive demands could be placed upon it. This system is the least costly, as shown by the cost figures in Table 16.2.

Alternative 2 is a design of a more elaborate nature. It provides for extensive future growth and affords the company operational flexibility, with possible time-sharing capabilities. Management realizes that the requirements of the personnel system will not tax the computer to its fullest extent. Thus the system, with minor modifications, would enable the company

IBM

INTERNATIONAL BUSINESS MACHINES CORPORATION

STORAGE LAYOUT

IBM 1240 - 1401 - 1410 - 1420 - 1440 - 1460

Form X24-6438-5
Printed in U. S. A.

APPLICATION STORAGE FORMATS – DISK

DATE 11 JULY __

APPLICANT STORAGE RECORD (DISK)

- SYMBOLIC: BRANCH CODE; SHIFT PRIORITY; HANDICAP CODE; MARITAL STATUS
- DATA: IN-QUIRY CODE | SOCIAL SECURITY NO. | LAST NAME | FIRST NAME | M.I. | TELEPHONE | JOB CODE | PRIMARY POSITION SOUGHT | SECOND POSITION SOUGHT | SALARY LEVEL DESIRED | START DATE DA./MO. | DATE OF BIRTH MO.-DA.-YR. | AGE | ADDRESS

APPLICANT STORAGE (CON'T)

- SYMBOLIC: YEARS OF EDUCATION; TOTAL YEARS OF INDUSTRIAL EXP.; YEARS OF EXPERIENCE IN FIELD; * AS REQ'D.
- DATA: CITY, STATE | ZIP | DEGREE REC'D | AREA OF MAJOR | MILITARY STATUS | POSITION AVAILABLE | CO.ID. OF COMPANY AVAILABLE | POSITION* AVAILABLE | CO.ID. OF * COMPANY AVAILABLE

EMPLOYMENT OPPORTUNITIES AVAILABLE RECORD (DISK)

- SYMBOLIC: QUANTITY; QUANTITY
- DATA: IN-QUIRY CODE | COMPANY I.D. NO. | COMPANY NAME | ADDRESS | CITY, STATE | ZIP | POSITION AVAILABLE IN CODE | SALARY RANGE AVAILABLE | POSITION AVAILABLE IN CODE * | SALARY RANGE * AVAILABLE | * POSITION AVAILABLE IN CODE

(continuation)

- SYMBOLIC: QUANTITY; QUANTITY
- DATA: SALARY RANGE * * AVAILABLE | * POSITION AVAILABLE IN CODE * | SALARY RANGE * AVAILABLE | *

* = THE GROUPS OF 3 FIELDS ARE ADDED AS REQUIRED, WHEN NEW JOB POSITIONS ARE ADDED. THESE REPRESENT JOB POSITIONS AVAILABLE.

Figure 16.15 Disk storage layout for applicant status records and employment opportunities available records.

IBM

INTERNATIONAL BUSINESS MACHINES CORPORATION

MULTIPLE-CARD LAYOUT FORM

GX24-6599-
Printed in U.S.A.

Company CALZONE

Application CARD FORMAT FOR APPLICATION RECORDS by ______ Date JULY -- Job No. ______ Sheet No. 4

CARD 1

Field	Columns
INQUIRY CODE	1–3
SOCIAL SECURITY NO.	4–12
BRANCH	13–14
LAST NAME	15–34
FIRST NAME	35–44
M. I.	45
TELEPHONE NO.	46–55
JOB CODE	56–60
PRIMARY POSITION DESIRED	61–65
SECOND POSITION SOUGHT	66–70
SALARY LEVEL SOUGHT	71–75
START DATE D /MON.	76–80

CARD 2

Field	Columns
SHIFT PRIORITY	1–3
DATE OF BIRTH M./D./YR.	4–9
AGE	10–11
HANDICAP CODE	12
MARITAL STATUS	13
ADDRESS	14–33
CITY, STATE	34–48
ZIP	49–53
YEARS OF EDUCATION	54–55
DEGREE REC'D	56–58
AREA OF MAJOR	59–63
MILITARY STATUS	64–67
TOTAL YEARS OF INDUSTRIAL EXPERIENCE	68–69
YEARS OF EXPERIENCE IN FIELD	70–71
	72–80

CARD 3

Field	Columns
POSITION AVAILABLE	1–5
COMPANY I.D. OF POSITION AVAILABLE	6–10
* POSITION AVAILABLE	11–15
* COMPANY I.D. OF POSITION AVAILABLE	16–20
* POSITION AVAILABLE	21–25
* COMPANY I.D. OF POSITION AVAILABLE	26–30
	31–80

MUST BE TOGETHER

NOTE: 1) IF NO POSITIONS ARE AVAILABLE DURING INPUT OF THE CANDIDATE DURING INPUT, THEY WILL BE ADDED AFTER THE MATCH-UP PROGRAM IS RUN.

2) AS MANY POSITIONS AVAILABLE, WITH RESPECTIVE CO. ID., WILL BE ADDED AS NECESSARY TO THE EMPLOYEE CANDIDATES RECORD.

Figure 16.16 Card format of applicant records.

IBM INTERNATIONAL BUSINESS MACHINES CORPORATION

GX24-6599-0
Printed in U.S.A.

MULTIPLE-CARD LAYOUT FORM

Company CALZONE

Application EMPLOYMENT OPPORTUNITIES RECORDS by ______ Date AUG. __ Job No. ______ Sheet No. 5

Card 1

INQ. CODE	COMPANY I.D. NO.	COMPANY NAME	ADDRESS	CITY, STATE	ZIP	POSITION AVAIL- ABLE, IN CODE	
1 2 3	4 5 6 7 8	9–28	29–53	54–68	69–73	74–78	79 80

Card 2

SALARY RANGE OFFERED	QUANTITY	POSITION AVAIL- ABLE, IN CODE *	SALARY RANGE OFFERED *	QUANTITY *	*	*	*	
1 2 3 4 5	6 7	8 9 10 11 12	13 14 15 16 17	18 19	20–24	25–29	30 31	32–80

FOR THIS COMPANY, THE POSITION AVAILABLE WILL BE LISTED IN ASCENDING ORDER (IN CODE).

* AS REQUIRED

Figure 16.17 Card format of employment opportunities records.

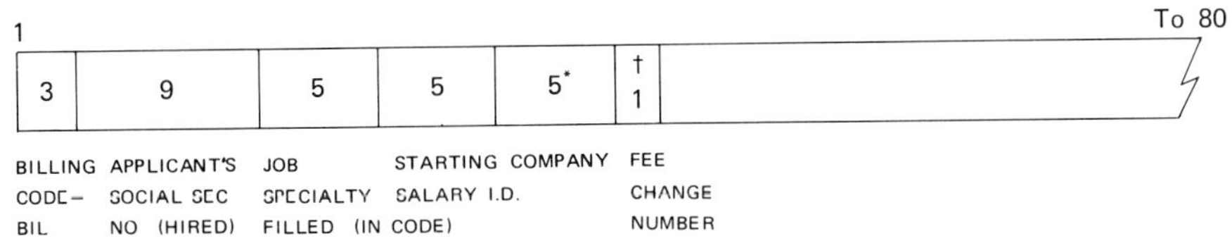

* IF THE APPLICANT IS TO RECEIVE THE INVOICE, FIVE 8's (88888) WILL APPEAR IN THIS FIELD

† THE NUMBER 1 INDICATES THE NORMAL RATE; THE NUMBER 2 A CHANGE FOLLOWED BY THE FEE RATE.

Figure 16.18 Format used for employee confirmation cards.

to rent unused computer time, to develop a small service bureau business, or to provide varied consultant/EDP services.

The costs for this system are listed in Table 16.3.

SUMMARY

Management feels that Alternative 2 provides the company with the greatest flexibility. They are willing to absorb the initial costs for a greater possible return. Alternative 2's system will provide for quicker services to all applicants and, thereby, will garner a greater portion of the personnel market. The usage of a computer system provides an advertising advantage, which it is felt will be financially successful.

The usage of terminals will enable the quicker processing of

TABLE 16.2 ALTERNATIVE 1

	Year 1	Year 2	Year 3	Year 4
Nonrecurring Costs				
System design	$45,000	$ 9,000		
Programming	25,000	5,000		
Training	4,000			
Physical planning	5,000			
Conversion and test	3,000			
Recurring Costs				
Personnel	14,000	29,000	32,000	35,000
Rental	15,000	24,000	26,000	28,000
Operations and overhead	7,000	14,000	16,000	18,000
Supplies	10,000	16,000	16,000	16,000
TOTAL COSTS	$128,000	97,000	90,000	97,000
	Estimated Income from the System			
Average hired per week	2	10	15	18
Average salary per week	$ 150	175	200	225
Operational weeks	26	52	52	52
Income	$ 7,800	91,100	156,000	210,000
Annual net income	$(120,000)	(5,900)	66,000	113,600
Cumulative income TOTAL	$(120,200)	(126,100)	(60,100)	53,500

TABLE 16.3 ALTERNATIVE 2

	Year 1	Year 2	Year 3	Year 4
Nonrecurring Costs				
System design	$85,000	15,000		
Programming	45,000	10,000		
Training	5,000			
Physical planning	5,000			
Conversion and test	4,000	2,000		
Recurring Costs				
Personnel	18,000	38,000	41,000	45,000
Rental	25,000	58,000	60,000	62,000
Operations and overhead	8,000	16,000	18,000	20,000
Supplies	10,000	16,000	16,000	16,000
TOTAL COSTS	$205,000	155,000	135,000	143,000
	Estimated Income from the System			
Average hired per week	6	15	25	30
Average salary per week	$ 150	175	200	225
Operational weeks	26	52	52	52
Income				
Personnel system	$23,400	136,500	260,000	351,000
Additional services	10,000	25,000	40,000	50,000
Total income	$33,400	161,500	300,000	401,000
Annual net income	$(171,600)	6,500	165,000	258,000
Cumulative income TOTAL	$(171,600)	(165,100)	(100)	257,900

data for the applicants. Terminal usage will ease the system's conversion or modification if extensive service demands are forthcoming.

The chart in Figure 16.19 shows the comparison of the alternative systems.

Figure 16.19 Implementation schedule for alternative systems.

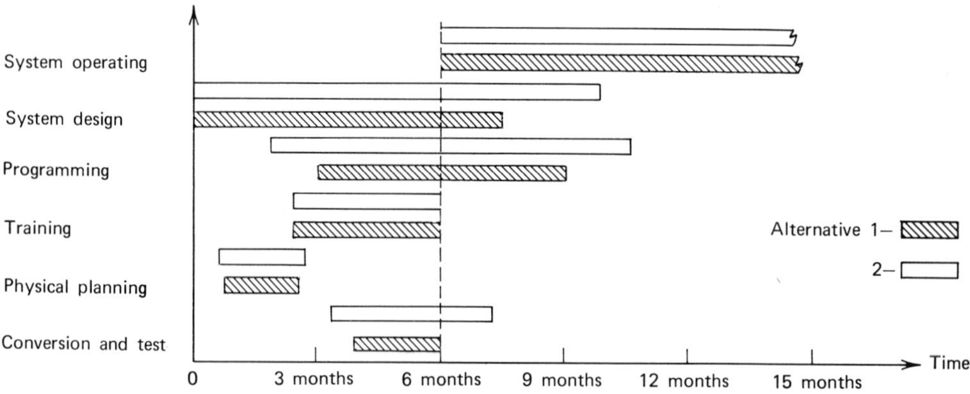

CHAPTER **17**

CASE STUDY—ACCOUNTS RECEIVABLE

In previous chapters we examined the fundamentals of analyzing systems and then of designing better ones. The purpose of this chapter is to reinforce the principles presented by applying them to an accounts receivable system that is currently a unit-record system.[1] The approach will be as follows:

1. Analyze accounts receivable system as it is currently operating in the Nanbeth Department Store
2. Prepare a problem definition
3. Design and document a new system

ANALYSIS OF CURRENT SYSTEM

Objectives

The basic objectives of the accounts receivable system in the Nanbeth Department Store are as follows:

1. To establish and maintain accounts for charge customers
2. To send monthly statements to each customer for payment
3. To suspend charge accounts for customers who are delinquent in payment for more than three months
4. To provide management with accurate reports for decision-making and planning purposes.

Constraints

Management will allow one man-year to analyze the current system and to design a new one.

Outputs

The basic outputs of the unit-record system are shown below.

1. *Monthly customer statement* (Figure 17.1). The company currently has 13,650 charge accounts, of which approximately 40 percent are active. By active, it is meant that one or more transactions have been made to the account within the last four months.

[1]Electronic accounting machines (collator, reproducer, accounting machine, etc.) are currently being used.

Monthly Statement

Nanbeth Department Store
Garden City, N.Y. 11530

Account number — Date:

Name
Address — Amount enclosed:

Please return this portion with remittance

Date	Ticket number	Description	Purchases	Credits and payments

Previous balance	Total purchases	Total credits and payments	New balance

Figure 17.1 Monthly customer statement.

2. *Daily accounts receivable register* (Figure 17.2). This report is prepared daily to show all transactions that have occurred during the previous day to affect charge accounts.
3. *Weekly accounts receivable summary report* (Figure 17.3). This report is run at the end of each week to show summary activity, by day, for accounts receivable.
4. *Customer name-and-address report* (Figure 17.4). This report shows the current name and address for all customers, by account number. It is produced every time any changes are made to the name-and-address file, which is discussed later. The name-and-address report is used as a double check that additions, deletions, and corrections to the name-and-address file have been correctly incorporated.
5. *Delinquent account report.* This report is prepared manually at the time when the monthly customers' statements are prepared. It is used by management to suspend those charge accounts for customers who are delinquent in payment for more than three months. See Figure 17.5.

Processing

The following systems flowcharts describe the current operations of the system.

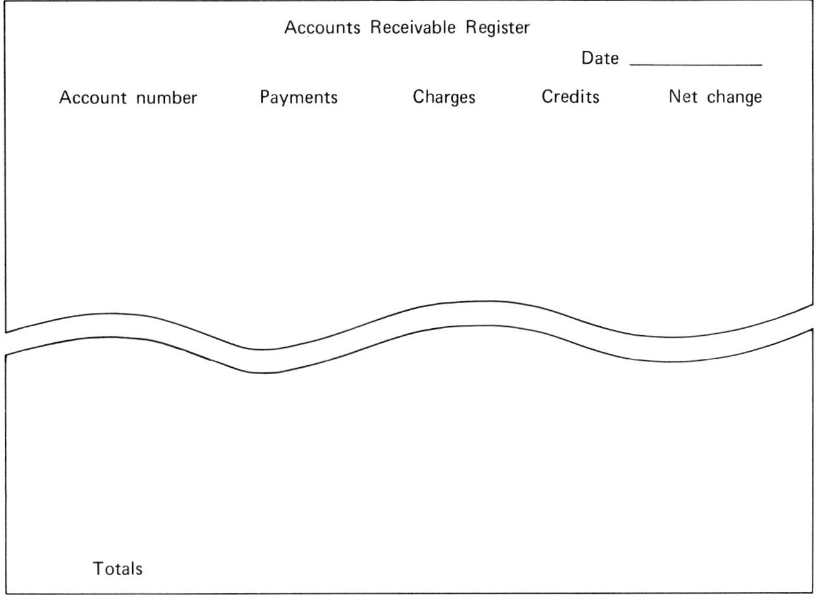

Figure 17.2 Accounts receivable register.

1. Processing of applications approved for new charge accounts (Figure 17.6)
2. Processing of sales slips, credit slips, and payment memos on a daily basis (Figure 17.7)
3. Processing of weekly accounts receivable summary report (Figure 17.8)
4. Processing of corrections to the name-and-address file (Figure 17.9)
5. Processing of monthly customer statements (Figures 17.10 *a* and *b*)

Inputs

The basic inputs used in the current accounts receivable system are shown below.

1. *Application for charge account* (Figure 17.11).
2. *Name-and-address card, and transaction cards for sales slip, credit slip, and payment memo* (Figure 17.12).
3. *Sales credit slip* (Figure 17.13).
4. *Payment memo* (Figure 17.14).
5. *Correction memo*—for changes to name-and-address file (Figure 17.15). If only the customer's name has changed, "Name from" and "Name to" are filled out, and his current address is entered under "Address from." If only the cus-

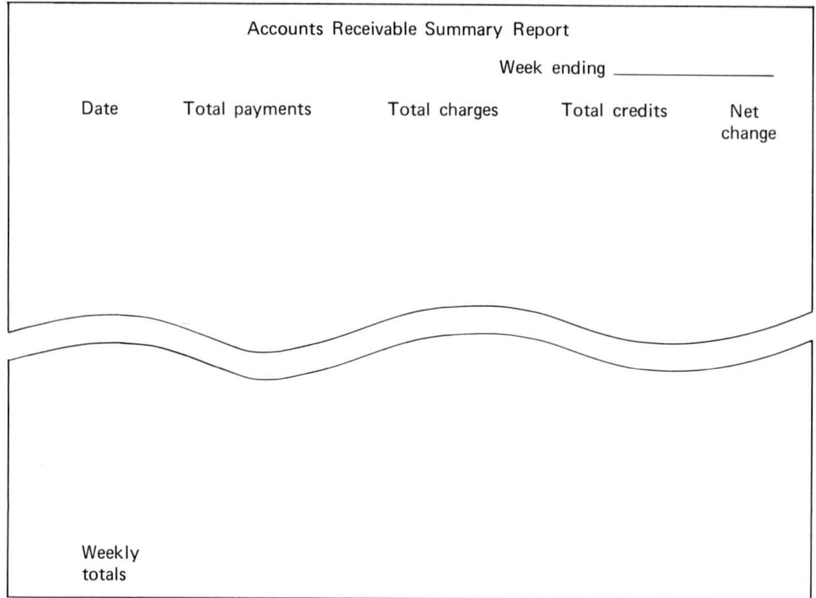

Figure 17.3 Accounts receivable summary report.

tomer's address has changed, "Address from" and "Address to" are filled out, and his name is entered next to "Name from."

Controls

The daily accounts receivable register and the weekly accounts receivable summary report are the primary controls used for making trial balances of accounts receivable.

The monthly cost of operating the current accounts receivable system is shown in Table 17.1. The information was obtained from interviews with the manager of accounts receivable and the manager of operations in the data processing department.

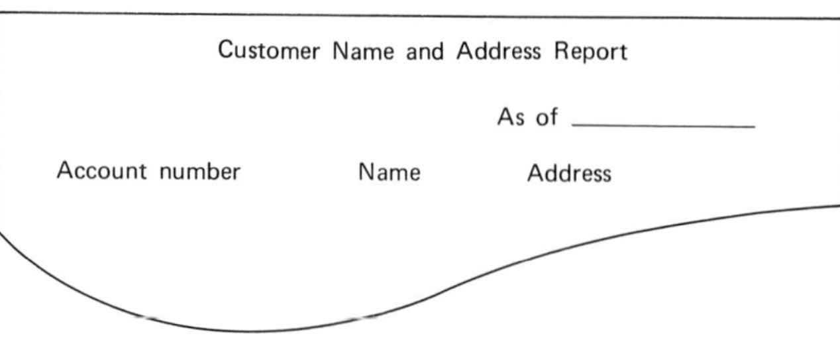

Figure 17.4 Customer name-and-address report.

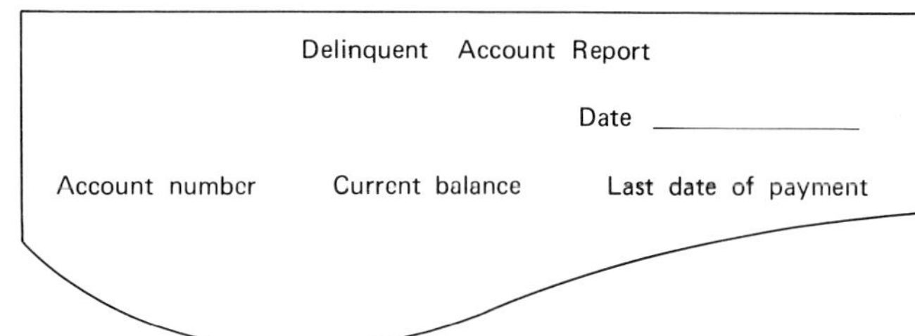
Delinquent Account Report

Date ______

Account number | Current balance | Last date of payment

Figure 17.5 Delinquent account report.

PROBLEM DEFINITION

Interviews with the manager of accounts receivable, and analysis of the current system have revealed the following facts:

1. The volume of activity in the system is expected to increase substantially now that the company is in the process of constructing a branch store in Queens and one in Brooklyn. Processing time on unit-record equipment will be excessive with an estimated number of accounts rising to 30,000.

TABLE 17.1 RESOURCE SHEET

Name and Description	Amount	Average Cost per Month	Notes
Personnel			
Manager of accounts receivable	1	$1500	
Accounts receivable clerks	3	1150	
Accounts receivable typist	1	475	
Keypunch operator	1	400	
Unit-record operators	.5	250	
Equipment			
Sorter	.2	30	Times allo-
Collator	.1	15	cated to each
Accounting machine	.3	75	device were
Keypunch machine	1	85	estimated by
Verifier	1	100	operations manager.
Supplies			
Punched cards	40,000	45	
Preprinted forms[a]	20 boxes	200	
Stock paper[a]	10 boxes	50	

[a]Primarily 2-ply paper, 1,600 sheets to a box.

TOTAL $4375

SYSTEM: Accounts receivable PREPARED BY: Robert A. Stern
DATE: 7/1/__

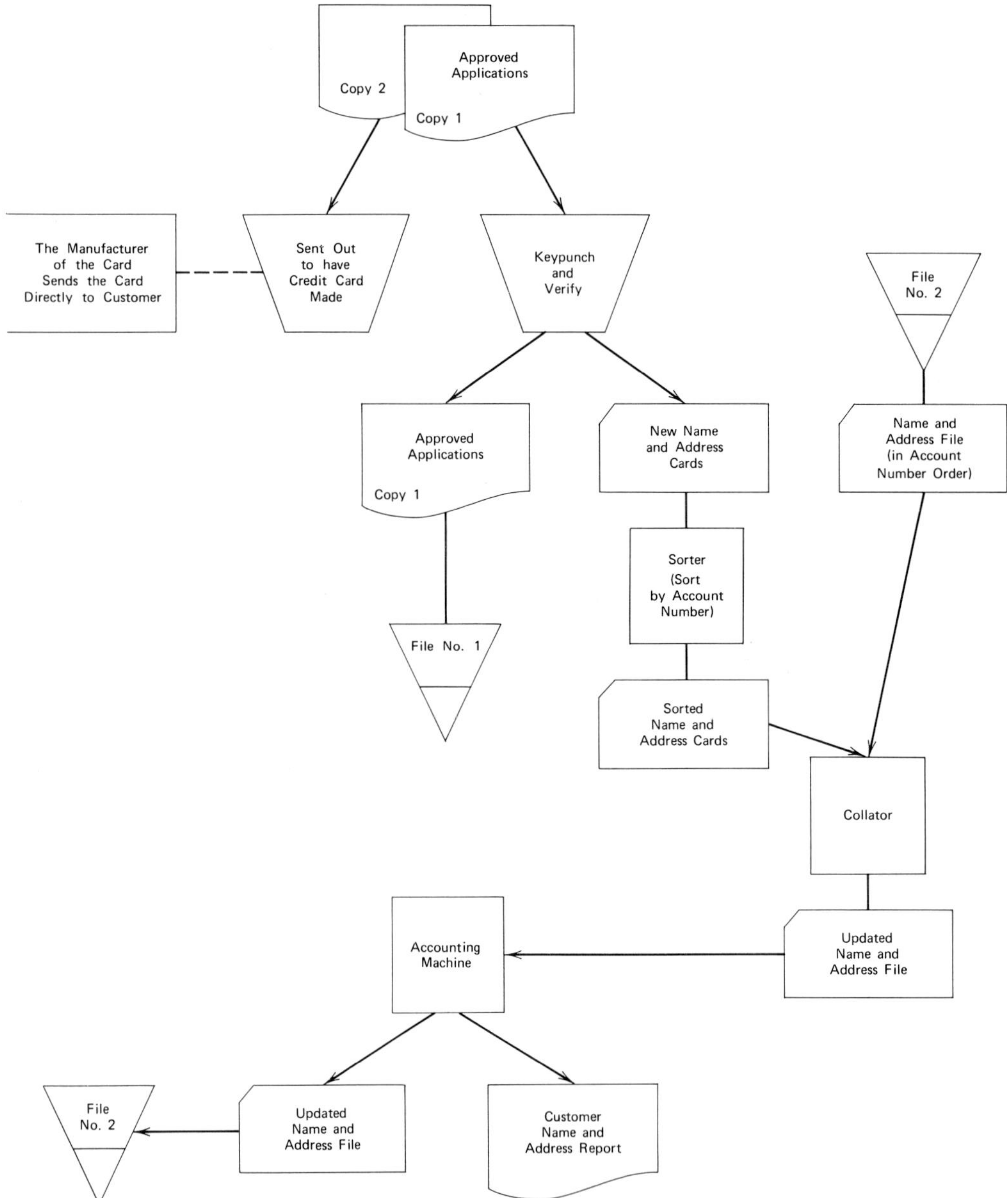

Figure 17.6 Processing of applications approved for new charge accounts.

2. Approximately 200 errors per month are caused because the incorrect item ("Sales" or "Credit") is circled on the sales/credit slip.

3. Management is dissatisfied with the higher number of delinquent accounts. Approximately 450 accounts have balances

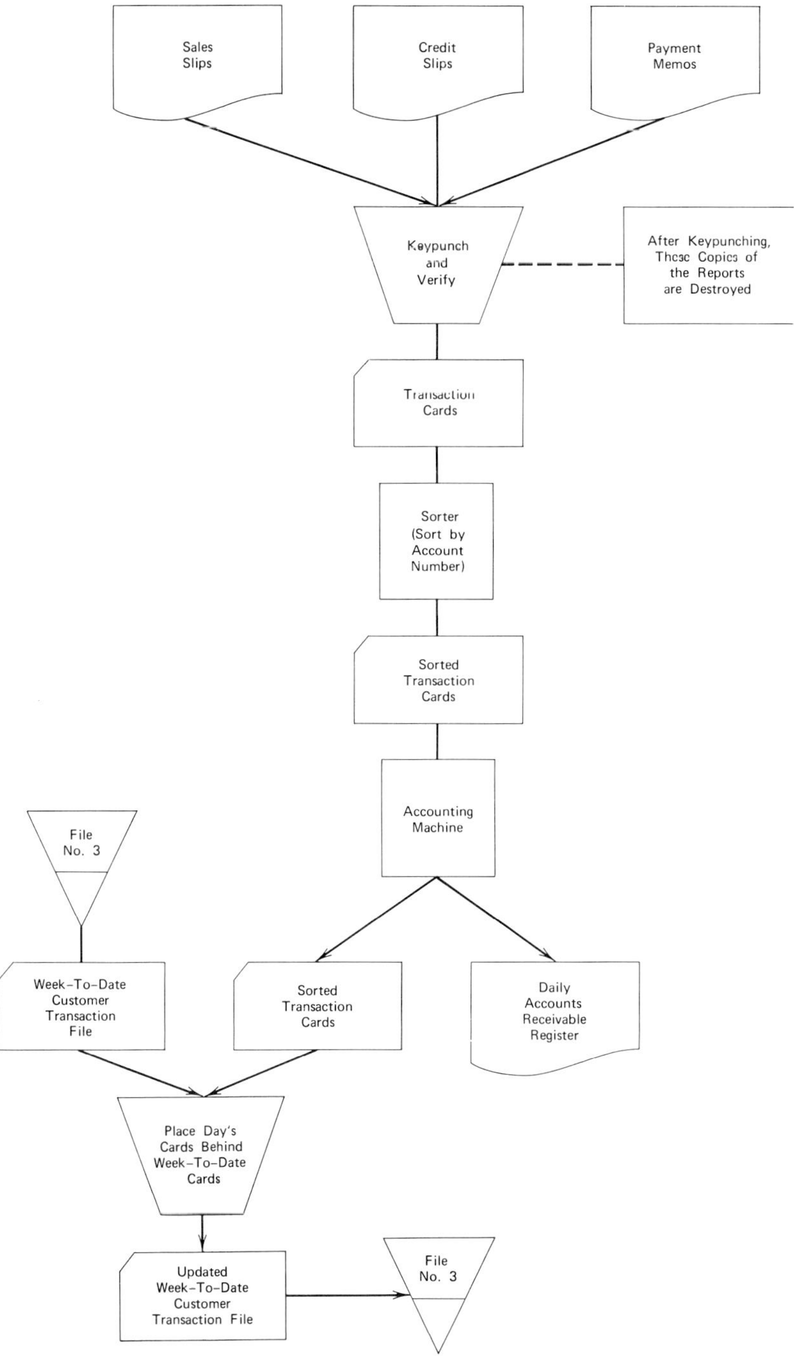

Figure 17.7 Processing of sales slips, credit slips, and payment memos on a daily basis.

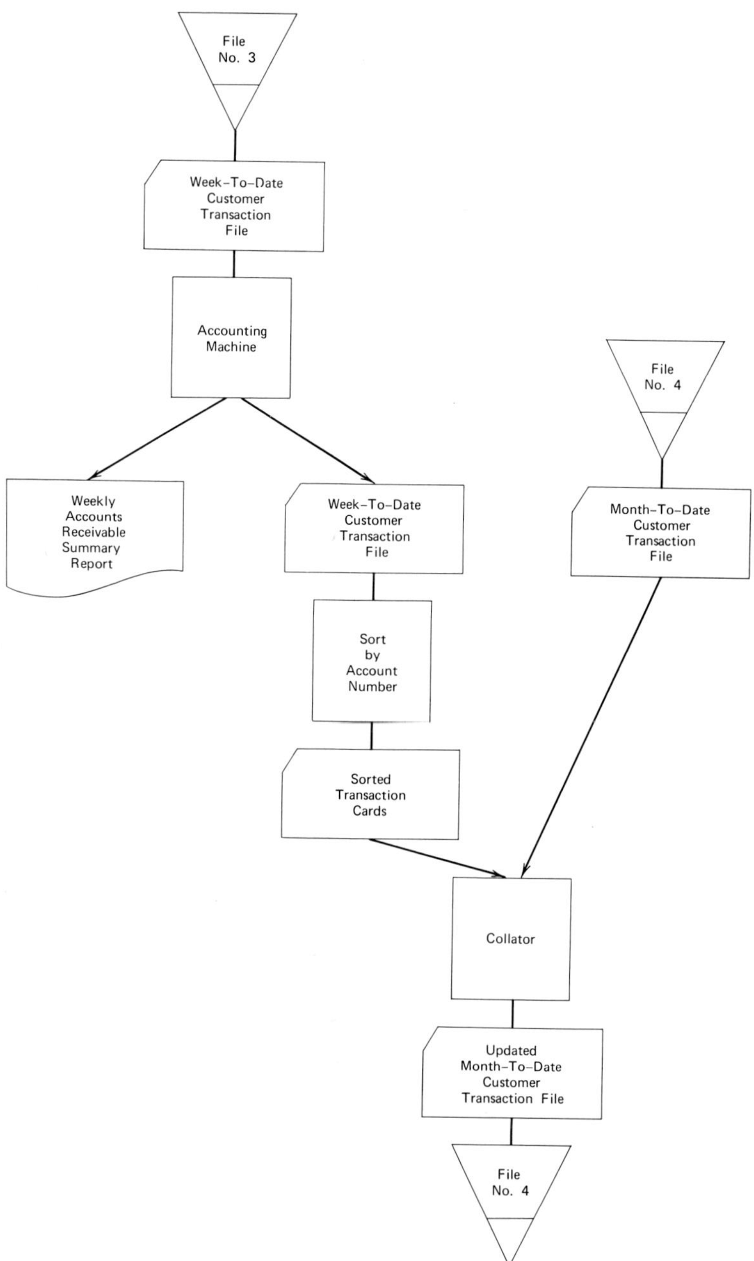

Figure 17.8 Processing of weekly accounts receivable summary report.

outstanding for three months or longer. Management would like to institute a financc charge as follows:

1½% per month on the first $500 of the previous unpaid balance, and 1% per month on any such balance over $500.

DESIGN OF NEW SYSTEM

Objectives

The objectives of the accounts receivable system remain basically the same. The following changes are to be made, however:

1. Management would like to have the capability to have sales personnel retrieve information from the computer immediately in response to customer inquiries concerning balances due.
2. Under the current system, if a customer forgets his charge card he must pay in cash. Management would like to add a service whereby customers can charge items without having their charge cards with them.
3. Management would like to incorporate finance charges for delinquent accounts.

Constraints

There are two basic constraints:

1. Management has allotted one man-year to completely analyze and redesign this system. Since two man-months have already been expended in the analysis of the current system, this leaves ten man-months for the design of the new system.
2. The company has on order the following computer configuration. The analyst cannot utilize hardware other than that described here.

 1 Central processing unit (CPU) with storage capacity of approximately 256,000 characters
 4 tape drives
 2 disk drives
 1 printer
 1 card reader-punch
 1 console typewriter
 6 display terminals

Basic Outputs from the Computerized System

The basic outputs are shown below, with changes from current outputs enumerated for easy review.

1. *Monthly customer statement* (Figure 17.16). The monthly statements will be prepared on preprinted forms on a ro-

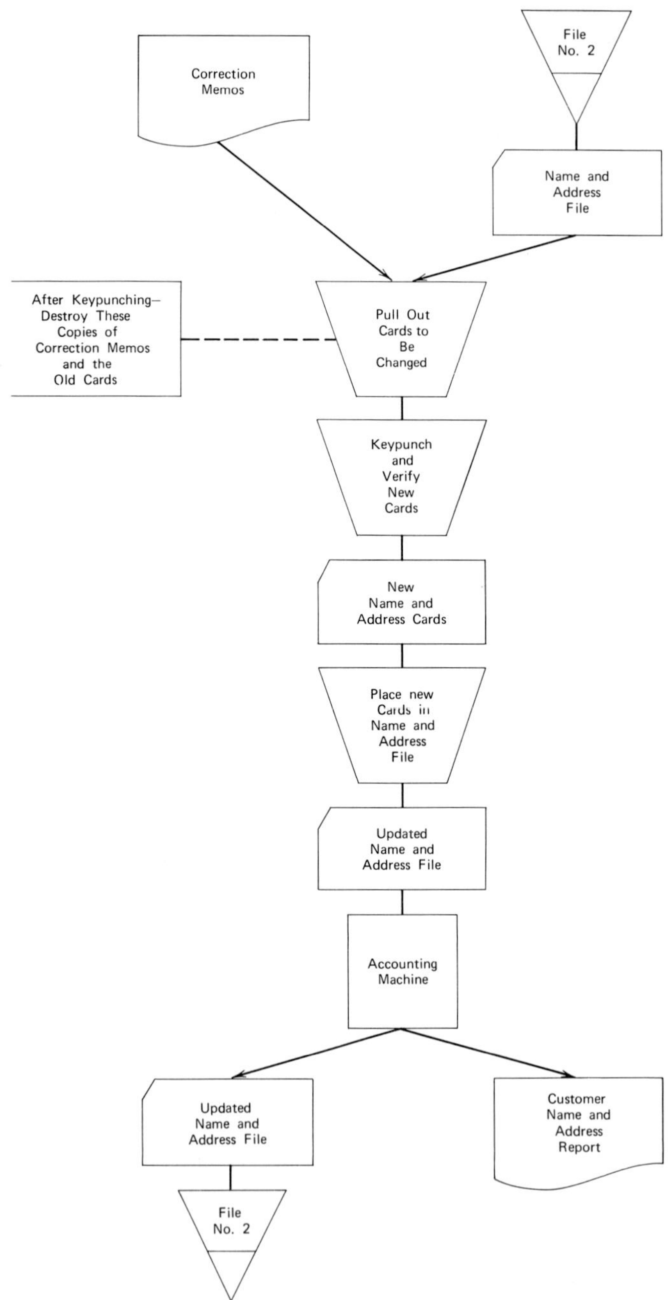

Figure 17.9 Processing of corrections to name-and-address file.

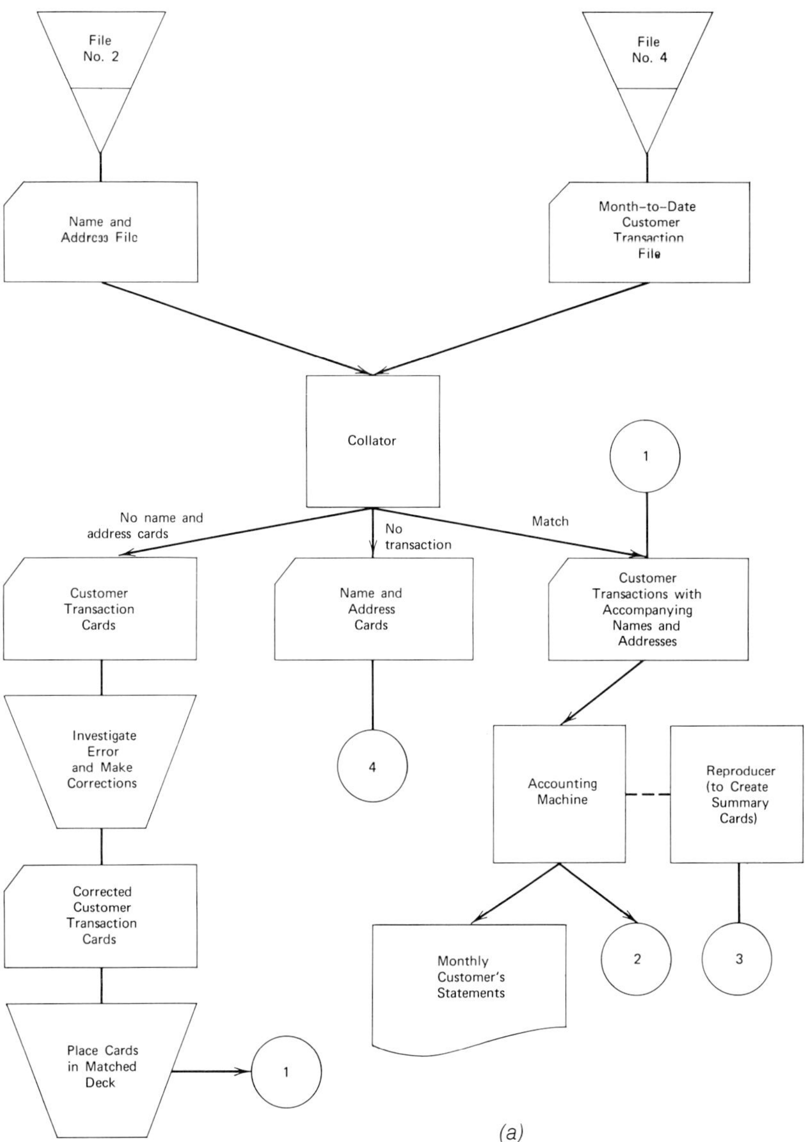

Figure 17.10 Processing of monthly customer statements.

tating basis. That is, the accounts will be subdivided into groups by account number, and statements will be rendered to each group on different dates. This will eliminate peak loads for the computer, which would occur if all statements were produced at the same time.

There are two changes in the monthly statement:

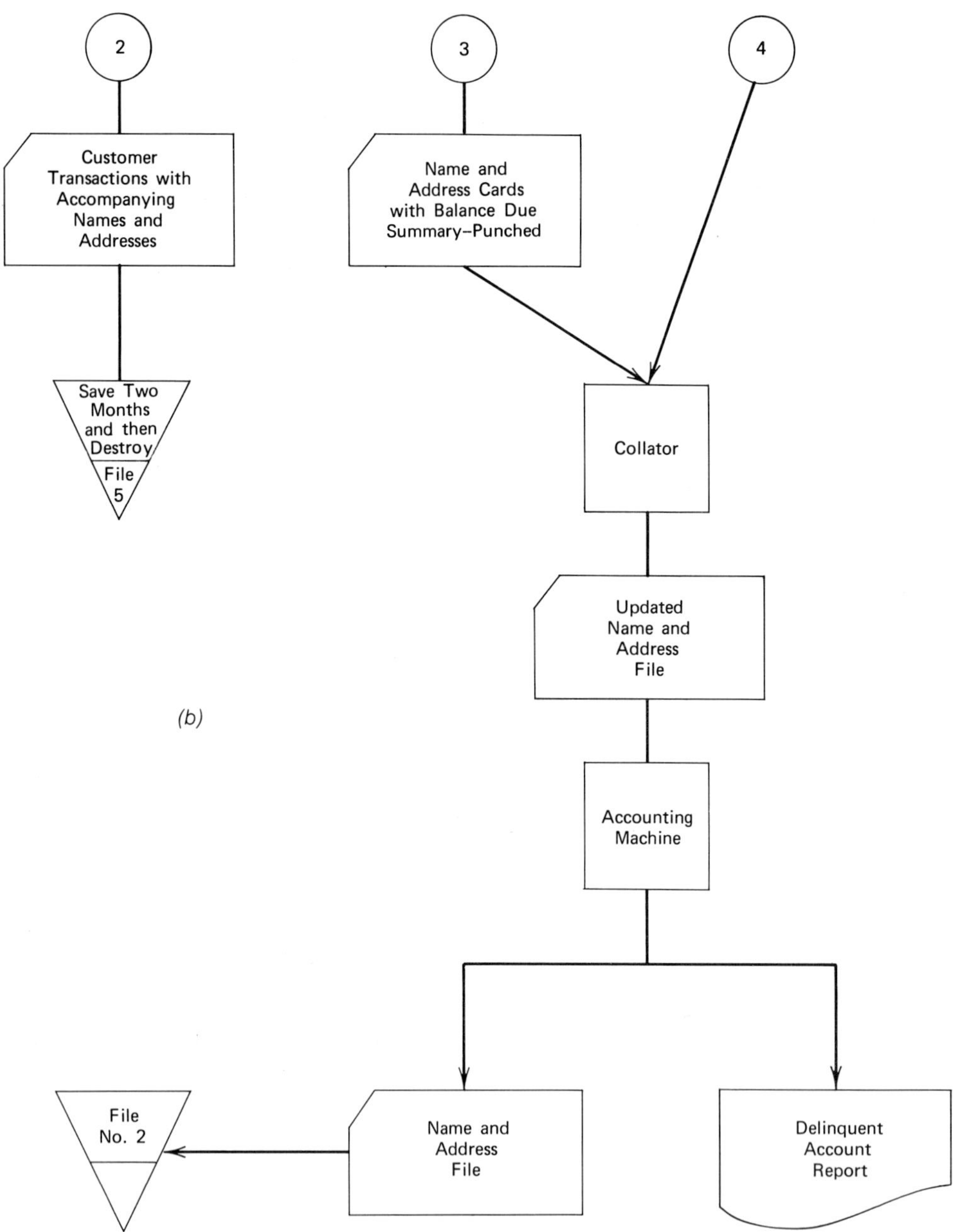

Figure 17.10 Continued.

a. Store identification has been added.
M = Main store B = Brooklyn branch Q = Queens store

b. Provision has been made to allow for finance charges.

Nanbeth Department Store
Garden City, N.Y. 11530

Application for Charge Account

Date ______________

Last name	First name		Middle initial	
Address		City	State	Zip
Home telephone				
Employer				
Business address				
Type of job	How long employed here			
Annual salary	Bank reference			
Age	Marital status			

Signature ______________________

For Office Use Only

Approved or disapproved: ______________
Date: ______________
Reason, if disapproved: ______________
Account number, if approved: ______________
Authorized signature: ______________

Figure 17.11 Application for charge account.

2. *Daily accounts receivable register.* This report will remain the same.
3. *Changes in customer information*—for accounts receivable use, prepared monthly (Figure 17.17). This report will be prepared on stock paper to be used by the accounts receivable department as a "double" check to ensure that information transmitted to data processing pertaining to additions, deletions, and corrections of customer accounts will be correctly incorporated. This will replace the customer name-and-address change report. It is felt that the new title is more meaningful. The codes will be as follows:

Code	Meaning
1	New account
2	Account deleted
3	Change of name
4	Change of address
5	Change of name and address

IBM

INTERNATIONAL BUSINESS MACHINES CORPORATION

MULTIPLE-CARD LAYOUT FORM

GX24-6599-0
Printed in U.S.A.

Company NANBETH DEPARTMENT STORE

Application ACCOUNTS RECEIVABLE (CURRENT SYSTEM) by R.A.STERN Date 8/3/-- Job No. ______ Sheet No. 1

NAME AND ADDRESS CARD — 4

ACCOUNT NUMBER	FIRST NAME	M. I.	LAST NAME	ADDRESS: STREET	ADDRESS: CITY	ADDRESS: STATE	ADDRESS: ZIP	PREVIOUS BALANCE DUE $	PREVIOUS BALANCE DUE ¢	DATE OF LAST PAYMENT MO. DA. YR.	DATE ACCOUNT ESTAB-LISHED MO. DA. YR.		
1–8	9–17	18	19–29	30–39	40–48	49–54	55–59	60–64	65–66	67–72	73–78	79	80

SALES SLIP — 1

ACCOUNT NUMBER	TICKET NUMBER	DATE MO. DA. YR.	ITEM DESCRIPTION	CHARGE AMOUNT $	CHARGE AMOUNT ¢	
1–8	9–14	15–20	21–31	32–35	36–37	38–80

CREDIT SLIP — 2

ACCOUNT NUMBER	TICKET NUMBER	DATE	ITEM DESCRIPTION	CREDIT AMOUNT $	CREDIT AMOUNT ¢	
1–8	9–14	15–20	21–31	32–35	36–37	38–80

PAYMENT MEMO — 3

ACCOUNT NUMBER	(X)	DATE	(X)	PAYMENT AMOUNT $	PAYMENT AMOUNT ¢	
1–8	9–14	15–20	21–31	32–35	36–37	38–80

Figure 17.12 Card formats for accounts receivable system.

Nanbeth Department Store
Garden City, N.Y. 11530

(circle) Sales Credit   Ticket No. ________

Name ________   Date ________

Address ________

Quantity	Description	Unit price	Sales amount

Subtotal ________
Sales tax ________
Total ________

Customer's signature ________   Salesman ________

Figure 17.13 Sales/credit slip.

The report will be used by the sales department for determining whether the number of charge account customers is on the rise or decline.

This report differs from the current one in that it will be an "exception" report. This means that only *changes* to the name-and-address file will be shown, not the entire list of customers.

4. *Delinquent account report*—used for suspending accounts, prepared monthly (Figure 17.18). This report will be prepared on stock paper and will normally be produced once a month. It will be used by the accounts receivable department to suspend charge privileges for customers who are delinquent in payment for more than three months. The report will also be available upon request by management for special use. As an example, prior to special sales for charge account cus-

Payment Memo

Date ________

Payment received from account number ________

Amount ________

Authorized signature ________

Figure 17.14 Payment memo.

Correction Memo

Account number ______________

Change ☐ Name from ______ | | ______ To ______ | | ______
First Initial Last First Initial Last

☐ Address from

Street ______________ To ______________

City ______________ ______________

State ______________ ______________

Zip ______________ ______________

Authorized signature ______________ Date ______

Figure 17.15 Correction memo.

tomers only, management might want the most current report to determine whether special consideration is to be given to these delinquent-account customers (e.g., suspension of charge privileges).

Figure 17.16 Monthly customer statement.

MONTHLY STATEMENT

Nanbeth's DEPT. STORE

NORTH CORAM, N.Y. 11727

ACCOUNT NO. 01045 DATE 9/26/77

NAME MRS. LORI STERLING

ADDRESS 25 HAWKINS DRIVE
CORAM, N.Y. 11727

AMOUNT ENCLOSED ______

PLEASE RETURN THIS PORTION WITH REMITTANCE

DATE	TICKET NO.	STORE	DESCRIPTION	PURCHASES	CREDITS AND PAYMENTS
9 16	175970	M	COSMETICS	10.50	
9 18			PAYMENT		25.75

PREVIOUS BALANCE	FINANCE CHARGE (MIN. $.50)	TOTAL PURCHASES	TOTAL CREDITS AND PAYMENTS	NEW BALANCE
25.75	+	+ 10.50	− 25.75	= $ 10.50

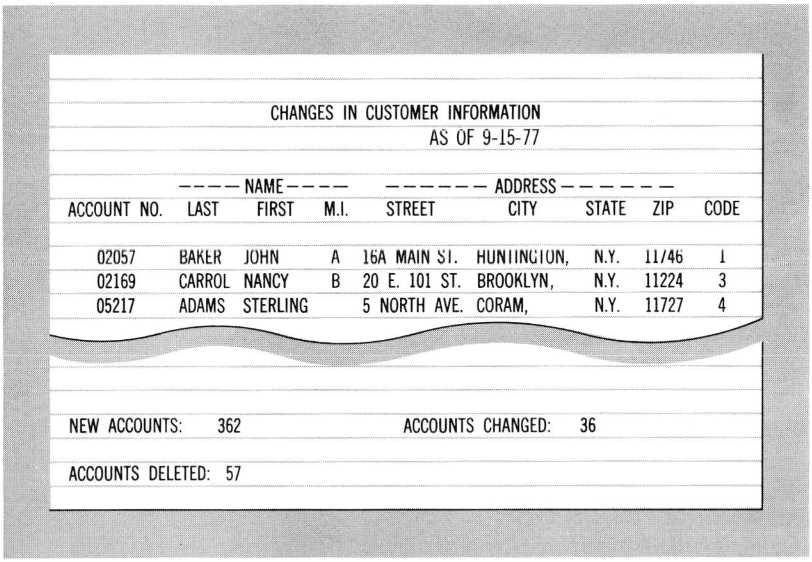

CHANGES IN CUSTOMER INFORMATION
AS OF 9-15-77

ACCOUNT NO.	NAME LAST	NAME FIRST	NAME M.I.	ADDRESS STREET	ADDRESS CITY	ADDRESS STATE	ADDRESS ZIP	CODE
02057	BAKER	JOHN	A	16A MAIN ST.	HUNTINGTON,	N.Y.	11746	1
02169	CARROL	NANCY	B	20 E. 101 ST.	BROOKLYN,	N.Y.	11224	3
05217	ADAMS	STERLING		5 NORTH AVE.	CORAM,	N.Y.	11727	4

NEW ACCOUNTS: 362 ACCOUNTS CHANGED: 36

ACCOUNTS DELETED: 57

Figure 17.17 Changes in customer information.

This report is similar to the current one except that it includes finance charges in the current balance.

5. *Weekly accounts receivable summary report* (Figure 17.19). This report is similar to the present one except that it has a breakdown of charges by store. This report is recommended for management's use in determining which store or stores might benefit from having special sales for charge account customers only.

Processing

The master accounts receivable file will be stored on magnetic disk and will be the major file used in processing information to produce all output files. All information pertaining to each customer will be maintained here, as depicted in Figure 17.20.

An on-line disk file has been chosen so that customer inquiries can be easily handled from terminals located on the sales floor.

There will be six terminals at specified sales counters linked electronically to the CPU and to the disk file, at the computer center. The *on-line* feature of this system will allow sales personnel to make inquiries of customer accounts at the specified sales counters via the terminals.

The random-access feature of this type of file was the primary factor in choosing a disk file over a strictly sequential file such as tape or cards.

DELINQUENT ACCOUNT REPORT AS OF 10-25-77

ACCOUNT NUMBER	CURRENT BALANCE	DATE OF LAST PAYMENT	---NAME--- LAST	FIRST	-----ADDRESS------ STREET	CITY	STATE	ZIP
05073	350.22	5-28-77	CRIMSON	JOHN	112 NORTH ST.	SELDON,	N.Y.	11728
06092	87.20	4-20-77	ABRAMS	JOAN	5827B JERSEY ST.	CORAM,	N.Y.	11727
06095	469.10	8-07-77	WATERS	ROBERT	11-05 E. 5 ST.	BROOKLYN,	N.Y.	11223

Figure 17.18 Delinquent account report.

The following system flowcharts represent the recommended operations under the proposed system.

1. *Initialization of master disk file for accounts receivable* (Figure 17.21). This will involve the conversion of the current name-and-address file, and the customer transaction file from two card files into one disk file. A copy of the disk file will be put onto tape as backup in case the disk file is inadvertently destroyed or damaged.
2. *Processing of applications approved for new charge accounts* (Figure 17.22).
3. *Processing of name-and-address corrections, sales slips, credit slips, and payment memos on a daily basis* (Figure 17.23).
4. *Processing of weekly accounts receivable summary report* (Figure 17.24).
5. *Processing of monthly customer statements* (Figure 17.25).
6. *Processing of customer inquiries* (Figure 17.26).

Inputs

The basic inputs to be used in the proposed system are discussed below. Differences from current inputs will be listed.

1. *Application for charge account.* This form will remain the same as the one currently being used.

A customer desiring charge privileges will be required to complete an application for a charge account. This document, once approved, will supply the information to be used for adding a new account to the master accounts receivable file to be stored on disk.

2. *Name-and-address card.* The card layout is shown in Figure 17.27. The card differs from the current one in two ways:

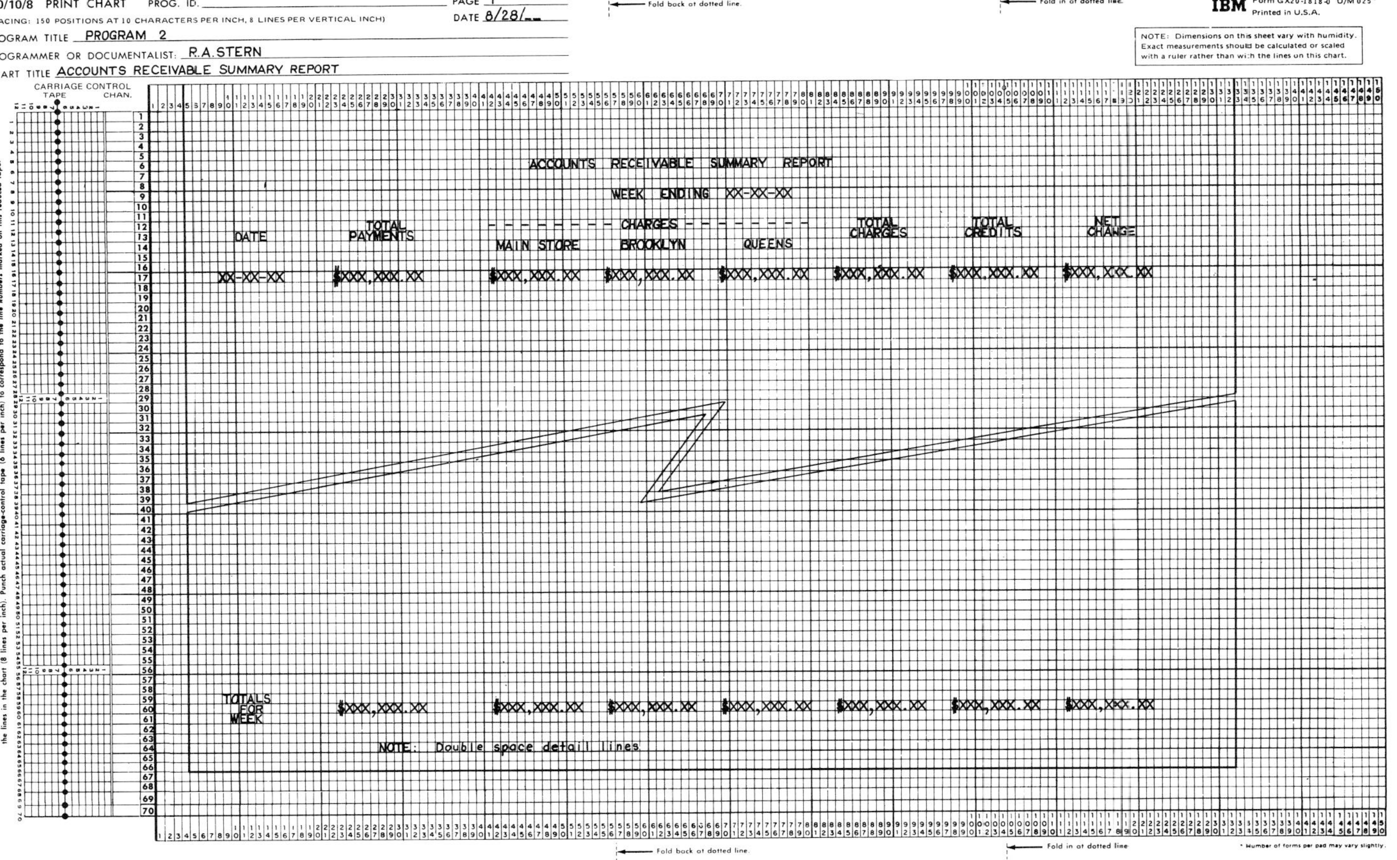

Figure 17.19 Accounts receivable summary report.

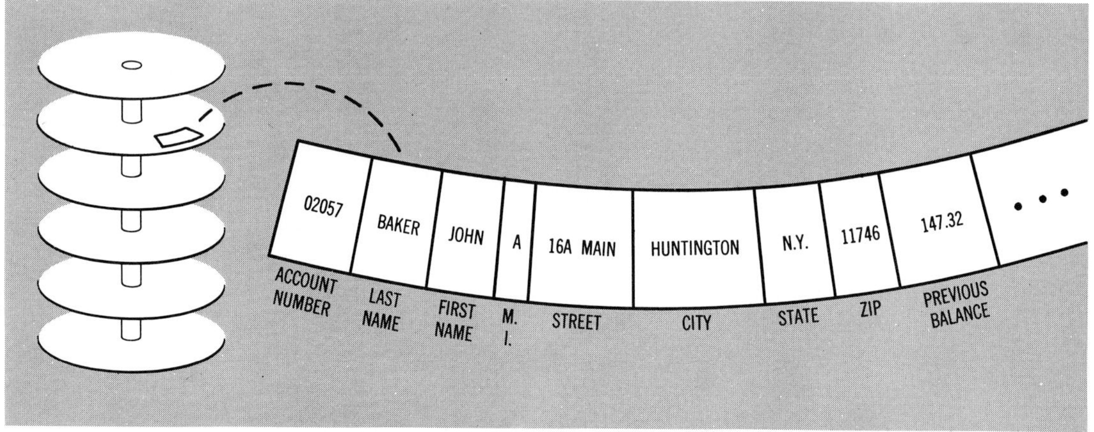

Figure 17.20 Master accounts receivable disk file.

a. It does not contain fields for the PREVIOUS BALANCE DUE and the DATE OF LAST PAYMENT. This information will be included in the master accounts receivable disk file.

b. Column 80 will contain a code as follows:

Code	Meaning
1	New account
2	Delete account
3	Correction—correct name punched
4	Correction—new address punched
5	Correction—correct (or new) name and address punched

3. *Transaction cards for sales slip, credit slip, and payment memo.* The source document in the original system utilized a single form for entering sales and credit information. The sales clerk was instructed to circle either "sales" or "credit" depending upon the transaction.

Analysis of the system has revealed excessive errors caused by failure to circle either "sales" or "credit." For this reason, the new design will include separate slips, one for sales transactions for charge customers and one for credits for charge customers. The original sales/credit slips will be retained for cash transactions. Figures 17.29 and 17.30 illustrate the new charge slip and credit memo forms. Sections 8 and 9 under Inputs provide more detail.

The card layouts are shown in Figure 17.27. The basic differences from the current cards are as follows:

a. The fields have been rearranged in order to facilitate keypunching. It is no longer necessary to skip spaces, for example, on the payment memo card.

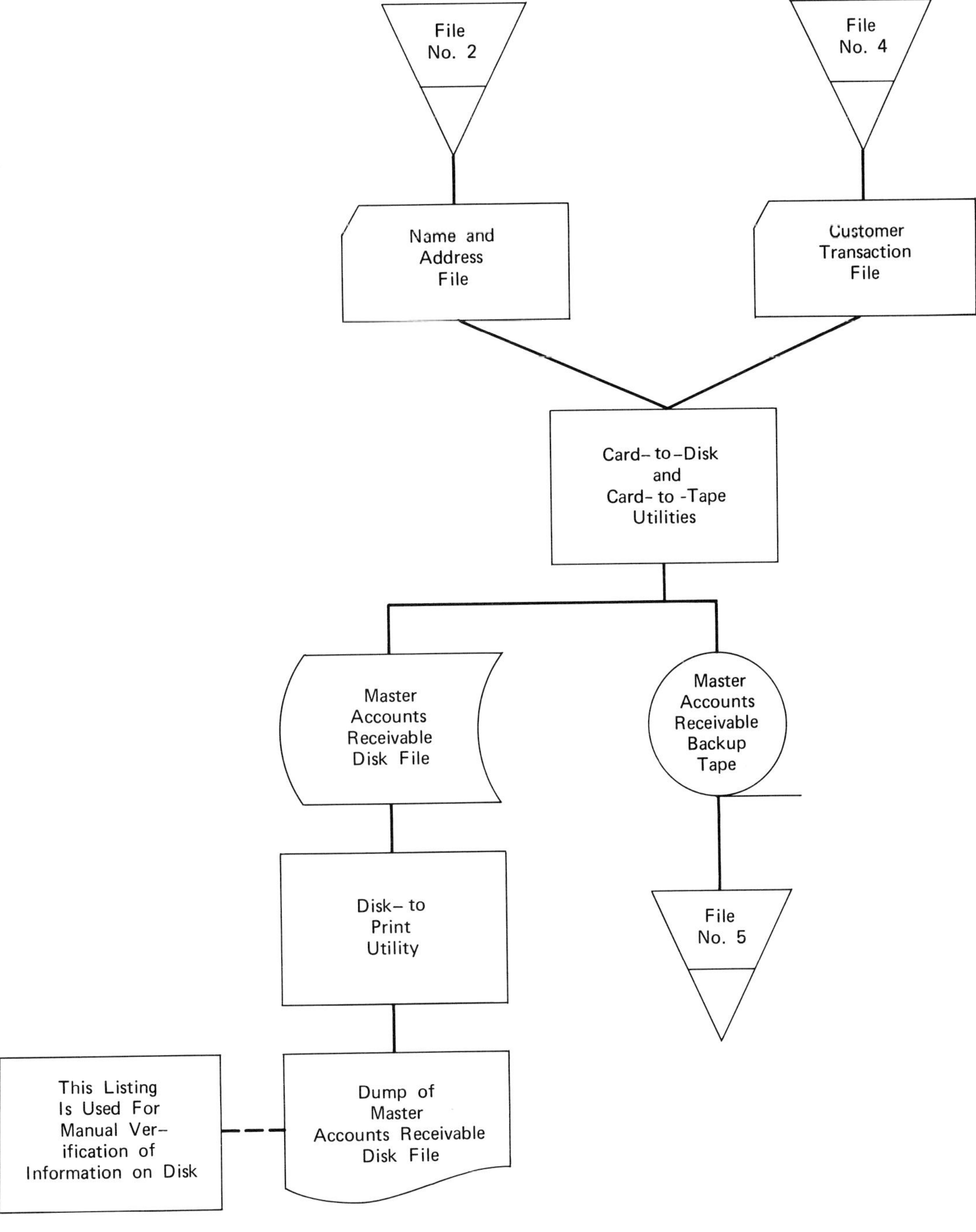

Figure 17.21 Initialization of master disk file for accounts receivable.

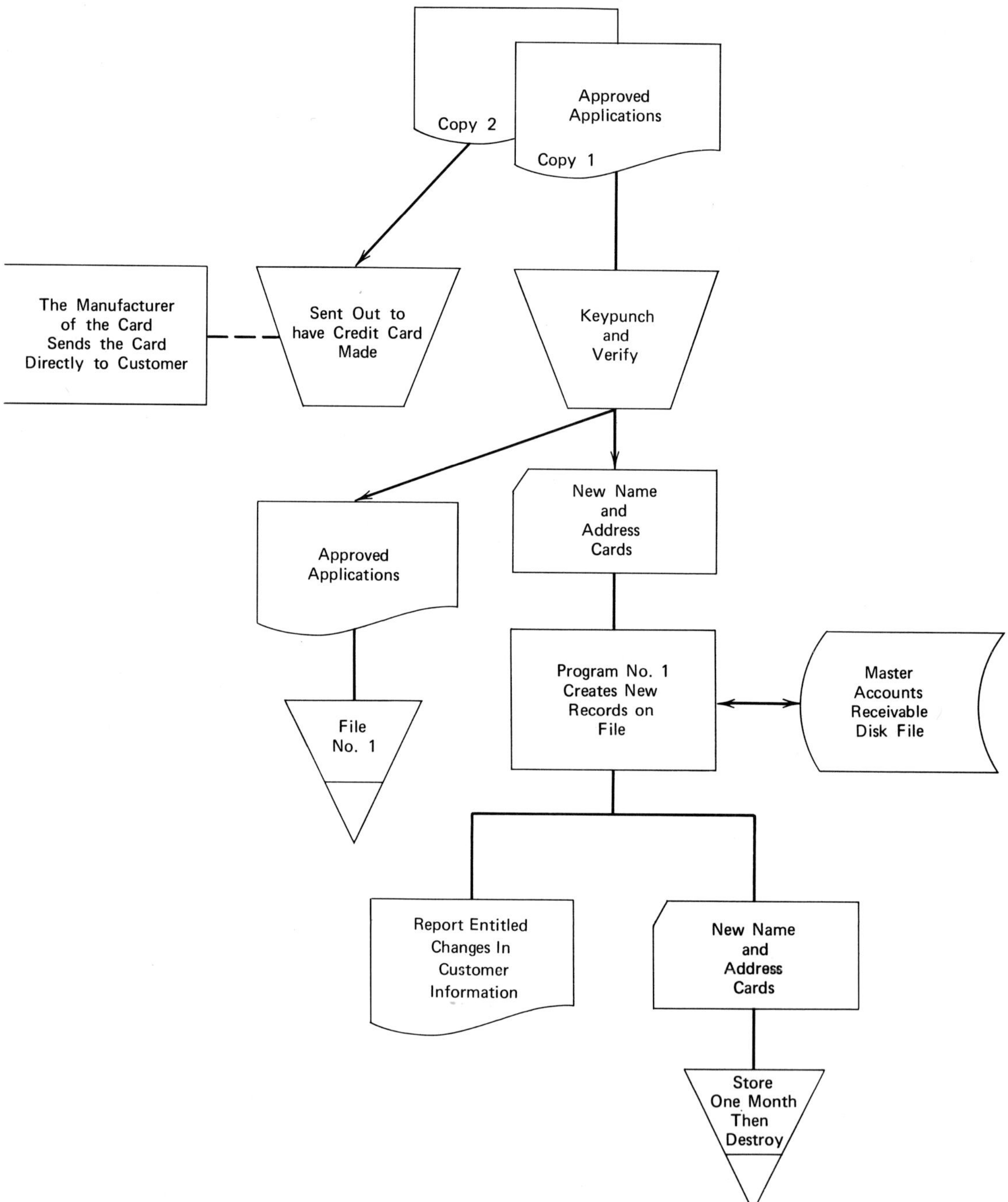

Figure 17.22 Processing of applications approved for new charge accounts.

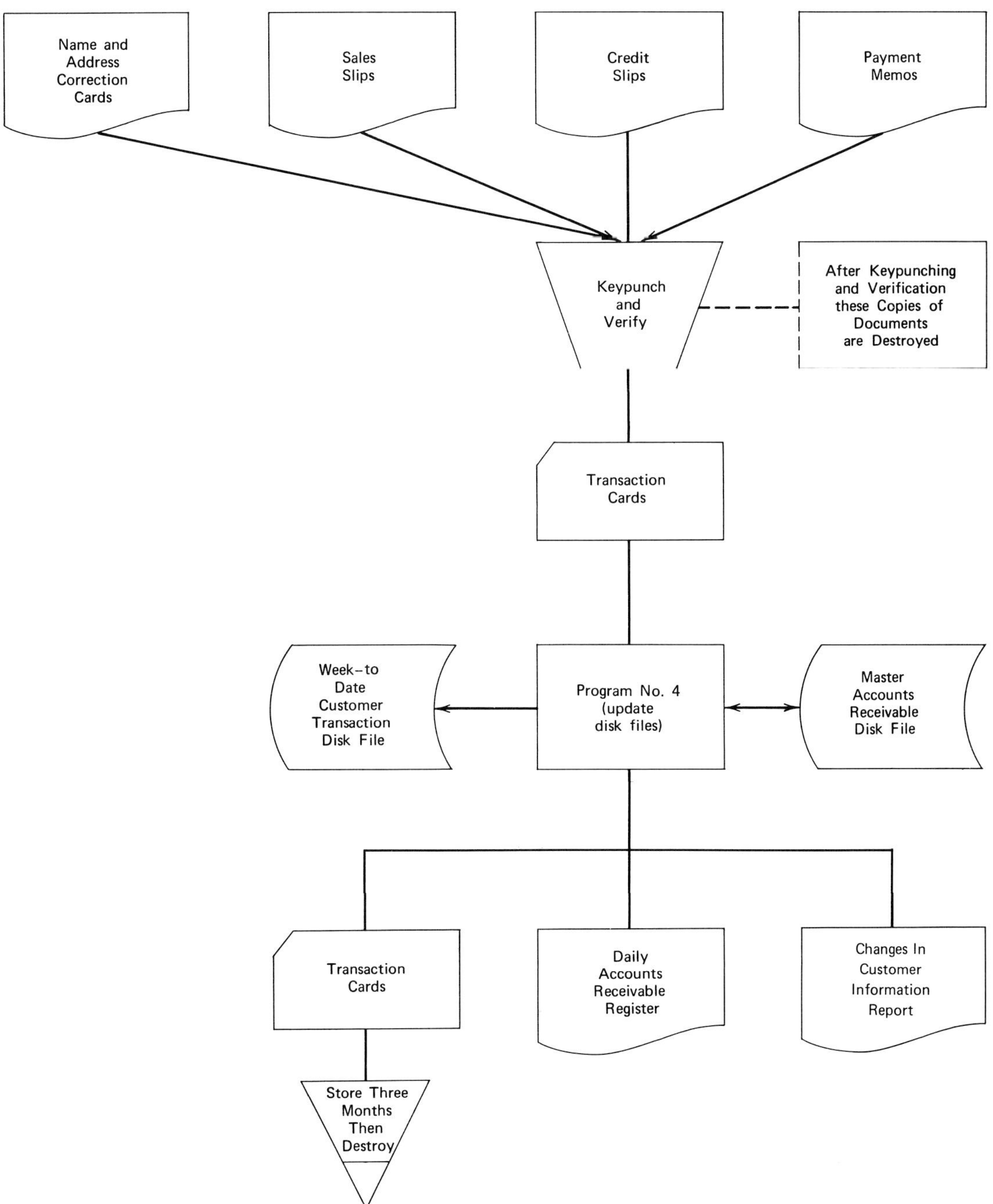

Figure 17.23 Processing of name-and-address corrections, sales slips, credit slips, and payment memos on a daily basis.

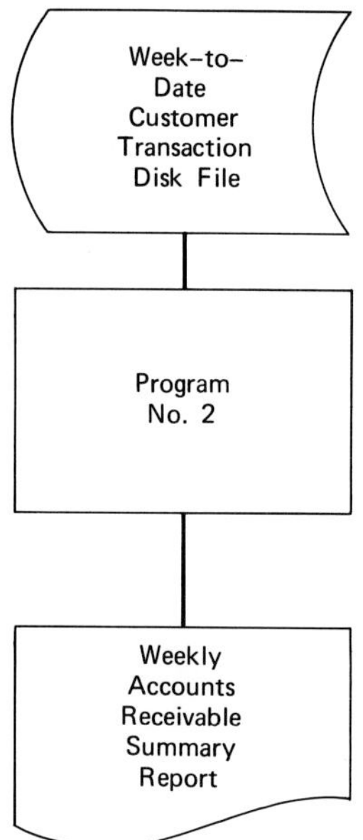

Figure 17.24 Processing of weekly accounts receivable summary report.

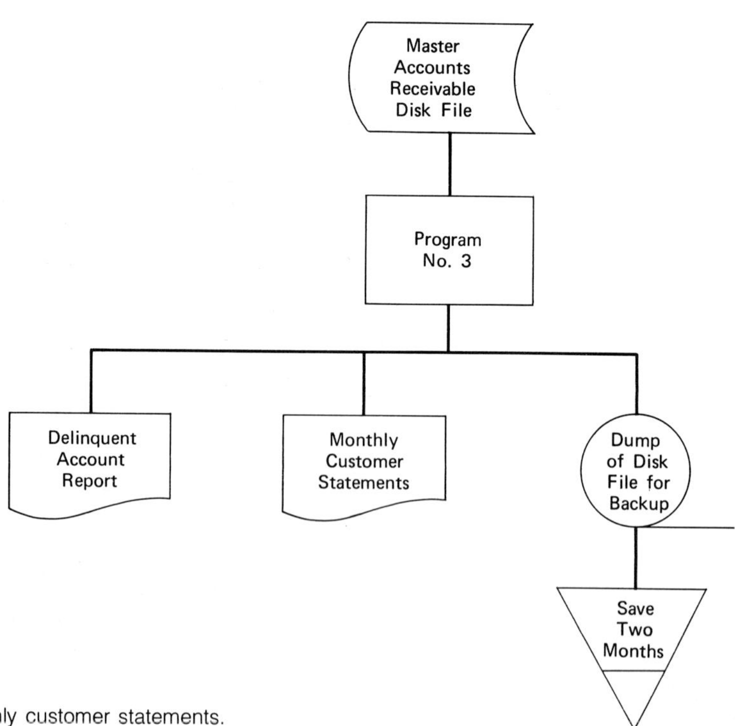

Figure 17.25 Processing of monthly customer statements.

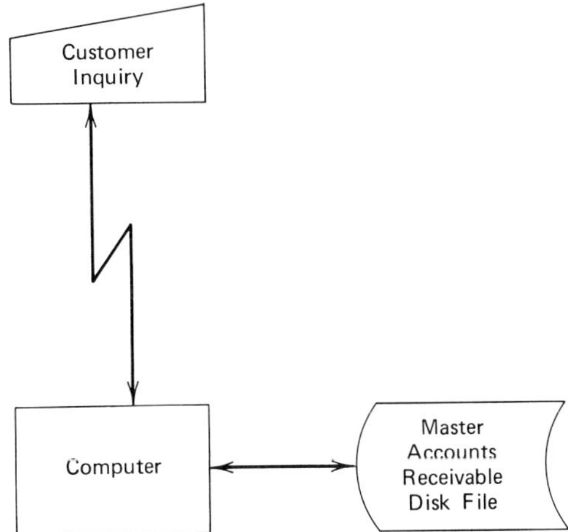

Figure 17.26 Processing of customer inquiries.

b. A field has been added for store identification on the sales slip card and the credit slip card. The code is as follows:

Code	Store
M	Main store
B	Brooklyn branch
Q	Queens branch

4. *Correction memo.* This form remains unchanged from the current one.
5. *Master accounts receivable disk file.* The layout in Figure 17.28 is for both the disk file and the tape backup. The disk file will be in account number sequence and will consist of variable-length records. It will be an indexed sequential file to facilitate customer inquiries. Based on a study of previous customer activity, provision will be made to accommodate up to 20 sales slips and 8 credit slips per month for each account.
6. *Week-to-date customer transaction disk file.* The file layout is shown in Figure 17.28. This file is used to store all transactions for the current week only. In this manner, the weekly accounts receivable summary report can readily be processed at the end of the week. If this file were not established, then it would be necessary to search the master accounts receivable disk file for all transactions that have occurred during the past week. Notice that a filler has been used in

IBM INTERNATIONAL BUSINESS MACHINES CORPORATION

GX24-6599-0
Printed in U.S.A.

MULTIPLE-CARD LAYOUT FORM

Company NANBETH DEPARTMENT STORE

Application ACCOUNTS RECEIVABLE (PROPOSED SYSTEM) by R.A. STERN Date 9/7/-- Job No. ______ Sheet No. 1

NAME AND ADDRESS CARD

Field	Card columns
ACCOUNT NUMBER	1–8
FIRST NAME	9–17
M. I.	18
LAST NAME	19–29
ADDRESS: STREET	30–39
ADDRESS: CITY	40–48
ADDRESS: STATE	49–54
ADDRESS: ZIP	55–59
DATE ACCOUNT ESTABLISHED (MO. DA. YR.)	60–65
(unused)	66–79
CODE	80

(Blank card: columns 1–80)

SALES SLIP

Field	Card columns
ACCOUNT NUMBER	1–8
DATE (MO. DA. YR.)	9–14
CHARGE AMOUNT ($ ¢)	15–20
TICKET NUMBER	21–26
ITEM DESCRIPTION	27–37
(unused)	38–78
STORE	79
CODE 1	80

CREDIT SLIP

Field	Card columns
ACCOUNT NUMBER	1–8
DATE (MO. DA. YR.)	9–14
CREDIT AMOUNT ($ ¢)	15–20
TICKET NUMBER	21–26
ITEM DESCRIPTION	27–37
(unused)	38–78
STORE	79
CODE 2	80

PAYMENT MEMO

Field	Card columns
ACCOUNT NUMBER	1–8
DATE (MO. DA. YR.)	9–14
PAYMENT AMOUNT ($ ¢)	15–20
(unused)	21–79
CODE 3	80

(Blank card: columns 1–80)

Figure 17.27 Accounts receivable card formats.

IBM

INTERNATIONAL BUSINESS MACHINES CORPORATION

STORAGE LAYOUT

IBM 1240 - 1401 - 1410 - 1420 - 1440 - 1460

Form X24-6438-5
Printed in U. S. A.

APPLICATION ACCOUNTS RECEIVABLE

DATE 9/11/_ _

 # 1 MASTER ACCOUNTS RECEIVABLE DISK FILE LAYOUT (VARIABLE LENGTH RECORDS)

Location	Data
0–5	ACCOUNT NUMBER
6–14	FIRST NAME
15	M. I.
16–26	LAST NAME
27–54	ADDRESS: STREET, CITY, STATE, ZIP
57–62	DATE ACCOUNT ESTABLISHED MO. DA. YR.
63–68	DATE OF LAST PAYMENT MO. DA. YR.
69–75	PREVIOUS BALANCE $ ¢
76–80	AMOUNT OF PAYMENT $ ¢
81–86	SALES: DATE OF SALE MO. DA. YR.
87–92	CHARGE AMOUNT $ ¢
93–98	TICKET NUMBER

FOR EACH ACCOUNT

NOTE: ALLOW FOR UP TO 20 SALES SLIPS PER MONTH AND 8 CREDIT SLIPS/MONTH

Location	Data
0–11	SLIP: ITEM DESCRIPTION (STORE)
12–17	CREDIT SLIP: DATE OF CREDIT MO. DA. YR.
18–22	CREDIT AMOUNT $ ¢
23–28	TICKET NUMBER
29–41	ITEM DESCRIPTION (STORE)

 # 2 WEEK-TO-DATE CUSTOMER TRANSACTION DISK FILE LAYOUT (3 DIFFERENT RECORD LAYOUTS)

Location	Data
0–5	SALES SLIP: ACCOUNT NUMBER
6–11	DATE OF SALE MO. DA. YR.
12–16	CHARGE AMOUNT $ ¢
17–21	TICKET NUMBER
22–35	ITEM DESCRIPTION
36–37	STORE — CODE = 1
38–43	CREDIT SLIP: ACCOUNT NUMBER
44–49	DATE OF CREDIT MO. DA. YR.
50–55	CREDIT AMOUNT $ ¢
56–61	TICKET NUMBER
62–76	ITEM DESCRIPTION
76–77	STORE — CODE = 2
78–84	PAYMENT: ACCOUNT NUMBER
85–90	DATE OF PAYMENT MO. DA. YR.
91–96	AMOUNT OF PAYMENT $ ¢

NOTE: FILLER USED IN PAYMENT MEMO RECORD TO FACILITATE PROCESSING OF FIXED LENGTH RECORDS

Symbolic	Data
MEMO	FILLER (locations 0–16)

Figure 17.28 Accounts receivable disk layouts.

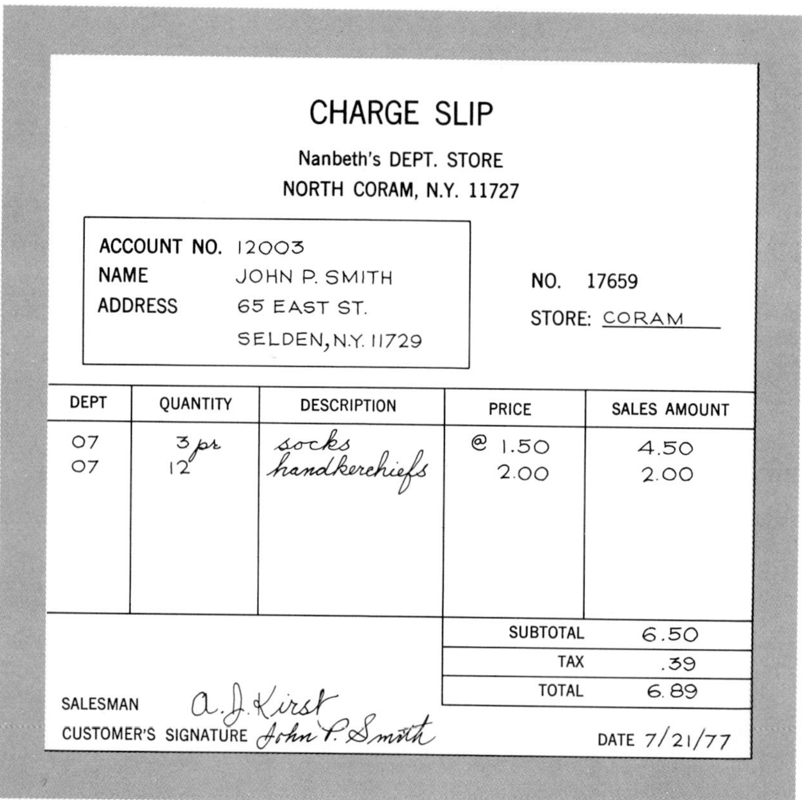

CHARGE SLIP

Nanbeth's DEPT. STORE
NORTH CORAM, N.Y. 11727

ACCOUNT NO. 12003
NAME JOHN P. SMITH
ADDRESS 65 EAST ST.
SELDEN, N.Y. 11729

NO. 17659
STORE: CORAM

DEPT	QUANTITY	DESCRIPTION	PRICE	SALES AMOUNT
07	3 pr	socks	@ 1.50	4.50
07	12	handkerchiefs	2.00	2.00
			SUBTOTAL	6.50
			TAX	.39
			TOTAL	6.89

SALESMAN A. J. Kirst
CUSTOMER'S SIGNATURE John P. Smith
DATE 7/21/77

Figure 17.29 Charge slip.

the payment memo record to facilitate processing of fixed-length records. All records in the file will contain 39 positions.

7. *Payment memo.* This form remains unchanged. The payment memo is generally completed by the credit office upon receipt of the customer's remittance and the remittance stub from the monthly statement. A copy is sent to data processing so that the customer's account can be properly credited.

8. *Sales slip* (Figure 17.29). There are three major changes from the current form:

a. It is no longer a sales/credit slip
b. STORE has been added
c. The color of the sales slip is white

9. *Credit slip* (Figure 17.30). The credit slip is a pink form to clearly distinguish it from the sales slip. It is similar in de-

sign, with the exception that it has "CREDIT" instead of "SALES" printed on it.

Controls

The daily accounts receivable register and the weekly accounts receivable summary report remain the primary controls used for making trial balances of accounts receivable. In addition, backup information is saved in case of a system failure. Every time customer statements are prepared, a dump of the master file is put onto tape to be saved for two months. Punched cards keypunched from source documents are saved for three months.

Feedback

In the event that errors are detected or that changes become necessary one of two forms can be used—the correction memo or the credit slip. These forms will be forwarded to keypunch-

Figure 17.30 Credit memo.

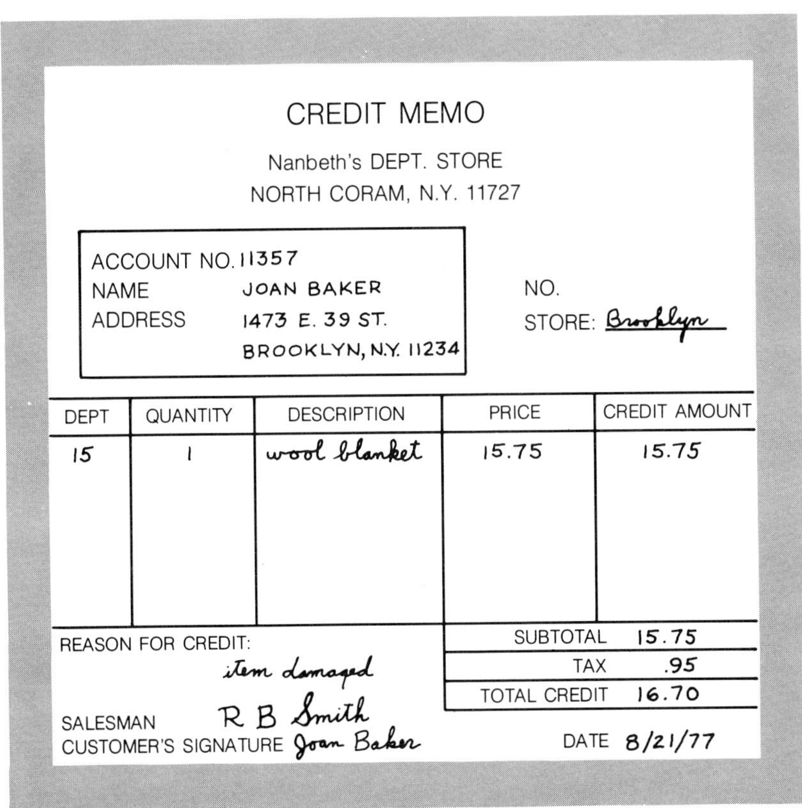

CREDIT MEMO

Nanbeth's DEPT. STORE
NORTH CORAM, N.Y. 11727

ACCOUNT NO. 11357
NAME JOAN BAKER
ADDRESS 1473 E. 39 ST.
BROOKLYN, N.Y. 11234

NO.
STORE: Brooklyn

DEPT	QUANTITY	DESCRIPTION	PRICE	CREDIT AMOUNT
15	1	wool blanket	15.75	15.75

REASON FOR CREDIT: item damaged

SUBTOTAL 15.75
TAX .95
TOTAL CREDIT 16.70

SALESMAN R B Smith
CUSTOMER'S SIGNATURE Joan Baker
DATE 8/21/77

ing so that cards can be generated to correct information on the master disk file.

COST ANALYSIS

Since the volume of the system is expected to almost triple with the addition of two branch stores, the current costs per month of operating accounts receivable have been adjusted for comparison purposes. A detailed comparison is shown in Table 17.2.

As can be seen from the comparison, the proposed system will cost $8,835 per month to operate as compared to the current adjusted figure of $10,125. Therefore, the proposed system will save $1,290 per month once it is operational. Since the design of the new system plus implementation will cost $36,100, it will take 28 months to write off the design of this new system.

TABLE 17.2. COST COMPARISON

Monthly Costs for Current System—Adjusted for Growth		Monthly Costs for Proposed System	
Personnel			
Manager of accounts receivable	$1,500	Manager of accounts receivable	$1,500
9 accounts receivable clerks	3,450	2 accounts receivable clerks	770
3 typists	1,425	1 typist	475
3 keypunch operators	1,200	3 keypunch operators	1,200
1.5 unit-record operators	750	.5 computer operators	300
Equipment			
.6 sorter	90	Computer system, including keypunch machines and verifiers—an allocation of 25% of the total anticipated monthly cost of $14,620 has been determined by management	3,655
.3 collator	45		
.9 accounting machine	225		
3 keypunch machines	255		
3 verifiers	300		
Note: Times allocated to each device were estimated by operations manager.			
Supplies			
120,000 punched cards	135	120,000 punched cards	135
60 boxes of preprinted forms[a]	600	60 boxes of preprinted forms[a]	600
30 boxes of stock paper	150	40 boxes of stock paper[a]	200
TOTAL COST	$10,125		$8,835

[a]Primarily 2-ply paper, 1,600 sheets to a box.

SUMMARY

The new accounts receivable system will operate at a savings of $1,290 per month after a 28-month write-off of design and implementation costs. The new system will accommodate the expansion of the store to two branch locations. It will minimize errors through the use of new sales slips and credit slips. It will incorporate finance charges for delinquent accounts. Three terminals will be provided so that immediate access can be made to the master accounts receivable disk file.

APPENDIX

COMPUTER CHARACTERISTICS FOR SELECTED COMPUTER SYSTEMS

[1] Reproduced with special permission from INFOSYSTEMS magazine, May 1974 issue, pages 39–59, Hitchcock Publishing Co., Wheaton, IL 60187,

Manufacturer / Model No.	Avg. Purchase Price ($1,000)	Avg. Rental Price ($/Mo.)	Central Processor: Speed (usec): CPU Cycle Time	Central Processor: Speed (usec): Add Time*	Central Processor: Storage: Medium**	Central Processor: Storage: Maximum Capacity (in characters)	Central Processor: Storage: Access Time (in usec)	Central Processor: Typewriter Console	Central Processor: No. CPU I/O Channels	Central Processor: Data Word Length***	Central Processor: Buffering	Readers: Data Collection	Readers: MICR	Readers: OCR
Basic/Four Corp.														
500	38	872 DI	1	9.6	C DI	48K	1	x	3	8	x			
Burroughs Corp.														
B300	240	5K	166Kc	492	C DI	19.2K	6	x		D	x	x	x	
B3506	510	12K	1	70	C	300K	1	x	10	B	x	x	x	x
B6715	1,987.3	41.4K	0.2	2.4	C DI	7,864K 36b	0.6 40ms		6	B	x	x		
B7748	4,440	90.2K	0.0625	0.125	C DI	7,864K 112b	1.75 40ms		56	B	x	x		
Control Data Corp.														
3300	700	15K	1.2	2.75	C DR DI	262Kw 4m 838m	0.8 17ms 80ms	x	8	B D	x	x		x
3500	1,100	24K	0.9	1.2	C DR DI	202Kw 4m 838m	0.6 17ms 80ms	x	8	B D	x	x		x
Cyber 70 Model 76	9,500	220K	0.0275	0.495	C DR DI	650K 5.12m 8,200K 800m	0.0275 17ms 100ms	x	15	B D	x	x	x	x
Honeywell Information Systems														
120	165	3.2K	3	69	C DR DI	32K 2.6m 149.6	1.5 27ms 75ms	x	3				x	x
415	450	9.6K	5.95	17.8	C DI	524K 120m	5.95 85ms	x	12	B D	x		x	x
2015	625	15K	1.33	15	C DI DR	262K	0.67	x	12		x		x	x
8200	2,900	40K 78K	0.75	3.12 128	C DR DI	2,096K 4.2m 300m	0.094 8.6ms 15ms	x	48-96		x		x	x
International Business Machines Corp.														
System/3	136-298	3.2K- 7.2K	1.52	35	C	128K	1.52m	x		B	x	x	x	x
System/360 Mod 20	99	2.2K	3.6	572	C DI	16K 10.8m	3.6 75ms	x	1	B	x	x	x	x
System/360 Mod 25	300	6K	1.8	110	C DI	49K 29m	0.9 75ms	x	1	B	x	x	x	x
System/360 Mod 30	420	8.5K	1.5	61	C DI	65K 233m	1.5 60ms	x	3	B	x	x	x	x
System/360 Mod 50	1,400	32K	2	23	C DR DI	524K 7.8m 699m	2 8.6ms 60ms	x	4	B	x	x	x	x
System/360 Mod 67	5,800	138K	0.75	3.9	C DR DI	2,096K 16.4m 699m	0.75 8.6ms 60ms	x	14	B	x			
System/360 Mod 75	3,600	80K	0.75	2.54	C DR DI	1,048K 16.4m 699m	0.75 8.6ms 60ms	x	7	B	x			

**this speed is the complete add time for two six digit numbers from memory to memory;*
***C = core, DI = disc, DR = drum, IC = integrated circuit, PW = plated wire, TF = thin film;*
****B = binary, D = decimal; K = thousand, m = million, b = billion, usec = microseconds, ms = milliseconds, ns = nanosecond, w = words, x = yes, mc = megacycle.*

Input / Output										Software								
Printers		Magnetic Tape		Punched Cards		Punched Paper Tape		Data Communications										
Lines Per Minute	Plotter****	7-Channel K/Char. Per Sec.	9-Channel K/Char. Per Sec.	Cards Per Minute Input	Cards Per Minute Output	Charac. Per Sec. Input	Charac. Per Sec. Output	No. Transmission Lines	Visual Display	Operating System	Time Share Capability	Multiprogram	Cobol	Fortran II, IV or VI	Utilities	Communications	Other
200		10	10	400/800		300	75	8	x	x	x	x			x	x	x
1,040		72		1,400	300	1,000	100	32	x	x		x	x		x	x	
1,100		96		1,400	300	1,000	100	36	x	x	x	x	x	x	x	x	
1,040		96	240	1,400	300	1,000	100	1,024	x	x	x	x	x	x	x	x	x
1,040		96	240	1,400	300	1,000	100		x	x	x	x	x	x	x	x	x
1,200	x	120	30	1,200	250	1,000	120	512	x	x	x	x	x	x	x	x	x
1,200	x	120	30	1,200	250	1,000	120	512	x	x	x	x	x	x	x	x	x
1,200	x	120	240	1,200	250	1,000	120	unlt'd	x	x	x	x	x	x	x	x	x
300-1,100		4.8-144	37.3-149.6	1,050	100-400	600	120	1-63	x	x	x	x	x	x	x	x	x
1,200	x	7.5-120	10-160	900	100-300	500	150	120	x	x		x	x	x	x	x	x
300-1,100		5.2-144	37.3-149.3		100-400	600	120	120	x	x	x	x	x	x	x	x	x
300-1,100		5.2-144	37.3-224	1,050	100-400	600	120	1-126	x	x	x		x	x	x	x	x
1,100				500/1,000	120/260			var	x	x		x	x	x	x	x	
300-1,100		15	30	1,000	500	1,000	150	1							x	x	x
240-1,400		30	30	1,000	500	1,000	120	26	x	x		x	x	x	x	x	x
240-1,400		90	180	1,000	500	1,000	120	224	x	x		x	x	x	x	x	x
240-1,400		90	320	1,000	500	1,000	120	256	x	x		x	x	x	x	x	x
240-1,400		90	190	1,000	500	1,000		256	x	x	x	x	x	x	x	x	x
240-1,400		90	320	1,000	500			256	x	x		x	x	x	x	x	x

Manufacturer / Model No.	Avg. Purchase Price ($1,000)	Avg. Rental Price ($/Mo.)	Central Processor: Speed (usec): CPU Cycle Time	Central Processor: Speed (usec): Add Time*	Central Processor: Storage: Medium**	Central Processor: Storage: Maximum Capacity (in characters)	Central Processor: Storage: Access Time (in usec)	Central Processor: Typewriter Console	Central Processor: No. CPU I/O Channels	Central Processor: Data Word Length***	Central Processor: Buffering	Readers: Data Collection	Readers: MICR	Readers: OCR
System/360 Mod 195	10,500	232K	0.54	0.154	C DR DI	1,240K 4m 233m	810 8.6ms 60ms	x	7	B	x	x		
System/370 Mod 125	377.8	8.2K	0.98	9.8	C	131K		x	16	B D				
System/370 Mod 135	472- 1,020		0.75		Mono- lithic	245	0.77	x	3	B	x	x	x	x
System/370 Mod 155	1,801- 3,736	37K 79K	m 2.1 ms B 115ms	C	C DI	2mb 800mb	2.1ms 300ms	x		B	x	x		
System/370 Mod 165	3,505- 6,719	71K 143K	m 2ms B 80ms		C DI	3mb 800mb	2ms 300ms	x		B	x	x		
National Cash Register Co.														
Century 100	135	2.6K	0.8	58.4	TF DI	32K 16.8m	0.8 43.7ms	x	2	8	x		x	x
Century 200	305	6.2K	0.65	12.4	C DI	524K 1.5b	0.65 43.7ms	x	4-8	16	x		x	x
Century 300	1,170	23K	0.24	6.2	C DI	2.097m 9.2b	0.65 43.7ms	x	11	32	x		x	x
Sperry Univac Computer System														
90/70	1,000	25K	0.6	20	IC DI	648K	27ms	x	22	32	x			x
1110	2,000	44K	0.12	1.5	C		0.32	x	96	96	x	x		x
9300	140	3.7K	0.6	60	PW DI	32K 12.8m	0.6 132ms	x	4 11	8	x			x
9480	350	85K	0.6	24.6	IC DI	262K	30ms	x	10	16	x	x		x
Varian Data Machines														
V72	43.2		0.66	12.8	C DI	64K 186.8m	10ms	x	48	B	x	x	x	
Xerox Corp.														
Sigma 3	200	5K	0.97	1.85	C DI	256K		x	28	B D	x			
Sigma 5	350	8.5K	0.95	3.1	C DI	512K 3b	0.9 17ms	x	256	B	x			
Sigma 9	1,000	30K	0.9	1.66	C	2,048K	0.9 17ms	x	256	32	x			
Xerox 560	700	17K	0.215	1.8	C DI		0.645 8.3ms	x	261	B D	x			

Input / Output										Software								
Printers		Magnetic Tape		Punched Cards		Punched Paper Tape		Data Communications										
Lines Per Minute	Plotter****	7-Channel K/Char. Per Sec.	9-Channel K/Char. Per Sec.	Cards Per Minute Input	Cards Per Minute Output	Charac. Per Sec. Input	Charac. Per Sec. Output	No. Transmission Lines	Visual Display	Operating System	Time Share Capability	Multiprogram	Cobol	Fortran II, IV or VI	Utilities	Communications	Other
1,100		90	300	1,000	500			196	x	x		x	x	x	x	x	
x				x	x			22	x	x							
2,000	x	90	320	1,200	300	120	120	var	x	x	x	x	x	x	x	x	x
2,000		90	320	1,000	500				x	x	x	x	x	x	x	x	x
2,000		90	320	1,000	500				x	x	x	x	x	x	x	x	x
450-3,000		10-40	40-80	300-1,200	82-240	1,000-1,500	200	1-256	x	x	x		x	x	x	x	
450-3,000		10-40	40-240	300-1,200	82-240	1,000-1,500	200	1-256	x	x	x	x	x	x	x	x	x
450-3,000		10-40	40-240	300-1,200	83-240	1,000-1,500	200	1-256	x	x	x	x	x	x	x	x	x
900-3,000		34-96	34-320	600-1,000	250	300	1,150	158		x		x	x	x	x	x	x
2,000		x	x	1,000				var	x	x	x	x	x	x	x	x	x
600-1,100		34	34-68	2,000	75/250	300	110	8	x	x		x	x	x	x	x	x
900-2,000		34-96	34-192	600-1,000	250	300	110	128		x		x	x	x	x	x	x
300-1,200		30	30	300-1,000	35-200	300	75	var	x	x	x	x		x	x	x	x
1,500		60	120	1,500	300	300	120	256		x				x	x	x	x
1,500	x	60	120	1,500	300	300	120	1,024	x	x	x	x	x	x	x	x	x
1,500	x	x	x	1,500	300	300	120	1,024	x	x	x	x	x	x	x	x	x
4,000		60	200	1,500	100	300	75	1,024	x	x	x	x	x	x	x	x	x

INDEX